Dear Stephen, Anita, Chandra, and Benjamin,
We hope you will enjoy reading, and
learning from this book. 12/11
        Happy Hanukkkah 1991
    Love, and kisses, Mom, and Dad

THE THREE GREAT CLASSIC WRITERS OF
MODERN YIDDISH LITERATURE

10/20/91,

To Steve and family,

    Best wishes
        Aunt Marion

Mendele Moykher-Sforim

THE
Three Great Classic Writers
OF
Modern Yiddish Literature

SELECTED WORKS OF
Mendele Moykher-Sforim

EDITED BY

Marvin Zuckerman, Gerald Stillman, Marion Herbst

Joseph Simon   Pangloss Press

Library of Congress Cataloging-in-Publication Data

Mendele Moykher-Sforim, 1835–1917.
  [Selections. English. 1991]
  Selected works of Mendele Moykher-Sforim / edited by Marvin
Zuckerman, Gerald Stillman, Marion Herbst.
      p.   cm. — (The three great classic writers of modern Yiddish
literature : v. 1)
  Includes bibliographical references
  ISBN 0–934710–23–6 : $34.50
  1. Mendele Moykher-Sforim, 1835–1917—Translations, English.
I. Zuckerman, Marvin S.   II. Stillman, Gerald.   III. Herbst, Marion.
1932–   . IV. Title V. Series.
PJ5129.A2 1991
839'.0933—dc20   90–63397
                                                           CIP

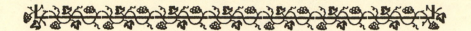

Contents

ACKNOWLEDGEMENTS

Thanks and acknowledgements are due to the following:

"A Chronology" from pages 11–12 in *Mendele Moykher-Sforim* by Theodore Steinberg. Copyright 1977, and reprinted with the permission of Twayne Publishers, a division of G. K. Hall & Co., Boston.

Pages 545–559, 575–582, 650–663 of *The Mare* from *Yenne Velt: Great Works of Jewish Fantasy.* Copyright 1976 by Joachim Neugroschel. Published by the Overlook Press, Lewis Hollow Road, Woodstock, New York 12498. $27.95 cloth, $15.95 paper.

Pages 179–202 of *Benjamin III* from *The Shtetl.* Copyright 1979 by Joachim Neugroschel. Published by the Overlook Press, Lewis Hollow Road, Woodstock, New York 12498. $35.00 cloth, $13.95 paper.

"Shem and Japheth on the Train," as translated by Walter Lever, as revised by Robert Alter, pages 19–38 in *Modern Hebrew Literature,* edited by Robert Alter. Copyright 1975, and reprinted with the permission of Robert Alter.

From *Of Bygone Days,* translated by Raymond P. Sheindlin, pages 342–358 in *A Shtetl and Other Yiddish Novellas,* edited, with introductions and notes, by Ruth R. Wisse. Copyright 1973 by Ruth R. Wisse, published originally by Behrman House, Inc.; since republished by Wayne State University Press. Reprinted by permission of Ruth R. Wisse.

"Selective Bibliography" from *A Traveler Disguised* by Dan Miron. Copyright 1973 by Schocken Books Inc. Reprinted by permission of Schocken Books, published by Pantheon Books, a division of Random House, Inc.

Preface

The main lines of Yiddish history are firmly drawn: almost everything in the modern era stems from the "classical" trio of prose writers, Mendele, Sholem Aleykhem, and Perets. So dominant are their literary personalities, so powerful the thematic and stylistic precedents they established that even those later writers who try to break away from them generally succeed in doing little more than confirm the very influence they would reject.
—Howe and Greenberg, *A Treasury of Yiddish Stories*

This is Volume One of a planned trilogy of the three great modern Yiddish classicists: Mendele Moyhker-Sforim, Sholem Aleykhem, and I.L. Perets.

This first volume of the trilogy is an anthology of some of the works of the first of that "classical trio," Mendele.

In 1911, the occasion of Mendele's seventy-fifth birthday, the Jewish writers and intellectuals of his day presented Mendele with the following tribute (Madison, *Yiddish Literature*):

You are the first to have concentrated in both Yiddish and Hebrew the total creative power of the Jews in past generations—and made both new languages; and you are the first to give us in both languages the artistic story and narrative with the accent which has become the Mendele stamp. No writer today is free from your influence, none who did not attend your school.

As A.A. Roback (*The Story of Yiddish Literature*), has put it, "Mendele . . . stands out as the first pillar of modern Yiddish literature . . . as the first master of Yiddish prose." I.L. Perets, the second author of that "classical trio," said of Mendele, "He was the first to create a Yiddish style." And according to Leo Wiener in his *The History of Yiddish Literature in the XIX Century,* "Beginning with Abramovitsh, style is regarded as an important requisite of a . . . [Yiddish] work."

Mendele Moykher-Sforim (Mendele the Bookpeddler), is the name of a character created by Sholem Yankef Abramovitsh (originally Broido, ca. 1836–1917), which then became the author's pen-name (it is ostensibly Mendele Moykher-Sforim who narrates Abramovitsh's stories).

Born in Kapulye, in the province of Minsk, White Russia, Mendele, as he was affectionately called by his readers, was dubbed by Sholem Aleykhem the "grandfather" (*zeyde*) of modern Yiddish literature.

As a boy, he had the traditional, exclusively religious Jewish education of the time, and a difficult, but interesting youth that provided him with much material for his later masterpieces.

As a young man he was tutored in the worldly subjects (mathematics, literature, and languages) by one of the learned daughters of Avrom Ber-Gotlober, a leading Hebrew/Yiddish writer of the nineteenth-century *haskole* (Jewish Enlightenment).

Early in his literary career, Abramovitsh wrote in Hebrew, but his strong desire to be "of use to his people" made him turn to Yiddish, the language of the Jewish masses of Eastern Europe. Although heavily influenced by the *haskole,* he transcended its didacticism to create a style and a modern literary language for both Yiddish and Hebrew sufficient to earn him the title as founder of the modern literatures in both these languages.

The publication in 1864 of his first Yiddish novel, *Dos Kleyne Mentshele* (*The Little Man*) marks the beginning of the modern period in Yiddish literature. This novel is included in its entirety here.

This anthology is the first comprehensive collection in English translation of some of the most important works of Mendele. It includes not only two complete novels, excerpts from several others, a short story, a memoir, but also a brief biography, a chronology, a selective bibliography, and a glossary of the Yiddish and Hebrew terms retained in the translations.

Mendele's work shows his love of nature, his devotion to his people, and his talent for satire. His collected works in Yiddish fill twenty volumes.

The works in this anthology are arranged in chronological order, except for *Notes For My Biography,* which is placed first to serve as a kind of introduction to Mendele by Mendele himself.

A NOTE TO THE READER
ON TRANSLATION AND TRANSLITERATION

Jorge Luis Borges is quoted by his translator-into-English, Gregory Rabassa, as having advised him: "Don't translate what I say, but what I *wanted* to say." The editors have selected translations for this anthology which, they hope, not only do that, but also attempt to stay close to what Mendele says. Yiddish can be a highly idiomatic language, maybe more so than others when popular speech is being simulated. Anyone who has tried to translate expressions like "a nekhtiker tog" or "s'vet helfn vi a toytn bankes" will have realized the good sense of Borges' advice to Rabassa. On the other hand, good translations cannot afford to stray widely from *what* the author actually says. This balancing act, we feel, has been successfully carried out by the translators of the selections in this anthology.

Some Yiddish words have been retained in the selections and are explained in the glossary at the end of the anthology. They are retained because the English equivalents lose too many nuances—even for the reader who knows little or no Yiddish. For example, to substitute "religious elementary school" for "kheyder" loses the entire milieu of a dark and dank, one-room school house with a long wooden table and long, hard benches on either side populated by bedraggled pupils; or substituting "person" for "mentsh." See the glossary for what can be lost.

Regarding transliteration, we have tried (without always succeeding) to make all Yiddish words, and names of referenced Yiddish writers and works, conform to the YIVO (*Yidisher Visnshaftlekher Institut*—Yiddish Scientific Institute) orthographic usage to render the accepted Yiddish pronunciation correctly. In a few cases, when such orthography differs from a very common previous spelling for the word, the latter is given in parentheses; i.e., "*toyre* (Torah)."

Finally, following the lead of Dan Miron in *A Traveler Disguised,* Hebrew words used within a Yiddish context have been transliterated according to the Ashkenazic pronunciation and accentuation (e.g., *Mas'oes Binyomin Hashlishi,* the Hebrew title of a Yiddish work). In this regard, it helps to know that Ashkenazic pronunciation generally accentuates the first syllable, while Sephardic pronunciation (current in Israel) generally accentuates the last; to wit: *Sha*bes — Sha*bat*; *toy*re — To*rah*.

And now, in the tradition of Mendele himself, the editors urge you, if you have any complaints, to let them know, as soon as possible, care of the publisher.

A remarkable historical document, this is a reproduction of the front page of
the daily newspaper, FOLKSTSAYTUNG, organ of the Jewish Labor Bund of
Southern Russia. Dateline: Kiev, Tuesday, November 28, 1917. The central
headline reads as follows:

> THE POLLS CLOSE TODAY AT 2 PM. HURRY TO GIVE YOUR VOTE
> TO THE TICKET OF THE JEWISH LABOR "BUND"

The black-bordered box in the lower, right-hand corner carries the following message:

> OUR DEEPEST SORROW AT THE DEATH OF THE IMMORTAL MAS-
> TER OF THE YIDDISH WORD—MENDELE MOYKHER-SFORIM

The revolutionary Yiddish press thus expressed its deep sense of loss, its love
for Mendele, noting his passing in the heat of battle, during the very birth-
pangs, the tempestuous days of the great Russian revolution.

(From *The Jewish Labor Bund: A Pictorial History, 1897–1957,* Compiled by J.S. Hertz,
© 1958 by Farlag Unser Tsait, p. 75.)

THE THREE GREAT CLASSIC WRITERS OF
MODERN YIDDISH LITERATURE

M. Usishkin, a Zionist leader, bars Mendele from the Society
of the Lovers of Hebrew *because he writes in Yiddish as well
as Hebrew (from* Der groyser kundes*).*

Chronology

c.1836 Born in Kapulie, Lithuania.

1850 Father's death. Abramovitsh travels to study in various small towns.

1853 Lives with mother and stepfather.

1854 Leaves home and travels through the Pale of Settlement with Abraham the Lame, ending up in Kamenets–Podolski. Marries.

1856 Becomes teacher in the Kamenets–Podolski Jewish schools.

1857 Appearance of Abramovitsh's first published work, ''A Letter Concerning Education,'' in the Hebrew newspaper *Hamagid*.

1858 Moves to Berdichev, marries Pessie Levin (having divorced his first wife).

1860 Appearance of *Mishpat Shalom (The Judgment of Shalom)* a collection of articles, including some of the earliest literary criticism in Hebrew.

1862 Appearance of Abramovitsh's first fictional work, *Limdu Hetev (Learn to Do Well)*, as well as the first volume of *Toldot Hateva (Natural History)*, his adaptation of a German work on natural history.

1864 Appearance of Abramovitsh's first fiction in Yiddish, *Dos Kleyne Mentshele (The Little Man)*, as a serial in the Yiddish newspaper *Kol Mevasser*.

1865 Appearance of the first version of *Dos Vintshfingerl (The Magic Wishing Ring)*.

1866 Appearance of *Eyn Mishpat (the Fountain of Judgment)* a second collection of articles, as well as the second volume of *Toldot Hateva*.

1868 Appearance of *Ha'avot Vehabanim (The Fathers and the Sons)*.

1869 Appearance of *Di Takse (The Tax)* and the first version of *Fishke der Krumer (Fishke the Lame)*. Leaves Berdichev and moves to Zhitomir.

1872 Appearance of the third volume of *Toldot Hateva*.

1873 Appearance of *Di Klyatshe (The Nag)*.

1878 Appearance of *Masoes Binyomin Hashlishi (The Travels and Adventures of Benjamin the Third)*, his last work until 1884.

1879–1881 Family problems (daughter dies, son arrested for political activities), poverty.

1881 Moves to Odessa, becomes head of the Odessa Talmud Torah. Assassination of Alexander II, followed by pogroms.

1884 Appearance of *Der Priziv (The Draft)*.

1886 Appearance of Hebrew story ''Beseter Ra'am'' (''In the Secret Place of Thunder'').

3

1888 Appearance of new versions of *Fishke der Krumer* and *Dos Vintsh-fingerl*.

1890 Appearance of "Shem Veyefet Ba'agala" ("Shem and Japhet in the Train Compartment").

1892 Appearance of "Lo Nachat be'Ya'akov" ("There is No Good in Jacob").

1894 Appearance of "Bymey Hara'ash" ("In the Days of Tumult") and "Byshiva shel Ma'alah Uvyshiva shel Mata" ("In the Heavenly and Earthly Assemblies").

1899 Appearance of *Shloyme Reb Khayim's (Shloyme, the Son of Reb Khayim)*.

1905–1907 Spends two years in Geneva.

1909 Tours Jewish communities of the Pale.

1911 Appearance of collected works in Yiddish.

1917 Dies December 8 at age of eighty-one.*

---

*The above chronology is from Theodore Steinberg's *Mendele Moykher-Sforim* (1977). For a more detailed bibliographical account of Mendele's work, see the bibliography by Dan Miron at the end of this book; for more facts about Mendele's life, see the "Introduction" following.

Introduction

A SUMMARY OF MENDELE'S LIFE, WORK, AND TIMES
by Gerald Stillman

MENDELE Moykher-Sforim wrote his *Notes For My Biography* in 1889, when he was fifty-three years old, at the request of Nokhem Sokolov,[1] who was compiling a series of biographies of prominent Hebrew and Yiddish writers for his *Seyfer Zikorn* (*Book of Records*). Mendele, as he is commonly (and endearingly) called, was then the director of the large reformed *Talmud-toyre* in Odessa, a position which allowed him to support his family but cheated him of time to write. "A cursed job," he called it, "which transforms me into a kind of dray horse...."

At this time, Mendele had started *Dos Vintshfingerl* (*The Wishing Ring*), an epic novel, which he wrote and published serially between 1888 and 1905. The demands on Mendele's time of his directorship and his writing, coupled with his natural aversion for discussing details of his personal life, account perhaps for the meagerness of the *Notes For My Biography* (see page 31). Many important details of his life are not mentioned. A later, unfinished novelette, *Shloyme Reb Khayim's* (see p.397), contains autobiographical material, but it too cannot be considered an autobiography.

This introduction aims to fill in some of the gaps and provide a more complete picture of Mendele—the man, the writer, and his times

Mendele's lifespan, from 1836 to 1917, encompassed a period of great change for the Russian Empire and for the five-and-one-half million Jews (according to the census of 1887) who lived in it. He was born during the oppressive regime of Nicholas I, and died three weeks after the Bolshevik revolution. At the beginning

5

of this period, Russia was a feudal country; the vast majority of Jews lived in conditions of indescribable poverty as a result of the brutality of the Tsarist government and the economic exploitation by *kahal,* the semi-autonomous Jewish governing body. Toward the end of the period, capitalism, and its attendant industrialization, made significant inroads in Russia. Among the Jews, nationalism and socialism had become important movements.

Throughout the nineteenth century, the economic condition of the Jews in Russia was one of misery. Aside from a few very wealthy Jews, most Jews were never sure where the next meal was coming from. The one certainty in life for them was its instability and the ever-present threat of hunger and disease. In *The Jews in Russia* (1872), I. Orshansky described the plight of the Jews in White Russia and Polesye:

> Half, if not three-quarters of the Jewish population consists of individuals who could be classified as go-betweens and middlemen, as vagrants and loiterers—not because these characteristics stem from laziness or lack of desire to work, but rather because these wretched people's sole concern is to obtain a crust of bread. They live in torment from day to day, not having the slightest means or opportunity to find gainful employment in productive work....These unfortunate families own nothing, live in filth and poverty, not knowing how or whether they will eat on the following day. Sheer necessity forces them to employ irregular means to provide themselves with the barest essentials of life...
>
> In Berditshev, there are as yet no welfare laws concerning the poverty-stricken and unsanitary conditions of the Jews. Some 5,000 families, about 25,000 souls, live from day-to-day only on what the Lord provides. They live in extremely crowded conditions. It very often happens that several families occupy one or two rooms in a ruined hovel, so that at night there is no free space on the floor between the sleepers....[2]

In 1847, Honore de Balzac traveled through Poland and the Ukraine to visit his betrothed, Mme. Hanska, on her estate. His journey took him through Berditshev, the city which Mendele called "Glupsk":

> Toward midday, I saw, rising before me, a height, upon which is perched the most illustrious city of Berditshev which, like its sister city Brody, belongs to the Radziwils. There, I saw, with renewed astonishment, houses dancing the polka — all of them leaning, some on their right haunches, some on their left, others with their heads thrown back; most of them falling apart, many of them smaller than our [Parisian] market stalls

6

and fit only as cattle pens. It is a spectacle so unexpected for a European, for a Parisian, that one must see it repeated in a number of cities before one gets used to it... One asks oneself, on seeing Berditshev, whether these houses, which three Parisian porters could carry away, have any occupants...[3]

Mendele, in a charming passage in *The Travels of Benjamin III*, conveys the pointlessness and hopelessness of the Jewish occupations in the Pale:

Ask a Jew of Tuneyadevke how he makes a living. His first reaction is to stand there paralyzed. The poor man is befuddled and doesn't know what to say. But soon he revives and begins to explain:
"Who, me? How I make a living? Me? *Et,* there is a God, I tell you here and now, who does not forsake any of his creatures. He has provided before and will probably provide some more, I tell you here and now."
"Still, what do you do? Do you at least have a trade or a craft?"
"Praise the Lord! I have, thank God, as you see here, a gift from His Blessed Name, an instrument, a musical voice, and I also recite the supplemental prayers during the Solemn Days. Occasionally, I am a *moyel,* and before Passover I knead dough for making *matses*—there isn't another kneader like me in the world, I tell you right here and now. Sometimes, I manage to make a match, I do. Also, this is between me and you, I have an interest in a tavern which can be milked a little. I have a goat which can be milked a lot, may the evil eye not harm her, and not far from here, I have a rich relative who can also, when times are bad, be milked a little. Now, aside from all these things, I tell you right here and now, God is a father and the children of Israel are both merciful and generous...[4]

Mendele Moykher-Sforim (literally, Mendele-the-Book-Peddler) is a pseudonym. He was born Sholem-Yankef Broyde[5] in Kapulye, a small town in the Province of Minsk. In his *Notes For My Biography,* he wrote:

My birth-date is nowhere recorded. Jews didn't pay attention to such things in those days, particularly in the small towns. But I have assumed that I was born in the year 1836, and my family determined December 20 to be my date of birth.[*]

---

[*]December 20, 1836, the date generally accepted as Mendele's birthdate is the date given here by Mendele according to the old Julian calendar in use in Russia at that time; according to the new calendar, the date is January 1, 1837, twelve days later. Contemporaries of Mendele's have said that he himself thought he might be seven or eight years older.

It was no accident that "Jews didn't pay attention to such things" during the reign of Nicholas I. In addition to other repressions, the Tsar experimented with various methods of Russifying and assimilating the Jews. He instituted severe conscription laws making ten Jews in every thousand liable for service in the army for thirty-one years, starting at the age of twelve. Jewish conscripts were transported thousands of miles from their native towns, far from any Jewish influence. Small wonder, then, that birth-dates of males were not recorded. The name would then not appear on any list, or, if the child were identified by the Jewish agents of *kahal,* his age could be falsified. Furthermore, it was not the custom among East-European Jews to take much note of birthdays. Birthdays were not celebrated as they were in the Christian world. (Among these Jews the date of death, on the other hand , was carefully noted so that the religious obligation to recite the yearly *kadish,* or prayer for the dead, could be fulfilled precisely on the anniversary of the date of death *(yortsayt)).* In Mendele's case, his lack of a birth record became a source of grief later in life, as we shall see.

Mendele's father, Khayim-Moyshe Broyde, a prominent and respected figure in Kapulye, was for many years the collector of the tax on kosher meat. There is a note of irony here.

The kosher-meat tax and the tax on salt were among the most oppresive levies on the tables of the Jewish poor. Mendele, with his keen sense of social justice, vehemently attacked the collectors of food taxes because of their impact on the life and health of the Jewish people. One of his best known works was *Di Takse (The Kosher Meat Tax),* a drama which dealt specifically with this aspect of Jewish life.

From available biographical material, however, his father was, despite his occupation, a kind and sensitive man, whose advice on all kinds of subjects was sought by the entire community. He served as crown rabbi[6] for the community without pay. He was also a fine Biblical scholar who wrote well in the stylized, flowery Hebrew current at the time. As he approached forty, his business affairs failed, and he died at the age of forty-one, leaving the family in poverty.

The thirteen year-old Mendele, the middle child of seven, left home to study at various Lithuanian *yeshives,* "lived in misery like the most learned of men...took meals at a different house each

8

day and experienced all the attendant humiliations."[7] After spending three years at *yeshives* in Timkevitsh, Slutsk, and Vilna, he returned to Kapulye when he was nearly nearly seventeen. Finding that his mother had married a widowed miller in Melniki, an isolated village near Kapulye, he stayed with a divorced sister in Kapulye. But he felt like a stranger in the town of his birth. He therefore jumped at his stepfather's invitation to come live at the mill. The village, with its woods and waterfall, was beautiful. In addition to tutoring his stepfather's children, Mendele spent many hours communing with nature. In the *Notes For My Biography,* he describes how he fell in love with nature here and "became betrothed to her for eternity."

Life at the mill became tedious, however, and he went back to the house of study in Kapulye to take up his religious studies again. At this time, Avreml the Limper, a well known tramp, returned to Kapulye from a lengthy journey through Volhynia and the south of Russia. He had a stock of wonderful tales about these regions and the good life of the poor Jews who, he maintained, lived more prosperously there than the wealthy ones in Kapulye, and ate braided *khales*, even during the middle of the week. The tales fired the imagination of the seventeen-year-old Mendele, and he left with Avreml. They wandered through Lithuania and the southwestern portion of Russia—through Volhynia, Podolye and the Ukraine—sleeping in poorhouses or on the benches in houses of study. They begged their way across the Jewish Pale of Settlement[8] for the better part of a year. The unscrupulous Avreml used Mendele, and an aunt of Mendele's who was traveling with them, to beg for alms. When they arrived at Kamenets-Podolsk, Mendele, with the help of a friend who lived there, escaped from Avreml's clutches. His travels in the broken-down wagon drawn by a gaunt old mare became the model for Abramovitsh's character, Mendele, and his van of books and wares, drawn by his wise, perpetually hungry horse—particularly in the opening chapters of *The Little Man* and *Fishke the Lame.* They also provided much of the material which Mendele used with such telling effect in his other novels and dramas.

He settled in Kamenets and was henceforth known as Sholem-Yankef Abramovitsh (son of *Abram*—the Russian version of *Abraham*) possibly naming himself after *Avreml* (the Yiddish diminutive of *Abraham*). In the house of study, his knowledge of the Bible, the *gemore*, and Hebrew grammar created a stir. It was suggested that he meet the finest scholar and grammarian in Kamenets. This turned out to be the poet and *maskil*[9] Avrom-Ber Gottlober[10], who was then a teacher at the local crown school for Jews. Gottlober encouraged Mendele to acquire secular knowledge and gave him the full use of his extensive library. With the help of Gottlober's daughters, Mendele applied himself to learning European languages and literatures, mathematics, science, and natural history. He also became acquainted with the works of the Russian critics Belinsky, Dobroliubov, and Pisarev. The notes he took were, at least until World War II, preserved in the Mendele Museum in Odessa. He became a teacher in the crown school when he was twenty, after passing the examination for that position.

The young scholar was an eligible bachelor and widely sought after. He married the daughter of a wealthy man who had some secular education. But within three years the marriage ended in divorce. Both his wife and his father-in-law showed great understanding for Mendele, and they parted as friends.

While working as a teacher in Kamenets, Mendele wrote a lengthy answer to a letter from one of his older brothers who was a *melamed* in a small town. His brother had complained about the misery of teaching. A friend of Mendele's found the first draft of his reply and sent it to Gottlober, who was then teaching in Staro-Konstantin. Gottlober forwarded it to the newspaper *Hamagid*[11] with a cover letter urging that the letter be printed not only in the original Hebrew, but also in Russian translation. Mendele's article, *A Letter on the Subject of Education,* created a stir among the readers of *Hamagid,* both because of its content and its Hebrew style. Y.H. Ravnitzky[12] wrote that it is impossible to appreciate its impact without being familiar with the trivial content and poor quality of writing in the first-year issues of *Hamagid.* Mendele's *Letter* was explosive, introducing, as it suddenly did, the thoughts "of a mature and developed person, who used fresh words, concisely and clearly, without convoluted flowery phrases, and introduced such new ideas as the need for a good teacher to understand the child's soul."[13]

A year later, in 1858, Mendele moved to Berditshev. There he married Pesye Levin, daughter of a prominent, well-to-do notary,

Zalmen Levin. His father-in-law undertook to support him, and Mendele plunged into his literary activities with renewed vigor.

Mendele's initial literary efforts were in Hebrew. By the time he was twenty-four, he had already gained a reputation as an innovative stylist. Hebrew was understood only by a select circle of intellectual *maskilim,* and it was the uneducated whom he wished to address. In his *Notes For My Biography,* Mendele described the dilemma facing a writer who wanted to publish in Yiddish:

> I observed the life of my people and wished to provide them with stories in the Holy Tongue based on Jewish sources. Most of them, however, did not understand this language, because they spoke only Yiddish.... Our writers... were interested only in the Holy Tongue and not in the people. They looked down upon Yiddish. If one in ten ever remembered the 'accursed tongue' and dared to write something in it, he did it behind seven locked doors and hid it beneath his holy prayer shawl so that his shame might not be uncovered to damage his good name. How great then was my dilemma when I considered that if I were to embark on writing in the 'shameful' tongue, my honorable name would be besmirched!... My love for utility, however, overcame my hollow pride, and I decided· come what may, I will write in Yiddish, that cast-off daughter, and work for the people. A good friend of mine...stood by me, and together we persuaded the editor of *Hameylits* [14] to publish a newspaper in the people's language... Enthused, I wrote my first story, *Dos Kleyne Mentshele.* [15]

The editor referred to was Alexander Tsederboym. [16] Mendele submitted the manuscript to him in 1864 under the pseudonym Senderl Moykher-Sforim, using the name of a real book-peddler who used to visit Kapulye from time-to-time. Since "Senderl" is the dimunitive form of Alexander, Tsederboym was afraid that his audience might suspect he had written the piece himself, so he changed "Senderl" to "Mendele," without consulting the young Abramovitsh. And that is how the grandfather of modern Yiddish literature acquired his *nom-de-plume.*

Mendele was almost twenty-five when Alexander II (reigned 1855-1881) abolished serfdom in 1861, ushering in a brief period of hope for reform among Russian liberals and intellectuals. The hopeful atmosphere affected the Jewish intelligentsia also, particularly the *maskilim,* and Mendele among them, who were in touch with the outside world. In dedicating *Fishke the Lame* to his friend Menashe Margolius, Mendele wrote:

11

You and I, dear friend, both began our work in Yiddish literature in the springtime of Jewish life here in our land. From 1860 onward, a new life seemed to have begun for Jews.

The hope was that the pitiful economic situation of the Jews could be reversed by improving their backward social and cultural conditions. The great majority of Jews were still living in the middle ages. Beyond the limits of their town or village lurked all kinds of unknown terrors. Their daily lives were filled with fears of elves, goblins, evil spirits, demons, and ghosts. Superstition governed almost every act. Whatever learning a poor child received came from a rod-wielding *melamed,* who, as Mendele would later put it, died three times a day from hunger himself. The child repeated by rote from the *khumesh* (Pentateuch), learning to read, but rarely to understand what he read.

Like other *maskilim* of the time, Mendele believed that the way to improve the living conditions of the Jewish people lay in popularizing science and mathematics, in urging Jews to use the Russian language, to learn useful trades, and to wear modern clothes. To this end, he wrote articles on education and published attacks against *khasidism,* which (as a true *maskil)* he regarded as a benighting influence. To make it possible for Jews to have access to natural science, he published a Hebrew translation of a then popular text on biology[17] under the title *Toldos Hateve* (*Natural History*) in three volumes—Mammals, Birds, Reptiles and Amphibians in 1862, 1867, and 1872, respectively. He also translated a history of the Russian people into Hebrew, so that ordinary Jews could become acquainted with the history of the people among whom they lived; and he translated various prayers and religious texts into Yiddish so that ordinary Jews could appreciate their beauty.

But Mendele was too well aware of the social injustices within the Jewish community, of *kahal's* economic exploitation, of the repressive measures of the Tsarist government, to believe that the appalling economic conditions of Jewish life could be reversed solely by education. His awareness of these factors distinguished him from most other *maskilim*. A healthy realism was already apparent in his early works in Yiddish.

Dos Kleyne Mentshele, Mendele's first major work in Yiddish, is a confessional novel in which the protagonist describes his climb from poverty to riches in a small Jewish town. It portrays the abuse of charitable contributions, the tax on kosher meat, the kidnapping of poor Jewish boys to serve in the army in lieu of rich ones, overcharging for medical services, graft, payoffs—all of which came out of the hides of the poor. *Di Takse,* subtitled *The Gang of Town Philanthropists,* is a drama which is even more outspoken, its cast of characters including various *kahal* officials, rich men, and their lackeys. But they were apparently too recognizable. The publication of the play caused such an uproar among the wealthy proprietors of Berditshev, that Mendele was forced to move, and he and his family resettled in Zhitomir. Even there, the long arm of the Berditshev *kahal* reached after him.

With the publication of *Di Klyatshe (The Mare)* in 1873, he parted company with the *maskilim,* poking fun at their short-sighted belief that Jews would acquire basic human rights as soon as they became enlightened and educated. The mare, a talking horse, is a symbol of the Jewish people; her story is an allegory of Jewish history. This work introduces the then nascent feelings of national consciousness among Jews. Here is a passage in which the mare lectures Yisrolik, the well-intentioned member of the Society for the Prevention of Cruelty to Animals (a parody on the influential Society for the Promotion of Culture Among the Jews—an official organization of the *haskole* movement) who pities her and wants to help her get out of the ditch into which she has fallen:

> I am the equal of others...of the same flesh and blood as any other... entitled to the same right to live. If someone commiserates with me, he implies that I am living on his merits. Thus he is privileged to live, while I am not! My very existence is due to him... I want to live on an equal footing with others—on my own merits, that is. Now, do you understand me, my righteous defender, my merciful master? As for your mercy and any possible advantage you may derive from me—I place no reliance on these possibilities... But if you were to treat me as you do others, fairly and squarely, we could have a friendly chat about all sorts of clever arts....[18]

In articles written in 1864 for *Hameylits (The Advocate)* and later published separately as *Eyn mishpat* (1867), Abramovitsh, according to Tsinberg's *A History of Jewish Literature* (Volume XII, p. 139ff) "comes forth...with a sharp critique and portrays the *haskole* literature in extremely dark colors." As Tsinberg puts it:

Mendele concludes that the *maskilim* also are "desirers of old things and maintainers of received things," that they still cling to the obsolete and remain faithful to the traditional forms. In their writings, too, the spirit of arid scholasticism and *pilpul* prevails in considerable measure. In the *haskole* literature, Abramovitsch declares, the breath of modern life is not felt. It is not organically bound up with real needs....A literature in which the echo of life is not felt is also incapable of affecting life....Abramovitsh addresses the maskilim: If you really wish to ameliorate the condition of your people, then throw away the old [threadbare] arguments about the barbarization and "superstition" of the people and request the government to grant us equal civic rights, to open for us the necessary sources of life. But demand it without any conditions, do not associate it with the question of education. (*Note by Tsinberg: It is interesting that Abramovitsh here [disagrees with] his own teacher Gottlober, who, in fact, argued in the same columns of* Hameylits *that Jews must learn to speak Russian as quickly as possible: "And the language of our country will be fluent in the mouth of all the* maskilim, *until it becomes the language of the people, for only then will we succeed in ascending to the levels of the natives of the country and to inherit the good of the blessed land, like all its inhabitants."*)

Fishke der Krumer (Fishke the Lame), first published in 1869, is a book about beggars and tramps. "It has been my lot to descend to the depths, to the cellars of our Jewish life. My stock in trade is rags and moldy wares. My dealings are with paupers and beggars, the poor wretches of life... the dregs of humanity," wrote Mendele in his introduction. As in the other works, he exposed the injustices within the Jewish community and their effect on the people:

Once a Jew has broken himself of the vile passion for eating, food ceases to be a matter of importance to him, and he can spend the rest of his life requiring virtually nothing. To this very day, in these modern times, many a Jew can be found who has only the vestige of a stomach—truly, the size of an olive pit. And there are great hopes that with the passing of time—if only the kosher-meat tax is retained and the activities of the charity workers and their brethren are not restrained—Jews will drift further and further away from eating, until among future generations there will be no trace left of a digestive tract at all, except for piles. Jews will then present a pretty picture to the eyes of the rest of the world.[19]

Mendele's beggars and tramps are a varied lot. Many are helpless in the face of forces far beyond their control. Others attempt to manipulate people, including their brother beggars, in an effort to survive. But there is anger, too. Here is a speech by Faybushke, the red-headed thief in *Fishke:*

Why should the rich sit around like princes, doing nothing, while others work for them? Doesn't everything they own come from other people's toil, other people's tears and sweat? They think they're fine folks. They take care of themselves and want others to work. A rich man, the fatter he is and the bigger his belly .the more honor and respect he gets. With us it's just the opposite. A healthy beggar has to be ashamed and hide like a thief. Otherwise people raise a hue and cry and want to know why such a healthy lout isn't working. It's time for a change....[20]

Despite the literary productivity of the years in Zhitomir, Mendele's life there was marked by privation. He had fled there in 1869 to escape the wrath of the *kahal* officials of Berditshev, who where infuriated by his too accurate descriptions in *Di Takse.* Tsvayfl [21] claimed that many of these individuals could not walk along the streets of Berditshev without being pointed at and called by the names of the characters in *Di Takse.* Even in Zhitomir, they made it difficult for him to find employment. Eventually, he obtained a certificate enabling him to teach at the crown school for Jews. But one of the characters in the drama, *Mendl der Geler (Mendl-the-Yellow-One)*, whom Mendele had described as "a hatchet-man, a thug, who danced attendance upon the charity workers and roughed up whomever they ordered," would not rest until he had taken his revenge on Mendele. He found out that Mendele's birth had not been recorded in Kapulye and that he had changed his family name to Abramovitsh. Disclosure of this fact could have been ruinous for Mendele, a man with a government position as crown teacher, with a reputation among government officials as a fine pedagogue, a learned Jew — and a recognized writer. *Mendl der Geler,* realizing the implications of his discovery, blackmailed Mendele and extorted large sums of money from him. From 1877 to 1884, Mendele stopped writing. During this time Mendele told his friend J. L. Binshtok[22] that writing "it seems, has become impossible for me. My brain is filled with lead, and my heart has turned to stone."[23] Two close friends eventually rescued Mendele from Mendl-the-Yellow-One by finding a way to have Mendele listed in the Kapulye registry. Gradually his creative powers returned. Concerning Mendele's last years in Zhitomir, the historian Dubnow[24] writes:

I cannot forget the description of the poverty that he experienced in the last few years before he moved to Odessa: "My expenses were large — a family of seven. The receipts from my books didn't even cover the rent. The publishers in Vilna and Warsaw cheated me. They reprinted *Di Takse, Di Klyatshe,* and *Dos Kleyne Mentshele* surreptitiously and sold each other the stereotypes of my books in secret. It came to such a pass that I wasn't sure how we would eat the next day. In those hard times, Baron Horace Günzberg,[25] who knew me in my youth in Kamenets, came to my aid. He heard about my difficulties from friends in St. Petersburg and began to send me a fixed sum of money each month — 100 roubles, if I remember correctly."[26]

In 1881, Mendele moved to Odessa, where he lived for the rest of his life (except for a two-year interruption in Geneva, where he fled following government-inspired pogroms in Odessa in the aftermath of the Revolution of 1905). In Odessa, he became the director of the large reformed *Talmud-Toyre.* There he wrote *Dos vintshfingerl (The Wishing Ring),* which was published serially between 1888 and 1905. It is an epic novel about the Jewish people in the Pale. Jewish life is portrayed in painstakingly realistic detail. Dovid Frishman[27] wrote that

if a flood were to destroy all that mankind had created, leaving this one book, we would be quite capable of using it to reconstruct the overall picture of Jewish life and Jewishness in the small towns of Russia during the first half of the 19th century... Not a detail is omitted, and, regarding his manner of writing—his descriptive powers have produced marvels again, even more so than in his previous works. [28]

The novel presents a social history of the period which cannot be obtained from any history book. Dubnow related that Mendele told him more than once: "I am an historian also, but of a different cut. When you will want to write a history of the nineteenth century, you will have to use my works to depict the life of those generations." The 1890's were years of political ferment in the Jewish communities of eastern Europe, particularly among the intelligentsia. Mendele, the social historian who knew on which side he stood when describing the past, remained unaligned in this active time, but not for lack of definite opinions nor for lack of sympathy for any of the announced programs. Dubnow writes:

16

He could not recognize any program as a necessity, or any system of principles as a proven solution. On social and political questions, he was by nature 'untamed.' He had moods, sympathies and antipathies, but no fixed principles, and his moods changed often as his personal, subjective perceptions changed, for example, in regard to this person or that representative of one party or another. He did not like the modern, clamorous political movements. The more adherents a movement had, the greater was his opportunity to see the negative or ridiculous aspects of individual adherents and the way ideals were distorted by individuals with little understanding. He, the artist who portrayed the way people lived, always proceeded from people to ideas, and not the reverse.[29]

Once, during a conversation in Dubnow's study, when Mendele was asked why he did not come out in support of those who were waging a struggle against the menace of assimilationism among Jewish youth, he flared up:

So I'm a bad Jew because I don't belong to the Nationalists! No, you are all Jews with labels: Nationalists, Zionists, Palestinians,[30] and I'm a plain Jew, but our entire people consists of such plain Jews.[31]

His non-alignment with any program or ideology may have enabled him to observe the weaknesses of each of them and depict them in his work of that period—the novels *Dos Vintshfingerl, Shloyme Reb Khayim's;* and the short stories *Tsurik Aheym (Back Home!), Di Alte Mayse (The Old Story) Shem un Yofes in a Vagon (Shem and Japhet on the Train), In a Shturem Tsayt (In a Time of Turmoil), Di Nesrofim (The Fire Victims).* The short stories deal with the turmoil in Jewish communities throughout the Pale after the persistent pogroms of the 1880's, following the assassination of Alexander II in 1881. These works depicted the aftermath of the pogrom period which, in the 1880's and 1890's, saw the dislocation of large numbers of Jews, the first waves of mass migration to America, the creation of Palestine-oriented societies, and of nationalistic and socialistic groupings.

In 1899, the first edition of *Shloyme Reb Khayim's,* subtitled "A Picture of Jewish Life in Lithuania," appeared. This unfinished autobiographical novelette was followed by further autobiographical chapters, published in various magazines in 1912, 1913 and 1917. In these later works, Mendele continued to reveal his

17

mastery as portrayer of all aspects of the life of the Jewish people but, now a new element entered—a conscious desire to preserve for future generations the knowledge of how their predecessors lived:

Let children's children know in what kind of houses their *zeydes* lived and spent their years, together with their children, big and small, and married couples who also lived with them.[32]

Although he lived most of his life in the larger towns of Berditshev and Zhitomir, and in the city of Odessa, most of Mendele's works are concerned with life in the Jewish villages and hamlets of the rural areas in the Pale, where, according to the census of 1887, more than half of the Jewish population of the Russian empire lived.[33] He used the beauty of the forests and fields, the hills and the valleys, the rivers and lakes which surrounded the towns and villages, as a contrast to life in the towns proper. He never forgot his adolescent experience at his stepfather's mill, where he had "betrothed himself" to nature and had "made a covenant with the trees in the countryside, with the birds and fruits of the earth."[34]

Mendele's trees, flowers, sunbeams, shadows, birds appeared to be members of the human community with similar joys and sorrows.

It is hushed and quiet in the forest in the fall during the High Holidays, like in Kabtsansk [Poor Town] on the Sabbath, when folks are napping in the afternoon and the stillness casts a melancholic mood over the town. The trees are pensive, worried...the buzzing of the leaves is a bitter wailing, a sighing, a moaning of a loving mother who remains alone after her children have gone off in all directions....The nests are abandoned. The little birds have flown away....[35]

Mendele's romanticism was at least in part an outgrowth of his familiarity with European literature. Hebrew reviews that he wrote as a young man in the 1850's, when he was studying in Kamenets, show that he had become acquainted with the works of the major Russian, German, and English writers. Alexander Binshtok (1866-1937), son of J. L. Binshtok, described Mendele's attitude toward certain classical English writers: "Swift's *Gulliver's Travels* was a favorite book of his. And in this book, the chapters he liked best were those dealing with Gulliver's stay among the Houhynhnms. He also had a very high regard for Thackeray, Dickens, and their predecessor, Fielding. I became acquainted with Fieldings's *Tom Jones* at Mendele's recommendation..."[36]

Writing did not come easily to Mendele. In this respect, he differed markedly from Sholem Aleykhem. According to Dubnow, the latter could write anywhere—on a train, in a street car, in the midst of noise and commotion—while Mendele would isolate himself in the furthest room and sit for hours rapt in thought before he wrote a single line. Dubnow relates an anecdote in which Mendele compared his manner of writing with that of Sholem Aleykhem's:

> A woman often takes several days to deliver a child. The whole household is aquiver. Everyone walks on tip-toes. People whisper to each other, waiting night and day until the good news is announced that, with luck, a child has been born. At the same time, a little hen sits for while in a corner, squeezes a bit, and there it is—an egg....[37]

Mendele was a severe critic of his own work. He continually revised and polished what he had written, mercilessly scratching out every inappropriate expression. He rewrote his works for each new edition, sometimes to such an extent that the later version bore little resemblance to the earlier one. This was particularly true when he translated works into Yiddish that he had originally written in Hebrew, or vice versa.

Mendele wanted the people to read and understand him. He used the language of the people, but it was far more than an ethnographic reproduction of their speech. He drew his inspiration from their language, from its sentence structure, its idiom, its colorful rhetoric. His respect for it was boundless. He took a language which, despite a literary and philological history which has been traced back to the twelfth century, was referred to as a "kitchen tongue" and a "jargon," and gave it literary status. He performed for Yiddish that service which Chaucer performed for English, Rabelais for French, and Dante for Italian. Much of the Yiddish literary heritage before the 1860's, when Mendele started writing, consisted of romances and minnesongs translated from the medieval French, German, and Italian troubadours; religious tales of a moralizing and didactic nature, *tkhines*—

prayerbooks for women with lachrymose commentaries on contemporary life; short novelettes of a sensational and shallow type; and *khasidic* tales. The written language was awkward, Germanized, and bore little resemblance to the language in daily use. The condition of written Hebrew was not very different and is graphically described by Mendele in the *Notes For My Biography*. Mendele's accomplishments in raising the level of both languages and literatures is summarized succinctly by Y. H. Ravnitzky:

> He is not only the creator of one literature, but of two—and simultaneously. This is such a rare phenomenon that it has no equal among other world literatures. Both in Hebrew and in Yiddish, Mendele had to hack out new pathways alone...Lucky were "the grandchildren"...Sholem Aleykhem in Yiddish and Bialik in Hebrew prose, that they came later...and had such an excellent model....[38]

In the summer of 1909, Mendele undertook a tour of four large Jewish cities in the Russian Empire. Dovid Frishman, who accompanied him, described the impact of the tour on the Jewish population:

> His trip was, in the fullest sense of the word, a triumphal journey...The triumphal arch extended from Vilna to Bialystok, from Bialystok to Warsaw, Warsaw to Lodz. No other writer, let alone a Jewish writer, ever had the honor of such a journey...Thousands of people waited at each station; thousands pushed and shoved to get close to him and were counted fortunate if they shook his hand or saw his face...In Lodz, tens of thousands of people gathered in the street in front of the hotel where Abramovitsh was staying. [39]

Mendele was astounded by the reception given him in each of the cities. He continued to marvel at the people's enthusiasm and warmth: "Now I begin to believe that my work was not in vain. Can you imagine? Porters, plain street-porters, came to greet me!" [40]

A year later, in 1910, preparations were under way to celebrate his 75th birthday. Y.L. Perets wrote an article in honor of the occasion and assessed Mendele's role as the architect of Yiddish literature:

Not only is he the oldest of our living writers, but he is also, and this is the heart of the matter, the first. A literature was being built, and it was he who laid the cornerstone. He was the first, after a brief period of side experiments, to write unselfishly, to create pure cultural values... And he was the first who did not consider his work to be a stepping stone from which "to lead the mare [*di klyatshe*] to pasture in greener fields."

He was the first to love and respect his artistic medium, the Yiddish language, and he developed it and kept it pure and clean—not Germanized, not Russified, not even Europeanized... and was thus the first to create a Yiddish style...

He was the first who said to his generation of *maskilim:* "You speak of reform, do you, and of enlightenment? The people need bread!" And the first who saw and depicted the officials of *kahal* in their true aspect....[41]

In the latter half of 1915, Mendele suffered a stroke which paralyzed the left side of his body. He recovered to some degree during the next year and a half. The February Revolution of 1917, which overthrew the Tsarist government, was a source of enthusiasm for the old fighter for Jewish rights. He sent a message of greeting to the Conference of Jewish Artists of Russia which took place in St. Vladimir's Hall of Kiev University on August 29, 1917:

Gentlemen! Need I tell you how sad it is, what a heartache it is, for parents not to be present at the festivities of their children, be it because of sickness, for example, or for lack of funds, and to have to stay at a distance, like strangers, while their friends and relatives gather from near and far to celebrate together?... If God will grant me health and life, I will come to visit you... and bring you new books..."[42]

But this hope was laid low by a second stroke which took away his power of speech. Mendele died in Odessa on November 25, 1917.[43]

· · ·

THE EDITORS thought it would also be useful to the reader to see what some of the writers, intellectuals, and Yiddish literary critics of Mendele's time (and also some from more recent times) wrote about Mendele's contribution to Jewish letters. In our English translation below, therefore, is appended a summary of some critical remarks from the end of the article on Mendele in *Leksikon fun der nayer yidisher literatur (Lexicon of Modern Yiddish Literature),* 1965:

21

The classic formulation, "Mendele's way," comes from the pen of Khayim Nakhmen Byalik: To create for a literature a 'way' [*nusakh*: style, version, form]—this means, once and for all, to contribute solid and lasting forms for the feelings and thoughts of the people, and thereby, at the same time, make it easier for the people to process these thoughts and feelings; it means to help the people to think and feel; it means to discipline the spirit of the people; to give form to what is formless; from raw earth to extract gold and melt it down into exchangeable coins; to present the people with a "way"—means to creep unnoticed into the people's bone-marrow; quietly to steal into their hearts, to pour oneself, perhaps to vanish forever, into their souls....this particular little piece of work is what the *zeyde* did. It is over fifty years since the grandfather with his spectacles over his sharp, pointed little eyes sits in his grandfather-chair bent over half a broadsheet, fashioning his pearls. So long did he work thus, until he fashioned for us all a language, a style—a literature."

"The style of an epoch," wrote S. Niger, among other things, "cannot be imitated. One can create it. In order to feel it, one must oneself have a deep and refined feeling for style. Mendele has it. Rarely among any of the Yiddish writers is the style so consistent and all of a piece as it is with Mendele."

Dr. A. Mukdoyni has related how highly I.L. Perets valued Mendele's style in his book, *Y.L. Perets un dos yidishe teater [Y.L. Perets and the Yiddish Theater]* "Perets once told me: 'Before I sit down to write, I read through a few pages of Mendele and I am led into the very thicket of Yiddish language. I don't copy him, but I soak up and am sated with the abundance of his Yiddish. I exploit that abundance in my own way.'"

Bal-Makhsoves saw as the chief virtue in Mendele's work the ability "to see in every particular, the universal, in every specific, the general, and to depict it all so artfully that out of every detail shines forth the greater whole. And this can only be accomplished by those who see life whole, with whom the stream of human continuity does not shatter into separate droplets. Only the soul that immerses itself in life larger than one's own individuality, which sees the world not just through the spectacles of its own narrow egoistic vision, is capable of always knowing and feeling the larger mass, the general soul of a community. There are few before or after Mendele among whom one can find such a broad synthesis as in his view of Jewish life."

Dovid Frishman, in his evaluation of Mendele's position in Yiddish literature, wrote that Mendele was not only the founder of modern Yiddish literature, but also embodied its highest achievement. In his evaluation of *Dos vintshfingerl*, Frishman said that the work mirrors the entire Jewish life of Mendele's time.

At the same time, the critics did not fail to see the artistic weaknesses in some of Mendele's work. Even S. Niger, who at every opportunity praised Mendele's artistic strength, wrote in his analysis of Mendele's drama *Der Priziv*, that "although it was already written after *Benjamin the Third* and he was already by this time more artist than publicist, and more humorist than satirist, nevertheless, the character of Alexander, just as his depicitions of all the intelligentsia of the new generation, is artistically pale: only the common folk breathe with life."

Perets also held a critical view of Mendele's work, although he greatly admired Mendele's style and without reservation recognized Mendele's position as a classicist in the development of Yiddish literature. Perets held that Mendele could not be the guide for the Yiddish writers of the younger generation. According to Perets, the picture of Jewish life that Mendele painted was not always a genuine and true reflection of the original. Mendele accepted Jewish poverty, the "old, big Jewish beggar's sack," as almost the only example of the Jewish reality, whereas in Jewish life there are many other more beautiful and more characteristic examples.

In more recent times, between both world wars, and after the Destruction (Holocaust) under the Nazis, many critics sharpened their critical approach to Mendele. Thus, for example, Yankef Glatshteyn wrote: "Mendele is an expression of the genius of the Jewish people. He was a spokesman for our brilliance, but that still did not make him more important than the Jewish people. Mendele rounded off an era. He came out of the *haskole,* which threw itself upon the Jewish people with harsh punitiveness. Jews never deserved such harsh punishment, because they are not, God forbid, worse than any other people. On the contrary, their great suffering and agony had so elevated them and refined them that even when they were wallowing in the muds of Tuneyadefke, they were always God's children....*Fishke the Lame,* is a very primitive work, and as if that weren't enough, Mendele's maskilic satire played itself out in the most heartless way. It is a pitiful story of a poorhouse, of the underworld, of beggars, of vulgarity and coarseness, and it is even worse that this work was interpreted as a symbol of the "great beggars sack of the House of Israel," as if the whole Jewish people consisted of such characters. We know that Mendele's work can make one feel quite downcast. One must enter into his orchard with great caution."

A negative approach to Mendele from the "Lovers-of-Zion" point-of-view recently provoked a controversy also in Israel. A. Kriv, who initiated the controversy, maintained that Mendele should not be taught in the schools of the state of Israel because they evoke in the students an antipathy towards the Jews of the exile [Interestingly, one of the editors of this volume was told by a New York publisher that he would not publish *Dos Kleyne Mentshele* because "it would be grist for the mill of the anti-semites.]

23

Soviet-Yiddish literary criticism had its own approach to Mendele's literary heritage. It highlighted, mainly, the social moments with which Mendele's work are so rich. M. Viner, the Soviet-Yiddish literary researcher, in his studies, developed various aspects of Mendele's work. In his work, "Mendele and the Traditon of World Literature," he pointed out clear examples of the influence of the classic writers of world literature, such as Cervantes, Gogol, Hugo, Dickens, et al, on the works of Mendele. "In his works for the masses," writes M..Viner, "Mendele strove to follow the highest examples. With the most refined artistic taste he uncovered in the Russian and European literary tradition what was most suited to his purposes; at the same time, however, he recreated that tradition in a national-specific, deeply original, and truly masterful way. In his best work, Mendele brought in not only the concepts, but also the innermost weave of subject and fable from the most excellent of the "European" traditions. He "Europeanized" (in the best sense of the word) his style, and he did not just make it superficially "modern," but deeply, internally so. For his "Europeanizations," he chose the very hardest path: organic "Europeanization."

In his general evaluation of Mendele's place in Yiddish literature (in his first essay about Mendele printed in *Der Yud*, 1901), Bal-Makhshoves wrote: "Mendele is the greatest talent that Yiddish literature in Russia can point to in the last few generations. Whatever he wrote was written with the divine pen that was created by the divine spark in the beginning of days. No-one before him painted pictures of Jewish life as he did. And the pencil with which he draws is as thin as a hair, capable of reproducing the finest line, the tiniest dot."

Zalmen Reyzn ended his detailed biography of Mendele in Volume I of his *Lexicon of Yiddish Literature* (1926) with a summing up from which we present excerpts below:

"In Yiddish literature, Abramovitsh occupies first place. He is not only the great original Yiddish author who drew from the deepest sources—from our folk-life and folk-culture and from nature; he is in general the first great artist in Yiddish. To the extent that a Yiddish literature existed before Abramovitsh, it displayed, with some significant exceptions, primarily religious or didactic purposes. Although Abramovitsh also had certain tendentious aims, he eventually transcended the tendentiousness of his generation and elevated Yiddish literature from its primitive state to a high level of artistic creativity....From the very beginning, he understands much more deeply the reasons for Jewish poverty and need than do his contemporary *maskilim*, who attributed all the problems of Jewish life to the benightedness and ignorance of the Jewish masses. Already in *The Little Man* and even more clearly in *The Meat Tax (Di Takse)*, Mendele displays for us the innermost social injustices in Jewish life....Abramovitsh ridicules the grotesqueries in the life of the people of Israel, but his laughter is bitter; a great compassion and a deep love for the terrible poverty of his people break through his incomparably bitter humor....We have Abramovitsh to thank for the first pure and truly artistic descriptions of nature in Yiddish literature; with him, all of nature acquires a Jewish demeanor; he paints here in truly Jewish folk images and metaphors, and because of this, his nature passages stand out in their classic simplicity and rare imagery. Through his nature descriptions, Abramovitsh showed that the Yiddish language possessed the kind of expressive means for mute nature that before him, had not even been dreamt of....Born in Lithuania, living for a long time in Volhynia in South Russia, blessed with a remarkable instinct for language, he created a Yiddish classic prose style on the basis of our chief dialects, exploiting in large measure the language-treasure of the folk literature of Old Yiddish."

The text above reads as follows:

"THREE IN ONE—MENDELE MOYKHER-SFORIM"

Cartoon on the right: "His friends claim he is the grandfather of modern Yiddish literature."

Cartoon in the center: "His enemies claim he has transformed the Jewish people into an old gray mare." [The Mare is the title of one of Mendele's most famous novels.]

Cartoon on the left: "The truth is, Yiddish literature has outgrown him."

(From Der groyser kundes, December 29, 1916.)

NOTES

[1] See footnote 1, *Notes For My Biography.*

[2] Quoted in M. Viner *Tsu der Geshikhte fun der Yidisher Literatur in Nayntsetn Yorhundert (On the History of Yiddish Literature in the 19th Century)*, Vol.2, p.117-118, Yiddisher Kultur Farband, New York, 1946 (my translation - GIS).

[3] Honore de Balzac, *Lettre sur Kiew,* in *Cahiers de Balzac,* p.70, Editions Lapina, Paris, 1927 (my translation - GIS).

[4] Mendele Moykher-Sforim, *Mas'oes Benyomen Hashlishi (The Travels of Benjamin III),* Vol. 2, p. 166-7, YKUF, New York 1946 (my translation - GIS).

[5] Y. H. Ravnitsky, *Sholem Yankef Abramovitsh,* an introductory article in *Ale Verk fun Mendele Moykher-Sforim (Complete Works of Mendele Moykher-Sforim),* Vol. I, p.10, Hebrew Publishing Co., New York, 1920.

[6] In 1835, Nicholas I decreed that all rabbis had to have a certain amount of secular education. Those communities whose rabbis did not possess such knowledge were required to employ an additional "crown rabbi" whose official function it was to record birth, marriage, and other civil records in Russia.

[7] *Notes For My Biography*

[8] In 1794, after the final partition of Poland, Catherine II of Russia issued a decree permitting Jews to live only within the confines of the former Polish Kingdom. This western portion of the Russian Empire was called the "Pale of Settlement" and consisted of 24 provinces containing 20% of the land area of European Russia. As some Jews acquired wealth and influence, they were granted privileges to live outside the Pale—revocable at any time.

[9] A *maskil (maskilim* - plural) was a proponent of the *haskole* (enlightenment). Started by Moses Mendelsohn in Germany in the late eighteenth century, this movement, in eastern Europe, tried to encourage Jews to learn European languages, to wear modern clothes, to engage in agriculture and industry, to learn mathematics and the sciences. It was, especially in its beginnings, a bitter foe of the *khasidic* movement.

[10] See note 23, *Notes For My Biography.*

[11] See note 21, *Notes For My Biography.*

[12] Yehoshua-Hona Ravnitsky (1859-1944); journalist, literary critic and publisher in Hebrew and Yiddish. He published Bialik's first poem, "El ha-Tsipor," in the literary collection *Pardes,* which he edited. He was a close friend of Bialik's and Mendele's. He established a publishing house in Odessa (1901) and in Palestine (1921).

[13] See reference in note 5, p. 10 (my translation - GIS).

[14] See note 26, *Notes For My Biography.*

[15] Originally translated into English by Gerald Stillman as *The Parasite,* Thomas Yoseloff, N.Y, 1956. Included in this anthology under the title *The Little Man.*

[16] See note 34, *Notes For My Biography.*

[17] See note 29, *Notes For My Biography.*

[18] *The Mare,* p.315 (my translation—GIS).

[19] *Fishke the Lame,* p.171.

[20] Ibid, p..242.

[21] See note 24, *Notes For My Biography.* Tsvayfl's claim is stated in S. L. Tsitron, *Dray Literarishe Doyres (Three Literary Generations)* Vol. I, p. 110, Szreberk Publishing Co., Warsaw (no date of publication given).

[22] See note 4, *Notes For My Biography.*

[23] Quoted in Z. Reyzn, *Leksikon fun der Yidisher Literatur, Prese un Filologye*

(*Lexicon of Yiddish Literature, Press and Philology*), Vol. I, p. 22, B. Kleckin, Vilna 1926 (my translation - GIS).

[24] Simon Dubnow (born 1860 - murdered by the Nazis in 1941) was one of the foremost Jewish historians of the twentieth century. He had a sociological conception of Jewish history, as distinguished from the customary spiritual one. He proposed that the Jewish people had always shaped its life in all its aspects and that it was a living nation with special characteristics resulting from its dispersion. His theories formed the core of the program of the National Jewish People's Party, which he helped organize in Russia in 1906.

[25] See note 22, *Notes For My Biography*.

[26] S. Dubnow, *From Jargon to Yiddish*, p. 116, B. Kleckin, Vilna, 1929 (my translation — GIS).

[27] Dovid Frishman (1860-1922), Hebrew and Yiddish journalist, poet, literary critic, short story writer, and translator. He was one of the early architects of modern Hebrew literature and, like Mendele, broke away from the stilted flowery style prevailing at the time.

[28] Quoted by Nakhman Mayzl in his introductory article, p. 9, to Vol. IV of *Geklibene Verk fun Mendele Moykher-Sforim (Selected Works of Mendele Moykher-Sforim)*, YKUF Publishers, New York, 1946 (my translation — GIS).

[29] See reference in note 28, p. 108-9 (my translation — GIS).

[30] "Palestinians" refers to those Jews who wanted to settle in Palestine, then under Turkish rule, without the consideration of creating a legitimate Jewish homeland. In the mid-1890's, when this conversation took place, homelands other than Palestine were seriously being considered. As late as 1903, six years after the first Zionist Congress in Basel, Theodor Herzl, founder of the Zionist Organization, was considering a British proposal to establish a Jewish homeland in Uganda.

[31] See reference in note 26, p. 122 (my translation — GIS).

[32] *Shloyme Reb Khayim's*, p. 10, in *The Complete Works of Mendele Moykher-Sforim*, Hebrew Publishing Co., New York, 1920 (my translation — GIS). Selection from this work reprinted in this anthology as *Of Bygone Days* (p. 399).

[33] Howard Morley Sachar, *The Course of Modern Jewish History*, p. 188, Dell Publishing Co., N.Y.,1958.

[34] *Notes For My Biography*, p.31.

[35] *Dos Vintshfingerl*, p. 55, in *Selected Works of Mendele Moykher-Sforim, Vol. IV*, YKUF Publishers, New York, 1946 (my translation — GIS).

[36] See reference in note 2, p. 37-8 (my translation — GIS).

[37] See reference in note 26, p. 47 (my translation— GIS).

[38] See reference in note 5, p. I (my translation— GIS).

[39] Quoted by Nakhman Mayzl in *Dos Mendele Bukh (The Mendele Book)*, p. 421, Yidisher Kultur Farband, New York, 1959.

[40] Ibid, p. 421 (my translation- GIS).

[41] Ibid, p. 360 (my translation - GIS).

[42] Ibid, p. 241-243 (my translation - GIS).

[43] Old-style Russian calendar; *Leksikon fun der nayer Yidisher Literatur* gives the date as Saturday, December 8 , 1917.

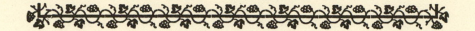

INTRODUCTION TO

Notes For My Biography

IN THE following selection (written in 1889 in response to a request by N. Sokolov for an entry about himself in a Hebrew literary lexicon; first published in Yiddish in 1911), Mendele tells us something about his youth (see selection from *Of Bygone Days* on p. 399 for more), how he became a writer, why he turned from Hebrew to Yiddish, and what he felt the function of literature among Jews in his time should be.

The passage beginning on page 41 with the sentences: "At that time, I observed the life of my people and wished to provide them with stories in the holy tongue. Most of them, however, did not understand this language, because they spoke only Yiddish. What profit accrues to a writer for all his work and thinking if he does not serve his people? The question—for whom am I working?—gave me no peace and caused me great perplexity...." and ending with "....come what may, I will write in Yiddish, that cast-off daughter, and work for the people," is often quoted to show why Mendele felt he must turn from Hebrew to Yiddish as the primary language of his creativity. He also tells us in the same passage:

Enthused, I wrote my first story, *Dos Kleyne Mentshele (The Little Man)*, subtitled, "The Biography of Avrom-Yitskhok, the Strong-Arm Man," published in Odessa, 1864(?)* in the newspaper *Kol-Mevaser* and in book form many times thereafter. This tale made a great impression on the Jewish public, so that it was soon issued in an edition in Vilna, 1865(?), and again in a fourth edition, but completely revised in Vilna, 1879. The book became the cornerstone of the new Yiddish literature.

---

*The question marks are in the original. Apparently Mendele at the time of his writing was unsure of the dates. See introduction to *The Little Man* (p.51) for the actual dates and places of publication.

(It is this novel, *Dos Kleyne Mentshele(The Little Man)*, that we have reprinted in translation (p. 53), in its entirety, as the first selection following this brief, introductory memoir, so that the reader himself may hold in his hand and read for himself this "cornerstone of the new Yiddish literature.")

In this memoir one can see not only why Mendele turned to Yiddish, but also how Mendele became so enamored of nature as a boy that his works later are studded with loving descriptions of natural beauty; how he took the first steps in his literary career; how his *haskole*-derived urge to reform, scourge, educate and uplift helped to shape him; and how even though he reveals himself in this memoir as a son of the *haskole*, the Jewish enlightenment, he was nevertheless steeped in the Jewish way of life of the times, with its bibilical and talmudic learning and piety, and later even became critical of some of the attitudes of the *maskilim* (proponents of the *haskole*).

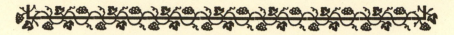

Notes For My Biography[1]

Translated by Gerald Stillman

MY BIRTHPLACE, Kapulye, is a small town in the County of Slutsk in the Province of Minsk. God did not bless the town with riches and treasure, nor did He favor it with trade and business. Instead, He endowed it with natural beauty, lovely forests, a tranquil life, valleys, and beautiful fields all around.

My birth-date is nowhere recorded. Jews didn't pay attention to such things in those days, particularly in the small towns. But I have assumed that I was born in the year 1836, and my family determined December 20 to be my date of birth.

My father, Khayim-Moyshe, of blessed memory, was a highly esteemed proprietor in the town. He was known in the region for his learning, his generosity, and his knowledge of world affairs. He divided his time in two. Half was allocated to God —he would study himself and teach others gratis. The other half was allocated to himself—to his needs, and to communal affairs, to which he devoted himself from conviction. The One-Above favored my father with a gift for oratory, and he often delivered beautiful sermons. He was a master of rhetoric in the Holy Tongue. His letters and sermons are, to this day, in the possession of those of his friends and admirers who are still alive. He loved me very much and chose me, among all his children, to be educated in a way which no one in our town could have imagined at that time.

When I as six years old and could already read Bible Hebrew, he hired one of the best teachers to teach me *Tanakh*[2]—verse by verse—and the *Targum*.[3] The teacher, Yoysef Ruveyni (you can find out more about him in L. Binshtok's[4] biography of me, in the magazine *Voskhod*[5] of 1884) sat with me and taught me up to twelve hours a day. After three years of study, I knew all twenty-four books of *Tanakh* by heart and was filled with God's wisdom.

And while I was still smacking my lips from the sweetness of the words of the divine prophets, enchanted by divine visions growing out of the great holy visions in the *Tanakh*, my teacher brought me into the domain of the *Talmud*, which has always been the giant—Og, The King of Beshan—the colossus of world literature. When I arrived there, I was like a person who comes to a great fair for the first time. He stands agape and cannot cease wondering at the bewildering array of merchandise and the variety of strange things. He is overwhelmed by the noise, the tumult, the cries on all sides. Buyers and sellers, brokers and merchants, hurry by noisily as the desire and passion to trade seizes them. They scurry about, excited and distraught, one with his jug, another with his keg. They shove, make inquiries, talk, wink to each other, and make no headway. They traffic and trade, haggle and higgle, and a roar and a racket dominate the crowd.

The power of my imagination endowed everything in the *Talmud* with shape and form. *Tanna-kamma* and *Ma'an D'Amar*[6] appeared to me like conceited people, men with flushed faces. *Raysho, Sayfo,* and *Metsiyasso*—like women who begrudged each other pleasure and who always contradicted each other — the one saying "So!", and the other saying "Not so!" —quarreling and clashing, so that there was no joy. And a host of others stood before me as though they were alive, each with his own shape and strange complexion.[7]

Their language was familiar to me as soon as I met any of them, because I had learned *Targum* as a child, but much of what they said was hidden from me. This was true only at first, when I had just entered the portals of the *Talmud*. With the passage of time, however, I got used to it and learned to love it. I "spent nights"[8] in the depth of *Halakha*[9] and was awed by the "towers that soared in the air" and the "mountains which hung by a thread" and other such marvels of subtle argumentation.

I came to love strolling in the garden of *Agadah*[10]. This is not like an orchard fenced in with gates and locks in which the trees are tall and planted in straight rows, each kind in its own bed, so that Nature is hemmed in by elaborate pickets. No, it looked like a broad expanse of field and forest which has no end and no fence, where there is no order, and the growth is dense and intertwined. Countless flowers grow there, and strange plants of all kinds are jumbled and as common as the grass in a field; the lily is the lily of the valley of Sharon, and the rose—the rose of the valleys, wreathed with a growth of green grass. Thousands, millions of shrubs provide a riot of intermingled colors. Fancy wanders freely and untrammeled in this garden, seeing wonders everywhere. Sometimes Heaven bows down toward Earth, and God's chariot descends, and sometimes Earth, rises up to Heaven, and people and angels kiss.

When I was twelve years old, I left the *kheyder*.[11] At that time, this was my daily routine of study: after my morning prayers, I studied the *mishne*[12] with my father at the House of Study;[13] in the afternoon, I stayed on and studied on my own. In the evening, after I had come home and my father was done with his business affairs, I studied *gemore* and all the commentaries with him. And, if he had no time for me in the evening, he would get up at dawn, wake me, and we would walk together with anticipation to the House of Study to study *toyre*.

True, it is indeed a pity for a young child to have to arise from sweetest slumber, particularly on a winter day, but once up and out of the house, deep down in my heart I enjoyed it greatly. And the reward—the reward for leaving home at dawn to study—was great: a divine stillness reigned over all the streets in a town sunk in sleep. The moon and stars, which still filled the sky, aroused my imagination, and I saw and heard many things. I saw Gabriel, who crows like a rooster and announces to the heaven that Night is departing. The angels in heaven begin to leap and dance and recite hymns with sweet song. Then the gates of Paradise swing open noisily, and the great God enters. The angels, seeing God appear in all His holiness, stand trembling, each at his post within his host. No one moves a wing, no one dares to breathe. Suddenly, God lets loose a powerful thunder and begins to weep. He weeps in the night because of His temple which has been destroyed; because of the city of Jerusalem, His crown, which is abandoned; because of His people, the dear children of Zion, who must wander among strange peoples; and because of the *Shekhina,* the Divine Presence, which is humiliated and must

33

wander along with them in Exile and suffer their sufferings. Tears fall from His eyes — this is the dew which falls to earth and leaves droplets on the fields!... Upon hearing God's voice, all the Saints of the world are struck with awe and weep bitterly together with the good angels. And I, imagining all this, begin to study with all my heart. I sing and hum while I study; I support my head with my hand and sing aloud. My heart desires to know all the secrets contained in God's *Toyre* and the *Talmud*. I concentrate on my work with redoubled energy.

This manner of studying had a two-fold effect on me. On the one hand, it sharpened my mind as it cut its way through the fine reasoning and turned me into an acute person — one who delves deeply and gets to the bottom of every subject so as to understand it in all its truth and simplicity. On the other hand, it awakened my emotions and my imagination with great, exalted visions which prepared me to respond to imagery and reverential feelings.

At that time, I was limited to the confines of *Halakha* and knew nothing aside from *Talmud*. I had not seen secular books, nor had I even heard about them. I did not know that there were such things as literature, theater, and the like, because my home town was an isolated nest, tucked away in a forgotten corner where a visitor's foot never trod. Being naive, I thought, like the chick in the egg, that the whole universe was right here within the shell, and that beyond Kapulye lay only bleak desert, beyond which lurked the Dark Mountains,[14] the river Sambatyon, and strange, fantastic creatures. In my eyes, the tiny houses of my town were palaces. And the *shul* and the *kloyz*[15] had no equal anywhere in the world. It was here that wisdom had its home, and the townsmen were the chosen of the world, all of them the wisest of the wise, particularly the older men with their long beards.

At that time, I held these principles: where there is age, there is also wisdom and knowledge; whoever has been blessed with a cow or a goat is as rich as Croesus and as happy as a lark; the *shoyfer* and the hurdy-gurdy, which accidentally came to reside in our town, were magical instruments; the simple musicians of our town, who play at every wedding, make the most beautiful music; happy is he who can blow the *shoyfer* so as to touch the listeners' hearts and make them shiver.

I already knew all of the Bible, but I had not yet attempted to write. When divine inspiration awakened in me, I did not pour it out on paper with flowery expressions, but I sat in silence while the waves of feeling raged and stormed within me. My heart wept, because I thought that this was Satan's work, that my Evil Genius was leading me astray with sinful ideas to distract me from studying *Toyre* [*Torah*]. To overcome him, the only remedy I could think of was prayer. There were days, when a strong urge would suddenly arise within me, and I would say to myself, "Pray to God!"...and I prayed.

In such prayers, I expressed my urge, experienced the sweetness of Paradise, and life became good. And then, if that scoundrel, my Evil Genius, caught up with me, I would lead him off to the woods, to the hills and mountains. There I would yield to the feelings in my soul and look at beautiful Nature and her glory. With time, Nature drew me to her with her clarity and beauty. I fell in love with her and delighted in her as a groom in his bride. Every day I would go out to the fields to see my beloved, and my visits with this beauty were spent in tenderness. I sought my love in the dense forest and the sparse woods, on the fields of grass, and at the river. She showed me all she possessed. She smiled to me, and I scrambled after her up the mountains, climbed the trees, and sat in the meadows listening to the lowing of the cattle. The nightingale sang for me, and the voice of the turtledove stood out in the chorus of birds. They sang love songs to my beauty, to that heavenly daughter. The love in my heart burned like fire, a spiritual love, a sacred love, which had no structure or form. It was a concealed love for the good, the beautiful, the exalted — a love which delights a man, refines and improves him, and elevates him above the mundane...The secret of this love, and the flood of feelings expressed in prayer and supplications — these are known to the poets, to the inspired ones. They are divine notes, the marks of God's song in the heart of his chosen ones.

And so I remained calmly in my nest until I was thirteen. I thought I would remain in my town forever. But things did not turn out as I expected. My father died suddenly at the age of 41 and left a wife and children in great need. Poverty forced me to roam far from home among the *yeshives* in the Lithuanian towns and cities. I will not attempt to describe here everything that happened to me, because there is a lot to tell, and I plan to write a separate book for Jews about this matter which will serve to commemorate their *yeshives* of that period. Suffice it to say that I fulfilled all requirements involved in studying *Toyre*. I lived in misery like the most learned of men; I took my meals at a different house every day and experienced all the attendant humiliations.

At the Slutsk *yeshive,* I studied with the well-known Reb Avrom-Borekh in the first class. I was soon promoted to the most advanced class, and after that, I became a student of the principal of the *yeshive*, the keen scholar, Reb Mikhl. Next, I was transferred to the House of Study, financed by its patron Reb Jonah, where I studied with the great Rabbi, Reb Avremele. I stayed in Slutsk for about two years.

For various reasons, I left for Vilna. There I studied with the famous Reb Senderl at Reb Meyle's *yeshive* and also at the house of study of the Vilna *Gaon*, Reb Eliyohu,[16] of blessed memory. There, I worked day and night and was up every night. I had originally come to Vilna at the invitation of a relative, the wealthy Nokhem-Khayim Broyde[17] who had promised to support me and be like a father to me. But I did not stay there long and returned home.

My mother had, in the meantime, married a miller in the village of Melniki[18] some ten *vyersts* from Kapulye. She and the younger children went to live with her husband in the village, while I remained in the town, alone and lonesome. I wandered about in sadness and was sick of life. I was a mere boy, still young in years, but sated with misery. I drifted dolefully and crestfallen, until my stepfather took me in, and in order to earn my keep, I tutored his children several hours a day.

The house in which my stepfather lived was surrounded by forests, large ancient woods. Wild animals lived there. Wolves howled at night, and even bears were seen from time to time. There were nests of all kinds of birds that twittered in the branches; there were wild geese and water fowl that screamed in the marsh grass. A wide river wore its way through the trees, flowing in a rush to the mill, where it dropped like a waterfall to drive the mill wheels with a roar and clatter. The thundering of the flowing waters and the mill was deafening.

Here, in this isolated place, my Muse—the beloved of my youth, from the time when I sat in *yeshives* with other poor youths, my beloved, whom I had lost hope of ever seeing again

— reappeared. She revealed herself to me in all her glory, and with the charm of her lips, talked me into following her into the forest to be together in sweet bliss under a young tree. At her urging, I made a covenant with the trees in the countryside, with the birds and the fruits of the earth. She taught me to understand their language and observe their mode of life. My heart was drawn to these friends of mine. They told me about the mysteries and the events of their world, about the greatness of God, who had created them and watched over them, and I told them about my feelings.

For the first time, I took pen in hand to pour out the feelings in my heart. I sang them a new "hallelujah" on paper. The river applauded and the mountain echo cheered me on. These first poetic attempts are in my possession to this very day, and they shall never see the light of day, because they are unripe fruits with the taste of crabapples. And, remarkably: as soon as I had begun to write and had completed my first piece, Satan, the scoffer, came to me — he still dominates me in the shape of Mendele Moykher-Sforim — and incited me to ridicule people and strip them of their masks.

At that time, I wrote a play in rhyme, using "The Folly of the Righteous" by Moyshe-Khayim Luzzatto[19] as a model. I didn't even know what a play was then; I had never read a book of that kind. My book was merely a prank and full of mistakes. It was the fruit of the young Satan in me who used to mock me. And when, on occasion today, I test my Satan and scoff at his youthful mistakes, he insolently retorts in kind: "Don't you know yet that the Eternal One himself hasn't created a finished product, and that everything he has brought forth still has to be refined? Development is an eternal law of the universe. So it is, and you should know it!"

My peaceful sojourn did not last long. It seems that it was ordained in Heaven, even before I was born, that I was to be a writer for my people, for the poor and the unfortunate, and that it was God's wish that I become acquainted with the customs of my people and observe their deeds. Therefore, he commanded me: "Wander, little bird, over the face of my world, that most unfortunate of unfortunates, and you will become a Jew's Jew!" And the wind carried me off—up and down the rungs of life; it carried me and shook me up, while one of God's angels thrust me along. The wind cast me among my suffering brethren on the very bottom rung so that I might live their life, know their sorrows, and feel their pain. I was allotted a double measure of their pain. At other times, it lifted me to the uppermost rungs, making room for me along our very wealthy—the satisfied ones, the Jewish elders—so that I might observe their conduct and deeds, their ways of doing business—but only to observe, not to enjoy, their prosperity.

From the time that God drove me from my stepfather's house, a new chapter unfolded in the book of my life, a chapter of wandering, trials and tribulation, followed by many other chapters in which the events of my life were woven into the cloth of Jewish life. These will be incorporated into separate books and will serve to memorialize the history of our people and its literature. A hint of the contents is contained in my biography by Dr. Binshtok, previously mentioned. Look into it.

I shall skip these chapters and events of my life and will only relate how I became a Yiddish writer, what the goals were that I set for myself and to which I dedicated my thought and my pen, and what kinds of books and articles I wrote.

Hebrew literature was a rare thing during my youth. There were no books, no daily or weekly newspapers, no monthly or annual periodicals, as there are today, whose aim it was to awaken the feelings of Jews and to arouse a love for our Holy Tongue in their hearts. There were no zealous writers.

While I was living in Kamenets at my father-in-law's, and also later, after I had divorced my wife and become a teacher in the crown school, I spent a great deal of time studying and investigating science and acquiring, with great hardship, the secular knowledge I lacked. If someone had told me then that I would become a writer among Jews, I would have thought he was making fun of me. I used to think naively that writers were all holy men, and who was I to attain such heights? But circumstances made me a writer, and it happened unexpectedly.

On a cloudy, foggy, dark winter night, the wind was howling, and I was sitting alone in my room feeling very depressed. To occupy myself and to raise my spirits, I picked up my pen to answer a letter that some *melamed* had sent me. I wrote a great deal all at once on the subject of education, covering both sides of a quarto-sheet.[20] The next morning, I copied part of what I had written as the answer to the *melamed* and tossed the original into a corner as a piece of trash. It lay in the corner for a long time, then in one place or another around the room. I had completely forgotten about it.

One day, the postman brought me a sealed letter from abroad. I opened the letter, curious to know who would write to me from a foreign country where I knew no one. I found issue number 31 of the first year of *Hamagid* [21] and was struck by familiar sounding words in the editorial which bore the title, "Letter on the Subject of Education," in large type. How great was my surprise when, at the end of the article, I saw my name followed by a note praising the article to the skies and requesting educated readers to translate it and have it printed in other languages. I was bewildered. There was also a cover letter of strong praise from the publisher of *Hamagid,* Reb Eliezer Lipmann-Silbermann, requesting that I send him my further efforts and that I conclude a "peaceful contract" with him and his *Hamagid.* This bewildered me even more. But it was not long before the matter became clear to me. My friend, the scholar M. Levin, secretary to Joshua Günzburg,[22] who was highly impressed by my letter, had sent it to Avrom-Ber Gottlober[23] for expert evaluation. That was how it got to the publisher of *Hamagid* and found its way into print.

These two learned men took my article and drove it like a spike into the framework of Hebrew literature. It was the beginning of all my future work in that literature.

I began to think seriously about our Hebrew literature, about its content and about the direction in which it was headed. I sought to find something useful in it — science and wisdom, delicacy and beauty — but I found very little of the sort there. That literature was a garden gone to waste, an abandoned garden, as in late autumn — no fruit, no fragrant flowers, no attractive plants; only rotting leaves and naked trees. Here and there were some weeds or some underbrush, but it was all neglected. And the writers? These caretakers of the garden lay in it, quietly and restfully, playing like naive children, amusing themselves, praising and admiring each other.

A writer of the time, E. Tsvayfl (Zweifel),[24] had written: "For the writers of Hebrew books, calm and peaceful times had come—good and prosperous times. Gone were the critics, and vanished the critical understanding that could disturb their peace or diminish their honor and glory. Every book and its sanctity had become like twins, the name of the author and his treatise— like father like child."

Tsvayfl was writing about times past, but because he was not overly perceptive, he considered this situation to be praiseworthy. But his description also fit the Yiddish writers when I was young, and I considered such a situation to be disgraceful, because times when critical understanding fades away are neither good nor happy times; and a literature which has no critics, in which each book and its sanctity are like twins, is like a garden without a master. The calf grazes there at will and destroys the seeds; the pig roots where he chooses; and the little foxes ruin the flower beds. If you walk into such a garden, and you crush and uproot things and even fill your pockets, it is no misfortune, for it is an abandoned garden and you can tell you are among Jews. Nobody sees, nobody cares. There is no law and no judge, except for God in heaven, and no one will say an angry word to you....I did a lot of hard thinking about these matters, and the result was my first book.

Mishpet Sholem (Peaceful Judgment) was printed in Vilna in 1860. The book, although it attacked E. Z. Tsvayfl, author of *Minim v'Ugav,*[25] was actually aimed as well at our writers in general and came like a bullet into the crown of placid writers who sat like wine on yeast. They regarded me as a disturber of the peace, as one who had come "to diminish their honor and glory." There was a loud outcry from the crowd, and a war of scribes broke out in the Hebrew newspapers *Hameylits* [26] and *Hakarmel,*[27] both of which had just begun to appear. I spoke up even more defiantly and, from time to time, challenged them with new articles. I had many supporters, and they were very encouraging. Whether I was right, and whether my barbs always hit the right target, others will have to judge. I know that I initiated a commotion in our literature: new critics appeared, and they went after the Hebrew writers. Many of the writers took the criticism to heart and mended their ways. The polemic among the writers became a living spirit that breathed new life into Hebrew literature and attracted many readers from the people.

It seemed to me that a writer must strive for the following three goals: to teach science to the people and develop good taste among them; to write about the life of the people so that they will identify with their literature; to help the people develop their lives into something useful.

I wished, with all my heart, that the writers and poets would get their heads out of the clouds, drop their empty fantasizing, and forget their plots involving Lot's daughters and Potiphar's wife[28] and other such beings and foolish ideas that had disappeared from the world long ago. Would that they would stop telling the living about the dead, come down to earth instead to observe the people's lives today, the kind of home and social life they lead and open their eyes! Let the writers exert themselves to refine the people's taste and improve their language. And let them also give the people some good lessons in science, so as to make them knowledgeable.

That was why I divided my literary work into three parts. The first work was *Seyfer Toldos Hateve (The Book of Natural History)* which discussed the three divisions on which the world is based: fauna, flora, and inorganic matter. I listed them all according to their species and families, with their names, characteristics, and properties — translated into the Holy Tongue from the work of the naturalist Lenz.[29] The first part of this translation, entitled *Mammals*, with eight pages of illustrations, was published in Leipzig in 1862.

Simultaneously, I attempted to compose a story in the Holy Tongue,[30] using simple language, based on the folk spirit and life of that time. I excerpted several chapters from this story and published them with an introduction as a separate book called *Limdu Hetev (Learn to do Good)*, Warsaw, 1862 (?)[31]

At that time, I observed the life of my people and wished to provide them with stories in the Holy Tongue based on Jewish sources. Most of them, however, did not understand this language, because they spoke only Yiddish.[32] What profit accrues to a writer for all his work and thinking, if he does not serve his people? The question — for whom am I working? — brought me no peace and caused me great perplexity. In my time, the Yiddish language was an empty vessel, containing naught but gibes, nonsense and fiddle-faddle, the jabber of fools who couldn't talk like human beings and had nothing to say. Women and vulgar folk read it without understanding what they were reading, and the rest of the people, although they knew no other language, were ashamed to read it so as not to expose their backwardness. And when someone could not resist the temptations of his Evil Genius and did read something in Yiddish, he would laugh apologetically: "I merely looked into the 'women's books' the silly females read. I was just fooling."

Our writers, masters of language, were interested only in the Holy Tongue and not in the people. They looked down upon Yiddish. If one in ten ever remembered the "accursed tongue" and dared to write something in it, he did it behind seven locks and covered it with his holy prayer shawl, so that his shame might not be discovered to damage his good name. How great then was my dilemma when I considered that if I were to embark on writing in the "shameful" tongue, my honorable name would be besmirched! I also listened to the admonitions of my admirers in *Hovivey Halosh'n Halvris (Society of Lovers of the Hebrew Language)* who predicted my loss of status and respect among Jews if I devoted my capabilities to this alien tongue. My love for utility, however, overcame my hollow pride, and I decided: come what may, I will write in Yiddish, that cast-off daughter, and work for the people. A good friend of mine, Joshua Mordecai Lifshits,[33] stood by me, and together we persuaded the editor of *Hameylits*[34] to publish a newspaper in the people's language. He came to the aid of his people with his newspaper *Kol-mevaser,*[35] may God remember it to his credit, and it grew to be a great success.

Enthused, I wrote my first story, *Dos Kleyne Mentshele (The Little Man)*, subtitled, "The Biography of Avrom-Yitskhok the Strong-Arm Man," published in Odessa, 1864 (?) in the newspaper *Kol-mevaser* and separately many times thereafter. This tale made a great impression on the Jewish public, so that it was soon issued in a third edition in Vilna, 1865 (?), and again, in a fourth edition, but completely revised, in Vilna, 1879. This book became the cornerstone of the new Yiddish literature.

I fell in love with Yiddish and bound myself to that language forever. I found for her the perfumes and fragrances that she needed, and she became a charming lady who bore me many sons:

Dos Vintshfingerl (The Wishing Ring) With Which Anyone Can

42

Attain Everything his Heart Desires and Thereby Be of Use to Himself and the World at Large. It was published in Warsaw, without the name of the publisher or the year of publication, in 1865 (?), I believe. The book is on the table before me now. I am considering expanding it and issuing it anew, together with all my works in Yiddish, which I am now preparing for a new deluxe edition.

Di Takse (The Tax) or *The Gang of Town Philanthropists*, Zhitomir, 1869, and reprinted in Vilna, 1872. It was translated into Russian by I. M. Petrikovsky, Belaya Tserkov, 1884. I don't care for this translation.

Fishke der Krumer (Fishke the Lame), A Story About the Jewish Poor, Zhitomir, 1869. I have just recreated him as a new character, and this will be the first of all my books in the new edition.

Der Luft-Balon (The Balloon), Zhitomir, 1869. A nice story, composed with the aid of my friend, L. Binshtok. It is now unobtainable at any price. I have looked everywhere and could not find a copy.

Der Fish (The Fish) Which Swallowed Jonah the Prophet, by the author of "The Balloon," issued by the editorial board of *Kol-mevaser* in Odessa, 1870.

Di Klyatshe (The Mare) or *Pity For Living Creatures.* To my mare in Pharaoh's chariot do I compare thee, O Congregation of Israel.[36] This is a tale which was found among the papers of Yisrolik the Madman, Vilna 1873. It was translated into Polish by Mr. Klemens Junosza,[37] a Christian by birth, Warsaw, 1886. His is a good translation.

Der Ustav (The Regulation), On Military Obligations. Published by the above-mentioned L. Binshtok, Zhitomir, 1874.

Yudl,[38] a story in verse. Ach, Yudl, my sick, sick, Yudl. Your life is a very, very sad song. In two parts, Warsaw, 1875.

Zmires Yisroel (Sabbath Hymns of Israel). Sabbath hymns,

translated as songs and clearly explained so that any Jew can appreciate their inestimable value and beauty — one of God's wonders. Zhitomir, 1875. There was a reason for my translating the hymns into Yiddish. I had seen them in the prayer book *Korbon Minkhe* (*Afternoon Prayer Offering*) for Jewish daughters; that translation had no taste and no aroma — you wouldn't want to put it into your mouth. So I decided that it was time to do something for our sisters, our Jewish daughters and just plain folk, to present them with a gift in a pure language. Their hearts, just like ours, yearn for God's sweet words, and they must not be deprived of good things, of knowledge and edification; it should not be hoarded for a small coterie of elite individuals. Our holy forefathers, too, translated the *Toyre* into the language of the people, and, later, the *Tanaim*[39] appointed translators again so as to give the people access to God's words. Why then should we not walk in their path and present wisdom and edification to their offspring in the language they understand? And why should we not, at the same time, care for our daughters and the whole populace? Why should they be deprived of the beautiful gifts and treasures in our prayers and be allowed to wander in darkness, to have only foolish and empty words which numb the mind, while we pay attention to only a very small part of our people? Are not all Jews equally holy, and does not God rest equally among them? I started my sacred mission with the translation of the Sabbath hymns. Then I translated the Book of Psalms into verse — I have it in manuscript form. Next, I translated into Yiddish:

Perek Shiro[40] (*Lesson of Hymns*), with an introduction in the Holy Tongue and clear, stimulating commentaries explaining, on the basis of common sense and the word of our sages, each sentence of every hymn. Published in Zhitomir, 1875. I had intended to publish a new *Korbon Minkhe*, but, I regret to say that for various reasons I have not yet been able to do so.

Maso'es Binyomin Hashlishi (*The Travels of Benjamin the Third*). The description of the journey of Benjamin the Third, who, in his travels, penetrated very far indeed, as far as the Dark Mountains, and saw and heard many novelties which have been disclosed in all seventy languages[41] and now also in our own language; under the auspices of Mendele Moykher-Sforim, Vilna, 1878. Translated into Polish by Mr. Klemens Junosza under the title *Donkiszot Zydowski (The Jewish Don Quixote)*, Warsaw, 1885. From Polish, it has also been translated into Czech.

Der Priziv (Conscription). A drama in five acts, with a picture of the author, St. Petersburg, 1884.

Der Nutslekher Kalendar (The Useful Calendar) for Russian Jews. It was published five times for five different years: 5637 (1877) and 5638 (1878)—in Zhitomir; 5639 (1879) and 5640 (1880)—in Vilna; 5643 (1883)—in Odessa. It contains useful essays and other good things.

Aside from the above listing, I have written many other articles, and now I will end the list with some of my earlier works:

Birds (part of *Natural History*), with eight pages of drawings and many references within the text and at the end. These explain the names of the various birds mentioned in the Bible, *Targum, Talmud* and *Midrashim*.[42] The notes also clarify many unintelligible verses and sayings of our sages, blessed be their memory. Zhitomir, 1866.

Eyn Mishpat (The Critical Eye). Contains two related articles which defend Jews. The first is an assessment of current Hebrew literature and the status of our schools and learned Rabbis; it also deals with methods of improving the condition of the Jews. The second answers questions about Jews raised by the government in the newspaper *Kievlyanin (The Kiev Citizen)*; it demonstrates the fine qualities of the Jews and their religious books to all peoples. Printed first in the newspaper *Hameylits* and again, with notes and much supplementary material, by the author in Zhitomir, 1867. I wrote the articles and sent them to the government after I had been requested to do so in a special letter of November 22, 1864. The government honored me with a letter of thanks on March 12, 1865. Both letters appear at the beginning of the book.

Haoves v'Habonim (Fathers and Sons), a novel, Odessa 1868. It was translated into Russian by my friend, L. Binshtok, St. Petersburg, 1868.

Divrey Hayomim Harusim (History of the Russian People). Translated clearly and simply for all Jews who wish to know the history of the people among whom they live, from the time they became a nation until the present. Odessa, 1867. I translated this book at the suggestion of the administration of the Society for the Enlightenment of Israel. For various reasons, I declined to continue the work, so that only a third of the original work was published. See *Eyn Mishpat,* page 51, and the note there.

Reptiles (part of *Natural History*), with seven pages of illustrations and notes within the text and at the end. These explain the names of crawling creatures found in the Bible, *Targum, Talmud,* and *Midrashim.* The notes also clarify many unintelligible verses and sayings of our sages, blessed be their memory. Vilna, 1872. The second and third parts were not translated from the work of the naturalist Lenz, as was the first. Instead, I culled material from texts by modern, well-known scientific researchers and compiled it for the use and pleasure of the Hebrew reader. I listed all the living creatures and found names for them, thereby giving them a place in Hebrew literature. I coined new names in the spirit of the Hebrew language. I also collected, like sheaves in a barn, the names of all living creatures in Biblical verses, *Talmud,* and *Midrashim,* and explained them in accord with explanations of famous learned commentators.

Luakh Hasokhrim (Merchants' Calendar). A collection of useful essays in the style of the *Mishne.* It is now a rare item. Vilna, 1879.

Aside from the above, I have written a great many scientific and critical articles which have appeared in the newspapers *Hatsefire, Hameylits, Hakarmel,* and in many others. I will mention the titles of a few:

Khokhmes Hakhemye (Chemical Science) in *Hatsefir*
Eymek Yehoshophat (The Valley of Jehoshophat) in *Hameylits.*
Ma Ani ?(What Am I?) in *Haskhar.*

46

and many similar articles which I am not in a position to list, because I don't have copies of the newspapers.

I also wrote about the religious elementary schools and their teachers when I was a member of the Commission sponsored by Governor Gresser of Volhynia in 1875. My article pleased the officials and helped solve some problems of the religious elementary schools and of their teachers at that time. This article remained in the archive of the Commission and, regrettably, I do not have a copy of it.

NOTES

1 The *Notes* were written in Hebrew and published in 1889 in Nokhem Sokolov's *Sefer Zikaron (Book of Records)*. The present English version is translated from a Yiddish translation by B. Appelbaum appearing in Nakhmen Mayzel's *Dos Mendele Bukh (The Mendele Book)*, Yiddisher Kultur Farband, New York, 1959. Sokolov (1859 - 1936) was a well-known journalist, writer, and editor. He was also a prominent Zionist leader, having served as president of the World Zionist Organization and the Jewish Agency.

2 *Tanakh*—the acronym for *Toyre* (Pentateuch), *Nviyim* (Prophets), *Ksuvim* (Scriptures) — the three divisions of the Bible (which Christians refer to as the Old Testament).

3 *Targum* is an Aramaic word meaning "translation." It usually refers to the Aramaic translation of *Tanakh*. In Yiddish, *Targum-Loshn* — literally, *Targum-Language* — is often used to refer to Aramaic. In the Middle East, Jews spoke Aramaic from the Fifth Century BCE until the Seventh Century CE, a period of over one thousand years. Much of the Talmud was written in Aramaic.

4 Judah-Leyb Binshtok (1836-1894) was appointed "Learned Jew" to the Governor of Volhynia by decree of his superior, the Governor-General of Kiev. In 1860, Binshtok established the first of two Jewish periodicals in Russian — *Siyun (Zion)* and *Rassvyet (Dawn)*. A close friend of Mendele's for years, he translated Mendele's Hebrew novel *Father and Sons* into Russian in 1868. He helped Mendele translate Jules Verne's first successful novel *Cinq Semaines en Ballon (Five Weeks in a Balloon)* into Yiddish as *Der Luft-Balon*. He co-authored *Der Ustav* and *Der Fish* with Mendele. In 1884, he wrote the biography of Mendele, referred to above, in honor of the 25th anniversary of Mendele's literary activity.

5 *Voskhod (The Rising)* was a Russian-Jewish monthly, with weekly supplements, established by Adolph Landau (1841-1902) in 1881 in St. Petersburg. Its content was literary and scientific. It ceased publication in 1906.

6 In the text of the *Mishne, Tanna-kamma* means "the first of the quoted authorities" and *Ma'an D'Amar* — "according to him who says." *Raysho, Sayfo, Metsiyasso* are grammatical terms, meaning respectively: the first clause of a sentence, the last clause of a sentence, and the middle clause of a sentence. When Mendele was introduced to the *Mishne* (see note 12) as a youngster, he thought that these grammatical terms and reference phrases were names of people, and he endowed them with personalities accordingly. It has also been suggested to me by Professor I. Goldberg of Queens College (CUNY) that Mendele was perhaps

47

gently poking fun at the custom of prematurely exposing bright young boys (Mendele himself must have been about 10 years old at the time) to the *Mishne*, which contains passages written for more mature minds.

7   Mendele lists another dozen terms (e.g., "adolescent female, " "barren woman," "maidenhood," "the ox who pushes into the cow," etc.) which also might have been beyond the ken of a bright young boy. For these, I have substituted the word "host of others," since the humor would have most meaning for readers familiar with the *Mishne*.

8   This and all other quotation marks in *Notes For My Biography* are Mendele's.

9   *Halakha* is that portion of the *mishne* text which deals with what a Jew is permitted and forbidden to do. It incorporates laws and rules dealing with monetary transactions, conduct of family life, conduct during the Sabbath and holidays, etc.

10   *Agadah* is the other portion of the *mishne* and includes all essays which are unrelated to *Halakha*. *Agadah* contains tales and parables which are poetic and imaginative and are more accessible to the general public. In the *mishne* proper, the *Agadah* and *Halakha* are intertwined.

11   *Kheyder* means "a room" in Hebrew. In the context here, *kheyder* refers to a religious elementary school, usually conducted by a *melamed* in his one-room house.

12   *Mishne* is one of the two major compilations constituting the *Talmud*. The other is the *Gemore*. The *mishne* contains commentaries on the Bible made during the course of several centuries. They were codified into sixty-three tractates by Yehuda Hanasi (Judah the Prince) in the latter half of the Second Century CE. The *gemore* contains commentaries on and expansions of the *mishne* by scholars in Jerusalem and Babylonia, resulting in a Jerusalem *Talmud* and a Babylonian *Talmud,* the latter being by far the more influential. The Jerusalem *Talmud* was essentially completed in the Fourth Century CE; the Babylonian in the Sixth Century CE.

13   The house of study (*Beys Hamedresh*) was used for praying, studying and for communal meetings, when necessary. Sometimes, *yeshive*-students or Jews who were traveling would sleep there.

14   According to *Agadah* legend (see Note 10), the ten lost tribes live beyond the Dark Mountains which are at the other end of the world. To reach the ten lost tribes, the river Sambatyon, which tosses rocks out of its waters all week except on the Sabbath, must be crossed. One cannot travel on the Sabbath, of course.

15   A *shul* was used for praying only and was regarded as being more holy than the house of study, which was usually located adjacent to it. A *kloyz* was a small House of Study, often restricted to a trade group, e.g., tailors, cobblers, etc.

16   The title *Gaon* was conferred on the heads of the *yeshivas* of Sura and Pumbeditha in Babylonia from the end of the Sixth Century CE to the middle of the Eleventh. The position of *Gaon* had official status, first with the rulers of Persia and later with the Caliph of Baghdad. After the official usage in Babylonia, the title *Gaon* became honorific and was occasionally conferred upon a great scholar. Such a scholar was Reb Eliyohu (1720-1797), an influential leader of orthodox Jewry, particularly in the struggle against khasidism. The house of study referred to by Mendele was the one in which Reb Eliyohu studied and was a landmark for eastern European Jewry.

17   Mendele's family name was also Broyde originally. His childhood writings were signed "Sholem-Yankev Broyde of Kapulye." He apparently adopted the family name "Abramovitsh" after his travels with Avreml the Limper (see *Introduction*).

18   In Russian, "melnik" means "miller."

19   Reb Moyshe-Khayim Luzzatto (known by the acronym *RaMaKhaL*), born in 1707 in Padua and died in Palestine in 1747 during a plague, was a renowned Hebrew poet, kabbalist, thinker and moralist. He is regarded as the father of post-medieval Hebrew poetry. "The Folly of The Righteous" (*L'Yisherim Toholo*) was an allegorical drama written in Amsterdam and published in 1743.

20   This event occurred in 1857 when Mendele was twenty years old.

21   *Hamagid (The Announcer)* was a weekly Hebrew Journal founded in 1856 at Lyck, East Prussia, by Eliezer Lipmann-Silbermann (1819-1881). Initially, it dealt with history and Bible interpretation. Under the later editorship of David Gordon (1826-1886), its scope expanded to include literary criticism and topical news. It ceased publication in 1892.

22   Menakhem-Mendl (Emmanuel) Levin (1820-1913) was an early pioneer of the *haskole*. He wrote a "Grammar of the Russian Language" in Hebrew in 1846 and was appointed as a teacher in the crown rabbinical seminary in Zhitomir. He was private secretary to Barons J. and H. Günzburg. Joshua (Joseph) Günzburg (1812-1878) was a member of the well-known Jewish family of bankers, philanthropists and communal workers in Russia. The hereditary title of Baron was granted to him by Alexander II. The Günzburg Bank in St. Petersburg was instrumental in financing railroad construction in the Russian Empire and in developing gold mines in the Urals and Siberia. Günzburg was active in trying to improve the physical lot of Jews in the Pale. In 1863, he was a founder of the Society for Promotion of Culture Among Jews of Russia.

23   Avrom-Ber Gottlober (1811-1899), a Hebrew and Yiddish writer and scholar, was one of the first *maskilim* in the Ukraine. In 1876, he established the Hebrew magazine *HaBoker Ur (Morning Light)* to explain and defend the principles of the *haskole* movement.

24   Eliezer-Tsvi Tsvayfl (Zweifel) (1815-1888) was the first *maskil* to dare defend khasidism and to recognize the beauty and inner warmth of the movement. His influence helped to develop neo-khasidism, a reflection of which can be found in the literary works of I. L. Perets, M.Y. Berditshevsky, and others.

25   A collection of scriptural commentaries, homilies and poems, deprecating the attitude of the *haskole* movement toward devotees of khasidism. Published in Vilna, 1858.

26   *Hameylits (The Advocate)* was established in Odessa in 1860 by Alexander Tsederboym (see Note 34) and later moved to St. Petersburg (Leningrad). It introduced the use of the editorial into Jewish journalism and mirrored Jewish life and literature. At first a weekly, it became a daily in 1885 and exerted considerable influence on Hebrew journalism until it ceased publication in 1904

27   *Hakarmel (Carmel)* was established in Vilna in 1860 by Samuel Joseph Fuenn. A monthly, it was noted for the high caliber of its scholarly articles. It ceased publication in 1880.

28   Lots' daughters — Genesis 19:31 through 19:38. Lot's two daughters slept with him after they had fled from Sodom, each bearing him a son.

Potiphar's wife — Genesis 39:7. When Joseph was brought to Egypt by the Ishmaelites, he was bought by Potiphar, a captain of Pharaoh's guard. His wife wanted Joseph as a lover but he refused, whereupon she told her husband that Joseph had tried to sleep with her. As a result, Joseph was imprisoned.

Mendele's reference here is to titillating subject matter, such as incest and fornication, which were then common in Hebrew and Yiddish novels.

29   Harold Othmar Lenz (1799-1870) was a teacher of Latin, Greek and natural

history in several German gymnasia. His *Gemeinnuetzige Naturgeschichtc (General Natural History),* published between 1834 and 1839 was, at the time, the most popular text on natural history in central Europe and had an unusually broad circulation.

30 Throughout this translation of *Notes For My Biography,* I have used the word "Hebrew" where Mendele uses *hebreyish,* and "Holy Tongue" where he uses *Loshn Koydesh* — GIS. (Neither of these is identical with *Ivrit,* the language of today's Israel.)

31 Mendele has a footnote here: "Wherever such a question mark appears, it is the result of my not having the book in my possession and my uncertainty as to the actual date of publication — since I have to rely solely on my memory."

32 In the original, Mendele uses *ivre-taytsh,* which, literally, means "the language used to translate sacred texts."

33 Joshua Mordecai Lifshits (1829-1878), a pioneering Yiddish lexicographer who published, among other works, a Russian-Yiddish dictionary in 1869 (with four subsequent editions) and a Yiddish-Russian dictionary in 1876. He had a broad background in physics, chemistry, mathematics, and languages, and was a proponent of the concept of a secular Jewish culture based on Yiddish.

34 The editor was Alexander Tsederboym (1816-1893). Although not formally educated, he became an influential Hebrew and Yiddish editor. In 1862, he established *Kol-mevaser (The Voice Which Brings News)* as a weekly supplement, in Yiddish, to the Hebrew paper *Hameylits* (see Note 26). In 1881, Tsederboym established the *Yiddishes Folksblatt,* which had contributors like A. B. Gottlober, M. L. Lilienblum, Jacob Dineson, and Elyakum Tsunzer (Zunser). Tsederboym's grandson, Julius Martov (1873-1923), was a close co-worker with Lenin in the Russian Social-Democratic Party and on the revolutionary newspaper *Iskra (The Spark).* He was also an early inspiration for the Bund, the Jewish section of the RSDP.

35 Although the first Yiddish newspaper, *Di Kurantin,* was published in Amsterdam in 1686, *Kol-mevaser* was the first one in the modern sense of the word. It ceased publication in 1873 after being banned by the Tsarist government.

36 "To a mare in Pharaoh's chariot have I compared thee, O my beloved..." — Song of Songs, 1:9.

37 Klemens Junosza (Klemens Szaniawski, 1849-1898) also translated Sholem Aleykhem's *Briv fun Menakhem-Mendl (Letters from Menakhem-Mendl)* into Polish under the title *Miljony (Millions)* and several short stories by I. L. Perets. He also wrote several novels in Polish dealing with the life of the Jewish poor in Poland.

38 *Yudl* — a Yiddish name. It also means "little Jew."

39 *Tanaim* — rabbis whose teachings in the first centuries CE are included in the *mishne.*

40 *Perek Shiro* is the name of an old apocryphal *Tanaitic* code which was not included in the *mishne* by its compiler, Judah the Prince. *Perek Shiro* states that all of creation sings hymns of praise to God every day: the heavens, the earth, the stars, all living creatures, and plants — each with a hymn suited to its individual nature.

41 Seventy languages — a concept based on the list of Noah's descendants given in Genesis 10, referred to as "The Table of Nations." The Jewish tradition that mankind consists of 70 nations is based on this table.

42 *Targum*— see Note 3. *Talmud*— see Note 12. *Midrashim* (plural of *midrash)* — collections of sayings of the sages in the *Agadah* (Note 10), portions of the *Talmud,* and also of later sages.

INTRODUCTION TO

The Little Man

Dos Kleyne Mentshele, subtitled "The Biography of Yitskhok-Avrom, the Strong-Arm Man," was the first work in Yiddish published by Mendele. Here translated as *The Little Man* (rather than, literally, as "the little person"), it is generally considered the work which marks the beginning of the modern period in Yiddish literature.

The first work by Sholem Yankef Abramovitsh to appear under the pen-name Mendele Moykher-Sforim, it was originally published in 1864 as a short story of several dozen pages in the Yiddish supplement to the Hebrew newspaper *Hameylits*. Mendele points out in *Notes For My Biography* (see page 31) that "this tale made a great impression on the Jewish public." A second printing was issued in Odessa in 1865, and a third in Vilna in 1866. A fourth completely revised and expanded edition was published in Vilna in 1879. This new version increased the number of pages by more than three-and-a-half times. A final revision was made by Mendele in 1907 for an edition of his complete works, published in Odessa. Aside from stylistic and grammatical changes, the 1907 version differs from the 1879 version in that it changes the sequence of some of the chapters and also omits the first introductory chapter of the 1879 version.

Gerald Stillman, one of the editors of this volume and the translator of *The Little Man,** used the 1879 edition, as published by the Hebrew Publishing Co., New York, in Volume I of *The Complete Works of Mendele Moykher-Sforim*, 1910: "I have also compared it to the 1907 text as published by YKUF Publishers, New York, in Volume I of *The Selected Works of Mendele Moykher-Sforim*, 1946. In a few scattered instances, where the sentence structure is clearer in the 1907 text, I have used some phrases or words from the latter."

---

*Published originally in 1956 by Thomas Yoseloff under the title *The Parasite*.

51

According to Mendele's friend, J.L. Binshtok, the figure of Gutman in the novel is modeled after Avrom-Ber Gottlober. The figure of Yitskhok-Avrom is modeled, according to Sholem Aleykhem, after a powerful man who "at that time cracked the whip in Glupsk (Berditchev) over the congregation of Israel."

A picaresque novel, it is a bitter attack on "toadies," or influence peddlers, who live off the people (milking the rich and squeezing the poor) without really contributing anything in return. As Gerald Stillman cogently observes in the introduction to the original edition of this translation (1956), since the protagonist learns that "the quickest and surest road to comfort and security lies in swindle and deceit, this very idea is in itself a profound condemnation of society."

Writing under the influence of the *haskole* (the Jewish enlightenment of Eastern Europe), Mendele not only attacks toadies and influence peddlers, but also the Jewish "establishment," as well as the cramped Jewish way of life of the time, especially its educational system and its cultural level. *The Little Man* displays Mendele's acid, bitterly satiric tone, as well as his desire to reform the life of his people.

By "condescending" to employ Yiddish as a serious literary medium, Mendele elevated both himself and it. He risked ridicule from his contemporary *maskilim* (adherents of the *haskole*) who looked down on Yiddish as a "jargon," not worthy of serious cultural effort (see "Notes For My Biography"). But Mendele demonstrated that Yiddish could be employed as a powerful literary medium by using the ordinary language of the people with grace, beauty, style, and authenticity—something which had never really been done before. No wonder Sholem Aleykhem's designation of him as the "zeyde" (grandfather) of modern Yiddish (and Hebrew) literature became so quickly and widely adopted.

In reading *The Little Man*, we not only read Mendele's first Yiddish novel, and not only the work that begins a new phase in the development of the literature in that language, but we also see reflected in it the life and state of mind of a large segment of the Jewish people at that time and place, as well as the then temper of the *haskole*. We also touch the heart, mind, and soul of a man—of Sholem Yankef Abramovitsh, called, affectionately, Mendele by his people, a great Yiddish writer, the "zeyde," who speaks to us magically across the chasm of time.

The Little Man

Translated by Gerald Stillman

CHAPTER 1

The first question that one Jew asks another, even a total stranger, as soon as they have met and shaken hands, is: "And what is your name?"

It occurs to neither of them that his response might be as follows:

"Tell me, brother, why is it so important for you to know my name? Are we going to discuss the betrothal of our children? I'm called by the name that I was given and let me be!"

But the question "And what is your name?" is a natural one. It is as much a habit as

feeling the material of someone's new coat and inquiring: "How much is it a yard?"

or asking for a cigarette when an acquaintance opens his cigarette case; or sticking your fingers into someone's snuff box and taking a whiff;

or dunking a greasy kerchief into another's bottle of liniment and giving yourself a rubdown;

or walking over to two people engaged in a conversation and listening in for a while;

or asking someone for no good reason how his business is going and then weighing him down with advice although he does not need it.

Such acts and many others are to be expected, since they are part of the order of things for all eternity. To protest against them would make a man seem raving mad and perverse.

Jews are fairly well convinced that, immediately upon getting one's foot in the door in the world to come, the Angel's first question will be: "And what is your name, brother?"

Even the Angel who wrestled with Jacob did not violate the eternal order of things and soon asked Jacob how he was called. A similar act on the part of a human being who is only of flesh and blood is therefore a foregone conclusion. I know very well that this, my first venture into Yiddish literature, will be greeted with the eternal question: "And what is your name, uncle?"

Mendele is my name! Thus, ladies and gentlemen, was I named after my great-grandfather on my mother's side, Reb Mendele Moscower, blessed be his memory. In his time, he was known as Moscower because he had once traveled to Moscow to purchase some wares. As a result of this journey, he had, in his little corner of the world, a respected name and much honor. He was considered a shrewd man, well versed in the whys and wherefores of the world. When any need arose, or if a petition was to be submitted to the government, he was always consulted first, but that is not my point.

I am, however, not yet properly introduced. After this initial question, Jews become curious in earnest. They bombard one with all sorts of questions, such as

Where are you from?
Are you married?
Any children?
What business are you in?
Where are you going?

and many others which have been accepted by the dispersed children of Israel as mandatory if the questioner is to be considered worldly wise and not a backward bench warmer. Sheer benevolence dictates that these questions be answered, just as one answers "A good year to you!" upon being greeted with a "Good Shabbes!" or a "Good Holiday!" Having no desire to go against the customs of the world, I stand ready to answer these questions as briefly and clearly as possible.

I was born in Tsvuatshits,* in the province of Teterivke, which is famous for its excellent cattle and even more for the deprecating grunt with which its inhabitants greet every remark. Tsvuatshits is known for this grunt throughout the world. In my passport, I am described as being fifty-two years old, but I wouldn't swear to my exact age. My father and mother, may they rest in peace, strongly

---

* Mendele, like Gogol, avails himself of the humorous device of playing upon place names. *Tsvua*, in Hebrew, means "hyena" or "hypocrite." The English equivalent of *Tsvuatshits* can be taken as "Hyenaville." *Tyetyerev*, in Russian, means "grouse"—a bird resembling a pheasant. *Teterivke* could be taken as "Grouseville."

disputed the calculation of my age. They both agreed that I was born at the lighting of the first candle during the Great Fire, but, according to my father's reckoning, this took place when the Great Frost descended upon our region and when my great-grandfather, blessed be his memory, was carried off. My mother, however, insisted that this happened approximately two years after the first Great Fright in our town, may we be protected from a similar occurrence today! As proof of this, she offered the fact that it was then that our red cow calved and she made *milkhike* jam-tarts for half the town, over which everyone licked their fingers, and to this day many an old man can still recall their taste!

My specifications in the passport read as follows :

Height—medium
Hair and eyebrows—gray
Eyes—brown
Nose and mouth—ordinary
A gray beard
An unmarked face
No distinguishing features.

But this is completely meaningless. I am merely a person like most other people and neither a tomcat nor an ass, God forbid. The question arises then, if the passpport did not describe one's features, one would still be a human being, for who ever heard of giving a passport to an ass? To which we make answer as follows: "It is not wise to ask questions."

The whole idea is—here is a description of my features, and there, you still do not know how I look. . . . And, in truth, suppose you knew that my forehead is high and wrinkled, that my nostrils are large and rather coarse, that when I part my lips I appear to be smiling very acidly. Believe me, even before we were married, my wife was not interested in such petty details.

She was told: "Congratulations, bride, you have a groom!"

Enough! Whose concern is it what kind of a nose he has or what kind of face? Whose business is it and why should it bother anybody? Anyway, ladies and gentlemen, now you know that I am married. It stands to reason that I have children, and plenty of them at that, may the evil eye not harm them, for who has ever heard of a Jew who is married and does not have a minimum of half a dozen little ones? Especially a poor Jew.

My business is selling books: *Khumoshim,* prayerbooks for

55

festivals, penitential prayerbooks, ordinary prayerbooks, and all sorts of religious works. I also have storybooks, including a few of the more modern novels. In my time, I have had many different jobs. Soon after leaving the room and board of my in-laws, I became a money changer, a spice dealer, an innkeeper, a grain dealer, a peddler, and a *melamed*. I went from one type of trade to another, as most Jews do, and remained a pauper. As the old saying has it: *You'll work all day for a wisp of hay.* Finally I took to selling books, and for a number of years, blessed be His name, I have done fairly well. Aside from books, I also carry prayershawls, venerable-looking *tsitses, shoyfers, mezuzes,* wolves' teeth, amulets, shiny patent-leather shoes for children, skullcaps, and sometimes brass and copper wares.

Exactly how brass and copper wares fit in with religious books, I am not quite certain myself, but it has been a custom of ours for years and years, since a Yiddish author must sometimes also be a matchmaker, just as a Polish janitor in a small *shul* must have a liquor concession on the side, or a tax collector will sometimes be a cook and butler at an affair given by the social elite, or a rabbinical assistant must have some confidential business deals afoot, or a rich idler must have his finger in the tax-farming pie. . . . But that is not my point. For years I have been on the road. I travel all over Poland and visit all its little towns and villages. I am as well known there, blessed be His name, as a counterfeit kopeck.

Usually you will find me at my wagon near the synagogue. My horse is there with me, facing the wagon and eating some oats (if there are any to be had) from a cloth which has one end tied to the trestle of the wagon and the other end to the yoke. Jewish children quietly steal behind and gleefully tear the hairs from his poor tail, and he, the *shlimazl*, stands there calmly, as if he were not bothered at all. Sometimes he drops his lower lip, at which time he seems to engage in a toothy laugh just like, forgive the comparison, a human being.

When there is nothing to eat, which happens on occasion, he stands thoughtfully with perked ears, looking at my display of books, and one could swear that with his horse sense he knows quite well what is written there, possibly better than many a. . . . But that, too, is beside the point.

I believe that I am now absolved of all introductory obligations. I have answered all the questions and it is high time to proceed with our story. Anyway, I am only human, and if I have left

56

anything out, believe me, upon my word of honor, that, just as soon as I remember, I will certainly include it in one of my narrations, which I plan, with God's help, to publish one after another. Furthermore, if there are any who are so impatient that they must immediately know the entire root of my being in complete detail, let them take the trouble to write to me and they will soon receive a clear answer. My address is:

Mendele Yudelovitsh Moykher-Sforim
Tsvuatshits, Teterivke

They do not have to bother adding the title "Reb Jew." The postal officials will be able to tell without that. . . .

Wait a minute, ladies and gentlemen—I completely forgot the most important thing! It is a good thing that I caught myself in time. It is the custom of our Yiddish writers, as is well known, either to mention directly the names of their modest wives in their books, or, by means of clever symbols, to praise their virtue and piety. Therefore, you will all probably want to know my wife's name and you will certainly be justified.

Ladies and gentlemen, her name is Yente!

57

CHAPTER 2

And now that we have become acquainted, ladies and gentlemen, try to imagine me, Mendele Moykher-Sforim, standing near my wagon somewhere along the road, deeply absorbed in thought, and apparently rooted to the ground. It is autumn. You will possibly think that my wagon is stuck in the mud and that I am considering the best way to extricate it? No! This is the year 5615, which will be especially noted in the almanac for its miraculously dry and beautiful autumn.

The weather was quite summery, warm, clear. The cattle grazed in the fields from which the dense young grain was shooting forth. The trees were garbed in yellow-green garments, somewhat faded, shredded, and moth-eaten. Yet it was plain that they had no intention of stripping completely bare in order to sleep their usual winter sleep. Long white gossamers floated through the air, a sure sign of good weather, although the almanac had, may I be pardoned for saying so, guessed wrong and had, as usual, told a big lie. But this is beside the point.

You will possibly think that I was standing near my wagon because I was lost? Wrong again! I knew very well that a little further, at the fork in the road, the road on the right leads to Glupsk* and the road on the left leads to another town. The problem was: which road to take—to the left or to the right?

I had to go to Glupsk in order to transact some business there—I wanted to unload some wares and waxen *Khanike* candles. On the other hand, I also wanted to go to the fair in the other town. Therefore, I stood undecided, going neither here nor there, as if chained to the spot.

I happened to glance at my horse. He was calm and unperturbed, scratching his neck against his harness. In general, he seemed very pleased at not being in motion. I stared as though expecting the sought-for advice from him. Then it occurred to me to leave the entire matter to his discretion.

Don't laugh, ladies and gentlemen! When in doubt, even wise people fall back on strange solutions. Tell me please, what is the

---

* A play on the Russian word *glupi*, "stupid" or "foolish." Glupsk can therefore be interpreted as "Foolstown."

point, for example, in slapping oneself on the forehead or casting a die? Of what value is it to flip a coin or to use any other similar device? A fool can be very useful in such circumstances: you ask him and take his advice. It happens quite frequently in this world of ours that wise men allow themselves to be led by fools. I know of many fools who play an important role with some businessmen, highly respectable people, too. But this is beside the point.

Climbing into the wagon, I flicked the reins and then dropped them, letting the horse lead the way. He chose the road on the right toward Glupsk. Well, lead me, lead me, horse o' mine. Maybe you're right. If you prefer Glupsk, let it be Glupsk!

Tuesday morning, having said my prayers, I arrived in Glupsk and, as usual, drove right up to the synagogue. Before I had a chance to catch my breath, I was surrounded. Old men and young men alike began to investigate the contents of my wagon, peeking into books, tapping my brass wares, examining the amulets and the wolves' teeth, asking me questions and asking each other questions, as is the custom among Jews. A gang of youngsters, the boys from the *Talmud-Toyre*, greeted their old friend, my horse, and were soon merrily plucking the hairs from his tail.

In the courtyard of the synagogue, I noticed groups of people arguing. They were talking, laughing, worrying, shaking their heads. Soon several little groups merged into one. Commotion, activity, noise, talking with hands and feet. Then the large group exploded, like a soap bubble, into a number of smaller ones. Apparently something had happened. Where there's smoke, there's fire.

I was very curious to know what was going on; after all, I'm also a Jew. My soul is, as the saying goes, not made of dough. One should know about everything that goes on in the world. One can never tell when this knowledge will be useful. There is many a Jew who earns his daily bread by poking his nose into every pot and sniffing; wherever there are two partners, he barges in to make a third and demands his share. Being united is a Jewish trait.

I listened to the conversation of a group which had just formed near me.

"Lord Almighty, blessed be Your justice! He was still a young man. I would say about forty. Such a man, such a man!"

"What are you so upset about, Reb Avremtshe, that you can't console your poor self! Pish, a great event! What was so wonderful about the man?"

"For you, Yosl, nothing is a great event and no man is ever wonderful. Reb Avremtshe is right. Such a man, such a rich man! It's a pity. As I am a Jew, it's a pity!"

"How d'ye do! Here's a new Mr. Pity! Leybtshe supports Reb Avremtshe with his booming bass and, like a good Jew, expresses his pity. Tell me, Leybtshe, what was it that you said a while ago?"

"What I said a while ago? I? What *did* I say, Yosl? Really, what did . . ."

"Certainly!, certainly! You yourself, with your kosher little mouth! Didn't you say: 'Is he also a human being, this Itsik-Avreml* the Strong-arm Man? He was, he may pardon me or not, a ruffian, a leech, a swindler, a liar, a brute and, to top it off, a lecher'?"

"Who? Me? Yosl! What? Well . . . good day! I really have no time."

"A good day and a good year! Come with me Reb Avremtshe. We'll go to the synagogue and have a drink. The caretaker has some good brandy today."

"You don't think that a little brandy would do any harm, do you, Yosele? Upon my life, you did a clever thing by getting rid of that liar. Let's not fool ourselves! What was that man anyway? He was, may he rest in peace, an ignoramus, a busybody, a swindler, a leech. It's all right, he left plenty of money—other people's money!"

"That's why I like you, Reb Avremtshe. Because you always like to tell the truth. . . ."

I unharnessed my horse, turning him around so that he faced the wagon, in order to feed him some oats. Then I got to work and began unloading the wagon. I had hardly put things in a semblance of order, stringing up on both sides of the wagon rings of amulets, satin skullcaps, a few sets of *tsitses*, a prayershawl or two, when the caretaker of the *Beys Din* came running toward me and shot out all in one breath:

"*Oy, g'vald*, Reb Mendele! *Sholem aleykhem*, Reb Mendele. The Rabbi, may he live long, cordially requests your honor to come to him quickly. Quickly, Reb Mendele!" The fact that the Rabbi had so soon become aware of my presence did not surprise me particularly. Glupsk, you see, is a Jewish town, and Jews become aware of things speedily. Let someone even so much as make a remark and it will immediately become known ten streets away.

---

* *Itsik-Avreml* is the diminutive form for *Itskhok-Avrom*. Diminutives in Yiddish are used either endearingly or sarcastically, depending upon the context.

As a matter of fact, the remark will be garnished and served up to all on a little platter. It's really much more effective than the telegraph. What surprised me was the fact that the Rabbi wished to see me. And why did he send the caretaker of the *Beys Din* after me in such a hurry? It occurred to me that a lawsuit must be involved. Yes, yes, there must be a little worm gnawing here somewhere. My heart skipped a beat. For where can you find a businessman who does not have some ugly little secret which, when found out, will allow others to prod their noses into his affairs?

In my mind, I quickly began to review all my business dealings. The first to appear before my mind's eye was my daughter's father-in-law. Maybe it is he who is stirring up the pot. Maybe he wants to force me to pay him the rest of the dowry and settle the whole affair. This father-in-law of my daughter's is a simple soul. He believes that whatever is written in a marriage contract must be fulfilled, and that whatever one has undertaken to pay must really be paid in full. He doesn't understand, the fool, that all that is mere talk and is written in black and white only for the sake of politeness. One must talk out of both sides of one's mouth so as to create a stir in the world, a custom which our fathers and their fathers before them developed.

Or maybe, I thought, God forbid, it is that book dealer with whom I did some trading last summer. I gave him *Shevues* prayerbooks, amulets, wolves' teeth, current novels, and sundry and varied trash. He gave me brass wares, books of religious questions and answers, prayer books for the guiltless, prayer books for festivals, and various other kinds of books. The point is that he may have reconsidered the whole transaction, felt that he had been cheated, and now wished, on the basis of an unfair price, to squeeze some more out of me! May the good Lord protect and defend a man from having any dealings with the book sellers of this area. One can get ulcers from their claims and demands! But that is beside the point.

Whatever the story, my heart grew heavy. Willy-nilly, I must go. I decided that I might as well take along some wares, small items, a brand new *Tkhine* to which the Rabbi's wife might take a fancy, which certainly would not do me any harm. I was annoyed with my horse. Why had he chosen the road to Glupsk? I only let him smell the oats. I insulted him with a few scathing remarks, left him and my wagon in the hands of the caretaker, and stalked away in anger. Let his friends, the boys of Glupsk, pull the hairs from his tail to their hearts' content! Serves him right! It was his choice. If it makes him happy, then I am happy and it is none of my affair.

No sooner had I stepped inside the Rabbi's door when he came to greet me.

"Oy, Reb Mendele! Oy, *sholem aleykhem*, Reb Mendele! Only the Lord Himself could have brought you here just when we need you, when we really need you, dear and hearty Reb Mendele. This is truly divine intervention, a veritable miracle. You did a wonderfully clever thing to come to Glupsk just at this time, Reb Mendele!"

"This wonderfully clever thing was done not by me, Mendele, but my horse." I laughed to myself and in my heart I apologized to the *shlimazl*. Obviously, I was not summoned for a lawsuit. Why was I wanted then?

Another person might easily believe that he was eagerly awaited because of his wagon full of wares. But since I am no numskull, nor was I born yesterday, I knew better. You see, I have found this to be a rule: it is deceit that makes the world go around. One who needs to buy a particular item plays crafty, acts as if the item were absolutely useless to him, so that he might pick it up for a song. Thus, for example, a customer wants to buy a prayerbook for festivals. Does he look at it? No! First he looks at a penitential prayerbook, then at some *tsitses*, then at some other wares. In the meanwhile, he picks up the prayerbook for festivals, as if in passing, lays it down with a shrug and a little smile, and says: "If you wanted only a few kopecks for it, I might buy it."

Believe me, the whole world is one big trading post. Some look for bargains. Some want to cut the other fellow's price. Some are waiting for others to lose something so they might find it. Still others look out for themselves first, and then, after the good Lord has helped them to snatch bargains by hook or crook, so many that they almost choke on them, they are genuinely interested in helping—themselves.

I could tell from the Rabbi's face that he was not interested in buying anything from me. If he were, he would not have made it so obvious that he was eagerly awaiting me. It is true that the Rabbi is a kosher, upright individual, so help me, but when one lives among wolves, one must howl like a wolf.

The Rabbi, long may he live, took me by the arm and led me into his private room. Within, apparently absorbed in thought, were seated the officers of the synagogue and many of the wealthy businessmen of the town. Well, wealthy businessmen always seem to be thinking and worrying, and they look at you with such a frowning glance that your mother's milk curdles in your veins. One feels compelled to leave and never to have to look upon them again. I really can't understand it: if one has money, why so much thinking, so much worrying, such serious faces? It seems to me that lofty thoughts are not particularly necessary in order to count coins. It seems to me, too, that one may have money in his coffers and yet look a person straight in the eye. Anyway . . . but that is beside the point.

"Gentlemen," the Rabbi addressed the rich men and the synagogue officials, "I have troubled you to come here because of an important matter. However, since, as if by a miracle, Reb Mendele arrived in our community today, I decided to have you wait a while longer so that I could ask him to favor us with his presence which is indispensable in this matter. Please forgive me a hundred times over. Now that we are all assembled here, I should like to tell you of a wondrous matter."

I was completely baffled by the proceedings and wondered what all this would lead to. But then I decided not to be so impatient; soon I would be a few minutes older, and have my curiosity satisfied. The Rabbi drew a thick packet of papers from his breast pocket and spoke.

"Look, gentlemen! These papers were sent to me at daybreak today by the new widow, Itskhok-Avrom's wife. Before his death, he requested that, as soon as his soul departed, the papers should be delivered to me. Bear witness, please, gentlemen—my name is written at the top of the first page. I shall not be mysterious about it, but I shall read the papers to you without delay. Be seated, Reb Mendele! Kindly place your wares on the shelf, and sit down here."

It became very quiet in the room. Not a sound could be heard. All present opened their eyes wide and, with bated breath, waited to hear what the Rabbi would read.

As if Satan had had a hand in it, the stool upon which the Rabbi had asked me to sit had a broken leg. No sooner had I seated myself, when I tumbled over and created a slight commotion.

CHAPTER 3

When I had seated myself properly, the Rabbi, may he live long, stroked his beard several times with all five fingers and, with a movement of his shoulders, began to read aloud the contents of the papers:

▲▲ These papers of mine contain my entire autobiography and the will which I have drawn up. I beg of you, Rabbi, to fulfill all my requests contained herein to the smallest detail. Forgive me a hundred times over for troubling your honor with such a long narration. When you reach the end, you will see that this is not, God forbid, meaningless prattle but that, on the contrary, this narrative of my life may be of great value. I really was compelled to write it.

I was born of poor parents in the town of Bezliudeff.* I do not remember my father, for he died while I was still in diapers. Upon his death, his estate consisted of a sickly wife with quite a number of little ones, myself included as an additional treasure. And that was all!

I can recall childhood events from the time I was five or six years old. So far as I can remember, I was not considered especially bright in my youth. All my actions and remarks were greeted with much laughter. I was certainly never petted or spoiled. I was never kissed, never caressed, never embraced as were other children. When I cried, I was never soothed with pancakes, candies, or toys. Instead, I got a few slaps or a beating.

The words *mercy* or *pity* were never mentioned in my presence. I never heard anyone say about me :

"What a pity! The poor thing hasn't eaten." "What a pity! His poor little face is all swollen."
"Shameful! The poor child hasn't slept."
"Mercy on us! He's frozen! He walks around naked and barefoot."
"What a pity! The poor child doesn't have an ounce of flesh on his bones."

---

* A play on the Russian word *liudyi* meaning "people" or "human beings." *Bezliudeff* signifies a town devoid of human beings, i.e., devoid of people with human traits.

The only comments I ever heard were:

"Look at that mug, that ugly snoot of his, those feet as red as beets!"

"Look at that glutton! The spittle is already dribbling from his mouth!"

"Look at that devilish creature. He's up to his little tricks again—trembling, shivering, and gnashing his teeth. . . ."

A poor man's child is always an unwanted thing in this world. He is always in someone's way. While still in the womb, death is quietly wished upon him. At birth, he is greeted like the plague. Before he has ever seen the light of day, he has made bitter enemies. Once he arrives, he grows somehow or other, incapable of awakening a feeling of pity or mercy in the breasts of even his own parents—unless he becomes deathly sick. Only then do the deep-seated parental feelings come forth and they pour out their grief at the bedside of their poor child, the dear and innocent creature, who has led such a desolate and dreary life, never having had an hour of peace and love. Then do they see their life in the sharpest colors and their hearts weep tears of blood. When a frozen heart melts, it can release a devastating flood. I have experienced this myself of late—it boils, it seethes, it erupts with terrible force! That is why poor parents lament their children much more vehemently and movingly than do the rich.

I grew like a wild horse on the steppe, crude, savage, with all the ugly habits of a wild street urchin. One of my habits was to watch someone's teeth while he talked or to stare into his eyes. My mother beat me within an inch of my life for this a number of times.

Once I was sick in bed and Mother was good to me. Somehow I began to look into her eyes. She allowed me to do so in order not to irritate me. I couldn't control myself and asked:

"Mama! Who is the little man in your eyes?"

Mother smiled and answered:

"My little fool! The little man is the soul. The little man cannot be seen in the eyes of any other creature, in the eyes of neither animals nor cattle. He can be seen only in Jewish eyes."

Mother's answer made a great impression upon me and awakened many fresh, vibrant thoughts. When a mother says something, she must know what she is talking about. After all, she is a mother and big, maybe ten times bigger than I. Her finger is thicker than my arm. I accepted her words as proven, confirmed fact and believed in them with all my heart.

From then on, my imaginative powers were busy with the little man. Really, isn't it a surprising, a curious thing? Even in my sleep, I could not forget the little man. I dreamed that I played with him, that I leaped into other people's eyes just as he did. In short, his image was my constant companion.

I developed a great desire to be a little man myself. Can you imagine—the little man is a soul! In size no bigger than a flea, and yet in him is concentrated the gist, the very kernel of life! The thought of how I could touch or feel the little man occupied my mind constantly.

Once I had a bright idea. While Mother was bending over in order to remove a pot from the stove, I ran up behind her like one obsessed—to this very day, I hardly understand the workings of my mind at the time—and, placing myself in God's hands, I struck her in the nape of the neck with my fist, so that the little man would be forced to leap out of her eyes, even for a moment! You can well imagine the blows I received for this act. All that day I went hungry because Mother had broken the pot of porridge with her forehead.

I was rewarded even more richly on another occasion. A thought, tinged with heresy, had entered my mind concerning my mother's words. I wanted to find out for myself whether a cow had a little man in her eyes or not. I took a walk down the street one day until I came upon a cow, and, while I was busy looking into her eyes, she gored me with her horns, mauling me very badly. The mark has remained on my left cheek to this very day. These misfortunes by no means forced the idea of a little man out of my mind. On the contrary, the idea became more firmly entrenched than ever.

I studied in the *Talmud-Toyre*. Everyone knows what a *Talmud-Toyre* is, so that it is really unnecessary to describe it. It is a grave in which poor Jewish children are buried, where their minds are mutilated and where they are removed from all contact with the world in which they live. It is a factory that manufactures good-for-nothings, ne'er-do-wells, and spineless, unfortunate creatures. It is a vast pit, an abyss, an unclean hovel standing on wobbly supports, even as are our *Talmud-Toyres* here—a shame and a disgrace for other people to see.

At the age of eight, I was studying the *Khumesh* and its associated commentaries, including those of Rashi, no small feat for a boy of my age who was not as yet very fluent in the Hebrew language itself. Apparently a person can be a scholar and a big fool; one has nothing to do with the other.

Mother used to call me *shlimazl*, and, in truth, she was quite right. In the *Talmud-Toyre*, I was more of a *shlimazl* than any other child. The *rebbe*, who by no means deserved the title Rabbi, was enchanted by one subject—beatings, possibly even more so than by a bit of brandy. For no apparent reason, he simply enjoyed torturing the depressed and persecuted little children, who received flayings aplenty without his attentions and who were so thin that their souls barely managed to remain united with their bodies. But he broke the already broken bones; he pinched and tore at the small bodies, and the best portion of his blows came my way.

Once, he became so annoyed with me and beat me so mercilessly that I barely escaped with my life and had to stop attending the *Talmud-Toyre*. This is what happened.

The *rebbe* had been explaining to me that passage in the book of Genesis which reads: *And Lamech said unto his wives...*

"Lamech was blind. Tubal-cain was leading him, and when he saw his grandfather Cain at a distance, he thought it was a wild beast." (The *rebbe* said "fox" in order to make it clearer). "He told the blind Lamech to aim at the fox. He did so and killed him. And when Lamech found out that he had slain Cain, he began to beat his palms together in sorrow and, in doing so, beat his son Tubal-cain to death. Because of this, his wives would not stay with him. He appealed for a reconciliation.

"*Vayomar Lamech*—and Lamech said, *l'noshiv*—unto his wives: '*Adah v'Zillah*—Adah and Zillah, *sh'man kohlee*—hear my voice, *noshee Lamech*—ye wives of Lamech! . . .' "

One fine day, a clean-shaven German* suddenly arrived at the *Talmud-Toyre*. I believe he had come from St. Petersburg. Together with him came all the tax collectors in order to audition the children. To my great misfortune, the German chose me to translate a passage from the Khumesh—none other than the one beginning with the phrase *Vayomar Lamech l'noshiv!*

---

* Any clean-shaven, beardless person was known as a "German" to the Jews and also to the Russian peasantry as a whole.

Since when was I accustomed to talking to grown-ups, especially to a German, a shaven one? I quivered and quaked like a fish out of water. There was a roaring in my ears and a beating in my heart. My hair stood on end and my blood ran cold. I felt that I would be unable to repeat such a long story as the one about Lamech. And here were these men standing over me, urging me on with one voice.

"Speak! Speak!"

What could I do? I had to speak. Completely breathless, I began to deliver a confused, stuttering explanation.

"*Vayomar*—a fox, *Lamech*—a blind man, *l'noshiv*—his wives left him, *Tubal-cain*—leading him, *Adah v'Zillah*—and he killed him. . . ."

The German was petrified. Beside himself with anger, he called the *rebbe* and said to him harshly:

"Hah! What is this I hear? Is that how you teach your pupils? Shame and dishonor! "

The *rebbe* scratched himself, picked his nose, and babbled:

"Good sir! The boy became frightened. He's really a good boy, upon my word."

Whereupon the German turned to me.

"Fear not, my child. Nothing will happen to you. Tell me, what is the meaning of the word *vayomar?*"

I no longer knew what was happening to me. With my eyes staring blankly like those of a statue, I shot out:

"A fox! . . . No, I mean, *vayomar,* he appealed to his wives. . . ."

The poor *rebbe* looked as if he had been dragged through a keyhole. He was fit to be buried alive. He submitted to all the abuse that was heaped upon him and had a miserable day. My turn came later, when he vented his spleen upon me. From that time on, he would pick on me and beat me until I could no longer bear it. I became very weak and had to stop attending the *Talmud-Toyre.*

CHAPTER 4

▲▲ My mother lived in great poverty and simply could not make ends meet from one day to the next. She darned socks, plucked chickens, helped other women during childbirth, and, when Passover came, rolled dough for *matses*. She worked day and night and barely earned enough to buy water for our porridge.

A woman's work has no value in our world and is but scantily rewarded. For what is a woman anyway? What is the worth of the whole woman? What kind of respect does she command even if she is an exceptionally capable housewife? Women, so the whole world believes, will never amount to anything. None of their jobs have any solid foundations. Work that requires deep thought, and is useful as well, is not for a woman's mind.

My father's estate had dwindled very noticeably: two girls and a boy had died, simply, it can be so stated, from hunger. One of the older boys had wandered off somewhere and has not been heard from to this day. With Mother remained a weak, sickly girl—not long for this world—and I, the *shlimazl*, who sat on her neck. My appetite, may no harm befall me, was excellent and the bit of food which I used to take from the poor thing was just enough to make my mouth water. I had one continual demand: food, food! Anything, so long as it was edible!

My poor mother suffered and did not know what to do with me. Friends advised her to apprentice me to a trade, but she would toss her head and object violently.

"Better should he perish than to go and work with his hands, disgracing me and his father lying in his grave. His father wouldn't be able to lie still! What do you think—Reb Tevl the *Melamed's* son should become an apprentice to a handworker? It hurts me even to think of it! Oh Lord, may my enemies never live to see the day!"

Finally, with the Lord's help, she managed to find a job for me in a general store. She delighted in the thought that her son was already a merchant.

But her son was no merchant, he was a watchdog! I will make this clear in a moment. My work consisted of pouncing upon any passerby and, with much shouting and commotion, dragging him into the store. As soon as someone appeared on the street, I was egged on like a watchdog and then let loose, shouting all in one breath :

"This way, Pan! Silk kerchiefs, linen, suspenders, knives, American galoshes, walking sticks, almond soap, pomade!"

This business was repulsive to me. One simply does not run out into the street with a yell to block someone else's path. Somehow it's savage! Consequently, I would fake a little and cut the performance short. This made my boss and his wife furious. They cursed me and made me feel as low as a worm. They upbraided me for gorging myself on their bread and salt without working, although I toiled and moiled more than my strength could bear, doing all sorts of work not only in the store but in their house as well.

In addition, the older errand boys used me as their erand boy. I had to go through fire and through water for them, crawling under their very fingernails, and I considered myself lucky if I caught nothing worse at their hands.

If an errand boy from another store happened to snatch a prospective customer out of my hands, I could bid farewell to my life. Everybody in the store would lash me, some with their tongues, others with their hands, and blows rained down upon me until I was sick. My mother and my father, Reb Tevl the *Melamed*, may he rest in peace, were also roundly abused. They were not, God forbid, forgotten.

On such a bitter day, eating was out of the question. I fasted. I was not even given a smell of food. I was told to eat my heart out, to chew the dust. However, as such fare was not meant for the human stomach, I simply abstained... Frequently, I practiced such abstinence several times a week.

When I finally realized that this was getting me nowhere, I went to work in earnest. As soon as anyone remotely resembling a possible customer appeared on the street, I rushed upon him like a dog off the leash, barked the whole list of wares in a thundering torrent, blocked his road and dragged him after me by his coattails. I often received a blow for my efforts, but I did my duty nonetheless. After a while, I grew so accustomed to this phase of the work that the yelling became a thing of joy and great glee. I was especially delighted when I laid hands upon a Polish landowner. I yelled in his ear and called out in Yiddish, among the other wares : "You can purchase, *Pan*, a Parisian heartache, may mine fall upon your head! Pomade, boils, the plague upon you, *Pan!*" My business dealings on the street brought me into conflict with the errand boys of other stores. They also pounced on customers with a hoot and a howl. We fought in the street just as our bosses quarreled indoors in their stores. But there was this big difference: while the bosses threw prices around and cut each other's throats, we threw each other around and got in some mighty blows. Since I was the smallest and weakest, it was considered a *mitsve*, sheer humaneness, to bestow the best-aimed blows and the most stinging slaps upon me alone. I thrived poorly on such generosity and gradually, as a result of too much humaneness, I began to lose the aspect of a human being, although, for the type of trade in which I was engaged, having a human aspect was not particularly necessary. One can be an errand boy without being human. Strength and health, however, are very important, and I—I ceased to resemble a living being; that is, my health waned, my strength ebbed, I could hardly stand on my feet.

Consider what I had to do: I had to serve and please anybody and everybody; my food was sorrow, my drink despair; beatings were bequeathed to me by one and all, strangers and acquaintances alike.

More than anyone else in the store, the oldest errand boy strove to make my life miserable. Somehow he was displeased with my sleeping in the kitchen. He used to steal in quietly and try all sorts of schemes to drive me out. I was like a thorn in his side. Still, I might have been able to bear the strain if not for the incident with the button.

Once I saw a mother-of-pearl button lying on the floor. It shone and sparkled with such beautiful colors that my evil genius began to work on me. I thought of my sick sister at home and of how I would make her a gift of the button. On *Shabes* or on a holiday, she would bedeck herself with it and would shine among her girl friends.

This notion gave me even more impetus. I picked up the button and put it in my pocket. The oldest errand boy, who had been standing in a corner all the while observing me, collared me with a shout.

"So, you crook! You little thief! You put it in your pocket? You see, boss, the other things that are missing must have disappeared the same way!"

This last remark was made with the calculated purpose of throwing upon me the blame for all his sins. I remembered, as if in a dream, that every now and then he would slip a little something to the serving-maid. . . . In short, I was beaten, insulted, cursed, and booted out.

Again I became a guest at my mother's house, at a fortunate and promising time. I do not say this in vain. At the time, Mother was rolling *matse* dough for a baker, and I was appointed to pour the water into the dough from a little pitcher. I felt as proud as if I were cupbearer to a king. I respectfully admired myself as an individual to whom another must turn for a favor and whose help was of great importance. At first, I had a little trouble in gauging the correct amount of water to be poured. As a matter of fact, several trays of *matses* were made *khomets* because of my faulty pouring, but soon I developed the knack and my road went as though greased. I considered myself to be *the premier pourer* in the world. Another such as I could nowhere be found, not even in Paris.

Among the many people who found it necessary to take odd jobs to make ends meet and therefore passed through the baker's establishment as helpers, there was a *melamed* who taught small children. He was very pleased with my method of pouring and even pinched my cheek. My mother, for some reason, engaged in endless conversations with him. One day she called me.

"You see, Itskhok-Avremtshe, Reb Ezriel will take you on as his helper!"

Then she turned to the *melamed*.

"I can't imagine why I didn't think of it before! His father was a *melamed*. His son should also be one! But it's the same old story, may your health prosper. My mind, may it never happen to you or to any Jew, is—O enemies of Zion!—my mind is worn out. You, Reb Ezriel, you can understand me. You knew my husband well, may you live long. It's the old story. It was probably written in the Books that the son should also be a teacher. If it pleases His beloved Name, it pleases me. May you, Reb Ezriel, never be the worse for the teaching. . . ."

But, alas, it was not, as Mother thought, for teaching that the *melamed* needed me. It was for rocking his child's cradle, for taking care of the goat and other such duties! It was to Reb Ezriel's wife that I was apprenticed. She tutored me and honored me with all sorts of work. To her I was a cork with which she plugged every leaking hole. As religiously as a Jew who will not miss his prayers, I had to take the goat out to pasture every morning. Rarely, rarely, did Reb Ezriel condescend to lead her by the horns while I prodded her from behind with a switch. Having finished with the goat, there

72

followed a program of bringing in the wood, picking stray slivers of wood from the dust heaps in the yard, emptying pails of slops, sweeping the house, and taking care of the baby, which, with its wet, rolled-up shirt, was continually crying, screaming for the breast, kicking its hands and feet, all of which resulted in its whooping and gasping for breath and covering itself with snivel. I had to hold it in my arms, inventing games for its amusement, blowing into my fist to imitate a trumpet, clicking my tongue, singing *Tsigele-Migele* or other children's songs. I dared not stop for a minute! If I did, Reb Ezriel's wife would open her sluices and drown me in a flood of curses and reproaches, holding the rolling pin in readiness to split my head.

After I had finished these duties in peace, I ran to collect the children for *kheyder*. This initiated a completely new set of activities: shining boots and shoes, pulling the soaked children out of bed, finding their clothes, buttoning their trousers, blowing the feathers off their skullcaps, wiping their noses, dragging them forcefully from their houses and shoving them outside. Thus I went from house to house until I had rounded up the whole command. Then began a wild march that had to be seen to be appreciated.

Before me and behind me were running boys, jumping boys, crawling boys, all with their shirt-tails hanging from their trousers. One walked sorrowfully, his head lowered as if he were being led to slaughter; another had a piece of bread and an egg which he was in the process of eating; a third one crowed "Cock-a-doodle-doo!"; a fourth imitated a goat, "Me-e-e-eh!" I walked importantly in their midst, my pockets and arms loaded with rolls and butter, bread and *shmalts*, crusts and herring tails, little pots of porridge, sour milk, cheese, onions, garlic, and sundry vegetables, and leading half a dozen boys with each hand. Some of them sobbed and sniveled. Others were stubborn and refused to go any further. Still others walked with their heads turned back howling "Mama, mama!" in high, piercing voices that could be heard all along the street.

Once we arrived at the *kheyder*, the *melamed* and his oldest helper took charge of the group of little prisoners and began to whip them. The *melamed* himself unbuttoned their trousers and laid the boys across the bench while I had to hand him the switches and hold down their legs. When the whipped children finally ran out to play in the pile of dirt in the yard, I sat down to take care of the baby, or I unwound a twisted tangle of thread, or I went to find

73

the chickens, and with a "Here chick, chick!" drove the rooster and his harem from the thatched roof.

A few hours later I went to gather the lunches for the children. I was kept busy in this way until nightfall when I took the children home. Now my stalwarts ran eagerly and jumped lustily. One had a blackened eye, another a bruised cheek; the ear of a third was a flaming red; a fourth had clumps of hair missing from his prayercurls. But no one made any fuss over these little matters. They romped, they chased, happily and merrily—they were going home. At this hour, the village herd was usually returning from pastures with the various goats in the forefront. I left my charges to their own devices and welcomed Reb Ezriel's goat with open arms. Grabbing her by both horns, I led her home to her stall. Thus I killed two birds with one stone: I prevented her from committing the sin of wandering into a stranger's garden and I spared myself the headache of looking for her until late at night.

Concerning my food, the arrangement was as follows: Reb Ezriel promised to board me with the parents of his pupils—one family was to feed me for eight days, another for two weeks, a third for a month—depending upon the circumstances. In reality, however, I was boarded out not to the parents but to their cooks. These good creatures frequently did not bother fulfilling Reb Ezriel's promises and simply let me starve. On the other hand, although my contract did not call for my helping the cooks, I could not possibly be so rude as to refuse when I was honored with an order to help. I prepared horseradish sauce, sharpened knives, scoured the pots, cleaned the brass *Shabes* candlesticks, went to the slaughterer to have the fowl killed, ran errands for the maid, and performed many similar household chores.

The time was *Tishe B'ov.* I was very busy preparing weapons of war for the boys—wooden swords colored with blackberry juice, spears, spikes—and I hoped to make a pretty penny at it. But a cloud appeared on my horizon and ruined my fond hopes. At this time, Reb Ezriel found it necessary to thrash the only son of one of the town's rich men who regarded the boy as the apple of his eye. The boy was badly hurt and had to stay in bed. His mother and father made a fuss and said that they must teach this Reb Ezriel a lesson that he would not forget. They would persuade all the other parents to remove their children from his *kheyder.* Reb Ezriel was frightened and sought a way to wash his hands of the matter. Therefore, he placed the blame on me, that is, he confessed that the whole thing was the fault of his helper. He pointed out that his helper was very mischievous and, in general, a wild creature! The little boy said nothing and was very much afraid, as usual, to tell about what took place in the *kheyder*. Consequently, I was acknowledged to be the culprit and both sides agreed that I should be soundly beaten and expelled from the *kheyder*. Thus I, the *shlimazl*, became the scapegoat and it was my hide that was tanned!

CHAPTER 5

▲▲ "There!" said my mother to a friend of hers while looking at me.

"How does the saying go, Esther? 'Man abides by what God decides.' For my part, I have taken steps and strides far and wide so as not to disgrace the name of my husband in the grave. But what can you do—O enemies of Zion!—when everything you touch shrivels beneath your hands? Look at him, Esther. I have tried to place him several times. Each time he could have been a success, a real success, so that God and people would have envied me. But, as if to spite me, Esther, everything I try works out just backwards. It's the old story—how does the saying go? 'When the wind blows, the willow must bow.' People say: 'If you can't cross over, then you must cross under.' And even, forgive the comparison, the *muzhiks* have a saying: 'When fish is not to be had, a crab serves as fish.' You're a wise woman, Esther. If you say that I should apprentice him to a handworker, maybe you are right. Probably it is so written in the books on high that Reb Tevl the *Melamed's* son should become a handworker. Woe—O woe is me! It's the same old story—who am I to ask the Lord questions?"

Several days later, I entered the household of Leyzer the tailor as an apprentice.

Leyzer the tailor was a thin little Jew with a pale face, high-spirits—and as lively as quicksilver. One could say he was both a men's and a women's tailor, or better yet, neither a men's nor a women's tailor. He undertook the sewing of men's and women's clothes. As a matter of fact, he would undertake to sew anything, and nothing, not even a cap, ever came out right. In his hands a coat would be transformed into a bathrobe, a bathrobe into a dress, a dress into a child's garment. In the measurement of cloth, he was truly expert; he always managed to have exactly enough cloth for the project at hand—and also a sizable remnant for his own use.

In autumn, which is the time when Jewish clothes undergo their annual transfiguration from one type of garment to another, he had work up to his neck. Whatever could be patched was patched; everything else underwent a transformation.

Leyzer was very proud and considered himself to be the best

tailor, if not in the world, then at any rate in Bezliudeff—simply because he did not realize how much he was lacking. When he was shown a good piece of work that was made elsewhere, he would smile and not even deign to try it on, let alone observe how it was stitched or patterned.

"Pish," he smiled deprecatingly so as to dampen the other person's enthusiasm. "What's the great wonder here? What's there to see? I've *fixed* such work a thousand times over. The only thing you need is luck."

His tongue was well-edged and very glib. When a customer tried to describe how he would like his garment sewn, Leyzer would not let him talk. He interrupted and did the talking himself.

"I know, I know! Don't you worry! With God's help, I'll do a better job than you know how to ask for. Do you think this is the first time I've done this type of work) Rest assured that you will be satisfied! "

When he delivered the garment and the customer complained that it was tight, it wrinkled, it didn't fit well, it was too small—Leyzer wouldn't listen. He unleashed a flood with the set purpose of drowning the other person in words.

"How can you say such things? It is not tight! Do me the kindness to pull it a bit, over there. It fits as if cast on your mold. It *must* not be tight! It doesn't even *begin* to look tight! Here's news: it's small! How can it be small if it dare not be small? You've just finished eating and you're full, so you *think* it's small. May I be sick in that hell-hole of a hospital we have here, if there was any material left over. Upon my faith as a Jew, I barely had enough to finish. The only thing that remained was a small piece of percale from the lining and, here, I've brought it to you. It cannot be sewn better than I have made it. Wear it a while, you'll get used to it. Wear it well!"

Then came the question of payment. Leyzer would talk for an hour, swearing, taking oaths, pouring forth "upon my faiths," praising his work to the sky, detailing how much each particular part of the work cost him, and making the typical tally of a tailor. Then he would call to witness the butcher, the baker, and the candlestick-maker. He made a studied attempt to bury the customer beneath a mountain of words until the latter threw in an extra ten kopecks out of sheer exhaustion.

"Tut!" Leyzer would say after all of this. "You might at least offer me a brandy!"

He started and ended all his transactions with a brandy. Not that he was, God forbid, a drunkard, nor did he lie in a stupor on the street, but he did like to drink.

"This business makes you like to drink" was one of his favorite expressions, and, in truth, he really liked a pony of brandy. Consequently, he was active in guild affairs, toadied to the guild-master, and was to be seen everywhere whenever elections were held. On all these occasions, the liquor flowed freely. Leyzer's soul somehow scented any opportunity where the bitter drop could be had. But it could not be said that he would sell his heart, his conscience, his sense of right and wrong, God forbid, for a drink. These things he would never drown in drink. He retained his sense of values and could recognize truth as easily as anyone else. The only thing that he drowned in drink was—his bitter gall.

As soon as I entered Leyzer's domain, he zealously began to teach me the ABC's of the trade. The ABC's did not consist of teaching me how to hold a needle or how to sew a stitch. It was much too early for that. It would be a long time before I was to be honored with this knowledge. First, I was introduced to things far more basic—the pail of slops and the woodpile and the other household chores, in short, the same ABC's as I was taught in the general store and at Reb Ezriel's. There were, of course, a few sartorial variations, such as going to the market for thread, putting irons into the stove to heat, looking under the tables a dozen times a day for a thimble or a missing needle, delivering a finished garment to a customer.

And—Leyzer had a wife. And this wife was not at all lazy. She was an expert housekeeper. She paid a lot of attention to me and always found some work for me to do. She made sure that not even for a second would I sit empty-handed.

As yet, my mother had no reason to be ashamed of my having been apprenticed to an artisan, and my father, Reb Tevl the *Melamed*, could still rest easily in his grave. Their son had as yet not besmirched the family honor, for a long time would pass before he held a needle in his hands.

Concerning beatings, there was no bargaining. Sometimes Leyzer would beat me and sometimes his wife would take a hand, and sometimes both of them beat me together. At times they would beat me in the following manner: Leyzer would send a few stinging slaps in his wife's direction; she would forward them to me with interest, on occasion throwing in a few pinches as a bonus. At other times, Mrs. Leyzer would, with her own hands, invest as many blows as her strength would allow in Leyzer, and he, not being able to bear it, would reinvest them all in me.

Leyzer and his wife lived like a pair of turtledoves, equal in all respects. They were both equally strange. They both had an equal voice in all their affairs. They were both equally afraid of each other. They both vented their bitter, pent-up emotions upon each other, kissed each other, embraced each other, and shared their very best and most warming blows.

This was no land of milk and honey for me. I worked like a horse and was beaten from every quarter. At that time I was under the impression that it was necessary to treat an apprentice in such a fashion, else he would never become a good worker—as if one must be beaten or he will never be a scholar. A good example for me was one of Leyzer's helpers, a thin, pale, humpbacked fellow who had spent his best young years at Leyzer's, had done all sorts of menial work, and had suffered until he was advanced to the level of holding a needle and sewing patches. Therefore I, the *shlimazl*, welcomed all blows with love and didn't even cry aloud.

Once, just before Passover, Leyzer called me.

"Itsik-Avreml! Run—may you be run over—down to the store and buy some thread for a groschen and then sew together—may your lips be sewn together—the upper and bottom parts of this dress. Lively now, *momzer!*"

I still remember the joy that I felt upon being honored with a seat at the worktable with a needle in my hand. It was as if I had been chosen to support the poles of the *khupe* at a wedding. I sat down at the table opposite the pale, humpbacked fellow. I was happy. I was excited. I held the bottom part of the dress as if it were a very dear thing, a veritable treasure. The tailor was singing in falsetto—first, a part from the *Kol Nidre* services, then he switched to a march, shaking his head and tapping his foot to the beat. Soon he said a little prayer for me and for the pale fellow while sticking out the point of his tongue. Then he sang in tearful voice like the master of ceremonies at a wedding.

"Lively there, Itsik-Avreml! Trim the candle, *momzer!*" he sang in the midst of his tune.

"Itsik-Avreml, a little more steam! Move, you *momzer*, let's not dream!"

And I? A stitch here, a stitch there, into the cloth or into my fingers, wherever the needle happened to strike. But who cared, when my heart was so full of joy? However, I was soon enveloped in a cloud of smoke. The whole house began to smell. We looked around and finally found that the bottom part of the dress was burning, the bottom part which I, the *shlimazl*, had sewn! Apparently a piece of burning wick had fallen on the cloth while I was trimming the candle. A hubbub, a racket, a commotion and slaps and blows rained down on me in profusion.

The tailor considered making sleeves and pads from the spoiled cloth. It wouldn't work! He even took from the chest the piece of cloth which he had appropriated for his own use. That wasn't big enough either! What could be done—O enemies of Zion! Try as he would, it was of no use! The burned piece of cloth had to remain as the bottom half of the dress. You can't make a hat from a pigtail!

"Listen to me, Itsik-Avreml," said the tailor."You little *momzer*! May your bones ache! I have no strength left to beat you any more. When the missus comes back from the market, she'll probably warm your bones for you, too. She has as much of a right to as I do, and she won't give hers up. But all this is nothing compared to what you'll get later. I'll fix you good!"

Then he sat down and began to study the piece of cloth very thoughtfully. Soon he was talking to himself.

"And why not a pocket . . . make a pocket at the hole?" " So what? . . . Pish! What's the difference? . . ."

Then he turned to me, staring so that his eyes started from their sockets, and bawled:

"Out, you *momzer!* You're only fit for dogs to deal with!"

I crawled out from under the table like a kitten and awaited my bitter end with a great lump in my throat.

This pitiful occurrence took place on a Wednesday toward evening. On Friday—I remember this as if it were yesterday—the boss told me to follow him to his wealthy customer with the dress. She took one look—thunder and lightning! A pocket right at the hem!

"What is this, my dear tailor!" she began to scream. "What do you call this—this? I will absolutely not accept such a dress!"

"Please," Leyzer answered her with an angelic smile and cut her short. "Please, don't yell, dear Brayndl! So help me God, this is a good piece of work! This dress is patterned according to the very latest fashion. Don't you know that the wives of all the Gentile landowners now wear dresses with a pocket near the hem? Only a madwoman would buy a dress today with pockets any higher! May the good Lord help me to get out of this business so that I no longer have to be a tailor!—[he always liked to use this oath which was standard among all Jewish handworkers]—if this dress does not look beautiful! It's a pity indeed that you can't see with your own eyes how much it adds to your charm! There's no need to feel it, Brayndl. It's excellent! Well, well. Wear it well, use it well, and tear it well! Please leave a tip for my apprentice here. He deserves it, by God. He almost lost his poor eyes from working so hard on that pocket. And I believe I could stand a little drink myself."

In Bezliudeff, Leyzer was regarded as one of the best tailors—one who sewed according to magazine patterns. Since her husband was one of the richest men in town, as soon as his wife was seen wearing a dress with a pocket at its hem, all the fashionable ladies ordered dresses with pockets at the hem. Although my pocket had thus become fashionable, Leyzer was afraid that I might produce other such new styles which would give him ulcers, and, because of this, he would not give me a stitch of work. He transferred me entirely to his wife and retained only the right to slap me on occasion.

"What use have I," he would say, "for such a plague, for such an artist?"

And he would finish with his little saying: "Ally-looly, [hallelujah] you're only fit for dogs to deal with!"

Once I did his wife some damage. By accident, I broke a pot full of eggs. Because of this, I was finally dismissed.

After this experience, I was apprenticed to all sorts of other craftsmen. I was, however, a *shlimazl*, and had no luck anywhere. Each new employer acquainted me with his household chores and harnessed me to his wagon.

One of my bosses during this period was a little shoemaker, a merry pauper. He always sent me to dirty places such as pigsties to tear bristles from the pigs' backs.

"Little fool," he would say, "a hair, even from a pig, is also useful. It's a *mitsve* in the eyes of the Lord to tear a hair from a pig."

When I would have to empty the pail of slops, this merry pauper accompanied me to the door with a little rhyme.

"Itsenyoo-Avremenyoo, carry it well! In your honor, I'll ring a bell! May I live to carry the wine to your wedding in a bucket. Carry it, my boy, carry it well! At your age, I had carried many a pail of slops!"

81

Deep in my heart, I liked the little shoemaker. He treated me better than any of my other bosses. I would have remained with him and I might even have learned something, but he became very ill. He began to cough up blood because he worked beyond his capacity in order to feed his wife and children. But all he had to eat was grief. Except for a meager crust of bread and a little something else with it, nothing passed his lips. He had long forgotten the taste of meat. While talking, he would sometimes make jokes.

"Meat? What! That's an un-Jewish thing! I try to convince myself, crazy fool that I am, that we have some in the pot for *Shabes*!"

The poor man was taken away on a little wagon to the pesthouse and it wasn't long before he died there.

CHAPTER 6

▲▲ It came to pass that a traveling cantor arrived in Bezliudeff and performed the *shabes* services with his choir. People came running from all the little *shuls* to hear him. Some, of course, tried to act dignified, and only came to hear him after having first said their prayers conscientiously. The crowding in the synagogue was terrible. People were packed in one on top of another like herring in a barrel. I pressed in with the crowd because, like all Jews, I loved singing very dearly.

The cantor had with him a little singer about my age. I envied him so, the way he stood at the reader's stand supporting his cheek with his hand and tra-la-la-ing the accompaniment. I would have given the shirt off my back to be a little singer like he was.

Later on, when I attended the services with the other boys, I looked at him with great respect. I felt very humble, and it seemed to me that there could be nothing better in the world than to be a singer. How could I compare to him? Every time he opened his mouth, I was enchanted, and had it been at all possible to leap into it, I would have done so with the greatest of pleasure.

On the way home from the synagogue, I tried to imitate him. When I sang the hymns after the *shabes* meal, I unleashed my voice and tra-la-la'd for all I was worth. My mother was very pleased. But I was not at all interested in the hymns. I wanted to imitate the little singer. Within me, everything was in song. My mouth wouldn't close for a second. We had already eaten, and I was still in full song. Finally the singing became an act of mischief on my part. I let loose with all sorts of wild cries. As soon as my mother realized that I wouldn't stop and that she wouldn't be able to catch her breath after having eaten the heavy *shabes* pudding, she boxed my ears and threw me out of the house.

Where can a young boy run on a *shabes* afternoon if not to the synagogue? There I found the whole gang, all the mischief-makers in town. I had thought that I was the only one who was imitating the little singer. Oh, no! The others were doing the same. One was bawling, another was howling, a third was booming like the bass, a fourth was in contortions, screaming in an effort to imitate the cantor, and yet a fifth was piping in falsetto. Then we all joined together upstairs in the women's gallery. We meowed, we

83

squeaked, we whistled, we howled and bawled until the caretaker spilled water on us and chased us out.

In truth, however, you must know that I had a clear voice and good intonation. I used to help Leyzer the tailor when he succumbed to the Muse. Leyzer would look at me and say with a smile: "Good, good, *momzer!* Keep it up! Sing, may you sing from pain!"

It occurred to me to ask my mother to apprentice me to the cantor. I insisted so long and so stubbornly that she had no choice other than to take me to him. He found that the poor and desolate widow was no sweet pill to swallow. Finally, having heard me scream, the cantor said that he would accept me. I thought that the whole world belonged to me. It would be impossible for me now to describe my joyous feelings at that time. Apparently my mother was also greatly pleased, for in a conversation with her friend, she philosophized as follows:

"It's the same old story, Esther, may your life be long.

"How can one person decide another's future? You can beat your head against the wall—O enemies of Zion!—you can rend yourself asunder and you will accomplish nothing! Nothing at all. When the good Lord, blessed be His name, decides to raise a person, to improve his condition, one can never tell how it will come about. Why am I saying this? I'm saying it in relation to my orphan. It's the same old story. People advised me to apprentice him to a handworker so I apprenticed him to a handworker. What would have become of him? But God in His goodness indicated that it should not be the way people were saying. He should be a cantor, thanks and praise, Esther, to His blessed Name! My orphan is provided for now. He will be a success, may the same happen to all my loved ones! I do not deserve such good fortune from Him. This could have happened only through the divine intervention of our blessed forefathers."

I traveled the country with the cantor for over half a year. I, the *shlimazl*, was miserable with him, too, more so than any of the other singers.

Whenever the cantor performed, it was customary for the choir to observe the audience to see if the people were pleased with his manner and to judge their reaction to his rendition of the prayers. Upon reaching home, the cantor would summon one of us by name, at the same time winking his eye in the peculiar fashion

84

which he reserved for this occasion. This was supposed to mean: "Well now, were they pleased? Speak up! "

Almost always, as if in spite, I was the one to be called. The reason for this may possibly lie in the fact that, after the services, the other singers dashed to the door and evaporated into thin air.

No sooner did he say "Avremke!" and give me the famous wink, then I, being naive and knowing no tricks, would promptly answer:

"Cantor, they were laughing. They were laughing very much."

Upon hearing this, he invariably fastened upon my ear. He twisted and turned it. He tried to stretch it, to test its strength and even remove it. I tell you, the beatings that I used to get from Leyzer's wife were mere child's play compared to this.

Once we stopped in a town for *shabes*. The weekly portion to be read from the *Toyre* was *Shekalim*. The cantor exerted himself more than he usually did because he was interested in getting a permanent cantorship in this town. That evening, he invited a number of the more important people to his room. Punch and wine were served. It was quite an event for me. Some of the people asked him to sing. He coyly complained that he had caught cold and would have to rest his voice for a few days. Nevertheless, he allowed himself to be persuaded and sang a few "Elijahs" and Rumanian shepherd songs.

It so happened that the cantor had to send for something, and so he called "Avremke!" giving me, so it seemed, the famous wink. The punch had already gone to my head, so I shot out: "Ha, ha, ha! Cantor, they were laughing at you!"

The cantor turned red and green like a tom-turkey. His face became unrecognizable and the people around him stood confused and shocked. I thought that the cantor did not want to believe me and, since the bit of punch had made me quite talkative, I unleashed my little golden tongue.

"Upon my word as a Jew, cantor. They were laughing at you! All these people were scoffing and sneering! Especially that one there, the man who is drinking and whispering in your ear—he really laughed during the services! I think he also said 'Windbag!' What is a windbag, cantor?"

The cantor bit his lip and tried to make a joke of the whole affair. He pointed out that I was a half-wit, slightly demented, and couldn't tell the difference between my thumb and my forefinger. In addition to all these virtues, he indicated that I was obviously quite tight. He would gladly get rid of such a plague as I, were it not for my excellent voice. The guests found the whole incident quite repulsive and left rather unhappily. You can well imagine my reward for the evening's performance. The cantor taught me the true meaning of justice, mercy, and charity as practiced in the world.

Once again we went on the road, picking our travelworn way through the many small Jewish towns and hamlets. One *shabes*, several months later, we arrived in Tsvuatshits. Here again the cantor had hopes of being accepted for a permanent position. He wheedled and coaxed, he pressed and provoked until the heads of the synagogue asked him to remain in the community through the Solemn Days, after which the matter of a permanent appointment could be discussed and arranged to everyone's satisfaction.

In the meantime, I had made the acquaintances of the young jackanapes and mischief-makers in Tsvuatshits and had, as a matter of fact, begun to occupy a position of honor among them. I was allowed to be first when chasing the village idiot, and when our attempts to steal the *shoyfer* from the synagogue attendant's drawer were crowned with success, I was allowed to blow the first blast. I was really beginning to feel both my feet on the ground. But all to no avail—I had no luck.

Listen to my final downfall with the cantor! You can imagine how the poor man strained himself on *Rosh Hashone*. He sang for all he was worth. He stretched each note, varied it, trilled it, modulated up and down the scale. He changed from a true note to a high falsetto and back again. A *hi-di-di-di-de* here and a *hi-di-di-di-de* there—he moved heaven and earth. The bass's voice was on the verge of cracking with all the additional variations and tricks. Again and again he was called upon for a *latum-dum-dum* and yet another *latum-dum-dum*. The tenor's falsetto no longer served him either. He had to strain his lungs to outshrill the bass. And I, the *shlimazl*, had to screech almost every second with a *tah-te-nyoo* or a lengthy *tra-ta-ta-tee!* In short, we strained every nerve and spared no effort.

Among the members of this congregation there was a rich young man—thick-set, robust, good-natured, something of a clown, with a secular outlook on the world. He enjoyed playing the fool with the children and was terribly annoyed with the cantor's airs and mannerisms. When the cantor had reached the climax in one of the eighteen benedictions of the daily prayer and was confidently marching along the highroad to success, strewing the flowery trills and variations as he strutted ahead, this rich young man—the clown—quietly came up to me and asked in a serious tone:

"Tell me, son, can you make a cherry?" And no sooner were these words spoken than his lips blossomed forth into a cherry, so red, so full and juicy, that I burst out laughing. At precisely this point, the cantor had finished chiseling a spectacular trill and was awaiting my *tra-ta-ta-tee!* The congregation, seeing that the cantor was silent, as though strangled, began to stamp their feet. The cantor turned to me and looked as if I had robbed him of what was rightfully his. Lightning flashed from his eyes. His face was as red as an overripe tomato. The bass turned his head toward me with a bellow, like that of a cow to her calf, commanding me to render my *tra-ta-ta-tee*. I had barely pierced the air with my shrill, when the rich young man stepped forth and once again blossomed his lips into a beautiful red cherry! In the midst of my note, I shot out with a tremendous peal of laughter! The cantor sputtered and spluttered, jumped the traces and ran off the main road, omitted a number of benedictions and made several blunders. The congregation began to stamp their feet and clap their hands, filling the synagogue with an amazed "Ay, ay!"

Upstairs in the gallery, the women became frightened and yelled in one voice: "Oy, a fire!"

This in turn frightened the men and everybody began to run toward the door. In short, the services were ruined. The congregation was extremely displeased with our performance.

On the morning following *Rosh Hashone*, the cantor chased me out and he, the poor man, left town in shame and disgrace, to wander once more over the countryside. I, the *shlimazl*, was left high and dry in Tsvuatshits. ▲ ▲

CHAPTER 7

The Rabbi, may he live long, laid the papers on the table in order to rest and catch his breath. He looked at the synagogue officials, at the wealthy men of affairs, and spoke:

"I hope that you will forgive me, gentlemen, for taking up your time with a story of this sort. After all, you're all people with business responsibilities, merchants, traders, and you undoubtedly have very little time. But I really have no choice. It must be remembered that it is a *mitsve* to fulfill the will of the dead. He, may he rest in peace, requested me to read this, and in any case his desire deserves fulfillment, as you shall all see at the end. Therefore, forgive me please, gentlemen!"

"That's quite all right, really," several magnates answered in a chorus. "On the contrary, Rabbi, the story pleases us immensely. We wouldn't mind sitting right through until the end, even if it required a day and a night. Furthermore, we all owe it to Itskhok-Avrom to give up some of our time and listen to the story of his life. He undoubtedly had some point in mind. The conclusion of his tale will probably be very beautiful and we shall not regret having heard it."

The door opened and the Rabbi's wife appeared to ask the Rabbi to step out, for someone wished to consult with him about a very pressing matter.

"Ah, Reb Mendele! How are you?" the Rabbi's wife said to me after the Rabbi had left. "It's a long time since you've been here. Any news? The men think that it's only for them that books are printed! Everything is only for them. Women have no souls. Women are not human and need nothing. They should be satisfied with the fact that they live, bear children and raise them, cook meals, take care of their husbands, and lead a miserable existence."

"Praised be God that we see each other again in the best of health!" I answered. "Don't worry. I didn't forget about you. I brought you a brand-new *Tkhine.* You see, dear *Rebitsin,* you're not right in accusing men. We do keep you in mind. Just think of all the *Tkhines* which are printed just for you. What more would you like? I think we've done more than enough for the women-folk."

"Ay-ay-ay!" smiled one of the businessmen teasingly. "Do you want to rouse our women to rebellion? If our wives listen to you, they'll become very independent and will begin to demand many things. They might even, God forbid, want to divorce us! But tell me, *Rebitsin*, since you've already brought up the subject, tell me, may your health prosper, why did Solomon write that among all his thousand wives he could not find a single good one:"

"He couldn't find one," retorted the Rabbi's wife, "for the very reason that he had a thousand. Men who seek to have many women will never be able to have one good one. Tell me, would you have acted any better if you were in their position?"

"Why then," exclaimed another gentleman, "does it say in one of our holy works that the entire wisdom possessed by woman is the knowledge of operating the spinning wheel?"

"It says that," answered the Rabbi's wife, "because that book was written by a man. Of course, you are the clever ones. You have the power and you hold womankind in the palms of your hands. The strong one is always the clever one, the righteous one. How does the saying go?

> Although he the Living does smite,
> The Angel of Death remains ever right!

"But sayings aside, how can you convince us of what, with our own eyes, we can see is untrue! Many were the women in the past who were Judges, Prophetesses, Sages; and many are the wise women today who stand head and shoulders above their husbands! I believe that even here, in our town, we can find a large number of women who have made their husbands what they are today, who pushed them and led them to their honor and their riches. If not for their wives, these men would amount to nothing. Yet, when any important issue arises which calls for thought and deliberation, it is these very property-owners, these ne'er-do-wells, who take counsel and make decisions for the entire community. The women don't even enter the picture. Everything is for and by the proprietors. Even when the town crier calls the people to the baths, he cries:

"Proprietors, to the baths!"

"You're very bitter today," said the first gentleman. "You're upset about something and you're taking it out on us."

"Believe me," said the Rabbi's wife, and tears welled into her eyes. Believe me, what I have said is not even a tenth of a tenth of what should be said. Oh, how dark and bitter is our condition! Woe unto us that we were ever born!"

She sighed deeply, from the heart, and wiped her eyes with a handkerchief.

"Here!" I said, and gave her the *Tkhine* which I pulled from my pack. "I know that this *Tkhine* will please you. It will suit you admirably."

"True, Reb Mendele," answered she. "For us poor women *Tkhines* are good. They are the only remedies for hearts that are full of boils and wounds. At least they make us weep; they allow us to empty the bitter dregs of our hearts in the flowing streams of our warm tears. But it's vexing, it's exasperating to see how the menfolk, who don't understand and have no desire to understand the turmoil within us, scoff at and joke about the women's *Tkhines* and begrudge us even this remedy. Let them sit in the women's gallery of the synagogue on *shabes* or on a holiday. Let them sit there and see the many poor and unfortunate women who barely managed to tear themselves away for a few moments from their work at home: one woman sits oppressed by the dark fate that has cursed her with such a husband; another is a desolate divorcee; still another has an embittered countenance because of her sick suckling child which keeps her from sleeping at night and torments her during the day; a fourth has swollen, scalded hands from standing at the oven all day; a fifth has a pale face and a worried look because of her continual serfdom, from endlessly plodding in the harness.

"All these sad and depressed creatures stand around the Sayer,* weep and wail and raise their eyes to the merciful and beneficent Father in Heaven. They bathe in their own tears and weep their very souls dry. If they, the menfolk, would observe all this and see it with their own eyes, they wouldn' t dare open their mouths to scoff at the women's *Tkhines.* . . . Thank you, Reb Mendele, for not forgetting me! I'll bring the money in a minute."

The *Rebitsin* silently wiped her eyes and left.

An embarrassed silence reigned in the room. It seemed as if everyone had lost the power of speech. The Rabbi's wife had cast

---

* A woman who leads the prayers in the women's gallery of the synagogue. She enumerates and dwells on the troubles of the world and of womankind, and at the same time she exerts a pacifying and tranquilizing influence.

90

a great gloom over the gathering. I sat sadly in a corner, thinking over the various points she had made. Her words were like toadstools swollen with sharp and bitter juices which pricked me and convulsed my heart the more thoroughly I grasped them. I felt as if I had just witnessed the autopsy of a living person, seen the removal of the warm, pulsing heart, opened it and cut it apart to see all that was taking place. With my mind's eye, I saw a dripping of blood, gall, and tears. With my mind's ear, I heard only groans and sighs.

I must have sat deep in thought for quite a while. Suddenly I started, as if from sleep, and looked around at the others in the room.

"Why are you sighing so, Reb Khone?" one gentleman asked another.

"I'm sighing, Reb Berish," answered Reb Khone, "because of the treasure we lost. Itskhok-Avrom was a very useful person. In him we all had a good friend, a man of action, a man who could keep his mouth shut. He died too early for us. He should have lived at least a few more years. What a loss! We may all bemoan such a loss. For no one is Itskhok-Avrom such a loss as for the town, for us I mean!"

"That's very true, Reb Khone," several gentlemen answered thoughtfully.

"You, Reb Fayvish, should know when the funeral will take place. After all, you're a leader of the Burial Society."

"The funeral, Reb Abba, won't take place until tomorrow. There were a number of questions that came up today which had to be settled first."

"I still have to attend a wedding today," said a judge. "I have to conduct the ceremony."

"And I am very hungry," said a second judge. "Of all things, I feel like having something to eat now. It's really time, you know. I haven't had anything at all aside from a glass of chickory."

"My hemorrhoids are giving me no end of trouble," a third judge volunteered. "Tell me please, what do you do for your hemorrhoids? I've heard that carrot mash is good for them. Is it? Until now, I've been a believer in stewed prunes."

"The best remedy for piles," chimed in both the former speakers, "is to ignore them and not bother with them. That is a secret we learned from our fathers."

I was sitting on pins and needles and counting every minute

until the Rabbi would reappear. I was anxious to hear the end of the story and to find out why my presence was so important. Every moment stretched into an eternity. I was exhausted with the waiting.

Suddenly the Rabbi entered. He appeared very disturbed. His brow was furrowed with wrinkles. He passed his hand over his face nervously, plucking hairs from his beard each time. Finally he turned to the people gathered in the room.

"Forgive me a hundred times over, gentlemen, for keeping you so long. I was busy with a most vexing question and now I have a headache. Besides, it is quite late. I would suggest that we postpone the remainder of the reading until tomorrow. Please try to be here early in the morning, right after the morning services, so that we may finish tomorrow."

Everybody left. I came back to the synagogue to find my hungry nag standing with pricked ears looking into my wagon.

"Well, my sage," I said and patted his mane, "come and have some mash. Today you'll have to manage with mash. If your wisdom holds out through tomorrow, then, my sage, you'll have real oats—and a full measure! "

CHAPTER 8

I tossed on my pillow until morning. I hastily said my prayers, gulped down a bit of food, left the wagon and the horse in the care of the synagogue attendant, and hurried off to the Rabbi's. The rest of the audience of the day before arrived shortly with the exception of Reb Fayvish. The Rabbi sat down, picked up the manuscript, and, after clearing his throat, said :

"I believe that we stopped yesterday at the point, 'I, the *shlimazl*, was left high and dry in Tsvuatshits.' Yes, right there. And now, gentlemen, listen kindly to what he writes further":

▲▲ On *Rosh Hashone*, I dined at the home of a man who beggars accurate description. It is difficult to decide just what kind of person he was. He was neither a *Khosid* nor a worldly individual—a bit of both, yet none of either. He dressed neither according to the old fashion nor according to the new—neither flesh nor fowl nor good red herring, but somewhat half-baked—a Jew who lived his own way. As I grew older, I met many such men, but I could never really understand what kind of people they were.

Upon finding myself stranded and roaming the streets like a lost sheep with nothing to eat and no place to sleep, I went to this man and told him my tale of woe. Not mean by nature, he was, however, a man of few words—a ruble the word. He listened to me silently, continually smoothing his mustache. When I finished, he signaled me to remain in his house and ordered a meal for me. Late that night, about ten or eleven o'clock, when even a mad dog couldn't be found out of doors, when it was dark enough to be a blind man's holiday, he took me to the other end of town to some back street. It was quiet there like in a graveyard. The only sounds came from the trees swaying in the wind, the rustling of the few remaining leaves, and the murmur of the dreary autumn drizzle dribbling lazily on the fallen leaves and dead grass. When the wind ceased for a moment, I could hear the grinding of a mill in the distance at the side of a roaring brook. When the wind blew up again, it brought with it all sorts of mixed sounds from town: the crow of a rooster, the lowing of a cow, the creak of a rusty gate, the rumble of a passing coach, the barking of a landowner's dog.

Apparently there no Jews lived along this street, for had there

93

been any, there would be no gardens and orchards, the earth would not be plowed and spread with dried leaves, and we would have had to feel our way carefully in the dark in order to avoid walking into a stray cow or tripping on the broken steps in front of every house.

The man walked on and on in silence. Finally we came to a small yard where we turned in. A candle was gasping for life in the tiny anteroom of a small, low-built house. The man took off his overcoat and went into the second room, telling me to wait. I happened to be standing near the closed door and overheard the conversation,*

"*Guten Abend*, Herr Gutman!"

"*Willkommen*, Herr Jakobsohn! What a guest! It is three weeks already since you have visited me. What is the meaning of it, Herr Jakobsohn?"

"My dear Herr Gutman! How could I have come sooner? You know that these are the Solemn Days and the Jews here are even more fanatical than usual. You know my position, how dependent I am upon these people. Suppose they saw me coming to visit you. . . ."

"You are absolutely correct, Herr Jakobsohn. If that is the case, then you are right. Yes, you are dependent. You have a family."

"Have you finished your book yet, Herr Gutman?"

"Oh yes, the book is remarkably successful. It is only a pity that we have so few people who can read Hebrew."

"Say better, Herr Gutman, that you get no reward for your labor but are frequently insulted and persecuted for no good reason."

"Believe me, Herr Jakobsohn. The writer, the poet, asks for no reward other than to be understood. Contempt, persecution, poverty—all these only spur his soul on to further activity. From these, he draws real inspiration. Earned contempt and dishonor are just as gratifying as earned respect and honor; to suffer for truth, for honesty, is actually not to suffer at all. To suffer means to lick someone's boots, to cringe, to deny one's self—to surrender one's conscience, one's heart, one's mind. Do you think that it is such easy work to be a bootlicker, a parasite? God forbid! It is just as difficult as it is to be a thief. The lickspittle, the toady, the parasite, these must always be on their guard; they must always be as wary

---

* This conversation is written in the original with a copious sprinkling of German words to indicate secularity on the part of the speakers.

as if they were thieves. Do you think that those who persecute me for my ideas on religion are truly pious and content? Oh, no, no! Many of them harass me because they are desperate and envious. It is quite simple—they feel themselves to be empty, ignorant, and worthless people. They are irritated because in me they see a person who knows them well and who can see right through them. They fear people with open eyes just as bats fear the light of the sun."

"Indeed, Herr Gutman, with your ability and your optimism, you are really fortunate. You are to be envied. By the way, do you know why I came to see you tonight? You have told me several times that you need a boy to run errands for you occasionally. I have found one and brought him here. He seems to be honest enough, although a bit dull, unpolished."

I understood almost all of this conversation, that is the words—not the meaning. The sense of it was beyond my comprehension, but I did understand words. Most of the words were in our language—Yiddish. I could guess at the German words because in my travels with the cantor, I had heard all sorts of people speaking. The cantor himself liked to throw in a German word or two on fitting occasions or to pronounce our Yiddish words with his version of a German accent. Why, he even boasted sometimes that he could sing from written music.

I also learned some German words in the *Talmud-Toyre*, in our word-for-word translations of the *Khumesh*. And in the general store, I heard German words from the errand boys who would collar a passer-by and belabor him in German. . . . Furthermore, all Jews understand German anyway. After all, it's their mother tongue.

Suddenly the door opened and I was called into the other room. The man who had brought me was bareheaded. The German took my hand and spoke to me in a most friendly manner.

"Well, dear young man! You would like to work in my house? You won't have any hard chores here. You'll only have to help around the house and run an occasional errand."

I stared so hard and looked so sheepish that the German couldn't control himself; he had to smile. But I liked him immediately. His face was good-natured and he spoke in a very friendly voice, not like the others—the tailor, the cantor, or even my mother. His features expressed such goodness when he looked at me that I somehow felt drawn to him.

I raised my hand to my sheepskin cap (I always wore my sheepskin cap, in the summer when it was very hot and I ran around barefoot, as well as in the winter) lifted it a bit, shifted it first to one side and then to the other, pushed it forward toward my face, then backward—a little higher, then a little lower, while my other hand scratched at my prayercurls or the nape of my neck. I simply did not know what to do with my cap until I finally worked up courage and suddenly snatched it from my head. I soon felt a cool breeze blowing over my bared head, as if I had been shorn. I felt compelled to touch my head every few seconds to make sure that all was in order. It was a peculiar sensation, as if I were in the public bath.

"Well, my dear child," said the German as he placed his hand on my shoulder. "You're a good lad! What's your name?"

I stood there in a fright, just as with that German in the *Talmud-Toyre*. My mouth hung open and I stared like a fool.

"What is your name?" repeated the German.

"How should I know?"

"You mean you don't know what your name is? Who knows then?"

"My mother used to call me Yitskhok-Avremtshe," I answered. "The *melamed* called me Itshe-Avremele; the tailor—little *momzer* Itsik-Avreml; the shoemaker used to tease me while I was carrying the slop-pail with Itzenyoo Avremenyoo; and the cantor—Avremke. So how should I know what my name is?"

"Right!" smiled the German. "Still, you don't have seven names like Jethro. You simply have a double name, Itskhok-*Avrom*, and a very nice name it is—in memory of our forefathers. I will call you Isaac-Abraham. Tell me then, would you like to remain with me, Abraham!"

"But don't beat me or hit me. I don't have one whole bone left in my body."

The German's eyes filled with tears. He gripped my shoulder and looked straight into my eyes.

"Poor lad! It seems he must have suffered very much. So young and already he hasn't a single whole bone in his body!"

He turned to Jakobsohn. "*Ja, Ja!* He is apparently very naive and rather dull, but a good lad."

Jakobsohn was silent. He smoothed his mustache constantly.

"No!" said the German to me. "I promise that I will not touch you. You are just as much a human being as I am and, besides, you are all alone in the world. Rest assured, I won't hit you. Well, will you stay with me?"

'"Yes!" I answered and remained there.

He was very poor. But in his home, poverty was not manifested by filth, slovenliness, sloth, or any of the other ugly signs of poverty which may be seen in most poor homes, especially those of the Jewish poor. The house was clean, everything had its place. Every last corner shone and sparkled.

Madame, his wife, inspected every nook and cranny, never allowing herself a moment's rest. She was continually cooking, baking, cleaning, sewing, mending clothes—all of which makes some women as wild as beasts, but she was always calm and quiet with a pleasant countenance. She had time for everything. No matter how busy she was, she managed to spare some time to sit down with a book in order to find out what was going on in the world. She admired and respected her husband. She thought the world of him and his writing, and allowed nothing to arise that might disturb him or interfere with his work. She was truly one with him, one soul and one body.

Their oldest daughter, a fine and gentle creature, helped her mother with the washing, ironing, and the other chores. In addition, she knitted very skillfully. She had only one dress, but it was always clean and fresh and looked as if it had just been bought. Every day, at a given time, she taught her two small sisters. She gave them a good education and always had them dressed in spotless white.

The oldest son was studying at the university. He frequently wrote home ardent and devoted letters in which he encouraged his family and begged them not to worry because they were in no position to send him money for his needs. True, he found himself in straitened circumstances, but he hoped that he would somehow pull through without starving.

"What you have done for me," he cheered them in his letters, "many rich parents are incapable of doing for their children. You have given me much more than money can buy. You have taught me and developed my understanding. You have refined my soul and instilled good traits in me: love for people, sympathy for the poor and oppressed, the ability to get along on little, to bear heavy burdens in difficult times with a happy demeanor. These are traits which rich parents, for all their money and power, are incapable of teaching to their children."

97

These letters were read aloud by all the members of the family, each of them deriving great pleasure from various passages, while the tears flowed copiously. In short, this was a very rare and beautiful family.

At that time, my understanding was so limited that I appreciated none of it in the manner in which I am setting it down here. I felt instinctively that Gutman and his wife were somehow a different kind of people, not, for example, like Leyzer the tailor and his lady, nor like Reb Ezriel the *Melamed* and his spouse, nor even like the rich owner of the general store and his fat, strapping wife—an Amazon with a tireless tongue—who wore a string of real pearls and a dress of real silk but who was encrusted with filth nevertheless. I saw only that this was a different kind of house, that the children were not the usual bedraggled and uncouth Jewish brats. To appreciate with any profundity the dignity of such a household was as yet completely beyond my capabilities.

The German sat in his room day and night. His books were scattered all around—on the table and under the table—but he was far too much absorbed to notice. His whole heart and soul were in his work and he obviously enjoyed himself immensely. Occasionally, he talked to himself, laughed, ground his teeth, exactly as if he were conversing with another person. If someone were to interrupt his reveries at such a moment, he would start suddenly, as if he had just fallen from the sky, and look confused. His answers would be topsy-turvy and completely irrelevant. More than once, I walked out of his room with a shrug because I couldn't understand what he was saying.

His boots needed no polishing because he rarely left the house. His robe and slippers, on the other hand, were terribly worn. My chief duty was to run errands. He sent me to the post-office frequently to receive or send off a letter or a package. Or I would be sent to deliver a message or a book to someone. One might wonder about this kind of job—surely, it must have been very easy. But no! There is no more bitter or more miserable type of work than this. When I delivered a message, the man who received it wrinkled his nose in disgust, as if he had just smelled some strong, freshly grated horseradish, and, with an angry face, he told me to return tomorrow. Tomorrow he said—the day after tomorrow; the day after tomorrow, he wasn't home. Upon visiting him again some time later, he would say: "What does this boy want with me? I can't get rid of him! "

Another man would simply order his servants to bar me from his threshold. A third would read the note, look doubtful, and leave without so much as giving me a glance. A fourth would look up and say: "Tell the Herr that I'm not at home! Understand?"

In short, I was chased and avoided like the plague. As soon as I was seen from afar, with either a message or a book, people either locked their doors or set their dogs or their errand boys upon me. The gentlemen to whom I was sent would fly into a rage every time they saw a book. Of what were they so afraid? I was not to understand this until much later.

The one person in ten who did bother to accept a book would fling it, like a hot potato, under a bed or chair and hand me a torn ruble without a serial number. Oh, that was a bitter time for me. May all my enemies have the experience of delivering books to the Jewish gentry, of listening to their gentle language, of observing their faces as they become indignant, their gorges rising and their cheeks and lips twisting with fury.

Herr Jakobsohn visited the German frequently at night. When I wasn't too tired, I would listen to their conversation, eavesdropping behind the door for no good reason—simply to pass the time. Once I overheard how Jakobsohn spoke with surprise about the actions of a Dr. Steinhertz.

"Tut," said Gutman. "What are you so surprised about, Herr Jakobsohn? Dr. Steinhertz is a little man and that is why he is so rich and leads others by the nose. Is it news to you? It stands to reason that if one becomes a little man, he can accomplish anything in the world!"

I was beside myself upon hearing these words. Gutman, *my* Herr Gutman, also says that a little man is rich and can accomplish anything! I hopped up and down with excitement. But just then Gutman called me. When he saw the foolish look on my face, he could not contain himself and burst out laughing. Jakobsohn looked me up and down and shook his head.

"Eh! He's still a dullard, the same lummox as before." A short while later, I again overheard a conversation. Jakobsohn was describing Issar Varger*, how rich and fortunate he was, a bigwig in town; his influence, his power was something really out of the ordinary!

---

* The names of Mendele's characters are often chosen, like Dickens', to reflect their character: *Gutman* means good man; *Steinhertz*—stoneheart; *Varger*—throttler.

"It is quite simple," said Gutman. "Varger is a little man who has gained the confidence—the very soul—of one of the biggest local magnates. That's nothing out of the ordinary. It is quite natural and nothing to wonder about."

"Yes, you are quite right," sighed Jaboksohn. "Only a little man has it good in this world!"

He soon said "Good night!" and went home.

100

CHAPTER 9

▲▲ Welcome back, little man! Once again my thoughts revolved about the little man. He was indeed a welcome visitor, returning at the very time when I was sad and depressed and sorely in need of a boost. After the foregoing conversation, I tossed restlessly in my bed all night, my thoughts racing endlessly and tripping pell-mell over each other:

"Issar Varger is a little man, a soul, a rich and happy man. It seems, then, that when one becomes a little man, one is rich, happy! Apparently, one can become a little man if one merely wishes to . . . and when one becomes a little man, one is rich and happy—one can have anything in the world. I was right in my desire to become a little man. Good! But the question remains, how does one become a little man? Just how does one cross this bridge? Suppose I twisted, turned, doubled myself up, I still wouldn't be a little man. . . It must be a trick that would amaze even a magician, a bigger trick than jumping through the hoop like a clown does. . . . There must be a secret at the bottom of all this, or else anyone could become a little man, a soul, a rich and happy person! . . ."

My thoughts ran on like this for a good part of the night until I finally fell asleep and dreamed all sorts of beautiful dreams. I saw a little man on the street. He was turning somersaults and cartwheels from one side of the street to the other, back and forth and back again. Suddenly he bounded to the house of the *Kahal*,* leaped in among the *Kahal* officials and began to play the fool with them. It wasn't long before they dug into their purses and paid roundly for his stunts. Then, like a demon, he sprang into the vest of one of the tax collectors and tickled him gleefully. They both roared with laughter. They seemed to be having a wonderful time, but when the little man leaped out of the collector's pocket, he was completely covered with gold. The tax collector spat three times and it was not long before he had a new type of pocket made for himself! . . . From the collector's pocket—boom—the little man was in the mouth of a shady character who, with others of his kind,

---

* The *Kahal* was the seat of administration of whatever autonomy was granted to the Jews by the Tsar. See Introduction.

101

was busily fixing the price of meat. He was just about to say, "Forty-five groschen a piece," when the little man grabbed his tongue and twisted it so that he sputtered "Sixty!" . . . From the pricefixer's tongue (which, may it happen to no Jew, was transformed into a piece of leather), he sprang like a fiend upon one of the local proprietors and, turning him around and around like a top, changed him into a leather cap-visor—from a cap-visor into a soupspoon!—from a soupspoon into a prayershawl and then into a jacket! And suddenly he was astride the village ox in the pasture with the herd of village cows! . . .

In short, the little man was busy doing anything he wanted to, and everything was done perfectly. I wanted so much to be like him that I began to contract, drew my feet under me, made faces, squeezed, held my breath—I stopped thinking, feeling, hearing, and seeing—and lo! suddenly I was a little man, no larger than a flea! I was delighted. All the two hundred and forty-eight parts of my body relaxed; I felt light as a feather. Soon I became the soul, the very life, of several important people and my fortune started rising. I rode in a carriage dressed like a prince. Everyone paid me great honor and respect. Nothing was good enough for me. My credit was excellent. I did whatever I wanted to and led the town by the nose. From a distance, people pointed at my carriage and exclaimed:

"Look, look! There goes the Soul! The Soul is speaking. *Akh*, just look at the Soul. Sh-sh! What is the Soul saying? What? You have dowry-money? Give it to the Soul! Do you have a lawsuit or a matter for arbitration on your hands? Go to the Soul for a decision! Do you need a favor? Your best bet is the Soul! A sage, a counselor, an honored adviser, a bigwig, a peer—that is what the Soul is!"

I began to straighten out and stretch. My eyes opened—and good morning to you, *momzer'l* Itsik-Avreml! There I was, sprawling as if I were in my father's vineyard. I pinched myself.

"Yes, it is I, as I am a Jew! I, the *shlimazl*, in person. How did I get *here?*"

How annoyed I was to wake up and find myself unaltered!

"Well," thought I. "All is not lost. I will find out how to become a little man if it's the last thing I do!

"While I was dreaming last night, it was only when I stopped thinking, feeling, hearing, and seeing, that I felt I had become a little man. The logical conclusion, then, is that one cannot become a little man unless one stops thinking and feeling. One must not

102

think or feel regardless of another person's pain or misery. But how can that be done? How can one stop thinking and feeling? That is the whole secret! That is where the treasure is buried!"

It occurred to me to ask the Herr, but I reconsidered.

"If Gutman knew the secret, the poor soul would become a little man himself! He would be rich. He wouldn't have to struggle so. He wouldn't have to send his books to unwilling subscribers and be the victim of everyone's opinion."

I considered the matter from all angles and remained confused. All that day I walked around in a fog. I had a splitting headache. Whatever I did went wrong. I broke two tea glasses, dropped several porcelain plates, upset an inkwell. I set up the samovar backwards: I put the coal into the water compartment and the water into the coal compartment. Everybody in the house looked at me in amazement and whispered with obvious reference to me. Gutman, indicating me, spoke quietly to his wife and placed a finger on his forehead.

"There's something brewing in the boy's head. He always looks somewhat doltish, but today he looks even more so. He looks very depressed, poor lad. He is so young yet!"

For a while, I was as mad as ten fiends. I made all sorts of faces and was disgruntled with the whole world. Everything within me was in a turmoil, as if there were a mill grinding without end. A voice seemed to be calling to me:

"Itskhok-Avrom! What is going to become of you? How long will you remain in misery, in loneliness? Become a little man, Itskhok-Avrom! Then you will live in riches, in honor. You will carry your head erect!"

The voice pecked away without giving me a moment's respite. My confusion led to indecision. I didn't know what to do or where to start. Then, like a lightning-bolt, the solution presented itself: why not become a lackey at Dr. Steinhertz's? There I would be able to observe him and discover the secret of becoming a little man!

One would have to be just such a blockhead, such a depressed child as I was in order to understand what was going on in my heart at that time. Everybody, even those people who have a wealth of experience in worldly effairs, as I found later in life, everybody has his moods, his peculiarities, his follies, his madness, his rationalizations of which he has convinced himself and which are seared into his heart. And to other people, his peculiarities appear to be wild—lacking in sense and in taste. Nobody can place himself in another person's position, understand his heart and remain patient with his follies. Everyone has sympathy only for himself. One person laughs at another and everybody is crazy!

I sought out an agent and promised him a good commission if he would get me employment as a lackey at Dr. Steinhertz's. It was not long before I left, almost fled, from my good Herr Gutman. I even forgot the farewells and flew to my new job at the doctor's.

CHAPTER 10

▲▲ My entry into the doctor's household could be compared only with that of a bedbug. A bedbug is an uninvited guest which waits impatiently all day until we humans are done with our business and get into bed. Then it can make our acquaintance and go about its business with us. The whole purpose of the bedbug's visit is, after all, purely business—to suck the blood of proud mortals.

Dr. Steinhertz, that proud mortal, was busy elsewhere with very important matters, filling his coffers with gold, no doubt. How could he suspect that that morning, he had taken into his household a bedbug, *momzer* Itsik-Avreml, who was going to observe his every move and thereby learn from him the secret of becoming a little man?

I worked all day at the chores that Madame assigned to me, but I could barely wait until I would see the little doctor. That evening, the door opened suddenly and in stalked a huge man, a behemoth, as massive as Gog and Magog together. When I saw him, I gazed at him with my usual half-witted stare. The behemoth was not at all pleased with my gaze. He pierced me with a glance and bellowed in Russian:

"What are you staring at, jackass?"

I had never heard this language before and didn't understand a word of it. I began to tremble as if I were being led to the gallows and, before I knew it, I stammered:

"My name is Itsik-Avreml . . . my name is . . . Avremke! ... I'm an orphan. . . a lackey. . . I work here! ..."

"You're obviously a big fool!" said the behemoth. "See here! From now on, when I enter the house, I want you to take off my sheepskin coat and my galoshes! Do you hear?"

I fell to the ground in a fright and embraced his clodhoppers with my hands in a frenzied effort to remove the galoshes. With God's help, I overcame my fright and the behemoth went into the dining room. A little later, I brought in the samovar, and all evening I served this handsome person and Madame.

All that night, I tried to guess who this behemoth, this bloated belly, might be. He sat alone with Madame all evening, caterwauling and philandering. He to her: lovey-dovey—and she to him:

105

kitten. What is all this about a kitten? And where is the little doctor himself?

Thus, for several days, the swollen paunch continued his prolonged visits. Whenever he entered or left, I immediately fell prostrate upon the ground to put on or remove his galoshes. He held his arms akimbo and gazed loftily at the ceiling, not at all concerned that his big hoofs had clamped my poor fingers to the floor. And still I didn't know who this healthy Esau was!

Having finished my work one evening and having left kitten playing with lovey-dovey, I went down to the kitchen to become better acquainted with the cook. I feigned a pious face and asked her as if in passing:

"Tell me, Dvosye, I beg you, who is that man who visits here so often? He seems to be an old crony of Madame's and sleeps with her in the bedroom."

"What's that!" exclaimed the cook in amazement. "What are you saying? What do you mean, *somebody* is sleeping in the bedroom? Who is *somebody?*"

"Upon my word!" I swore. "May I be struck down if it is not so! May I live to hear the Messiah's trumpet, as I have seen and heard him go in there with my own eyes and ears! May we both live long and be healthy! What does she call him? Kitten or tomcat! The devil knows! "

"Well, and the boss?" asked the cook with a gleeful grin, and a little fire was reflected from her eyes as it was when she baked bread in the oven.

"The boss?" I stammered. "The boss apparently doesn't sleep at home nights. He must have gone to some other place to do his work."

"Well, if that is the case," said the cook with a sly giggle, "then I must go and see for myself. I'll find some excuse. It is worth seeing that the ladies are no better than the maids. . . . Let them not put on such fine airs!"

Several minutes later, she came storming down the stairs, her eyes ablaze like the fires of hell. A barrage of deathly curses belched from her mouth.

"Why, you little spider! You should be torn limb from limb! Some nerve, from a little snotnose, from a stinking piece of carrion, from such a wormy brat! What is destined for all of Israel and for me, O Lord, may it not happen to you—may you not arise from the dead on Judgment Day! So young, and already the little backbiter's

106

tongue runs on wheels! May you not rest in peace! . . . It's the boss himself who is sitting with Madame in the bedroom!"

"God be with you, Dvosye! What are you saying?" I attempted to repair my fortunes with the cook. "Just think what you are saying, Dvosye! You mean that behemoth, that bloated belly?"

"The devil take you and your ancestors, you brat!" she screamed and grabbed the rolling pin. "How dare you call the boss a behemoth, you brat! Out! Get out or I'll split your skull!"

I speedily slipped out of the kitchen and went upstairs without a sound. I lay down on my bed in the anteroom and couldn't sleep a wink for sheer astonishrnent. My thoughts carried me away:

"What is going on here? The doctor is tall, fat, and heavy. Then why did Gutman say that he is a little man? Would Gutman tell a lie, such a big lie? No, it can't be! Gutman never fooled a soul. Whatever Gutman said was always as true as could be. What *is* the matter then? There must be some magic here. If people can change themselves into wolves, werewolves, and assume all sorts of shapes—and this is the truth because I heard it myself from old Jews with snow-white beards—then it must certainly be possible that they can also change into little men and make a fortune! If a man can become a wolf, a vicious beast that runs wild, howls, and devours everyone he meets, then it must be easier to become a little man. In short, one looks like a normal person—the same body, face, features—but instead of being big, one acts small. Yes, I think I am on the right path. That is probably the whole secret! There must be some hocus-pocus, some witchcraft, here. I must keep my eyes open and find out what it is even if the world should come to an end!"

With this new approach, my childish mind, as you can see, made a step forward. Whereas my previous conception of a little man was very naive, infantile—that little men simply sprang full-blown upon the earth—it had now be come more refined, more polished. It now had a purpose, a drive, a spiritual strength behind it, namely, that all men are born equal into the world, but some of them change and sometimes become little men with the help of demons and fiends. In this there was something of the supernatural. . . . "

Several days later, I was eavesdropping at the door leading to the doctor's office. I overheard a strange conversation between the doctor and the apothecary.

107

"This week, doctor, you've done very well, may the evil eye not interfere. I pushed quite a bit of business your way. I fulfill my half of the bargain to perfection. Everywhere I go, I proclaim your wisdom, that you are the only doctor worth seeing, and yet you ignore me, doctor! "

"What are you saying, Getzl? What about yesterday?"

"Why, what happened yesterday, doctor?"

"What a short memory! Do you mean to say that you have forgotten already, Getzl? For whose sake do you think I prescribed thirty leeches yesterday? For the patient? Between you and me, he needed your leeches as much as you or I. A damp rag on his forehead would have turned the trick. Feh, shame on you, Getzl, upon my word! Only because of you, honestly, was I a little man yesterday!"

"As you say, doctor, you were a little man yesterday. But for your sake, I am a little man every day. Between you and me, did that patient today need a doctor? All he has is a simple cold. Only because of me did he call you and now we have hopes that he will be calling you twice a day for the next few weeks. The man is filthy rich—he can afford to be sick for a couple of weeks."

"Well, then, Getzl, what would you suggest?"

"Leeches, doctor! I have lots of leeches!"

"Rest easy, Getzl. You will apply leeches to him. But do you at least have good ones? You know that I am very fussy about these things."

"Very fresh leeches, doctor. So help me God! I, too, hate to fool people in these matters."

"O-ho! So that's the story! " I thought after hearing this conversation. I was lying in bed. "Apparently, from what I see and hear here, to be a little man does not mean that one must be small in size, as I foolishly thought. One can be full size, even a behemoth, and yet be a little man. And one can remain full size while one is a little man. To be a little man, one must be a parasite, a blood-sucker, and cheat others of their money. So that is the key to success! Now I've begun to understand the matter properly. That is the virtue of getting about in the world and meeting people! But what is the use of my knowing the secret when I am neither a doctor nor an apothecary? Nor do I know how to let blood with leeches. I must find another way in which to let blood—without leeches. There must be many such methods of cunning to be mastered. How then shall I go about it?"

108

Then I thought of Issar Varger.

"Not a bad idea. Somehow I must get into his service. As I am a Jew, I must! My heart urges me on, 'To him, to Issar Varger!' He also is a little man who is doing very well!"

These were the thoughts that whirled through my feverish brain all night and kept me tossing on my pillow. That night, I grew several years older. A big change came over me.'

The following day, without further ado, I hunted out my agent, promised him an even better commission than before, and several days later I entered the service of Issar Varger.

CHAPTER 11

▲▲ Issar Varger was one of the foremost men of substance in Tsvuatshits. Rare was the man who dared say his soul was his own when Issar spoke. People were terror-stricken and stammered nervously: "What do you mean? Issar himself said so!"

Issar himself did not engage in trade. He lolled in the lap of luxury and did not even lift a finger—yet his house was as busy as a beehive. Everyone, from the cradle to the grave, had some business to transact with Issar.

Was he, do you think, a man of great learning or of noble lineage? Not at all! He wasn't even a man of small learning. He could barely recite his prayers and was, as a matter of fact, a dullard in matters of religion. Still, he had a prayershawl and a large bag for his phylacteries. This bag was made of the smooth skins of several kids which had been removed alive from their slaughtered dam's womb. It was trimmed with red embroidery. Within it were to be found the *Derekh Hakhayim*, a religious work containing all the necessary rules of daily life, a book of psalms, and several other religious articles.

In matters of penmanship, he had a heavy hand. His pen and he were always at odds. In spite of his coaxing, the pen insisted on having its own way. It balked, squirted, blotted, burrowed into the paper, and finally refused to budge. Every letter wore him out. By the time he managed to get his signature *Issar* down in black and white, his eyes started from their sockets and he was covered with sweat. After each such accomplishment, he mopped his brow with his sleeve or his coat-tail and was as breathless as if he had just felled a tree.

One of his virtues as a writer was that he was not, as are many others, particularly insistent upon the conventions of orthography. He gave no preference to one letter over another. He was not at all concerned with questions of priority or seniority. What mattered it whether the letter belonged at the beginning or at the end of the word, or if it were left out entirely? People would get the general idea. If, occasionally, he encountered an especially difficult problem, his pen came to his rescue. It would embark upon its own course, make a line, a blot, and a dot and the problem was solved. As a sample of his erudition, I present you herewith with

110

a version of his spelling of the word Noah—*kNowhAh*—with all seven errors.

So much for his learning. Nor was his lineage anything to boast of. His family had no gilt coat of arms, nor did he, in his youth, dine on white rolls and butter. The truth of the matter was, as I found out later, that he was a little man, and was far more successful with this talent than are many others with skilled hands or learned heads.

Issar had the richest man of Tsvuatshits in the palm of his hand. Whenever a problem arose, this man always consulted with Issar. Issar was his right hand, his very soul, his be-all and end-all, and therefore Issar was accorded much honor by everybody who amounted to anything in the town.

Many were the things that I learned from this Reb Issar. He, and only he, was my true master. He took me in hand and opened my eyes. He set me right on the question of what makes the world go around. He answered embarrassing questions for me. He explained the innumerable contradictions of life. He put me on my feet, polished me and refined me and turned me into a jewel. In a word, he uncovered for me the mystery of becoming a little man.

By nature, Issar was a very secretive and reserved individual. One could never divine even his most petty thoughts. He never meant what he said and never said what he meant. Even his own wife could never wheedle any information out of him. He kept her and his children at a distance. Everyone in his household respected him. He talked little, never argued, but when he gave a command, it had to be fulfilled immediately. The expression on his face was always the same, somewhat serious and thoughtful. He never laughed outright. Only rarely would the shadow of a smile flit across his face. This sour little smile was an orphan—nothing more than a tug at one corner of his thin lips. The rest of his face had no inkling of the smile at his lips but remained stony and cold, his eyes glassy as before.

He had a crony, however, with whom he was very intimate. With this man he was talkative and not at all withdrawn about the slightest thing. He enjoyed spending an evening with him over a glass of wine discussing one thing or another. At these times, Issar was a completely different Issar. His heart was wide open. His crony could enter at will and read there all of Issar's secret thoughts. And when Issar was a trifle tipsy, he really laid bare his mind: whatever was concealed in his lung was soon disclosed by

111

his tongue. He and his crony would meet in his private room and merrily chat away.

I had long ago acquired the habit of standing behind the door and eavesdropping. I would like to record here a typical conversation between Issar and his friend which will give you a picture of Issar, his view of life and the world, and his method of attack, to all of which I subscribed without the slightest deviation.

"Listen, brother o' mine!" Issar called to his friend after they had entered, happy and somewhat intoxicated, and had sat down in his private room. "Listen to me, you blockhead! I tell you that in the whole wide world there is no other people so dear, so good as the Jews. Really, a good people, a golden people. Upon my faith, they will give you their last—groschen! "

"It would be better, Issar, to say a foolish people. Such fools as Jews don't exist anywhere else in the world!"

"Correct, brother o' mine! What's true is true. There is no other people, so good, so useful, so golden, and so foolish as our brothers! There just isn't!"

"What is all this talk directed at the temples of Israel? Enough of it! Tell me about today's meeting."

"What meeting is this?"

"Out with it, Issar! Do you mean to tell me that you have forgotten about the meeting—today's meeting about the meat?"

"Am I supposed to know what you are talking about, you blockhead? An important thing, the meeting. . . . It was as significant as all of their other meetings. You should have been there. You would have seen something pretty. When I entered, I found the place in an uproar. People were buzzing about like flies. I decided that there was no point in getting myself involved in these petty discussions, so without further ado, I spoke up nonchalantly, you know:

" 'What is the big problem if the price is a few groschen higher? It is certainly better, believe me, than if the tax collector should get angry and, God forbid, resign! Believe me, it's so!'

"If you think I knew what I was talking about, you're mistaken. But you should have seen how several respectable gentlemen, men who consider themselves cunning, piously turned up the whites of their eyes, smoothed their beards, and shrugged sheepishly: 'True, indeed. There is nothing to talk about. It's most certainly so. . . .' The whole place quieted down. No one had anything to say, as if the whole matter had been settled. They stood there in a stupor. Nobody thought it even necessary to ask: 'Why is it true?' Only one, an upstart on whom I've had my eye for a long time, wouldn't give in and insisted: 'Then let him resign! Let him! People can live without a tax collector! ' The cunning gentlemen, who think they understand business, looked upon him as upon a child who should be seen but not heard. But I want to take care of this upstart. You'll have to write me a letter of praise about him which will throw his reputation into the gutter. . . . You know that in matters of writing I have a heavy hand."

"Let's leave that for another time, Issar. But will you ever get around to telling me how the meeting ended?"

"You mean you can't guess, blockhead? Do you know of any other people that is so good, so golden as the Jews? They agreed to everything. The prices were raised even more than I had expected and everybody left in an elated mood. I, of course, am certainly pleased."

"You may, of course, be pleased, Issar, but . . ."

"But what? Numskull! But what? Maybe you want to say: 'But it is a pity on the poor'? You silly fool, with your empty, meaningless word—*pity!* Pity was invented by the weak, by the unlucky ones, by the sheep, who, knowing that they are weak and incapable of obtaining what they desire because they lack the teeth and claws to fight, have invented this word *pity* and use it as their weapon. They preach morality. They ask for pity. They walk around with pious faces, their eyes turned heavenward, and think that they will accomplish something in this fashion. It's a swindle, brother o'mine, an utter swindle! I can see through all this morality and all these moralists. I know which way the wind blows and why. I have, blessed be His Name, a fair knowledge of the ways of the world, although I am no great scholar. It's not scholarship that is needed here, but good hard common sense. One doesn't need much insight to realize that the world consists of two opposing camps, the strong and the weak: wolves, the wild animals—and sheep, the tame animals. The former do the skinning and the latter give their skins. It just can't be any other way. Reverse the order of things and the end result will still be the same. No sooner will the weakling grow strong, than he will swim up to the surface and kick hard. Let the lamb feel that he is sprouting teeth and claws, and he will begin to sharpen them and tear you to bits. Try this: take one of your pity-mongers, one of your good-for-nothings and moralists, and appoint him to a position of power in the *Kahal*. As

113

soon as he smells power, as soon as he grips the whip in his hand, he will begin to wield it, and wield it he will without pity! Make one of these weaklings a tax collector and he will teach everyone the ABC's of taxation—he will tear and scrape the flesh from your bones. 'God grant that the *muzhik* never become a landowner!' says the proverb. It is a true, a fitting saying. The landowner would have to be stark raving mad to give over the reins to Ivan. Keep your pious little face, you good kosher soul, you pious lamb! You can preach morals to me as much as you wish, but if you had teeth and claws, it would be worse a thousand times over!"

"God forbid, Issar! What are you talking about? Who is talking about pity? How do you like that, pity! I'm talking about something entirely different, Issar. I say that you may, of course, be pleased, but I . . . "

"Well, then, speak up, man! So the story is that you, too, would like to be pleased! Pardon me, but you may go to blazes! Dip your paw in the pot and you'll also have a taste. You 're old enough to take care of yourself. The devil won't take you! Tomorrow, brother o'mine, the *Kahal* will deal with a new series of measures."

On another occasion, Issar said to his crony: "I'm very glad that you came, blockhead! I'm walking around with my mind full of thoughts, like a chicken with an egg. I can hardly contain myself any longer. I must get things off my chest at least once in a while. To hear all and see all as I do, and say nothing, is almost beyond human endurance. If I did not have such an awkward hand, I would sometimes like to sit down, let myself go, and write a comedy, upon my word. Just taste this wine! What do you say to it? I received it as a gift for a little favor."

"This is good stuff, Issar! But tell me, what kind of a favor was this?"

"Ta! A little affair, concerning Leml. He has been bothering me for quite a while to see what I could do for him, as if I were a lawmaker. The fools in this city think that everything lies in my power, just so long as I am willing to extend myself. Can I help it if a few minor officials eat fish at my house on an occasional *shabes* because their mouths water for the taste of Jewish cooking? But the town thinks that therefore all the officials, from the big fish to the small fry, are my bosom friends and that they would do anything for me. Let it be that way, brother o'mine. Let the town believe it, the fools, and come to me for favors. I always have the same answer for them:

" 'We will see, we will see. . . . As long as we are alive there is hope.'

"And they think that I have seen fit to take action in the matter, although all I have seen is what I can see in a coalbin at midnight—but I take a nice fee. If the deal falls through, they think it did because I refused to take any action, but that if I had wanted to, everything would have come out all right. Let them be angry. Let them come and hang me. In the meantime, my reputation as a man of influence remains unblemished. They'll be angry for a while, and when they need another favor, they'll be back again. And I will have my usual answer for them: 'We will see, we will see.' Do you understand? . . . I answered Leml the same way and along with that I gave him some advice about greasing the proper palms. I knew very well that any action on my part would be of as much use as milking a ram. Leml, however, was certain that I had taken a hand in the matter and that I was prodding the magnate to decide in his favor. Well, you should have seen what happened while I was walking down the street today. Leml and his wife extolled me to the skies with tears in their eyes before a big crowd of people:

" 'Reb Issar, our father, our savior! Only with God's help and yours was our request fulfilled. Without your intercession, we would have been unable to acomplish a thing. We'll tell the whole world, Reb Issar! '

"From this I gathered that Leml must have taken my advice to heart. But I didn't let on. Instead, I winced as if to say: 'You will never know at what cost, in strength and health, I succeeded! You cannot imagine the effort it took!' Later on, Leml sent me my commission and several bottles of good wine to boot. Well, what do you think of the wine, brother o'mine?"

"God grant, Issar, that no worse should be said about you, about your fools, about the whole swindle. . . . To your health, *lekhayim!*"

"Choke on it, blockhead! Swindle, he says, swindle! Why do you call it a swindle? What are all transactions, what is business and trade in general if not swindle? From top to bottom! I tell you, all transactions, not excluding those dealing with the world to come. Do you understand? How is any business conducted and what does it lead to? What is the very basis of business? Truth and honesty, do you think? Not at all! Brother o'mine, *truth* is only a word which everyone interprets in the way that suits him best, and this interpretation is never the one that really should be applied in the particular instance. There is no such thing as true *truth*, and there cannot be, because our minds could not grasp it. Furthermore, it would not be a very good thing for business. Thousands of offices, thousands of stores, and thousands of other enterprises which you see every day would disintegrate like spiderwebs, leaving neither trace nor sign of their existence. A lot of our rich men would be tramping about with knapsacks on their backs.

"Maybe you think that all this is based on work? God forbid! Do you know who works! The lumberman, the water carrier, the porter, the handworkers, and the like. But you will never earn much from working. Even if you break your back at your job, you will still starve ten times a day with hunger pains. Go ahead, spare no efforts running Leml's silly errands. You will spend all your time on it. You will wear your fingers down to the bone with the necessary writing, and then, providing you have succeeded, what will you be paid? You won't even be able to buy water for your porridge! And now, God forbid, suppose you haven't succeeded. Then all your work is thrown to the winds and the whole world thinks that you are stale, flat, and unprofitable—a cripple, a good-for-nothing who doesn't know his knee from his elbow— that all you have is foul fish and rotten herring!

"Don't wrinkle your brow like that, brother o'mine! This is not some deep philosophy, but plain everyday sense. Philosophy is also worthless. It is not good to be too smart—the world will hate you and avoid you like the plague. Great minds, good scholars, all of them walk around in torn boots without soles. The little man does much better in this world. You don't need any special trade or knowledge, but you must be able to cringe and crawl, you must be a lickspittle and be able to beat around the bush. What can you do? One must have money. Without money you amount to nothing, you're a thousand times smaller than the most petty little man.

"What does a pauper amount to, brother o'mine? Can you possibly imagine how much rich men hate a pauper? They speak to him sometimes, and even appear to pity him occasionally, but the truth of the matter is that they can't bear his sight. He distorts their whole field of vision. They wonder why this creature is allowed to wander over the face of the earth. In their eyes, he is scum, a leftover bone, a cancerous growth, a misfortune, a plague. Whenever they see him, they get a gnawing at their hearts—they see in him a threat to their lives and to their moneybags. Believe me, I lack the proper words to describe this feeling to you. Brother, if you're a pauper, you're an outcast in this world. Your former friends, if they are rich, will keep you at a distance. They may pay you an occasional visit, but the impression you get is the same as when you see a newly rich woman stealing away to the small poverty-stricken town where she was born to visit the grave of her father, a pauper, while she is all bedecked in pearls and diamonds—so that the poor town may be proud of her. Either in the *Khumesh* or in the *Song of Songs*, I believe, there is a remark which says that the pauper smells of the grave. Money is the root of all wisdom, brother o'mine, everything. . . . If you have money, both this world and the one to come belong to you. But in order to have money, you must be a little man, a parasite. You must lick boots, you must cringe, you must play your cards right! *Lekhayim*, brother o'mine!"

"To your health, Issar. May we have a continual supply of such Lemls.* Well, Issar, what about your rich man, the one whose guiding genius you have become? What kind of man is he?"

"I don't wish to speak about him, brother o'mine, do you understand? Ever since I have become his concessioner, I do not discuss him."

"What do you mean by '*his* concessioner,' Issar? Here's news! Do you mean you have a concession on *him*? What is he, a mill or a tavern, that you have a concession on him?"

"What is the difference, blockhead? What is the difference between a rich man, a mill, a tavern, a demon, a fiend, or the devil knows what else? As long as you have the concession! Ha, ha, ha, brother o'mine! You are still naive, a schoolboy. Everything must be digested for you. Well, I will explain it to you somehow. Let's start as you suggested—with a mill.

"Flowing water or the wind both possess great power. Along comes Man who wishes to use everything: he sets up a structure with wheels and stones so arranged that the water or the wind will turn the wheels. The wheels turn the stones, and the mill grinds away. Do you understand? Now, we'll go further. The thing that makes the world go around is power. A rich man is one of the powers of this world. All bow to him. Everyone grovels and scrapes before him, even those who get nothing for it, who never had even a glass of water from him, have none now, and never expect to have one from him in the future. Why? Simply because

---

* A play on words, since *Leml* means a lamb in Yiddish.

117

a rich man deserves honor, because he deserves everything. But I, Issar, say that the only thing to value in a rich man is his money. Do you understand? His money is number one and he himself is number two. A rich man who is of no use to you has a value of zero. If he is of no value, then why fuss over him? Pay no attention to him. Ignore him as you would last year's thunder!

"The next thing for you to understand is that a clever person must make use of everything in the world. Do you understand? Now I will repeat it for you once more. Say after me, little blockhead, say after me:* 'Everything is based on power. A rich man with much money has much power. A clever person must make use of everything. Therefore, he must find a way to make use of the rich man.' And what do you think—should one take the rich man's money? No, no! One must erect a windmill near him so that he may turn its wheels with the power he possesses. Then the mill will grind away! In other words, one should use the rich man like the showman uses his comedy or like a gypsy uses his bear. If you've given me my sack of grain, then you may grind yours in my mill. Have you paid for your ticket?—then you may come and watch my comedy. If you will give me a few groschen, then I will make my bear dance for you. . . . Do you understand?

"I have a concession on my rich man. Would you have any dealings with him, that is, with my windmill, then give me my sack of grain—I am the concessioner. Would you like to see the comedy, to be entertained with make-believe? Then pay me for the ticket—I am the showman. Or would you rather have my rich man stand up on his hindlegs for you and roar? Then out with a few groschen, and you'll kindly pay as I command, for I am his gypsy! . . . Now do you understand! Well, enough for the present! *Lekhayim*, brother o'mine!"

"*Lekhayim*, Issar, to your windmill, your comedy, and your bear. May the wheels turn, the show go on, and may the bear dance! . . ."

---

* A parody on the method of instruction used by a *melamed* in a *Talmud-Toyre*.

CHAPTER 12

▲▲ It stands to reason that Issar's outlook on life was at first too deep for me. Many of his words were beyond me, and I simply could not make head or tail of them. But this much I grasped immediately:

"To have money, you must be a little man, a parasite. You must cringe, you must crawl, you must play your cards right. . . ."

Here I had the secret in a nutshell. However, I did not as yet understand what was really meant by cringing or crawling. In general, at this point, I did not know what was morally permissible and what was forbidden.

My conception of a sin was

not using a rooster as an expiatory sacrifice during Yom Kippur;

or clipping one's fingernails in order, rather than on alternate fingers;

or forgetting to add to the nail clippings three slivers of wood, carved from a synagogue pew or a table, which would serve, in the world to come, as kosher witnesses against the evil eye;

or not believing in good spirits;

or not believing in perverse spirits;

or doubting that ghosts pray in the big synagogue at night;

or doubting the existence of a world of chaos, namely, that there are many people among us who, to all intents and purposes, engage in trade, business, go to fairs, buy and sell, while in reality they are only ghosts, poor deceased people, from the world of chaos;

or not believing that when the Rabbi of Bezliudeff delivered a judgment, there were ghosts present who were marched away in a column, like recruits, by their guardian angel;

or not believing that this self-same Rabbi had seven-league boots, was an honored guest in Heaven, and knew the secret of making rain, snow, and children;

or not believing in incarnate spirits, that is, that the holy souls of men can be reincarnated as cattle, animals, and birds;

or doubting that a certain magnate had been reincarnated as a swine; another, also a fine man, as a calf, God keep us from a similar fate; still another, a great quibbler, as a bird with a sharp whistle, may all Jewish children be kept from such a fate; another, a slippery character, was reincarnated as a fish, with the voice of an eel; and still another, a do-gooder, somehow became a cat, God forbid. . . .

119

In short, such things were sins in my book. But cringing, crawling, fawning, being a little man? After all, a little man is rich and happy. Nobody dares to beat a little man into a pulp, and beatings hurt so terribly! When a tailor or his wife clout you, you see stars before your eyes. And when a cantor decides to twist your ear, your mother's milk curdles within you. Nor is it a pleasure to fall prostrate to the ground to remove or put on galoshes for a behemoth who stands with his arms akimbo staring at the ceiling.

Of course I would be a little man—to the very smallest detail! I would be rid of all my troubles at once and live in riches and in honor. For this reason, I always stole up to Issar's door when he was closeted with his crony. I heard many things which I later attempted to figure out. As time passed, I understood him very well, much better than I had understood my *melamed* at the *Talmud-Toyre*.

It is true that I was rather a dunce in my youth, very foolish. But it became clear later on that I was not so by nature. Why, then? Ever since childhood I was an outcast, an orphan, uncared for, and depressed. I was raised on whippings and blows, from foot and fist. Whoever so desired fell upon me and drubbed my thin bones. What does the proverb say? "If one sins, one thins"—from many beatings, one gets beaten down. What befell my poor, dried-up, frail little body in those days was no joke! I suffered hunger and cold. Many were the times that I felt my strength ebbing, when every bone in my body ached, but instead of being pitied—after all, it was a child that was waning, a human being, created in the image of God, flesh and bone—instead I was pinched, struck, and kicked even more. It seemed as if everyone had designs on my body, to see just how much it could endure.

Then, too, it must be remembered that I was born and raised in Bezliudeff, which is only a small town, and a provincial person, apparently, remains a provincial. Small-town people, upon my faith, are different! They have different senses, different tastes, neither here nor there, neither flesh nor fowl nor good red herring.

I have gone into these particulars merely in order to clarify how a dolt, like I was, could eventually find his way in the world. It was not that I had screws missing in my head; they were simply not tightened down sufficiently. That is why I was capable of learning and mastering Issar's theories.

I served Issar for many years. During this time, I became

polished. I came to understand all things which should be known by a little man. I listened carefully and was an ardent student. I learned how to deceive and hoodwink others. My fondest sport was to draw a herring across the trail, wait for someone to catch the scent, and then bamboozle him, while I slipped out of the situation unscathed. The feelings of justice and mercy had never developed in me beyond the embryonic stage.

"Justice," said Reb Issar, "is like a rubber band. You can stretch it any way you wish—a highly elastic material. Mercy? A contrived, meaningless word—a complete swindle! I, if I am stronger than you, am the dispenser of justice, and you, if you are weaker than I, want to mislead me with mercy!"

I was a devoted disciple of Issar's and tried to please my master in all respects. He was very satisfied with my services and would not, as the saying goes, have traded me for my weight in gold.

As I grew older, I began to think more about my future, when I would be on my own and stand on my own two feet. After all, I was getting to be a young man! It was true that I had mastered Issar's theories with all their refinements; however, it was not the Learning but the Application that was essential.

I pondered this question so long that I finally hit upon a scheme.

"In truth," I said to myself, "what a fool I've been! Issar himself says : 'The clever man must make use of everything in the world. He must gain the confidence of a rich man, became his concessioner, make him dance to his tune, and earn a pretty penny.' Then what am I waiting for? Isn't Issar a rich man? I will become his concessioner. He will be my bear. I will be his soul! Isn't he a power in this world! Then I will erect my windmill and let him turn my wheels! Oh Lord! Here I am begging for food while the roast doves are flying straight into my mouth!"

To make a long story short, I began to cringe and crawl for Issar. I sought every possible way to ingratiate myself with him and unlock the portals of his heart. Finally, I found the master key and began to take possession of my bear! Issar was, for all his pretensions, only a human being. He enjoyed being flattered, petted, fawned upon, and admired, although he was perfectly well aware of the value of all this toadying. He himself, for example, would say to someone: "You're a sage—a good, pious soul, a kosher, honest man!" But what he meant was just the reverse:

"You're a simpleton, a brute, a toad, a stingy dog—a thieves' thief!"

But it is apparently the way of all flesh that each man enjoys being pandered, enjoys fooling himself. However, all this is easier said than done. It was long before I became Issar's prime minister.

You may possibly wonder how a lackey manages to become a prime minister? If so, then pardon my saying so, you don't understand the ways of the world! Almost all lackeys are prime ministers and almost all prime ministers are lackeys.

When people began to realize that I had become Issar's guiding genius, his honored lackey, they began to truckle to me. They went out of their way to greet me and say "Good day!" Such is the custom the whole world over: in order to petition the master, the practice is first to approach his honored lackeys, soothe them, engage them in a conversation with honeyed words, become chummy with them, and, last but not least, grease their palms. There are several lines of reasoning behind these actions :

"Let me, first of all, close *their* mouths. Let *them* not snarl or bark and the battle is half won."

Or: "It's all right. Let them breathe a favorable word into the master's ear. A lackey can frequently influence his lord in unsuspected ways, which are even beyond the ken or power of great men. The lackey knows his lord's heart and knows what to say and what not to say."

If anyone needed to see Issar (and who didn't?), he now had to polish *my* doorknob first—he had to pass through my chambers in order to reach Issar. Tips and gratuities were now the order of the day. The petitioner was under the impression that so long as he had persuaded me to speak to Issar on his behalf, his request was as good as granted. I knew that Issar's intervention would be of as much use as, in Issar's own words, milking a ram. But who cared? Let the petitioner have illusions and hand me the money. And supposing that Issar were in a position to help, then *he* would take the money and act without my intercession. In any case, Issar would take his fee and say as usual: "We will see, we will see." But, then, who would need me as middleman? I didn't care: let the petitioner have his hopes and give me gold.

In this fashion, my fortunes rose. I began to put on weight and accumulated a substantial amount of money. ▲▲

CHAPTER 13

"Only one word with the Rabbi. Please, only one word!"

A deep voice was heard behind the door and a moment later a bustling little Jew entered. He wore no coat—only a patched sweater from which peeked the tattered edges of a greasy prayershawl, the *tsitses* of which bounced aimlessly on his knees. His trousers were made of coarse material and were supported by a pair of heavy, oversized boots, each of which dragged along a *pood* of mud and emitted a peculiarly strong odor of sweat and iodine.

"Ah, Benny!" said the Rabbi, glancing at this person. "What do you have to say, Benny?"

"What should I say?" answered Benny, scratching the nape of his neck. "Ett, I've nothing to say. You have already paid me for this month, and I brought you your water last night. I was carrying water nearly all night. Itskhok-Avrom's death almost carried me away, too. The landlords who live in the neighboring houses poured out their water and had none all day—nothing even to cook with. Who is to blame? The water carrier! *He* decided to die so it's *my* fault! Go, carry water for them all night!

"Toward daybreak, just when I finally fall asleep, my mother, long may she live, wakes me. 'Benny, Benny! Get up and lock the door behind me. I have to go to the synagogue for early services and from there I must go to the cemetery because today is my memorial-day for the dead. Keep an eye on the porridge. I've left it on the hearth.' Well, I get rid of Mother and lie down again. I just about close my eyes when I hear 'Peck, peck, peck.' The hens and the rooster have come off the roost and are standing on the table merrily pecking at a crust of bread. I try to scare them off while lying in bed, but it's no use. Suddenly, I notice a wooden spoon, a *fleyshik*, lying near me. I pick it up and start after the chickens, when suddenly I hear the pot boiling on the hearth. Without thinking twice about it, I stir the *milkhik* pot with the *fleyshik* spoon and make trouble! That's why I'm here, Rabbi, for your decision. You see, the spoon is *fleyshik*, not, God forbid, because it was ever used for meat, but because it cost less than three rubles. May my health prosper as this is true!

The pot, on the other hand, is *milkhik* simply because no meat was ever cooked in it—ever since my goat died, no milk has crossed our threshold. So, tell me, Rabbi, does the porridge have to be thrown out!"

"Is it a big pot, Benny?" asked the Rabbi.

"Bigger than my head. It's almost like a pail. When I eat it all, I'm as tight as a drum and can work all day without a break."

"It's kosher!" said the Rabbi.

Before Benny was able to leave, a woman came running in wailing and weeping.

"Rabbi, I just can't bear it any longer! I don't have the strength! You no doubt meant well when you tried to convince us not to be divorced but to live together—but I wish that only my enemies should live together like that! Your dear words made as much of an impression on him as a pea on a wall. He does just as he pleases—that man will be the death of me yet. I am at my wit's end with begging, borrowing, and selling chickens and eggs or what have you, so as to maintain the lives of my poor, hungry children who are always in rags and tatters. And he? He is busy with one thing only—his *Khasidim*. He spends all day with them huddled around the stove, drinking and blabbering away, and when he comes home, he expects everything to be just right. He doesn't even glance at the children. They are not his affair—as if they belonged to strangers! He never says a kind word to me, as if I had been sold to him in bondage, a serving-maid who is not even worthy of washing his feet and drinking the water. The only words I hear from him are: 'Goose! Old crone! Sloven!'

"As soon as there is any sort of holiday, he takes the last bit of food and money from the house, rides off with his *Khasidim* to their Rabbi and rots there for weeks on end with his cronies who are just like him. He has no responsibilities for a home, for a wife, for children who are thankful for a crust of bread and are wasting away. If I dare to breathe a word about all this, he threatens to cast me off, to desert me, to teach me that a woman should know her place.

"This morning, he comes home from his *shtibl*. The house was so cold and damp that even wolves would flee—it's more than two days since any smoke has come out of my chimney. The children are trembling and shivering with cold, begging for food. The little one in the crib is hoarse from yelling. I would suckle him but I have no milk—I haven't seen any cooked food for over two days now. 'Goose!' he says to me icily. 'Pack my shirt and my *shabes* coat into the traveling bag.' I see that he is about to leave with his gang—after all, *Khanike* is almost upon us. My heart was full of gall, so I say to him: 'Monster! Who do you think you are? Look at your children, how they suffer and waste away! And all you have on your mind are your foolish, empty matters! Granted, your wife is a goose, a nag, a crone. But your children, O Lord, your children! . . .' No sooner do I finish than he falls upon me with an angry roar. 'So! Goose! You dare to scold me and call those holy ideas foolish, empty matters, which your woman's mind can't even begin to comprehend! So! This is the last straw. I will cast you off forever and make you an outcast, deserted woman. I'll remarry somewhere again—I'm allowed to, it's my privilege. I must teach you a lesson. You'll learn your place!' He wasn't satisfied with mere words. He started pinching me. Here, look at my arms! My whole body is black and blue. Rabbi, save me! Let him divorce me. I simply don't have the strength to put up with it any longer!"

"Go, go home!" said the Rabbi. "I'll send the synagogue attendant to bring him to me today."

While the Rabbi was thus occupied with his rabbinical duties, the gentlemen in the room were strangely absorbed in thought. The rich men puffed their cheeks with annoyance and were highly excited, as if they had been publicly called swindlers.

"Why are you sitting like that, Reb Khone?" groaned one of them.

"Ett, Reb Berish," winced Reb Khone. "I really don't see what Itskhok-Avrom was driving at with his tale. He uses words which don't fit him at all. How do you like the taunting phrases, Reb Berish? Do you realize in which direction the bullets are flying? Who knows how long this reading will take . . . and I hardly have the time. I'm sitting here on pins and needles."

"Indeed, I'm on pins and needles too," answered Reb Berish. "Do I realize in which direction the bullets are flying? Oy, oy, I realize it full well! Feh! I would never have expected this from Itskhok-Avrom. He certainly was no man's fool and understood the ways of the world. . . . Maybe the best idea would be for us to leave right now. After all, we are busy men. Upon my word, take my advice. Let's leave now."

"God forbid! No, no!" exclaimed several of the gentlemen in a chorus. "Then it would look as if we felt guilty. On the contrary, let us sit it out until the very end."

Reb Khone sighed deeply. Reb Berish enveloped his nose with his hand and growled in anger.

"Ah! Good morning, good morning!" Reb Fayvish entered the room. He was radiant. His face was scarlet, a sure sign of a man who has had a few drinks. "I was very busy and couldn't tear myself away until this very minute. What's wrong?" he asked as he glanced around the room. "Why are you all so gloomy?"

"What makes you so cheerful this morning?" someone grumbled.

"The Rabbi must have continued the reading without me," said Reb Fayvish. "Upon my faith, it's a pity that I missed part of it. It must have been very pleasant."

"May your coming year be as pleasant," growled Reb Berish under his breath.

"Don't worry, Reb Fayvish. There's enough left for you, too," one of the gentlemen called out.

"Ah! Good morning, Rabbi!" said Reb Fayvish as the Rabbi seated himself at the table. "Pardon me for coming late. I was very busy with the details of Itskhok-Avrom's funeral. The Burial Society has just arrived at a settlement of the burial fees. Both sides were a bit stubborn, adamant. But the Society was right and carried the day. It's not every day that such an affluent body comes between their fingers and thumbs. It's a pity indeed that I missed part of the reading. Such a tale should be heard. Believe me, I was in ecstasy yesterday listening to the words pouring from your pious lips. The end of the story must be quite unusual!"

"Of course, Reb Fayvish, we've read quite a bit during your absence, but there is still a good deal left. I'll get on with the reading now. Possibly we can finish without any further interruptions."

CHAPTER 14

Without further delay, the Rabbi proceeded with the reading:

▲▲ As is the case with all newly rich lackeys, my greatest pleasure lay in dressing and arraying myself in the most garish clothes possible. A newly rich lackey is concerned with wearing gleaming chains and rings, having his boots polished to such a high luster that one's face can be seen in them—so that the whole world might be adequately impressed. On *shabes*, I would bedeck myself like a lord and go strolling with my friends in order to give the world the opportunity to notice and envy us and so that we might inspect the girls and young ladies who promenaded about in little giggling groups. I was acquainted with almost all the serving-maids in town. I was therefore well-versed in the very latest gossip concerning many of their young ladies, among whom I also had a number of acquaintances.

One *shabes*, as I was taking the usual stroll with my friends, observing the various young ladies who were festooned in silks and velvets, draped in pearls and all sorts of jewelry, a girl passed in the opposite direction. She was clad very simply in a cotton dress which was clean and neat as a pin. Her face sparkled like the bright morning-star. She twilighted the others with all their pearls and diamonds. They compared to her as candles compare to the sun. Escorting her was a personable, well-favored young man.

Her beauty so affected me that I remained standing in confusion, neither hearing nor seeing what was going on around me. When I finally took notice, I no longer saw them. She had disappeared into the crowd like a falling star disappears into the summer night, but her image was so deeply engraved in my heart that thenceforth I could not get her out of my mind. Her face, her form appeared before me continually, and, at night, her blazing eyes shone, twinkled at me out of the darkness like two brightly burning candles. I felt as if I had known her for a long time, as if I had seen her somewhere before, but I could not remember when and where. I promised myself to find out who she was and where she lived.

Late one afternoon, I happened to be walking along a street in the outskirts of the town. The clear blue sky was bordered at the horizon by a black mass of cloud against which, from time to time, could be seen flashes of lightning. The street was quiet. No sound of life could be heard and I walked along brooding, deep in thought. Suddenly I heard a piercing cry. I looked up and saw a man running toward me with a package, like a thief attempting to flee.

"Stop!" I yelled and placed myself stoutly in his path with my thick cane uplifted. He became very frightened, dropped the package, and fled. At a nearby fence, I noticed a prostrate figure. I ran to it with the package, but it didn't move. Meanwhile, the mass of black cloud had advanced overhead. It had become dark. I raised the person's head and tried to revive him. Flashes of lightning struck all around, one after another, and I saw a pair of blazing eyes looking at me. My heart began to pound furiously. I felt faint and stood there in a daze. I recognized *her*. It was *she*.

She told me how she had been walking alone on the street when suddenly a man sprang out of nowhere, struck her hand sharply, and snatched the bundle of linen which she had collected from her customers for mending. Had I not appeared at this opportune moment, she said with tears in her eyes, she would not only have been unable to keep the wolf from the door, but, worse yet, she would have gotten a bad reputation and people would no longer have given her a stitch of work. She thanked me from the bottom of her heart, blushing deeply. Each glance from her blazing eyes burned and scorched me. I felt my heart melting within me like wax.

"May God repay you!" she said at last with a trembling voice and turned to go her way.

"No, no!" I exclaimed excitedly. "Under no circumstances would I allow you to go your way alone now. I must escort you to your door."

She seemed to hesitate, the expression on her face saying that she would feel uncomfortable arriving home at this hour with a strange young man. But I gave her no chance to protest. I quickly took the bundle and accompanied her.

We hardly spoke a word all the way. I glanced at her out of the corner of my eye and shook as if in a fever. Each time she touched my hand with hers as she tried to take the bundle from me, a shiver passed up and down my spine. My blood froze in my veins. I couldn't catch my breath. We walked together until she brought me to a little house in front of which hung a small white sign with black handwritten letters saying: "Here lives Golda Jakobsohn, Seamstress."

"Jakobsohn!" I exclaimed with astonishment as I recalled the Jakobsohn who had once helped me in a time of need.

"Yes," she said. "My name is Golda Jakobsohn. Why are you so surprised?"

"I have known your father for a long time. He once helped me in a time of dire need."

"My father has been dead these last few years," she sighed and, before we could bid each other farewell, a thunderclap brought on a drenching downpour. She invited me to wait in her house until the rain ceased. Needless to say, I accepted with great joy. I was very pleased with this rain. For my part, Noah's flood could come again and I would seek refuge here—in his Ark.

The house consisted of one room partitioned with a drape. Half of the room was a bedroom, the other half a sitting room. One could see at a glance that the inhabitants of the house were poor but not lazy or demoralized. There were several old stools and a sofa, covered with a yellowed, threadbare cotton spread. Near the wall stood a chest of drawers covered with a cloth as white as snow. On it were arranged various knickknacks: a pair of porcelain shells with red flowers, two polished blue vases, a little mirror, several perfume bottles, and a few more odds and ends. These constituted the sole luxuries of the house with the exception of several flowerpots on the windowsills and a portrait, embroidered in silk, of Moses holding the Commandments in his hand. On a workbench near the window were stacked linens, threads, and all the other implements of the seamstress' trade.

Upon entering the house, Golda introduced me to her mother-a thin, emaciated woman of about fifty years—and related to her how we had met in the street a few moments before. Her mother made me welcome and asked me to sit down. At the other end of the table, a little girl of about eight was seated on a stool, ostensibly sewing, but every so often she would steal a glance at me out of the corner of her eye. Golda also sat down at the table and unpacked the bundle which she had almost lost. For a few moments I sat like a bashful bridegroom and couldn't say a word. My heart jumped for joy as I watched Golda's plump, white little hands busily working away.

Then a conversation developed about the weather and how much this rain was needed. The old lady must have repeated at least ten times that it was not rain that was falling from heaven, but bread. She expressed the hope that after this downpour the price of flour would fall a few groschen. Golda, in the meanwhile, winked to her mother and left the room. The old lady remained sitting near me and brought the conversation around to her husband's death, may his sojourn in Paradise be bright, and to how he had been ill for a long time until every last copper was gone. Then he died, leaving her a destitute widow with two children to feed. But, the Lord be praised, He had blessed her with a daughter the like of whom could not be found in the whole wide world. Her Golda is gentle and pious. She has every virtue. She works, the poor thing, night and day, sews, knits, ruins her eyes with the needle in order to eke out a meager existence.

"We live in poverty, in misery. Her bitter drudgery hardly suffices for the bare necessities, but we don't complain because, after all, we're still alive. God knows what would have happened to us if not for Golda.

"Of course, I should be happy—I should be overjoyed with this gift from Him. But my heart weeps within me," she said with a deep sigh as the tears started into her eyes, "when I see Goldenyu toiling for all of us, straining every nerve. . . . She risks her health, her life, and doesn't allow herself to spend even, one may say, a broken farthing. I say to her: 'Goldenyu! My dear soul! Take pity on your own life. Buy yourself a trinket, a delicacy, anything! And rest a little, my child.' And she always answers me with a little laugh. 'I don't need any delicacies, Mama! I'm not ill, God forbid. Let them buy delicacies who sit with folded hands and don't know what to do with themselves. And so far as resting is concerned, for that we have our glorious *Shabes*.' That's how she always answers me, with a joke, and she continues working, quietly, like a dove. May her troubles fall upon my head! "

As she finished talking, Golda entered with a tray on which were four glasses of tea.

By the time we had drunk our tea, it had stopped raining. Golda told her little sister to go to sleep.

"Go, Sheyndele," she said, patting her head. "It's time for you to go to bed. You'll get up earlier. Your teacher probably won't be here today."

Sheyndele kissed her mother, then her sister, said "good night" to everybody and went to sleep. It was time for me to leave also. I got up, said goodbye, and left.

130

The half-moon was like a golden ship gliding through the great blue ocean of air which was still, without the slightest breeze. The sky, like an enamored bridegroom, looked down with thousands of starry eyes upon his beloved earth which was bedecked in a green dress of grass, garlanded with all sorts of flowers which emitted sweet and captivating scents like the most expensive perfumes. The frogs croaked lustily in the ponds and somewhere, in a garden, the song of the nightingale was heard. The nightingale—is there another such singer in the world?—far better than all the cantors taken together!

My heart was in song, too. I hummed as I walked, neither knowing nor caring about the melody. When I approached my house, I was taken aback, for suddenly I realized that I had been humming Leyzer the tailor's chant, the one which was sung as the bride was prepared for her wedding!

"Go to hell!" I jokingly scolded Leyzer and, with a joyful smile, sent him to blazes.

Yet, after such a happy encounter, I had sad dreams all night. I dreamed of people crying out their very eyes—cries of people from the bowels of the earth: "Lord! O Lord! What do they want from us?"

131

CHAPTER 15

▲▲ I became a frequent visitor at Golda's house. I was drawn there as if by a magnet. Was I attracted by her virtues, or by her excellence of character, or by the sweet patience with which she supported an old mother and a young sister by the sweat of her brow? No! A disciple of Issar's could not appreciate such things.

Money, that was the measure for judging the qualities of a person, that was the scale on which to weigh his virtues. A sharp fellow, a man of the world, was he, in my estimation, who had money and lived in luxury. How he came by this money, at whose expense he was rolling in riches—this was no concern of mine. Only paupers, ne'er-do-wells, concern themselves with such trifling thoughts. They do so from vexation and envy, and because they conceal their own faults by such gossip. They smooth away the very reason for their being paupers, ne'er-do-wells, good-for-nothings. This gossip soothes their own hearts and throws dust in the eyes of the world by saying that they are poor only because they have good character, only because they couldn't be like others—false-hearted and unscrupulous.

No! It was not Golda's purity of character that attracted me. It was only her pretty face. I was drawn to her with a wild, uncontrollable emotion. Where this love was driving me, I had as yet no idea. In the meanwhile, I continued to visit her. At first, I brought her work. I had her sew my shirts, sleeves, cuffs. Afterwards I came as a good family acquaintance.

During my visits, I frequently met the young man with whom she had been strolling that *shabes* when I first saw her. He was very much at ease in the house, as if he were part of the family. He gave lessons to Sheyndele, helped with the various household chores, brought home things from the market, and even lent them money when they were badly in need. He was addressed with the familiar "thou" and was called by his first name—Michael.

Michael was a writer who earned his living by teaching boys and girls to read and write. From one of my conversations with the old lady, I realized that Michael was a pillar of strength for the family, that without his support they would be in a very bad way indeed. He was a distant relative of theirs and was practically

132

engaged to Goldenyu. For the time being, this was still a secret to outsiders, but she hoped that, in a very short time, she would be able to have the marriage contract drawn up and publish the banns. These words pierced me like daggers, but I feigned nonchalance, as if I weren't bothered in the slightest.

Henceforth, I regarded Michael as my worst enemy. I began to entertain thoughts of getting rid of him. I would sidle up to Golda and her mother, as innocent as a little kitten, with soft, sweet words. I would play with Sheyndele, frequently bringing her candies and toys, in the hope of gaining a foothold in the house and thus brushing Michael aside. I even tried to offer them some money once when I noticed that they were sorely pressed, but Golda returned the money to me with a smile that taught me my place and was, in effect, much worse than a slap. This increased my hatred for Michael a thousandfold. Inside, I was burning with the fires of hell, but the more my hatred increased toward Michael, that much more did I disguise it always speaking to him with honeyed words, always greeting him with a pleasant mien.

Disguising my feelings was a well-known art to me by that time. That is one of the first things that a little man must know. When Issar finally convinced himself to dig someone's grave, to assassinate his character, he began to greet the victim with great warmth, running to meet him, and practically falling on his neck. The kiss of death should be given gently, quietly, so that it will pass unnoticed in the world. That was Issar's policy.

I would come to see Golda decked out in my very best, my hair thickly pomaded so as to please her and discredit Michael in her eyes—Michael, who was always dressed simply. But Golda was not at all impressed by fine clothes. She once informed me very gently that it was easy to catch cold from the pomade on someone's hair. At that, Michael smiled, while I fumed and foamed inwardly.

"Feh, Michael!" Sheyndele exclaimed once. "Look at how you are dressed! Reb Itsik-Avreml looks splendid. He dresses nicely. He shines with red cheeks and lips like a pretty girl."

"Silly child," Michael answered calmly. "What can I do if I am poor and don't have a position which brings me money for everything I want?"

I felt that Michael was poking fun at me for being a lackey and was trying to discredit me in the eyes of the others. But I swallowed my pride, bit my lip, and said nothing.

The summer and part of the autumn passed in this fashion. I was almost beside myself with uncontrollable emotion, but there was nothing to be done. Michael was like a bone in my throat. If I did not hasten to remove it, I would soon choke on it. The day was approaching when Golda and Michael were to be married. The old lady loved him like her own son and could hardly wait for the day when the two of them would be united eternally. Sheyndele jumped for joy. She teased Michael and clasped him to her with both her little hands. Golda looked at them with moist pleasure in her blazing eyes and blushed as red as a beet. At this time she was simply dazzling—her face was aflame and shone like the fiery sun—so pretty was she. I expressed feigned pleasure, as was to be expected from a good acquaintance who shared the joys of the family. But my heart was a seething inferno. Upon leaving, I ground my teeth and swore that I would find a good method to clear this obstacle from my path.

It was not long before I found the desired solution. When the levy for new recruits was imposed upon the town, I worked it out quietly, through Issar, so that Michael was taken away as a soldier!

At Golda's, it was like the destruction of the Temple. When I arrived, the household was steeped to the lips in misery. The old lady was in bed, sick, with a wet kerchief tied around her head. Golda was as pale as the plastered wall, her eyes red and swollen. She wandered around aimlessly, her hair unkempt, forlorn, completely overcome. Sheyndele was a different person—crouched in a corner, her hands crossed listlessly in her lap, staring blankly at the ground. They burst into tears as I entered the house, the sizzling, wordless tears which seize people stricken down by misfortune upon seeing their best friend.

"What has happened here?" I asked innocently and remained standing in dull amazement.

For several minutes there was no answer. Then the old lady spoke in a tearful voice, choked with sobs:

"Woe is me! Michael . . . no more Michael! The recruiting gang—O woe is me!—has snatched him!"

And a new reservoir of tears burst its floodgates within her. Golda sat near her on the bed with her face in her hands. Her mother patted her head and all of them wailed and moaned as if at a funeral.

I exhibited as sad an aspect as I could muster. I sighed and groaned, but my heart was glad as I looked at Golda and saw that no one barred my way now. I devoured her with my eyes, from head to toe, as the wolf must size up the lamb he is about to swallow. And I said to myself:

"You will be mine. You won't escape me now! . . ."

CHAPTER 16

▲▲ The months rolled by. Michael had been shipped far, far away. Golda's household was in ruins. The little family was crushed and undone. The flowers wilted in their pots; no one had a mind to water them regularly. The knickknacks on the chest of drawers were in disorder and a thick layer of dust coated the silken portrait of Moses. He brooded morosely and peered from his glassed-in frame with resentment and wrathful indignation. At any rate, that was my impression and I was careful not to look at him. Sheyndele's lessons had ceased and she no longer had anyone to play with. She lost weight and seemed to flicker like a dying candle.

Golda's face was the color of ash. No longer did her sunny smile light it with its golden rays. It was as if she had lost all desire to live. The old lady looked at her children, wistfully shook her head, and bathed in her tears. Occasionally, her strength failed her and she had to lie in bed.

I began to visit more frequently. I sat with Golda while she worked and encouraged her with sweet and honeyed words, seeking by these means to establish a foothold in her heart. Poverty gripped the household ever more tightly. Golda's work, no matter how much she struggled, sweated, and fought, did not suffice to supply even the basic necessities. It became ever more clear what a mainstay Michael's assistance had been and how they had depended on it. Now this help was no longer forthcoming, and, to make matters worse, there was very little work for Golda.

Once, it was necessary to fill a prescription for the old lady at the druggist's and there was not even a groschen in the house. I suggested to Golda that she borrow some money from me. Golda flushed, lowered her eyes, and didn't say a word. It was obvious that a storm raged in her heart, a storm of bitter feelings. I made it clear to her that it was a loan for a short time, until she could repay it, and that she must accept it because her mother needed this prescription on which, possibly, her life depended. Just then, the old lady groaned loudly in her bed and Golda became agitated. She hurriedly took the money with a hand that was cold as ice, wrapped herself in a shawl, and ran from the house. . . .

Late one night, I lay in bed tossing on my pillow. Sleep had deserted me. My love for Golda tortured me cruelly. It allowed me no peace. I wondered how it would end. How long would I torture myself like this and do nothing to bring the matter to a head? And what was my aim? Marriage? But marriage was a difficult thing for me to think of. It did not pay! First, I would have to give up my position with Issar, and leaving Issar meant leaving easy money, an easy life with no troubles, no bother, no headaches. It meant giving up all my plans for the future. Second, what would I get from her? Nothing! She would come to me stripped and shorn, naked as a new-born babe. She would bear me many children who would eat me out of house and home—and then? Then I would be a pauper, a good-for-nothing, a helpless creature who suffers, who is buffeted about like I was in my youth. And all this, for what? For love! Issar, I thought, would laugh himself sick when he heard about it!

"Love is nothing but a pretty face, a soap-bubble which plays before one's eyes with all the colors of the rainbow and suddenly—poof! It's gone, you don't know how or where. It's a plaything, a trifle, which should be purchased for no more than a trifle. It can easily be had if one is not a fool. Love is a pretty cover which makes it easy for one person to ensnare another. It is a cleverly woven web for the capture of weaklings who melt like snow under the first warm rays of the spring sun." This was Issar's definition.

Should I not be a fool and try to accomplish my purpose in such a crude fashion? Out of the question! Knowing Golda as I did, it was impossible for me to entertain any such idea. Her bearing was so dignified that one had to respect her. Even the tongue controlled itself so as not to utter anything verging on the vulgar in her presence. I had, on one occasion, made a remark which was not quite proper, although most people wouldn't have noticed it, let alone comment upon it, but Golda's face took on such an expression that a cold chill traversed every limb of my body. No! Women like Golda could not be purchased or ensnared, even if one had the cunning of ten devils.

Should I spit at the whole affair and forget her? This, I felt, was beyond my strength. Rather would I surrender my life than her. Love may be, as Issar said, only a plaything, but I had to have this plaything. I could not live without it. I considered and reconsidered and came to the same conclusion each time—I had no choice, I must marry her!

And the harm done to my affairs? Well, I would have to find a means to keep my affairs intact and my love satisfied. I had to get married, the sooner the better. I had no strength left to struggle any

137

more. I had to bring the situation to a head. Golda must be mine! With this thought I fell asleep and dreamed sweet dreams.

The following morning, I awoke rather late and decided that I would declare my intentions to Golda that evening, come what may. It was just before Passover and Golda was very hard pressed for money for the holidays. This would be a most favorable time for me.

When I arrived, I found her sitting alone over her work. The old lady was in bed behind the partition with Sheyndele. All that could be heard from the other side was a coughing—first the old lady and then Sheyndele, as if they were competing to outdo each other. In a corner, a cricket chirped sadly. The combination of these sounds resulted in a chilling, macabre concert. Golda was worried and sewed without letup, continually wielding the needle, not allowing herself to raise her eyes from her work for a moment.

I began by admonishing her for working beyond her capacity, for endangering her health, for having pity neither on herself nor on the household which depended entirely upon her nor on her friends to whom her health was very precious, her friends who would give their lives for her. Upon hearing these words, Golda glanced at me. I gained courage from this meaningful glance and spoke with great ardor. Finally I came out with my proposal that she was dearer to me than life itself and that I would consider myself undeservedly fortunate if she would be my wife. The needle dropped from her fingers and she sat in confusion, supporting her head with her hands. I remained silent for a few minutes. I was bathed in sweat and my heart pounded violently, as if I had just climbed a mountain.

The coughing and wheezing from behind the wall grew louder and louder. A broken pane in the window rattled and beat in morbid harmony with the howl of the wind outside. Once more I spoke, with great warmth and conviction, in order to convince Golda. I painted for her the situation in which she found herself, how she was pressed to the wall from all sides. I pointed out the state of her sick old mother and Sheyndele, how they were both suffering and wasting away. If for no other reason, then only because of them, she had to agree. I would be able to provide for all. With me they could all be happy, so that God and people would be glad. Golda looked at me. The hot tears, in large droplets, like pearls, fell from her eyes.

"Leave me, for a short time," she exclaimed in a beseeching voice. "I would like to think a little and talk it over with my mother. Then I will give you my answer."

When I arrived the following day, I found Golda sitting with her sick mother. The old lady took me by the hand, and, with her head indicating Golda, said that she was willing to turn over to me her precious gem, her treasure, her gift from His dear Name, but that I must promise to cherish and appreciate her. She also said that I must give up my position because, despite the homage accruing to me, I was in reality no more than a lackey. She felt that it would be a blemish on her honor and on that of her family to give her Goldenyu in wedlock to a lackey.

I objected to this condition and explained that it would be neither wise nor well to leave such a lucrative position which yielded me a fine income and which would help me to establish myself.

"There are many men of distinguished birth," I boasted, "who lie at my feet and envy me and who will envy me even more as time goes on. But, today, I'm just as distinguished as any of them. The point is that to quit now would be a great mistake, a transgression. For the time being, it would be much more sensible for me to remain with Issar even after we are married. What's the difference? Let us suppose that I am a storekeeper and sit in store all day, or that I am a peddler traveling on the road all week. When I am free, as well as on *shabes* and on holidays, I will be home. For the present, it must be so. As far as the future is concerned, after all God is our Father. . . . Everything will probably turn out for the best. But if you feel that being a lackey is disgraceful, then we can arrange to have a quiet ceremony, without pomp, without commotion, and without all the people of distinguished birth . . . as if it is even worth talking about them."

The upshot was that my words were accepted and we shook hands on the bargain.

"But remember! Take care of my jewel! Respect my child, my dear soul!" the old lady appealed again and burst into tears. Golda and Sheyndele also cried and sobbed, while I didn't know what to do with myself for joy and for having been able to fulfill my wishes so easily and so smoothly.

One fine day, it was Lag B'omer, Golda, her mother, Sheyndele, and I rode to a nearby village where we were married before the necessary quorum of ten Jews.

CHAPTER 17

▲▲We lived together very happily for a time after the marriage. Everyone in the house was pleased. I remained with Issar as before. I clung to him, working my gold mine as never before. Not for a moment did I forget that I was now a married man in need of money. I thoroughly reviewed all the rules and regulations of being a little man, together with Issar's commentaries and my own annotations. With eminent scholarship, I studied and delved deeply into the science of being a little man. It was high time for me to disclose to the world what an acute scholar, what a source of retribution I could be. Let the world discover that I now had a wife and debts to pay. Let it pay for my expenses! The world was large enough to absorb such a blow easily—the devil would not take it! That was the decision I had reached and I raised my prices for favors accordingly.

Issar's rich man, the big bear, danced in Issar's circus exhibition, and Issar himself, the little bear, danced in my private side show. We were both amply rewarded. The foolish public came to us at every opportunity, beseeching us to do a favor, to use our influence, to help, to act, and they paid for all this through the nose. Our affairs prospered exceptionally well. We were both highly pleased with the returns.

I had developed an overpowering love for money—the more I earned, the more I wanted. I found it difficult to part with a single ruble. At home, we lived in a miserly fashion. I tried to save and store at every opportunity and I looked as black as thunder whenever an extra groschen was spent. The old lady scowled at this and said that I counted each grain of barley in the pot and that I begrudged them their food. These complaints put me out of humor and I returned her scowls with spiteful words—that it was easy to be openhanded with other people's money and that if money grew on trees, then fine, I wouldn't be a miser! Golda sat on thorns during these exchanges. Her face became ashen, and, not infrequently, we became embroiled in a quarrel.

On one occasion, I lashed myself into such a fury that I had a very bitter argument with Golda, insulted her as only a lackey can insult, and stormed out of the house, slamming the door behind me, not to return for a week.

140

My former ardent love cooled considerably with the passing of time. Golda's attractive features became a commonplace for me. I no longer saw anything outstanding in them—a face like other faces, with a nose, with eyes. She lost her charm for me. She was just another woman. In the depths of my heart, I regretted my marriage.

"For what reason," I would think, "did I have to bind myself to such a load, to a whole family which eats me out of house and home? It was an evil hour when I permitted myself to be led astray by a pretty face into such an extravagance. Where was my mind then? Where was my reason?"

I was astonished at my thoughtlessness. I recalculated time and again how much this foolishness had cost me and how much richer I would have been had I not committed it. These thoughts so stirred up my bile that I would stalk about the house glowering at everyone, incapable of uttering a civil word. During the course of a few years, Golda drank deeply from the cup of misery. She kept her control and quietly swallowed all the ventings of my spleen. She did not even weep aloud.

And then, suddenly, the rich man, the big bear, whose soul lay in Issar's hands, died. The windmill ground to a halt. The wheels would no longer turn! With his death, Issar's circus exhibition was finished and so was my side show. It was not long before the public became aware of the new state of affairs and ceased to request favors from Issar. He was no longer a concessioner—his bear was dead.

In addition, Issar had aged a great deal. He was senile. No longer did he have the wit, the cunning, the imposing front of former days. Since he was no longer the power behind the throne, I was shorn of all my influence. In fact, I was of as much use as a counterfeit kopeck. It was true that I still had influence with Issar, but as soon as I realized that he could no longer serve any useful purpose for me, I lost all interest in him. These were his own tenets, his own words, his own precepts! I did not hesitate long and abandoned Issar about whom the reek of death hovered.

A deceased body never makes so pitiful an impression as a creature which is to all intents dead but nevertheless exhibits certain signs of life. I mention this not only with regard to myself, but also in relation to certain species, such as former tax collectors, boastful peddlers of influence shorn of their influence, deflated windbags, and all the associated specimens who, at one time or another, had profited from communal funds. A corpse is at least a corpse—it is dead and needs nothing. However, these other specimens, who had been pushed off their rung on the social ladder, are also corpses, but living and pulsing corpses, corpses which have to eat and drink and need all the other necessities of life. But what is the use, if they are helpless? They have mouths, but no arms or legs to serve them. It is heartbreaking to observe such living corpses, such helpless, stinking creatures!

Just such a creature had I become after I left Issar. I did not know what to do or where to turn. Aside from my profession as a little man, I was good for nothing else. Those were bad times indeed for me. We lived on my reserves: I brought forth the rubles and we ate. The loss of every ruble was like a pound of flesh to me, like the loss of a limb. I walked around the house in a constant fury, begrudging any and all their lives and picking quarrels at the slightest pretext. Every groschen that I gave Golda for household expenses was paid under protest.

"What do you want from me? I can't support such a family!"

I planted so many thorns in the old lady's breast that she finally became critically ill. One could see how the life within her was ebbing. She was not long for this world. I must confess that I secretly wished her to die as soon as possible. My heart anticipated with gladness the time when I would be rid of a mouth to feed.

As befits a little man, I masked my feelings and acted as if her sickness had touched me to the quick. I freely spent money for the doctor and for medicines—if only she would speed her departure. I served her as would a faithful child. I sat up with her all night giving her the prescribed doses, while my mind harped on one question only: "Oh, when will the Angel of Death come for you?"

I rose greatly in the estimation of the others for my devotion and selflessness, so much so that they forgave me my past sins. Golda often begged me to leave her mother's side and get some sleep. I never yielded.

"Go," I would say to her. "Poor thing, rest yourself and I will remain here alone. It's all right."

I recall with horror that winter night when the old lady lay in a coma with glassy eyes, mumbling feverishly, with a terrible rattling in her throat which could be heard all over the house—like the sound of wood being sawed. Golda sat nearby on a chair, more dead than alive, her eyes red with weeping, cracking her knuckles. Thin, emaciated little Sheyndele stared with frightened eyes at her

142

dying mother and sobbed, her sobs breaking into fits of coughing. Suddenly, the old lady sat bolt upright. She looked at her children and sighed deeply.

"I beg you," she called to me weakly. Then she stared at me for a full minute with a glance that pierced me through, chilling the marrow in my bones. "I beg you, have mercy on my children! They remain all alone in the world—like solitary rocks, orphans, without father or mother or relatives. I will depart this world more peacefully, I will rest in my grave with more tranquility, if you will swear this to me and fulfill it."

Again she sighed deeply, placed one hand on Golda's head and the other on Sheyndele's and blessed them both so quietly that only her lips were seen to move. Both children melted into tears and threw themselves upon their mother who hugged, kissed, and pressed them to her bosom. She soon fell back helplessly, turned her face to the wall, and, with a loud rattle, slept her final sleep.

Golda and Sheyndele wailed so pitifully that a stone would have turned. I covered my face with both hands, and, although it is a foul and shameful thing to admit, smiled with pleasure, having just been rid of a heavy burden.

The old lady was, for the time being, my second victim. A short time later, my third victim would go—thin, emaciated little Sheyndele!

CHAPTER 18

▲▲ I grew ever more irritated with sitting at home, my arms folded, doing nothing, allowing my talents to go to rot. It was a sin, upon my faith, to allow such capabilities to waste away, such talents to gather mold and become leftovers on the inventory list. This was the time when I was still young and full of ambition, when I could drive the very hardest of bargains.

"Does the whole world consist then only of Tsvuatshits?" I asked myself. "Are there no other Jewish cities where I can market my wares successfully? The world, blessed be His Name, is big. There are other Jewish cities. Jews have everywhere the same customs, the same characteristics. And Jewish bigwigs and magnates abound, may the evil eye not harm them, like pebbles on the beach, and I, probably, can gain their confidence and make them dance to my tune! Why then do I waste my time at home? Shall I wait until I eat up my last ruble so that I can suffer from poverty, misery, and torment as I did in my youth? Whenever I think of that time, I get chills and my hair stands on end! No! I must not sit here like this! While I am still young and have substantial reserves of cash, I must leave and try my fortune."

"Farewell!" I said to Golda, who was with child, one fine morning, and left for the wide world.

Glupsk was the city that attracted me most. Glupsk is a large Jewish city with many fools who love to be led by the nose. They come running to greet you, thrusting their noses forward, shoving each other, each one striving to offer his nose first, because they believe that to be so led is an obligation—a Jewish custom which should not be violated. Glupsk is a city with many societies, heads of synagogues, officials, and magnates. And the good Lord who feeds all, from the horned buffalo to the larva of the louse, also provides for these creatures as well. In short, Glupsk pleased me immensely, as if it had been designed for me. Glupsk was for me what the stagnant, slimy swamp is for the frog, a place where it can croak and enjoy its domain.

At the time, I was twenty-four or twenty-five years old, or, who knows, perhaps twenty-six or -seven. I didn't count my years, and, like many Jews of the time, I never did know the date of my birth. It was never recorded. Furthermore, of what use was such knowl-

144

edge? A birthday was for me, just as for other Jews, no occasion for rejoicing. A Jew remembers an anniversary of a death; but an anniversary of birth—what for?

I had money with me and therefore it was easy to become acquainted with the magnates of Glupsk. I announced that I had come to do some business, but in reality I was out to gain the confidence of the right man, because, aside from being a lackey, I was not worth a straw. My desire was to obtain the concession on the soul of the richest magnate in Glupsk and make him my bear, as Reb Issar had once done with his magnate.

As you well know, the richest magnate of Glupsk carried great weight in the entire province. His influence and power were beyond question. Yet, powerful as he was, he loved gossip; he enjoyed hearing about the most trivial occurrences in the city; he had to know what was cooking in every pot. It was as if we had been made for each other—gathering such information was my specialty. With such a tower of strength as this man under my yoke, I felt that not only could I make the wheels grind but I could make the earth itself follow my commands. But how could I gain his confidence? I saw that the only possibility of accomplishing this lay in my becoming fast friends with the synagogue officials and politicians of Glupsk. I devoted much thought to the possible procedures to be adopted.

As time progressed, I became more and more acquainted with the city. The matchmakers did not allow me a moment's rest. They buzzed around me like bees around a rosebush. For some reason, they were under the impression that I was a widower. How they arrived at this conclusion, I never knew. Apparently, the sight of a male who lived for a length of time without a female was sufficient reason for them to conclude that I wished to be married. No other explanation made any sense to them. They fell upon me like a swarm of locusts and made propositions to me. I always listened with a tolerant smile, thinking all the while that it cost absolutely nothing to listen. On the contrary, it was a pleasure to discuss young brides, to while away the time talking about pretty women with pious Jews who extolled their charms, their virtues, their upbringing, and licked their fingers over each tasty morsel.

"For my part," I thought, "let them talk—even until they're blue in the face! Who cares?"

In the meanwhile, the matchmakers proclaimed my virtues all over the city. They spread my good name and my qualifications

145

in the finest homes: that I was wealthy, made of money; that I stemmed from a distinguished family; that I was clever and worldly wise; that I could sing beautifully. In addition, I had a most pleasant disposition, a Jewish heart with no gall.

"Very good!" I thought. "Talk! Talk, children of Israel.

"Here, have another brandy and talk to your heart's content!"

One of the matchmakers proposed a match which made me think twice. There was not much money in it, but the girl's father stemmed from a very distinguished family. In a word, it was a question of buying into an exceptional pedigree.

This sire of unusual extraction had a four-tiered name: Reb Yoisef-Markl son of Reb Monish-Leybele. He was saturated with distinguished ancestry—his lineage derived from the legendary Rabbi of Glupsk. He never did a stitch of work. His pedigree guaranteed him and his family a fine living. God had endowed him with many skinny, swarthy, ugly daughters, who, beside their many other talents, could not even pick up a dish without dropping it. Moneyed men, such as, for example, newly rich lackeys or freshly baked little men, would go to any lengths in order to become sons-in-law of Reb Yoisef-Markl son of Reb Monish-Leybele so that they might buy into his pedigree. No sooner did one of his daughters reach the mature age of fourteen or fifteen than a customer would appear who pushed all others aside and made off with the great bargain, paying a fine sum of money to boot. The daughter that was proposed to me was even swarthier and uglier than her sisters with a shriveled and shrunken face like a dried fig! To compare her to Golda was to compare an ape to a human being. But the matchmaker found no fault with her charms. In his eyes, she was full of Jewish charm.

"So what?" he asked. "So what if she is a little dark, or a little light, or who knows what? What's the difference? Who ever looks at such trifles? Who is ever concerned with them? What does a Jew care if it's a little darker or a little lighter? It's all the same, believe me! The chief thing is the stock, the pedigree. That's what you should be concerned with. That the stock I'm offering you is good, even a blind man can see."

It stands to reason that I laughed when he launched upon this little speech of his. Nevertheless, I enjoyed listening to him, and the more I listened, the more convinced was I of the practicability of the idea. The fog lifted from before my eyes, and it became clear to me that the only possible way to obtain my sought-for concession was through just this type of match. Reb Yoisef-Markl son of Reb Monish-Leybele was, after all, a politician, a communal official, a busybody, a synagogue head, a director of many of the societies, and very well acquainted with my magnate. The magnate honored him and respected his judgment, frequently consulting with him concerning matters of faith. Now, if I were to be his son-in-law, how easy it would be for me to gain the magnate's confidence! I would make him dance to some wonderful tunes. I would have thousands and live in such splendor as I had never dreamed of before. What difference does it make if she is ugly? And if Golda is beautiful, what profit do I have from her beauty? Everything tastes good with bread. . . .

The thought of Golda vexed me greatly. She was chained around my neck like a millstone. I cursed her inwardly and considered how I could best rid myself of her.

The matchmaker did not sit idle during this time. He persevered in his task. He pecked and pecked at my mind, warning me that, if I did not move quickly, another customer would appear who would snatch this kosher bargain from under my very nose. I would be very sorry then but it would be too late. I allowed myself to be convinced and, in a trice, the matchmaker, like a magician, introduced me to Reb Yoisef-Markl son of Reb Monish-Leybele. He told him about me and sung more praises in my behalf than are customarily found on a Jewish tombstone. Everything was fine and acceptable. The only condition upon which the bride's father insisted was that I should have no children from my first marriage. He absolutely refused to saddle his daughters with any strange children. I assured him that I had no such children and the matchmaker supported me, swearing to it upon his holy faith and his share of the Paradise to come.

We shook hands on the bargain and decided to delay the betrothal for a short time. I began to think in earnest about ridding myself of Golda in so quiet a fashion that never a soul should know and never a cock should crow.

CHAPTER 19

▲▲ Three weeks after the conclusion of the agreement, a carriage drove into Tsvuatshits one evening and stopped in front of Golda's door. The cold autumn wind moaned through the branches, stripping them of their few remaining yellowed leaves which fell to the ground and lay whispering to each other in tones so mournful that the onlooker's heart was gripped by deep sadness. A figure climbed out of the carriage, walked slowly to the door, and remained standing before it with a countenance that expressed revulsion at the thought of grasping the knob.

This being was none other than my own honorable self.

Upon entering the house, my heart sank. I stood speechless at the door. Golda sat alone on the floor in a corner of the room, supporting her head face down on a bench as if she were dozing. She did not notice my entrance. A wax candle burned with a red flame on the windowsill. Near it stood a glass of water and a piece of linen. I soon realized the significance of these objects and many feelings awakened within me. I recalled my first visit to this house, how happy and attractive it had appeared at that time. How joyously a poor family had lived here! They had all loved each other, hoped for the future, and lived cheerfully and contentedly with their hopes. Then, like the cat that steals into the nest of a brood of happy, peaceful doves, I appeared and ruined the members of this family one after another. Michael was somewhere at the other end of the world. I had driven the old mother and now Sheyndele to their graves. And here I was, come to ruin Golda! I stepped into the room. Golda started, as if from a trance, and stared at me in confusion for a moment. Her pallid face, which told the story of all the sufferings she had undergone, and her swollen, red-rimmed eyes, which reflected the somberness of her features, momentarily awakened unexpected human feelings of pity in me. Involuntarily, I spoke to her.

"How are you, Golda?"

"A dear guest, in truth!" she exclaimed with a deep, bitter sigh and turned her face away. "After maintaining an unbroken silence for such a long time, he finally remembered that he has a wife somewhere! Here, you see how I am . . . I am wearing sackcloth and ashes. . . . *Akh*, Sheyndele, Sheyndele!"

148

"Golda!" I exclaimed. Somehow my tongue was wagging by itself without my being aware of what I said. I was very much smitten by her last words. They were spoken with a sadness deep enough to move a stone.

"Dark and dreary is my life. I would gladly wish death upon myself were it not for him. . . . Come!" She said this more softly as she got up from the floor. Behind the partition lay a sleeping baby in a little crib. Two clenched little fists covered his little mouth over which a smile flitted from time to time.

"This is why I go on living!" she said, pointing to the infant, her face much softer and almost happy now.

The baby opened its eyes, began to suck upon a little finger, and made all sorts of noises and faces. The mother was thrilled and forgot, for the moment, her bitter troubles, as if she herself had become a child. "Look here, sonny!" she said in baby-talk. "See who is standing here? It's *tya-tyee* ! See your guest? Here is your *tya-tyee!* "

Suddenly my blood boiled within me. I had promised my future father-in-law that I would bring him no children and here, before me, lay the crown prince who could ruin all my fond hopes. The feeling of pity was quickly extinguished within me. I stood as taut as a bow, staring with animosity at the unfortunate child which turned its face away and began to scream.

"Sh, shush!" Golda tried to quiet him. "Shush, my silly baby! Are you afraid of your *tya-tyee?*"

While she was bent over the child, I drew a paper from my breast pocket. Pressing it hastily into her hands, I said:

"There, you have a divorce from me!"

Golda looked up uncomprehendingly, as if she had been struck with a sledge-hammer. Her eyes glazed and she could not utter a sound.

"Listen to me, Golda! The fact is that you are no longer my wife. We have nothing to do with each other any more. But if you won't be a fool and won't make a fuss, and if you will keep the child, then I probably won't forsake you and will send you some money from time to time." At these words, Golda burst into a fit of wild laughter.

For a moment I thought that she had lost her reason.

Then the maddening laughter became a wild cry.

"Get out! Monster! You're not worthy of staying in this house one moment longer—in this house where honest people lived once who have since been sent to their graves by you! Rest easy. I won't run after the likes of you. I'm only ashamed to have to admit that you were once my husband. You can remarry without any worries! My child and I have no need of your help! As long as my body and soul are together, I will be able to earn enough with my ten fingers in a kosher manner to take care of our needs. Get out of here, I say! Forget that you have a child! Get out! O-O-out!"

I fled through the door into my carriage and departed that very night.

CHAPTER 20

▲▲ My father-in-law, Reb Yoisef-Markl son of Reb Monish-Leybele, was the golden key that opened all the doors for me into the inner world of Glupsk politics. Having bought into his distinguished pedigree, I became a man of honor myself and was finally able to worm my way into the confidence of the richest man of Glupsk. As was well known, this magnate loved to bask in the warm rays of public adoration, and the whole city—from pauper to prince, from cradle to the grave—fawned upon him and rendered homage to him. But never did he shine forth as he did after I made him play the bear *à la* Issar Varger. Jews had to open their purses for every favor. Issar's slogan became a tangible reality for me:

"In the whole wide world there is no other people so good, so golden, and so foolish as the Jews!"

My confession, which follows, will indicate to you only a tenth of a tenth of the philosophy which governed my course of action in life:

I Sinned in Being a Little Man. "I will be a little man," I said, "and may the devil take all other trades! One can never become rich by plying the other trades. One is continually insulted and oppressed. One is always the underdog, always the scapegoat, always starving at every meal. Let others work until their strength has been sucked from their marrow—I want to breathe, to loaf, to live well!"

And I Sinned in Gaining the Confidence of Others on False Pretences. Being a confidence man, a very easy and profitable business, turned my heart to stone. I did not believe in truth, in decency, in pity, in friendship, or in any of the other valuable human feelings. I believed only in that which was useful and necessary for me. I did not hesitate to tear the last crust of bread from the mouths of orphans and widows. When a pauper cried tears of blood, I was not in the least bit moved. "What use have I for your tears?" I would say to myself. "Pay me!" In other words: Dog, give me the money and choke on your tears!

And I Sinned in the Corruption of Human Dignity. Although one must not debase human beings, I did so constantly. I took a magnate, one of God's creatures with two feet, a face, and the appearance of a human being, and of him I made a bear! I fully

151

agreed with Reb Issar Varger that a rich man is one of the powers that makes the world go around. It is the custom among us Jews to praise the rich man, to agree with everything he says, and to emulate his actions. In all the actions of the public—in their dealings with each other, in their singing of praises to their children, in their life at home and in the market place, in their attitude toward matters of religion—can be seen the reflection of the tastes and character of the magnate. This behavior may be good or bad, clever or foolish, depending to a very large degree on the type of person that the local magnate is. Therefore, when I made my rich man do foolish things whose sole purpose was to fatten my purse, I also caused many other people to lose their dignity and act foolishly. The more foolishly they acted, the more did they think that their actions were truly in keeping with Jewish tradition. Fools became very important people and ignoramuses reached the greatest heights. . . . I, woe is me, observed this chaos and was delighted with my fools. I looked at them as a cattle dealer looks at his cattle, estimating, with glee in my heart, the amount of income that would accrue to me from each of them.

And I Sinned in Making My Own Laws. The justices, the judges, the interpreters of the law were all at my beck and call. They did as I wished. Their interpretations were unheard of, wild, but they suited my purposes. What was permitted, they prohibited. What was kosher, they made *treyf*—as long as it suited me. They could not afford to cross me for fear of losing their means of earning a livelihood. For example, they decided that large roosters were a variety of eagle and consequently *treyf*, unfit for eating according to our laws. I had them make this decision because I had an agreement with the tax collector who levied a fixed tax for each slaughtered fowl regardless of size. If the public were to eat these large roosters instead of the smaller ones, both he and I stood to lose a good deal of money.

And I sinned in the Use of Blackmail. If anyone were so bold as to complain about the manner in which I controlled the city, if he could not bear the corruption and the way in which the public was being fleeced, if he protested against the arrogance with which the people were being led by the nose into a filthy mire of swindle, I and my colleagues sent a note of denunciation to proper quarters. We silenced many a critic in this fashion.

And I Sinned in the Use of Deception. I squeezed blood from a turnip and milk from a stone. I made black into white and white into black. I made sages of fools and fools of sages. When I so desired, a rooster became an eagle and a broomstick became a gun. My tricks were so varied that the best magician would have been bewildered.

And I Sinned in the Fixing of Elections. Any man running for office must have certain qualities: honesty, understanding, intelligence, an ability to speak and to write. These are qualities which maintain the reputation of the government in the eyes of the world and which improve the welfare of the people. So far as I and my clique were concerned, however, these qualities in a candidate were the gravest of vices. I needed candidates who would neither maintain the reputation of the city nor improve the welfare of the people—what was good for the people was usually bad for me. I needed a charlatan, a good-for-nothing, a yes-man who would bend in whatever direction I dictated, who would sell his soul for a groschen, who would dance attendance upon me and my clique. Since the people of Glupsk were like foolish little children, they always cast their vote for my yes-man in the communal elections. They voted in a hurry and regretted it at their leisure. Does a child ever consider the future? He is ready to fulfill your slightest wish so long as you reward him with a cooky or a sweet. It is true that later his belly will hurt and he will twist and turn in pain, but he never thinks of that. The public, those foolish children, had neither the cooky nor the sweet from me, but they had the belly-ache all the same.

And I Sinned in Being a Member of Societies. Philanthropic societies attracted me very much because of the revenue that they were capable of yielding. Do-gooders acquire prestige—they are humanitarians and protectors of the faith. They also quietly amass a comfortable fortune by their good deeds. My father-in-law had earned the title of "Secret Dispenser of Funds," that is, he was a man in whose trust the funds of the various societies were deposited, who kept them under the closest surveillance, and who was the only one who knew how the money was spent. I, too, was very active in many societies and earned the title of "Trusted One"—in short, I was a do-gooder whose word was holy. Whatever course of action I proposed or undertook was assumed to be wise, and I was accountable to no one. Each of us, however, according to our natures and ingenuity, made certain that a substantial share of the funds found its way into our pockets.

And I Sinned in the Collection of Taxes. The tax on meat is collected by the tax bureau or "The Box." "The Box" is a stinking,

153

filthy place which breeds vermin, reptiles, and serpents. "The Box" produces the little men, the vampires, who suck the lifeblood of the people and contribute nothing but damage. "The Box" is a plague which spoils the blood, shrivels the spirit, poisons our lives and all Jewish activities and undertakings. Because of the tax, Jews are sick, undernourished, and emaciated. Because of the tax, they suffer from various debilitating diseases which are transmitted from generation to generation—only because they can never afford to eat enough meat. The tax gives us the excuse for fleecing the public. And I, woe is me, was one of those little men. I suckled on the breast of the tax and was its staunch defender whenever it was attacked. I knew that as long as Jews have a tax on meat, they will always be in the power of the little men, like me and my clique, who will be able to control them like children and make them sing their tune. I supported the tax and the tax supported me. I ate the choicest cuts of meat for nothing. The poor paid through the nose and gnawed on bones. They, the poor, were the lambs and I was the wolf. I throttled, I devoured, I sucked enough Jewish blood during my lifetime.

And I Sinned in the Misuse of Fear of the Lord. I cloaked all my swindles with the mantle of piety. I did everything in the name of the Lord whose Jews I was protecting and whose status quo I was maintaining. For me and my clique, the most desirable status quo was that the people should remain fools, down-trodden and oppressed. Whenever anything was suggested to better the life of the people, I and my crowd promptly labeled it as a scheme of the devil and exerted all our cunning to eliminate the plague. We considered it an infernal scheme, for example, that Jewish children should be taught to read, write, and figure in order to earn an honorable livelihood. We considered it an attack on our faith when it was proposed that Jews should discard their contemptible medieval garb, which had been forced on them centuries before by their enemies, and wear more modern clothes. Certainly, any suggestion to abolish the meat tax was immediately labeled an attack upon our Jewishness. We never suffered from these plagues. On the contrary, we made a pretty penny from them, and many of us still do.

And I Sinned in lying, in using vulgar language, in blasphemy, in spreading gossip and slander, in being disrespectful, in making false accusations, and so on and on. There is no need to dwell upon these, for their meaning is plain for all to see.

CHAPTER 21

▲▲ I have said previously that I was not inherently a fool or a dolt, but rather that I was down-trodden and neglected. Similarly, it appears, I was not inherently cruel, but I was misled. The terrible trials to which the world exposed me in my youth, combined with Issar's philosophy of life, had turned my heart to stone and made me vicious. After having committed a particularly cruel swindle, I frequently found myself the subject of momentary torment by a very uncomfortable feeling which pricked me like a pin—but only for a moment. Then it disappeared. Take Gutman, for example! Such a courageous, decent man—who had treated me with every consideration—I avoided him and all his friends like the plague! When anyone like him crossed my path selling his books, I would trip him up as if he were my worst enemy. Of course, it was evil on my part, but I had no choice other than to hate such people.

"The people who produce those little books should never have been born. They should be hated! One should beware of them as one bewares of fire! Their sole occupation is to crawl under another person's skin, delve into his soul, and create disturbances with their descriptions and telling thrusts. For them, everything is either round or pointed—there is no middle road. As it is fortunate that the ass has no horns, it is equally fortunate that such pests have no money. They haven't a groschen to their names, and, praised be the Lord, they are compelled to come to us for a few coppers. There is only one effective means to prevent these vermin from biting, and that is to stuff their mouths with a few groschen. This generosity on our part also corrupts them and digs their eventual graves!"

Thus spoke Issar Varger. And for me, Issar's word was the holy truth!

This was true while I was under the spell of my evil genius which urged me ever onward to acquire more and more money, when the specter of poverty was continually before my eyes, striking fear into my heart. Under these conditions, what room was there in my soul for decent feelings?

Later, however, when I grew unshakably wealthy, satiated as it were, when the fear of poverty had become a remote image of the dim past, my evil genius weakened. My hibernating good genius

155

bestirred himself, crawled from his hiding place in the recesses of my heart, and began to reproach me, quietly at first, in a dignified manner, but growing ever louder and more insistent, until my mind was filled with an angry roar. Certain events and circumstances, especially in more recent years, have been like oil on the fires of the hell that was within me.

It is said that the woman makes or breaks the home. In other words, as the wife is, so is the house. My experience has proved this to be true. I do not wish to speak here about my wife. I forgive her . . . the point is what happened to my home. My home, I say, was no home. It was neglected; expensive furniture, trimmings, decorations but dirty, filthy, hideous to see, with the aspect of a corpse. The house was dominated by a feeling of gloom. It smelled of decay, not at all like a home. When I was younger and engrossed heart and soul in the hunt for gold, I overlooked it—pish, it's nothing at all! And if I sought pleasure, it was away from home, among strangers. As one grows older, however, there comes a desire for peace and quiet. One would like to sit with one's family in one's own house. It was then that I realized my misfortune, how lonely I was, how desolate. I had no home. My life ceased to be pleasant. I reconsidered my way of life and began to regret my actions.

"Heavenly Father, how I have sinned! Good Lord, of what use was all this effort, all this commotion?" I asked. "Of what use are these riches, for whom?"

My two children, weak and sickly, had recently died. This broke my heart. I was thunderstruck. With a bitter countenance, I asked myself again and again: "These riches, what good are they when I am all alone in the world, when I have no home? Heavenly Father, I have sinned terribly—and for whom?"

At times like these, I always thought of Gutman. He was so friendly, so warm to everyone he met. The poor man was a pauper, but his home sparkled. The remotest corner was spotless! And how much pleasure he had with his dear wife, who was expert in managing her household, and from his fine, educated children who sincerely loved and respected him! He suffered from poverty, but he was always gay and happy.

Once, I remember, his wife wept bitterly. The Passover holiday was almost upon them, a matter of a few days, and there wasn't a groschen in the house to buy what was needed. He sent me out all day with his books, but no one would come near them. His faithful wife, the good woman, who loved him dearly, was broken-hearted and wept miserably.

"*Akh*," Gutman encouraged her. "Don't sin, my dear soul, with your tears! We are still better off than the rich swindlers who feast with their unholy gold. We haven't, God forbid, stolen from anyone or hurt anybody. We're suffering? But it's much better to suffer with the truth than to be happy with a lie. Don't worry, dear heart, don't! God has helped before and God will help again. After all, He has no choice. He will have to do something. What use have I for two jackets and an overcoat? I wear only one jacket at a time. And the overcoat? Soon it will be eaten by moths. Here, Avreml, upon my word, be a good boy—take the jacket and the coat, pawn them, sell them, do what you want with them, and we'll have the *matzoh*, the bitter herbs, the parsley, and all the things we need!"

I recalled this scene frequently. I realized that Gutman was happy without money. Apparently, then, happiness was not embodied in money but consisted of something else. Somehow, only honest people were really happy. I recalled what he had once said to Jakobsohn :

"One suffers when one grovels, when one toadies, when one is a lickspittle. The sneak, the parasite, always worries. He must be on his guard forever like a thief."

Only now did I begin to realize fully how true his words had been. Gutman understood intellectually—in his mind—that a sneak was as badly off as a thief who must at all costs evade detection. But I felt this emotionally—in my heart—without offering any logical reasons. I felt that a false person could never be happy. Somehow he has a weight around his neck, his blood curdles, his head throbs—the fires of hell are within him. He feels that he is being pursued and he can find no place to hide. With what joy would he spring out of his own skin and run away from himself!

I had many terrifying nightmares. I used to dream that I held a butcher's knife in my hand which I wielded continually. All about me I heard groans, sighs, and wailings woe. The skirts of my coat were drenched in blood.

Michael, the good quiet Michael, frequently appeared before me with his face as white as a sheet. He looked at me with sorrowful eyes, showed me the chains in which he was bound, and spoke in a pained voice:

"My God! Itskhok-Avrom, what did I do to you?"

157

The old lady and Sheyndele both appeared suddenly as if they had sprung from the ground, coughing and gasping. They ate into me with their fiery, accusing eyes and screamed :

"There is our Angel of Death! There he is, the monster, the murderer! '"

And just as suddenly they collapsed into a heap of bones from which crawled worms and poisonous reptiles who dashed at me with ravenous mouths, snapping and biting, slashing me with their knifelike teeth.

But more than all others, the thought of Golda tormented me. I imagined her sitting dismally, despondently, woebegone, with a piece of work in her hands. She pricks her finger, but she doesn't feel it. She doesn't even wince. She sews on and on like a machine. She rocks a heavy cradle with her foot and sings in a maddeningly melancholy voice. But the cradle is empty. There is no one in it! "Golda!" I shout. "Where is he? Where is the child?" Golda sings on without even glancing at me:

> Ah, lyoo-lyoo-lyoo, how cruel, how wild!
> Woe to the mother and woe to the child!
> In the little crib, lying fast asleep,
> Lie a snow-white goat and a coal-black sheep.
> Baa, baa black sheep! Baa, baa, baa!
>
> Don't cry then, dear. Don't groan!
> In this world, you're all alone.
> Baa, baa, black sheep! Baa, baa, baa!
>
> Dark and dreary is your world,
> You will always suffer from hunger and cold.
> Baa, baa, black sheep! Baa, baa, baa!
>
> There, outside, do you hear? Do you hear?
> Howls the wolf and growls the bear!
> Baa, baa, black sheep! Baa, baa, baa!
>
> Empty, empty is the little crib
> No one lies there fast asleep,
> No snow-white goat, no coal-black sheep!
> Ah, lyoo-lyoo-lyoo, how cruel, how wild! Woe to the mother
>   and woe to the child!

With these words, Golda rises. Bloody tears roll down her

cheeks. She extends her hands before her and wails wildly: "Oh, my little white kid is gone!"

I flee from the house to the wolves and the bears. They are cracking young bones with their hungry teeth. In the distance, I hear the pitiful cries of an unfortunate little kid . . . .

These nightmares, these bitter feelings, tormented me so much this year that I began to ail considerably and felt that I was not long for the world. I wrote a letter to Golda in which I begged her to show mercy and forgiveness toward me for the way in which I dealt with her. I begged her, in God's Name, to visit me with our son, if he was still among the living, so that I might repent by word of mouth and depart more peacefully from the world. But several weeks have passed now, and I have had no word from Golda!

I beg you, Rabbi, to intercede in my behalf with Golda to forgive me for having made a desolate desert of her life. As you know, according to the law, Golda was not permitted to remarry. She undoubtedly lived in poverty and misery at a time when I lived in riches and honor, when I completely forgot her and the unfortunate child with which I had saddled her.

She kept her promise and forgot about me as well. She never troubled me after I had deserted her and, for shame, never mentioned who had been her husband. Golda is proud, but she is good. When you beseech her to forgive me, tell her that Itskhok-Avrom was misguided and never understood how to appreciate her, but rather, like many another husband, he thought that a wife was not entitled to any special consideration, that there was no need to cherish and respect her. Tell her, please, that before he died, Itskhok-Avrom came to love her *truly*, and that only then did he realize that

> A virtuous and loving wife
> Is the dearest thing in a man's life.

159

CHAPTER 22

▲▲The Scriptures say that, if a man's heart is troubled, he should relieve it. To suppress undisclosed troubles, to maintain silence under all conditions, is an unbearable torture, a bucket of seething molten metal which can explode at any time if the confined gases find no means of escape. My heart was raging far more violently than the confined gases in a bucket of molten metal, for within it burned the fires of hell! The sum total of all my sinful actions, my bitter regrets, and my fantastic nightmares all these, taken together, were tearing each other, and me, apart like the flaming pillars of a fire-spouting volcano. It is much better for a sinner to be in hell, than to have his hell within him.

A man can make of his life either a heaven or a hell. His judge sits within him. Lord, if I could have only poured out my heart to soften my pains a little! But I had no one to speak to. Of gold and silver I had plenty, but good friends—not one.

I consider it an act of charity on the part of Him who is our Father that He showed me the way to voice my feelings. The same God who indicated how water might be struck from a stone in the desert showed me how to lighten my sufferings—by means of the pen.

In my worst, darkest moments, when I was most sorely troubled, I poured out my flood of bitter feelings on paper as well as I knew how. At first it was difficult for me. I was not used to it. Later, the words flowed of themselves, as if I were talking to a good friend and uncovering for him my innermost feelings. In the course of time, these writings grew into a history of my life, and upon rereading them from beginning to end, my sufferings were greatly eased! The crimes did not appear to weigh so exclusively on me, that is, these were not only my own crimes, the crimes of an individual, but in large part—perhaps for the most part—they were attributable to society and its evil customs.

Take our Jewish *Talmud-Toyres* for example.

Poor Jewish children, orphans, are driven into a hovel, a stable in truth, where they wallow in dirt and filth, where they are whipped and beaten as much as their poor bodies can stand, and where they learn—not a single word. They are turned into miserable, unhappy people who are useless to God and man. And no better than the vicious *melamdim* are the pious solicitors of charity

160

funds who go from door to door with their collection boxes, collaring anyone and everyone for a donation ostensibly to educate poor Jewish children. They explain their activity by saying that they are trying to make Jews of the poor unfortunates—but, in reality, they make them inhuman. They make them into beasts, cattle!

What I, a poor neglected orphan, underwent in the *Talmud-Toyre* as a child is not to be underestimated! I am not speaking of the torments which were inflicted on my emaciated body; after all, I was born in poverty in order to suffer from hunger, cold, and beatings. But good God, what did they want with my soul? They corrupted my human feelings! It was bad enough that I was not taught how to live in the world like a human being, but they went further. They killed in me the feeling of human dignity, of the value and worth of the human being, with their foul treatment, with their curses, with their filthy, vulgar language. Such is the *Toyre*, the Jewishness, which our pious philanthropists inculcate in poor children!

And another example, take the attitude toward handwork.

Working with one's hands has fallen into terrible disrepute among Jews. Just as a ne'er-do-well, a parasite, is regarded as a swindler, so is the craftsman regarded as a blot on the family honor. Anyone who by any stretch of the imagination can call himself an independent business man, although his belly be swollen with hunger, will not teach his children a trade that is even remotely connected with handwork. For this type of work God has provided enough castaway orphans, children of the lowly common people. It is the latter who become apprentices to the handworkers in whose good graces are entrusted their education and future development. The apprenticeship generally starts with the dirtiest work: carrying the slop-pails, fetching water from the well, watching the baby, carrying the mistress' purchases home from the market, delivering finished work all over the city, being a flunkey to each and all, and suffering all manner of insults and gibes. For dessert, the apprentice is privileged to listen to the vile language current among handworkers, love stories with pornographic twists, which will almost certainly extinguish any remnant glowing embers of human feeling that may accidentally have survived in him. That is how the apprenticeship begins. How does it end? With nothing at all! One becomes a rag-patcher, and a sloppy one at that.

Nor is it entirely the fault of the handworkers. They, just like me and thousands of other poor children, have led bitter lives. They, too, started by carrying pails of slop and garbage. Only now did I understand the tragic humor of the little shoemaker's song, the one with which he would accompany me when I carried out his slop-pail :

"All honor to Itsenyoo! Carry, carry it well, Itsik-Avremenyoo! When I was your age, I had carried many a pail of slops!"

Good Lord in heaven! I am a sinner, but the sins do not rest entirely upon my shoulders. I give thanks to you, O God, for having opened my eyes!

O God! You have not opened my eyes in vain! I want to do what I can to protect others from these evils and to point up to Jews the right road—how to redress the injustices which have been inflicted upon generations of poor little children.

According to my will—of which I am sending you a separate copy, Rabbi—I want my big house to be made over into a *Talmud-Toyre* for poor children and also into a school where they can learn some decent trade. The income from my various enterprises and part of my investments shall be used for the upkeep of both schools. I desire that, along with Jewish studies and the holy tongue, the *Talmud-Toyre* shall also teach the language of our country and various secular subjects, so that the children may become both good Jews and good human beings, of use to both God and man. In the other school, the children shall be taught *Toyre* and useful crafts together. The apprentices shall be subjected to no humiliations, no insults, no corrupting influences. Let them learn to be well-educated craftsmen who will know their own worth and who will therefore be able to compel others to appreciate and understand their value.

In order to accomplish these aims, it is imperative to have good teachers in these schools, people with compassion and understanding, with hearts as well as minds, who love their work. The main idea is Love, because, after all, they will be dealing with poor, neglected, castaway children who yearn for love. Love is something sought for by every young heart, even among other living creatures, and these children lack it dreadfully. An encouraging word from one who loves them is infinitely more effective than all the scoldings and moralizings in the world. They will be ready to go through fire and water for someone who loves them well. I felt like that myself occasionally when I was a child.

162

All these plans demand good administrators who will see to it that the intent and purpose which I have set down here will be fulfilled. I desire that you, Rabbi, and Herr Gutman, should be in charge of both institutions. Under your guidance, the new schools will unite both learning and wisdom. You, Rabbi, will look after the Jewish subjects and Herr Gutman will look after the other matters.

Since I know both of you fairly well, I feel that you will both get along well together. Both of you desire the best for the children of Israel and each of you will do all he can to serve them well. The payment for this work is stipulated in my will.

The income from funds which are to be used for the general welfare shall be allocated as the two of you see fit. If, for example, there would be the possibility of establishing a city school for many children, with honest *melamdim* and teachers, a school which will teach Jewish and secular subjects, where the children will be taught to be good Jews and useful, educated human beings, I would be very pleased if you would allocate a sum of money annually from the general welfare funds toward the maintenance of such a school—but with the proviso that you and Gutman should be in charge of its administration.

I know that a city school, administered by such people as you and Gutman, would be a blessing for Jewish children. But I also know that, because such a school would be a blessing, there will be many little men who will not like the idea. They will oppose the idea and they will cloak their opposition with a mantle of piety, claiming that such an institution is anti-Jewish. They will seek, with all the means at their disposal, to prevent the establishment of such an institution. Nevertheless, Rabbi, you will kindly try to do all that can be done to further this idea.

What will be done for poor children here, in my city, is not enough. One swallow does not make a summer. Others must be moved to do the same thing in every city where Jews live. Therefore, I request that my confession and my will be published so that they shall ring in the ears of the rich, the politicians, among the Jewish people wherever they be. If my words do not convince them to improve themselves during their lifetime—to understand how to work for their unfortunate brethren, to do good deeds, to live like human beings—then maybe they will learn how to die like human beings. I have met many rich men in my time and all of them remained to the very last what they had been throughout their lives—they died like fools. Let them listen to the words of my confession and, observing me, let them at least learn to depart this world like wiser men.

Until my confession can be published for others to read, Rabbi, I would like you to read it, before my burial, to all our local rich men. For me, it will be an exposition of shame; for them, it will be a moral lecture. It's all right, let them hear it!

For the correction of these papers, for the elimination of the obvious errors, for the addition of salt and pepper, a bit of spice, so that this chronicle may be more readable, for their publication and dissemination among people we have an expert in Reb Mendele Moykher Sforim. I remember him from Tsvuatshits when he was still quite a young man. Please give these papers to him. I hope that he will fulfill my wishes to the best of his ability. Naturally, he should be well paid for his work. ▲▲

CHAPTER 23

When the Rabbi finished reading and laid down the manuscript, the wealthy gentlemen stirred uneasily. They were very irate. Some of them sat quietly, biting their lips with restrained fury. Others sighed, groaned, or growled.

"Why are you sighing like that, Reb Khone?" asked one of the gentlemen, sighing heavily himself.

"Ta-ta-ta!" Reb Khone shook his head. "So that's where. . . that's where he landed! Now how can you trust people? I must say, the world has certainly fallen low . . . very low. . . . It's no longer recognizable. Wha-a-a-t a shame! Wha-a-a-t. . . . What's that you say? A horror, upon my word as a Jew! It would appear that. . . What a story, Reb Berish!"

"But I saw directly from the beginning in which direction the bullets were flying!" said Reb Berish. "Ai, ai, I have a keen nose for such things, Reb Khone. And why did we sit here like fools, waiting like cattle to be led to slaughter? Didn't I say right at the start: 'Feh, feh! Let's go!' Why then did you remain? To listen to all the needling reproaches until the bitter end? But then, on the other hand. . . . True, it's a bit . . . painful, but it's not so terrible. We've heard such things before. Why the commotion? Ta! A fool remains a fool, and the rest of the world goes on, yes, goes on just as it did before."

"No, no, Rabbi!" several gentlemen protested with deeply offended voices. "This is unprecedented! To tell people such things right to their faces! Where is justice?"

"To make people into . . . into . . . who asked him to do it? Speak for yourself, write for yourself, but what business is it of yours to pick others apart? What right do you have to delve into other's. . . No, Rabbi! It's a great injustice."

"Well, Reb Mendele?" the Rabbi approached me after the wealthy gentlemen had left. "Tell me, who is this Herr Gutman in Tsvuatshits?"

"It's been a long time since I've lived in Tsvuatshits, Rabbi. Soon after I became a book seller, I moved my family from there to Kabtsansk and today I'm a Kabtsanskan Jew!"*

---

* The Hebrew-Yiddish word *kabtsn* means "pauper." Hence, Kabtsansk is the equivalent of "the city of the poor," or Pauperville.

"But do you know Herr Gutman, Reb Mendele?"

"Yes, I remember him very well—a German with a trimmed beard, but a very honest and good-natured person. It is said: 'Better a Jewish heart without a beard, than the beard without a Jewish heart!' "

"Then I beg you, Reb Mendele, to go without delay, tomorrow morning, to Tsvuatshits. Look up this Herr Gutman, deliver this letter of mine to him, and do what you can to persuade him to come here immediately so that we can fulfill the will of the dead. Furthermore, I must ask you, Reb Mendele, to take the manuscript and publish it in many copies at a cheap price so that it may be widely read, and spread it in all corners of the world, wherever Jews are to be found. As far as payment is concerned, there's no point in talking about it—it will be fair."

Upon returning to the synagogue, I found my horse in a deplorable state. The brats and mischief-makers had torn almost all the hairs from his tail, leaving him some forty to switch with. All he had to eat was dust. He was standing very seriously, his lower lip hanging down, as he contemplated the books in the wagon. What does a horse think about when he looks at books? That's not for our minds to grasp. All I know is that my *shlimazl* was looking at them and thinking, maybe in his own horse-language, but thinking nevertheless.

"Well, my sage," I said to him, taking him by the mane. "Today I owe you lots of oats. You acted very wisely in bringing me to Glupsk. Your wisdom has profited both me and literature. Do you know, horse, what you have done? Do you realize what a fine novel I will be able to produce now for the rest of the world, only because of you, because of the workings of your brain, because you decided to come to Glupsk? From now on, you will lead me, horse o'mine! My sage, I lay aside the whip and reins from this day hence!"

On the morrow, I made ready and we left.

Upon reaching Tsvuatshits, I found that Gutman had moved from the city without leaving a trace. I attended to the other part of my assignment and have made haste to publish this book. I've spared no pains to make it, as the saying goes, round and pointed.

I wish to add the following:

HEAR YE!   PUBLIC NOTICE   HEAR YE!

Ladies and Gentlemen! If any of you know of the whereabouts of one HERR GUTMAN, should you meet him by chance or by design, please speak to him and convince him to go immediately to Glupsk, where the Rabbi is eagerly awaiting him, in order to work with him toward the establishment of a renowned *Talmud-Toyre* and a school for the training of craftsmen, as well as many other fine projects.

Take pity, ladies and gentlemen! Do it for the sake of poor Jewish children!

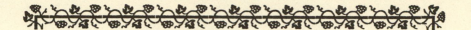

INTRODUCTION TO

Fishke the Lame

When S.Y. Abramovitsh (Mendele) was seventeen years old, he was induced to follow a wandering beggar by the name of Avreml the Limper. Mendele became part of this beggar's entourage, wandering through Lithuania, and then throughout the whole Southwest of Russia: Volhynia, Podolye, and the Ukraine. What he learned during his time (several months) as a beggar with Avreml—about the depths of Jewish poverty, Jewish communal poorhouses, Jewish charity, beggars and begging—he used in *Fishke der Krumer*. Various versions of *Fishke* (subtitled, "A Story about the Jewish Poor") were published by Mendele over the years: in 1869 in Zhitomir as a 45-page booklet, some sixteen years after Mendele's travels with Avreml; in 1876—a second version never published; in 1888—the version translated here, as released by Yiddish Bukh, Warsaw, 1953; and in 1907 a fourth version in Hebrew retitled by Mendele *Seyfer Hakaptsonim* (*The Beggars Book*).

It is true, of course, that Mendele wanted to portray the dreadful poverty of so many Jews at that time, to describe the world of the Jewish beggars and their eternal *torbe* (beggar's sack); but Mendele also wanted to, as always, upbraid a world—both the internal Jewish world and the surrounding non-Jewish world—that forced people to live this way and did little to help them. There are many interesting, pointed scenes in this novel; e.g., the scenes in Odessa where Fishke follows a young *maskil* (adherent of the *haskole*, the Jewish enlightenment) around who is trying, without success, to sell his writings to the enlightened Jewish burghers of the city: they would rather give Fishke-the-beggar money than buy an enlightened book from a *maskilic* author. Not only is this episode pointed, it is full of typically Mendelian irony and humor.

In *Fishke*, Mendele-the-Book-Peddler does more than just frame

169

or introduce the story as he usually does in Abramovitsh's other works. In *Fishke* we get to know Mendele-the-Book-Peddler himself quite well—he plays a role in the narrative itself.

Leo Wiener in *The History of Yiddish Literature in the Nineteenth Century* (1899) says of *Fishke the Lame:* "This psychological study of the impulses of the lowest dregs of society is probably unique in all literature." Theodore L. Steinberg in *Mendele Mocher Seforim* (1977) calls *Fishke der Krumer*

> Abramovitsh's most artistic novel (114)....quite simply, a masterpiece (111)....in terms of pure literary artistry, in terms of the control that Abramovitsh had over his materials, *Fishke* is unquestionably his greatest work. It is a beautiful, moving novel that can stand comparison with some of the great works in world literature; and its greatness is all the more remarkable in light of Abramovitsh's position as the pioneer of Yiddish literature. Clearly he was influenced by writers such as Swift, Sterne, Fielding, Dickens, Sue, Hugo, Dumas, Gogol, and others, but the genius that enabled him to use these writers in order to fashion a distinctively Jewish-Yiddish literature cannot be praised too highly (112).

Fishke marks a new period in Abramovitsh's creative life; rather than being experimental, bitterly satirical and didactic, or humorous and hopeful, Mendele in *Fishke* saw that "Bitter social criticism [as in *Dos Kleyne Mentshele*] would have been too cruel, and Horatian laughter [as in *Benjamin III*] would have been out of place, so Abramovitsh sought another mode. The result was *Fishke der Krumer*, in which, as Viner* says, Abramovitsh both 'celebrated the people as no one before him had and berated them for their backwardness. He was truthful rather than romantic' " (Steinberg, 112).

Perhaps *Fishke the Lame* also prefigures in many ways that great short story of I.B. Singer's, "Gimpel the Fool"; the parallels are clear.

Fishke is not a "perfect" work, but overall it continues to have lasting aesthetic value. It is one of the wonders of early modern Yiddish literature, full of humor, satire, social criticism, wit, love, and warmth. It is virtuosic in its use of the Yiddish language—one of its characteristics that, unfortunately, cannot be conveyed in even the best translation.

---

* M. Viner, *Tsu der Geshikhte fun der Yidisher Literatur in 19-tn Yorhundert*, vol. 2 (New York: Yidisher Kultur Farband, 1946), p.46.

Fishke the Lame

Translated by Gerald Stillman

To my dear, beloved friend
Menashe Margolius*
I dedicate this book from the depths of my heart.

Dear friend,

Sad is my melody in the symphony of Yiddish literature. My works express the very core of a Jew who, even when he does sing a merry tune, sounds from afar as if he were sobbing and weeping. Why, even his festive *shabes* hymns sound as if they were taken out of the Book of Lamentations. When he laughs, there are tears in his eyes. When he tries to make merry, bitter sighs escape from the depths of his heart—it's always *oy-vey*, woe is me, *vey*!

I am not, God forbid, trying to give myself airs by saying that I am a nightingale in Yiddish literature, although, in one respect, there is a great deal of similarity between me and him. This melancholy poet of the birds pours out his sad heart and sings his avian melodies precisely in springtime when all the world is newborn, when the buds burst into bloom, when delicious aromas tickle the nostrils, when everything looks bright and rosy and one's heart skips a beat for joy.

You and I, my dear friend, both began our work in Yiddish literature in the springtime of Jewish life here in our land. From 1860 onward, a new life seemed to have begun for Jews—a more relaxed life, a life full of hope for the future. At that time, we were both still very young. Each of us seized his pen with zeal and began

---

* A Jewish-Russian writer who was a good friend of Mendele's. He wrote a number of reviews of Mendele's works in the Russian Jewish press in the period around 1890.

to work away lustily, each according to his own bent. The people licked their fingers from your writing. They were thoroughly delighted to read the sweet words you wrote about many important matters in Jewish life. You were an advocate of righteousness among Jews and lectured them gently, in friendly fashion, on how to know themselves, to learn how to live and become the equals of other peoples. Pearls fell from your lips, lustrous pearls which shine and will always be an ornament for Yiddish literature.

I, too, hummed a tune in my own way during those happy spring days, but there was always one note which repeated gloomily and cast a spell of melancholy over the listeners. Some of them listened readily, although with heavy hearts; others made faces, scratched themselves unhappily, and were annoyed because I reminded them of unpleasant things and made their ears tingle. Be that as it may, I sang my song the only way I could.

That promising spring has long since passed. Woe, oh woe is to the life of a Jew! Trouble has made me lose my desire to write.* It has been a good while since I have lost my tongue.

And if I now take my gaunt and shriveled pen in hand and again attempt to use my voice, it is only thanks to you, you whose company has restored my balance and renewed my strength. Your clever words, your unrelenting labors in behalf of our people have refreshed me and inspired me with the desire to undertake some useful labor also. A spark has risen from the holy fire which ever burns in your Jewish heart and has alighted in my breast where it burst into flame and is now burning with the vigor of my youthful years.

Yes, we both commenced our literary labors at the same time, but our fortunes have not been the same. You scale the great heights. There you deal with the gems and jewels of Jewish history. You put our best foot forward by exhibiting our most sparkling antique diamonds, the best and dearest in the life of our people. You deal with Rabbi Hillel, Rabbi Meir, Rabbi Akiba and other greats—men of the highest renown.

On the other hand, it has been my lot to descend to the depths, to the cellars of our Jewish life. My stock in trade is: rags and moldy wares. My dealings are with paupers and beggars, the poor

---

* Mendele refers here to the period from 1877 to 1884 which he described to his friend Binshtok (see Introduction) as a time when writing "has become impossible for me. My brain is filled with lead..."

wretches of life; with degenerates, cripples, charlatans and other unfortunates, the dregs of humanity. I always dream of beggars. Before my eyes, I always see a sack soaring—the old, familiar Jewish beggar sack. No matter which way I turn my eyes, the sack is before me. No matter what I say or do, the sack comes soaring up to me! Oy, it's always the sack, the Jewish beggar sack! Yes, dear friend, through you the fire for writing has revived in me and has again produced a punishment for our numerous iniquities, a sack! A *Fishke der Krumer** with which I am appearing before the public after such a long period of silence. I know that my *Fishke der Krumer* is not the most suitable gift with which to express my gratitude for your friendship, but knowing your warm heart and your understanding of people, I dare to hope that you will accept my poor Fishke with a "Welcome!" Possibly, you will invite him into your home and introduce him to your family and friends. Fishke will gladly rest with you for a while, put his basket aside and tell you tales which you will enjoy. With this picture before my eyes, I smile with pleasure and thank you from the depths of my heart,

The Author

* *Fishke the Lame*, the English title of the present work.

CHAPTER I

Just when the bright sun begins to shine proclaiming another summer to the land, when people feel newly born and their hearts fill with joy at the sight of God's glorious world—just then the time for wailing and weeping arrives among Jews. This time of sorrow brings with it a host of mournful days: days of fasting, days of self-torment, days of grief and tears—starting at the end of Passover and lasting well into the damp cold and deep mud of autumn.

This is the very time when I, Mendele the Book Peddler, am busiest. I travel from fair to fair and from town to town to provide the children of Israel with all the wares needed for shedding tears: Books of Lamentations, Penitential Prayer Books, women's Books of Supplication, ram's-horns for the Day of Atonement, and prayer books for festivals. In short, while Jews weep and wail all summer long, my business thrives. But that's not the point . . .

Early one morning on the road, it was the seventeenth day in the month of *Tammuz,** I sat on my wagon in my prayer shawl and *tfiln,* my whip in my hand, in an altogether Jewish manner. My eyes were shut to keep the distracting light of day from interfering with my prayers. Satan would tempt me, though. Nature, or whatever it is called, was wondrously beautiful, a sight to behold. I was strongly driven, as though by witchcraft, to steal a glimpse. I wrestled with myself for quite a while.

My Good Mentor said, "For shame! You mustn't!"

"It's all right! Enjoy yourself, silly!" prodded my Evil Genius and at the same time forced open one of my eyes.

As if for spite, I was overwhelmed by the exquisite panorama which greeted my eye.

Fields peppered with blooming buckwheat as white as snow were embroidered with stripes of golden-yellow wheat and pale-green stalks of corn; a pleasant valley, the sides of which were covered with groves of nut trees; and below, a brook—clean and clear as crystal—into which the rays of the sun ducked and leaped out again in a shower of blinding golden sparks. In

---

* Yiddish words in italics will usually be found in the glossary at the end of the book.

174

the distance, the cows and sheep at pasture looked like gray and red specks.

"*Fe, fe!* For shame!" my Evil Genius mocked and flung the well-known precept at me: "Should a Jew, while traveling, interrupt his prayers and say, 'How pretty is the tree, how beautiful the field,' he commits a grievous sin." But, at the same moment, he blew into my nostrils the delicious fragrance of the stacks of newly cut hay, of herbs and roots—fragrances which trickled into my very extremities; the tricky melodies of the myriad songbirds drifted into my ears and tickled my soul. He sent a soft warm breeze across my face; it rippled through my prayer curls and whispered: "Look, enjoy yourself and be a man, silly Jew that you are!"

I babbled and gabbled, and truth to tell, I myself did not know about what. My thoughts ran away with themselves; curses and sneers pecked at my brain:

"Cadaverous creatures! Neither substance nor soul! Creatures with their souls absorbed in eating! Creatures without taste or smell. Dried out, useless rubbish!"

I began to rock back and forth with forced devotion so as to keep my mind from wandering. But I suddenly heard my mouth twist the prayer to say, ". . . he who returns to the dead carrion their souls."

Why? To whom did this refer? I almost jumped, so ashamed did I feel of my ugly thoughts. To smoothe over my error against the One Above, I acted as if I had meant something entirely different: it was this horse of mine. I flicked the good-for-nothing with the whip and growled, "A-a-a-h! You carrion, you!"

This was indeed a clever act, but today it was of little use. Somehow I was deeply concerned that such thoughts should occur to me today of all days—on this day, when we bewail and lament the great misfortune that once befell us children of Israel: the army of Nebuchadnezzar, King of Babylonia had entered Jerusalem and razed it to the ground. Forcing myself to feel contrite, I said the penitential prayer for this day in a tearful voice which mounted in pitch until it reached a climax of sorrow at those bitter words of the refrain:

"And the horned monster, the Tatar from the North, swept me from my feet like a jet of water and carried me far, far away . . ."

Once a Jew has shouted a psalm to his heart's content or talked himself hoarse repeating penitential prayers, he feels greatly relieved and, like a child who has had a good cry after a whipping,

175

is quite happy again. So I felt now, half reclining in my wagon, smoothing my beard, with a beaming countenance as if to say: "Well, my share is done, I've done my duty. And now, *Gotenyu*, the rest is up to You; show Yourself, O Father, Merciful and Just One!"

"Come now, come! Forgive me!" I looked at my horse with good will, apologizing in my heart for having called him "carrion" before. My *shlimazl* was kneeling on his forelegs, his head bowed to the ground, and groaning as if to say:

"Your lordship! How about something to eat?"

"True! You're as bright as the light of day," I said, signaling that he might rise now, that is, get up on his feet. Not in vain is it stated in the Book of Lamentations: "Zion, even your cattle and poultry are clever . . ." But that's not my point.

This profound thought led to others concerning the children of Israel; I mused about their wisdom, their mode of living, their communal leaders, and their sorry condition. My thoughts strayed hither and thither. Before me I saw the horned monster, Nebuchadnezzar and his army, bloody battles, confusion and commotion. The army tore down walls, smashed out doors and windows. Jews, many with packages of wares and old clothes, cried for help and mustering their courage—fled. I seized a stick and was about to—when boom! I found myself stretched out flat on my back on the ground.

Apparently, let it not be repeated to others, I had been napping in the midst of my prayers. My wagon, I saw, had run into a puddle, of the type known in the coachmen's jargon as "an inkwell." The axle hub of another wagon was caught in my rear wheel. My poor horse stood in agony with one leg over the shaft, all twisted in the harness and puffing like a goose. From the other side of the wagon flowed a stream of deadly curses, in Yiddish, interrupted only by a spell of coughing and choking.

"A Jew," I thought; "then there is no danger." And I strode in anger to the other side of the wagon. There, underneath, lay a Jew smothered in his prayer shawl and *tfiln*, his whip entangled in the leather thongs of his *tfiln*, struggling for all he was worth to free himself.

I shouted, "What do you call this?"

And he: "What do you mean, 'What do you call this'?"

"How does a Jew dare to fall asleep while praying?" I exclaimed.

"How can a Jew snore away like that?" he retorted.

I cursed his father and his entire generation and his mother and hers. I whipped his horse and he, freeing himself, ran in a fury to whip mine. Both horses reared on their hind legs. In a frenzy, we flew at each other like two raging cocks and were about to seize each other's prayer curls, when we stopped and stared at each other for a silent moment. It must have looked strange, indeed: two Jewish champions in their prayer shawls and *tfiln*, facing each other in a rage, ready to exhibit their prowess and slap each other, right in the middle of this open field, as though they'd been arguing in a *House of Study,** forgive the comparison! It would really be worth going to some trouble to witness a charming scene like this one. We stood there, ready to slap each other in a moment, when suddenly we both jumped back several paces and, in great surprise, shouted in one voice:

"*Oy*, Reb Alter!"

"*Oy, oy!* Reb Mendele!"

Alter *Yaknehoz*** was a powerful little man with a big belly. His face was overgrown with a thick mat of dirty yellow hair of which there was enough to provide for prayer curls, beard and mustaches not only for himself but for several more Jews as well. In the midst of this sea of hair lay an island—a broad, fleshy nose which, being stuffed almost all year, defeated its own purpose. But occasionally a change in its condition would occur, say, in the spring just before Passover, when everything else was in thaw, when the ice floes on the river crashed with thunderous blasts, like those of the *shoyfer* on *Yom Kippur*. The whole town of Tuneyadevke,*** reverberated to its clarion calls which, together with gobbling of the tom turkeys, made for a real spring concert. Everybody in the town stood gaping, and offerings of snuff and good wishes for health poured in from all sides.

In Jewish towns especially, noses break into song at this time of year. Perhaps the odors and aromas of the season have something to do with it. Or, maybe it is the order of things, for does it not say in the Scriptures . . . But that's not my point.

Alter Yaknehoz was a book peddler from Tuneyadevke, an acquaintance of mine of many years standing. He was a man unto

---

* See glossary.

**See glossary.

**Mendele uses the humorous device of playing on place names. *Tuneyadets*, in Russian, is a sluggard or parasite. *Tuneyadevke* might be translated as "Sluggardtown."

177

himself, not too sharp, a man of few words, always gruff as if angry with the world, although he was not at all a bad sort.

After a round of warm greetings, we began to inquire after each other's business. Among us Jews this investigation usually involves a peek into the other fellow's wagon, possibly accompanied by a searching hand or a nose sniffing for a clue—a revealing odor.

"And where is a Jew going!" I tried to feel Alter out.

"Where a Jew is going? *Ett* . . ." Alter answered with a question since it is the custom among Jews not to answer such a question directly but rather to put the inquirer off with an "*Ett*," which could signify a lot or a little depending on how adept one is at taking a hint.

"A Jew is going! He's going to the dogs, that's where! And where is Reb Mendele headed?" Alter was trying to feel me out in return.

"Yonder! Where I'm usually headed this time of year."

"I'm afraid I can guess where 'yonder' is: Glupsk!* Just where I'm headed myself," Alter said, his face expressing worry about the possible effect of competition on his earnings. "But why, Reb Mendele, by way of a side road? Why not with the main highway?"

"It happened to be more convenient this time. I'm glad. I haven't been this way for a long time. And you, Reb Alter? Why the back road!" I tried to feel him out again. "Where have you been?"

"Where I've been? On the road to ruin, that's where! I've been to the fair at Yarmelinets—may it sink into the earth!"

While my Alter was fuming and cursing Yarmelinets and its fair, some peasants in wagons approached. They shouted and demanded why the road was blocked. When they came closer and saw Alter and me in our prayer shawls, with the big leather *tfiln* boxes held on our foreheads with broad leather thongs, the shouts became coarse and mocking:

"Hey, there! Look at that pair! What a sight! Hey, the devil take your mothers' mothers! Clear the road! Snappy there, little Jews, lazy bones!"

Alter and I began to work on the wagons quickly and with vigor. Several of the peasants, although not children of Israel, but the truth must be told, had the goodness of heart to come and help us in this, our time of need. By dint of their pushing, my wagon was soon out of the "inkwell." Were it not for them, we would have

---

* Again, a play on place names. *Glupsk* stems from the Russian *glupi*, meaning stupid or foolish. *Glupsk* can be taken as "Foolstown."

puttered around for God knows how long and would probably have torn our prayer shawls to tatters. But together with the peasants it was an entirely different story: they pushed in real earnest, for the hands were the hands of Esau; but with us it was only the voice, and the voice was the voice of Jacob. We grunted and groaned and struggled as if we were really pushing. . . . But that's not my point.

As soon as the road was cleared, these vulgar louts went their way, turning only to mock and jeer at us for being dressed like orthodox priests, forgive the comparison, and for walking alongside the horses, serving the Creator with whip in hand. Some of them, grasping the lower corner of their coats to form the shape of a "sow's ear," pointed them at us, shouting: "Jewish swine!" Alter was hardly bothered. "Remember whence it comes," he shrugged. "Who is there to get insulted at?" But I was deeply hurt by their mocking. *Gvald*, Father in Heaven, why? Why?

"Almighty God!" I began in the plaintive style of the women's *tkhines*. "Ope Thine eyes and do mark, from Thy retreat which is the Heaven above, how Thy dear Name is holden by them, for in awe do they stand of Thy might, and Thy word do they cherish most reverently. Do Thou then cause to descend upon us Thy compassion that we may find Favor and Grace in Thine eyes and in the eyes of all people. Do Thou then shield Thy most surely beloved sheep and let Thy Mercy dwell among Thy constant worshipers. Do Thou also improve my fortune for having this day praised and glorified Thy Name in deep reverence. Cause to descend upon me, Thy slave Mendl, son of Thy maid Gnendl, and upon all of Israel, some good bit of business that our spirits may be at ease, Amen!"

CHAPTER II

Without further ado, we climbed up on our wagons and off we went. My wagon was in front. Behind me rode Alter in a van with tattered matting, four crooked wheels with wedges between the spokes and rims tied together with rope. The greased wheel blocks tossed from side to side on their axles, creaking and groaning, unable to find themselves a comfortable position. A tall, strikingly lean beast put itself to the trouble of drawing this van—a scrofulous mare with a flea-bitten back full of blisters, with long ears, a twisted and tangled mane matted with wisps of hay and wads of cotton padding which were coming out of her collar.

All that remained to be said of my morning prayers were the last few verses, about which, even under ordinary circumstances, little fuss is made. Having done with my prayers, an entirely new contest developed with my Evil Genius.

"Go ahead," he urged. "Take a sip of brandy! It will refresh your heart."

"*Ai, Ai!*" I wrinkled my nose in refusal. "On the seventeenth of *Tammuz!* On such a day of fasting!"

"*Ett!*" came back a reply. "There's a bit of difference between a Jew today and one in the times of Nebuchadnezzar! There are bigger troubles today and yet . . . nothing. Don't be silly. You're old and weak, poor man. There's no harm in it!"

I swept my hand across my face as if to brush away a troublesome fly and in the meanwhile stole a wee glance at the little satchel back in the wagon—the little satchel where I always kept a good bit of brandy, buckwheat cookies, rye cakes, garlic, onion, and other greens. My mouth watered, my heart grew faint, my stomach growled:

"*Gvald*, help! A drop of brandy! *Gvald*, something to eat!"

I turned my head away swiftly and fixed my attention on the fields about me in an effort to drive away these evil thoughts.

The sky was blue and clear without a trace of cloud. The sun baked and broiled. There was not the slightest breeze, not even a breath of air, for relief. The stalks of grain in the fields, the trees in the woods stood stock still—as though petrified. The cows at pasture lay fatigued, their necks outstretched, wiggling their ears from time to time and chewing their cud. Some dug up the earth with their horns and pushed it underneath them with their hoofs while bellowing from heat. The bull lifted his head and went galloping madly, tossing his head from side to side, stopped suddenly and lowered his brow almost to the ground. He sniffed, blew hard through his nostrils, let out a great bellow and stamped his feet. Near an old, gnarled, half dried-up willow, split in half by a thunderbolt long ago, stood a herd of horses, their heads thrown over each other's rumps to create some shade; they whisked their tails to and fro to get rid of the troublesome flies. High up in a tree, a magpie swayed back and forth on a branch. It looked, for all the world, as if she wore a little white prayer shawl with the blue stripes in front and was praying with a rocking motion. She bowed her little head in supplication, hopped and chirped a few times . . . then remained still again, without a sound, extending her little neck and staring into the world with sleepy little eyes.

Along the road there was only silence, not the slightest sound, not a peep; there was not even a bird in flight; only mosquitoes and midges carried on like demons, flying by with a hum and a hiss, whispering a secret into one's ear and then—gone again. Only in the haystacks, among the stalks, crickets chirped incessantly; they were in full cry.

It was hot. It was quiet, and wondrously beautiful. Hush! God's creatures were resting. . . .

On account of the heat, I sprawled in my wagon in my shirt sleeves, pardon my appearance, and prayer shawl. I had pushed my stitched felt cap to the back of my head and rolled my heavy woolen stockings, from Breslau, down to my anklestockings, which, in expiation of our manifold sins I wore even during the summer, and perspired profusely. Because I love to perspire, I would have enjoyed the heat if the sun were not beating directly into my eyes; I could lie for hours on the upper bench in the steam bath in the very greatest heat. My father, his memory be praised, had accustomed me to it even as a child. He was a hot, smoldering, burning, fiery Jew. He loved to steam himself through and through and thereby made a name for himself. He was greatly beloved among the people, for the very gist of Jewishness is to be found in this fiery nature. Therefore they regarded him as a respectable Jew who was close to God. They spoke of him with reverence:

"Oh, yes, as far as whipping goes, he is a deep scholar.

He's a past master on the subject 'steam bath.' He knows . . . he knows all there is to know about sweating!"

181

Sweating is a Jewish thing. Not a Sabbath goes by, not a holiday, when a Jew does not find himself in a good sweat. Who, among all the seventy nations of the world, has sweated more than the Jew? But that's not my point.

And while I lay there sweating, how I did need refreshment! My throat was dry, my lips were parched and crying for a drink, I was dying for some food. My Evil Genius seized upon me again, stronger than ever, and enumerated the whole list of Jewish delicacies:

"Broiled *ledvetsa* with porridge; sweet-and-sour meat; a *lokshn* pudding with a 'thief' (a stuffed neck of chicken hidden within); boiled *farfl*, fried with bits of chicken skin." I became faint; my limbs turned limp. My appetite was ferocious. But he went right on:

"Thin dough stuffed with meat, jellied calves' feet with liver slices; radish and onion; the crop of a tom turkey in a candied parsnip sauce . . ."

And suddenly, I don't know how it happened, the little satchel appeared before me, as if it had sprung out of the earth.

"*Lekhayim*, to your health, silly!" the demon spoke through me. "You've been foolish enough for one day, you dolt!"

My hand stretched forth, by itself somehow, opened the satchel and swiftly snatched the bottle. I looked about like a thief when suddenly my horse's eye brought me to a dead halt. In the process of scratching his neck on the shaft, he had turned his head toward the wagon and scowled at me with resentment, as if to say:

"Here, look! My hind leg is all swollen and bandaged with rags; one of my eyes keeps on watering; my neck is chafed; my mouth, a useless organ, has forgotten the taste of oats. Still and all, what can I do? I just drag along, hungry, sick, and wretched—not even thinking of throwing off the yoke, God forbid."

The bottle slid out of my hand, back into its resting place. I pushed the little satchel away from me in great shame, groaning from the depths of my heart:

"So this is what has come to pass! This is who must serve me as an example; from him must I learn wisdom! *Milpani mibheymes hoerets*—he teaches us by means of the cattle of the earth. . . . No, horse o'mine! I will not throw off the yoke either. We'll live somehow, Reb Horse, the devil won't take either of us! *Adam ubheyme*—man and beast—*toyshiah adonai*—are both saved by the Lord!"

Once a Jew has broken himself of the vile passion of eating, food ceases to be a matter of importance to him and he can spend the rest of his life requiring almost nothing. To this very day, in these modern times, many a Jew can be found who has only the vestige of a stomach, truly the size of an olive pit. And there are great hopes that with the passing of time—if only the kosher meat tax is retained and the activities of the charity workers and their brethren go unhampered—Jews will drift further and further away from eating until among future generations there will be no trace left of the digestive tract at all, except for piles. Jews will then present a pretty picture to the eyes of the rest of the world. . . .

The point of this discourse is that, having pushed the little satchel away, I somehow felt much stronger. I lay back thinking about business and hummed a sad little tune. Everything appeared to be in order. But the devil had to bring into being a peasant lass, ugly as they come, with a pot of mushrooms, my favorite dish. Any pious man in my position would have taken it for granted that this was the Evil Genius himself, disguised in the form of a female in order to . . . But not I! I had to take a good look. It really was only a simple peasant lass! And asking me to buy the mushrooms together with the pot for only ten groschen, she pushed it right under my nose. I was almost overcome by the aroma. It went to my heart. My mouth watered and I felt faint. Oh God, how I wanted it! Fearing that I would lose control of myself, I jumped off the wagon as if I were running from a fire. It was a sheer miracle that I did not break nape and neck. I shouted with a voice that was not mine: "Reb Alter!" My purpose was that Alter should be my chaperon.

There, in his wagon, my Reb Alter lay flat on his back, both hands under his head, red as a beet: his shirt was open, forgive his appearance, and his woolly red-haired chest exposed, burnt, roasted, and so covered with sweat, oh enemies of Zion, that my heart almost broke to see him thus.

"Wh-a-a-at?" called Alter without stirring when he heard my cry. "What's the matter?"

A quick glance told me that she of the mushrooms was gone. It was as though she had evaporated. Since I had to say something, I asked Alter:

"Tell me, what time do you think it might be now?"

"What time do I think it might be now?" repeated Alter in a hollow voice. "How should I know? Our eyes will probably pop from their sockets waiting for the first stars to appear. That's certain. My, it's awfully hot!"

"A delicious heat, eh? Are you sweating, Reb Alter?" I asked, walking alongside his wagon. "I think it's time to rest. Our lions are weary, they are barely dragging along. It is still many versts to Glupsk; and then maybe a couple more. Down yonder where the woods start, I see a good spot on the left for the horses to feed. It's not far."

A few minutes later, we turned off the road to the spot where the woods started, among pretty fields and a good green meadow. We unharnessed our lions and let them feed in freedom at the edge of the woods. We lay down under a tree.

CHAPTER III

Alter Yaknehoz breathed heavily because of the heat. His moans and groans affected me so that my heart melted with pity. To cheer him up a bit and partly to make the time pass more quickly, I engaged him in the following conversation :

"Well, Reb Alter, is it hot enough for you?"

"*Beh!*" Alter answered briefly and somewhat vexed, as he slid further under the tree in an effort to hide himself from the rays of the sun which cut through the branches.

"*Feh!* This day of fasting is making me sick! Is that you groaning like that?" I probed Alter again, having firmly resolved that though I should die in the attempt I would get him to speak.

"*Beh!*" Alter answered, and slid still further under the tree.

I was not disposed to be happy with only a "*Beh!*" for an answer. "Aha!" I thought. "You hide-bound old mule! I'll fix you! I'll make you talk. If heat and sweat won't do it then the subject will have to be business—the best, in fact the only topic to make a silent Jew talkative. A Jew, even if he be on his deathbed, will come alive as soon as he hears something about business; he comes alive and even the Angel of Death cannot come near him at that moment. God help the man who must cross the path of a rich merchant when he is occupied with business: he will demolish anyone, even his best friend, his own brother, with his glance . . . But that's not my point.

I turned to Alter and said: "You and I, Reb Alter, are going to do some trading, I think! I'm glad that we met each other today. Oh, I have some stuff with me today that is worth its weight in gold!"

My new tactic had its effect. Alter was a changed man. He raised his head, turned toward me and pricked up his ears. I continued to feed the fire:

"This time, Reb Alter, all our trading will be on a cash basis. You say you're coming from the fair at Yarmelinets, so your pockets must be bulging with money, may the Evil Eye not harm them."

"Bulging pockets, yes! A heart bulging with trouble is all I have," said Alter testily. "I tell you, Reb Mendl . . . but—nothing . . . an unlucky man would be better off if he hadn't been born. I was looking for deals, special deals! Had it been someone else, heh-heh-heh! But with me, it all came to nothing. Everything goes

185

downhill with me. Only misfortune comes my way! It hurts to talk about it. Cut your nose to spite your face . . . it's no more than nothing."

It was clear that things were not going smoothly with my Reb Alter. He had troubles. But as long as his tongue had loosened, a wee little push was all that was needed to keep it wagging. I was of no mind to prevent this. I gave him a good push, and my Alter was on the move, telling about his misfortune in his unique way:

"Anyway, I go to the fair in Yarmelinets. When I arrive at the market place, I unhitch the wagon in the square, you understand, and unpack my bit of goods. Well, to make a long story short— nothing! I stand there waiting for customers. What brought me to this fair, God only knows. I, it shouldn't happen to you, am in a tight spot right now. The printer wants his money. Well, that's a small matter—so he wants it. But he wants, you understand, to stop giving me goods! My older daughter is not getting any younger. A girl of her age, you understand, should be getting married. So I have to find her a husband. There are plenty of bachelors, but a husband, you understand, a husband is not so easy to find! And then, with all this going on, my wife decides to have a baby boy, and when? Just before Passover! You understand me? A boy! You know what that means? But—nothing!"

"Don't be offended with me," I said to Alter, "for interrupting you. But why, at your age, did you marry a young wife who has children so easily?"

"God protect you!" cried Alter in amazement. "I had to have a housewife to take care of the household. What does a Jew want to get married for at all? All the poor man wants is a good housewife."

"Tell me then, Reb Alter," I asked, "why did you divorce your first wife and ruin her life? She was a good housewife."

"*Beh!*" Alter winced, looking wretched.

"Nor was she a sterile woman, glory to His Holy Name, this first wife of yours," I persisted in the same vein. "What happened to your poor children by your first marriage? Do you know?"

"*Beh!*" Alter scratched under his prayer curl uncomfortably, waved his hand helplessly and sighed from the depths of his heart.

"*Beh!*" is a priceless word for us Jews. It has so many meanings and serves to answer so many difficult questions.

"*Beh!*" can be used at any time during a conversation and will always be in place. A Jew in a difficult situation, with his back to

186

the wall, can always wriggle out of it with one word: "*Beh!*" A swindler or a bankrupt will use "*beh*" as a payment to his creditors when they press him too hard. "*Beh!*" stands by a man in time of need, as, for example, when the poor fellow is caught telling a lie. "*Beh!*" is a fitting comment to one who has been drumming in your ears for hours on end and you haven't listened to or heard a word of what he said. "*Beh*" is the apology of a bigwig who has hoodwinked the public; of a man of reputed virtue whose true character has finally been uncovered. In a word, "*beh*" has a variety of tastes and all sorts of interpretations, such as, for example: come, if you dare! the goose is cooked! I'm on your side! do your worst! a plague upon you! A Jewish mind will always divine the proper meaning of "*beh*" under the given circumstances. The direction in which the barb is aimed will always be clear.

Alter's last "*beh*" was a bitter one. Contrition, repentance and self-accusation seemed to be wrapped up in it. Surely, his mean treatment of his first wife and their children must have left a wound in his heart. He must have seen in the many misfortunes that had befallen him a punishment for his sins. This was clearly expressed by the bitter heartfelt sigh, by the helpless way he waved his hand, and also by the sheepish scratching under his prayer curl, as if to say: "Bite your lip and keep your mouth shut! The devil take you!"

I was angry with myself for having scratched Alter's old wounds. That is the trouble with a Jew who must needs butt into someone's personal affairs and get under his skin with all sorts of questions, while all the time the poor man is choking down his troubles in silence. In addition, I was angry with myself because I would have to start all over again. After loosening Alter's tongue so that it was merrily wagging away like clockwork, I had to touch a little wheel and make the pendulum grind to a halt! I fell back on my former tactic. Once more I fed him hints about the possibility of our trading. I was not stingy; I gave him a full measure of tongue loosener. I found the little key that fitted him, wound him up so gently that he did not even notice, and soon the pendulum was swinging merrily again.

CHAPTER IV

"Well, I was waiting for customers near my wagon," Alter began again where he had left off. "In short, I stood there, looking around and watching the fair. Well, a fair is a fair—it's noisy. The crowds are big. Jews are busy, carried away; they're really living. A Jew at a fair is like a fish in water—it's lively, if you know what I mean. Our Father Jacob's blessing: 'And ye shall multiply like fish in the waters of the earth!' That's the way it goes, doesn't it, Reb Mendele? And don't we always say: 'There's a fair in the air way up there'? That means that for a Jew Paradise is a fair. Anyway, whatever it means, people were hard at it. They ran around. They bargained. No one stood still for a minute. Among the storekeepers, I saw Berl *Teletse.** He used to be a flunky once, then an errand boy, but today he's Reb Ber with a big store in the market place. He stood in front of it and argued so loud you could hear him all over the square. In short—nothing! It was all hustle and bustle. A man ran by, then another, and a third—all in a sweat, their caps pushed back on their heads. They tapped something here, felt something there. They talked with their hands and all at the same time. Then they suddenly stopped to think. They chewed the tips of their beards quietly—a sign that they'd soon agree. Then, uproar again. Brokers flew by gasping for breath, matchmakers, traveling repairmen, commission men, women with little baskets, Jews with big baskets, young gentlemen with canes, older gentlemen with bellies, all of them with flaming faces. Nobody had time! Time was a rouble a minute.

"Well, in short, nothing! It looked as if any one of them would strike it rich in a minute. *Ai,ai*, how their luck filled me with envy! There they were, earning money, raking in gold, and I, *shlimazl* that I am, what was I doing? Standing with folded arms like a clay statue near my tattered van! *Oy*, my van with the prayer shawl tassels and little charms dangling on the outside, and inside, the packs of books and other junk. The whole thing is a joke, I tell you. Go ahead, try to make a living and marry off a daughter when a whole pack of *tkhines* brings in no more than three roubles! In my heart, I cursed the whole lot of

---

* Teletza (from the Russian *telionok*) means a calf.

188

them—my daughter, the van, that dried-out mare of mine! I wished that I'd never seen them. Enough, I had to get down to work, and try my luck too! Maybe the One Above, blessed be His Name, would have mercy. Why not?

"In short, my cap flew to the back of my head, my sleeves rolled themselves up, my feet carried me to my van by themselves, a straw found its way from the wagon right into my mouth. My mouth began to chew on the straw and my mind began to work: it took only a few wrinkles and furrows before I slapped my forehead I had it! A good idea—a match between two merchants, both of them with big stores here on the market place. Respectable men, both of them. Do you know whom I mean? Reb Elyokum, Reb Elyokum Sharograder was one of them! The other one—Reb Getzl Graydinger! I decided to get down to business. To hell with the wagon, the mare, and the printer! I went to work in real earnest. Luck was on my side and it looked like something might come of it. To make a long story short, I cracked the whip and things started moving. I ran from Reb Elyokum to Reb Getzl and from Reb Getzl to Reb Elyokum. I was now running around, blessed be His Name, like the best of them. I sweated and strained. The match had to go through, and right here, at the fair. Why not? Is there a better place than a fair?

"To make it short, the two merchants were in a big hurry: they looked each other over in passing, liked each other, wanted each other—wanted each other badly! *Nu*, who could ask for anything better? The two of them were straining at the leash.

I tell you, I could have hugged myself! My commission was as good as in my pocket. I had decided how much dowry to settle on my daughter. I was already bargaining with a ragpicker for an old satin coat for myself. Shirts were my last worry. They could wait until later. The good Lord would provide . . . Well, to make a long story short—nothing! Just listen to what had to happen to me! I tell you, a man with no luck is better off not being born. Just as we were ready to break the pots in celebration, we happened to remember the bride and groom, and what do you think? Believe me, it hurts to even talk about it. The whole thing was a flop! No, it was ten times worse than a flop! It just blew up in my face! Listen to my misfortune and how the wrath of God descended on me: the two merchants each had—what do you think they had? They each had a son!"

"What do you mean, Reb Alter?" I shot out in a peal of laughter.

"How can that be? You would never do anything as foolish as that! How could you arrange a match before finding out which of the two parties has a son and which a daughter?"

"Of course, it's simple enough!" Alter winced in vexation. "I still have as much sense as anyone else and nobody has to teach me how to live! Who ever heard of a Jew who doesn't know how matches are made? Reb Mendele, you know what our customs concerning matchmaking and marriages are like. Then why are you so surprised at my misfortune? It could have happened to anybody.

"I knew that Reb Elyokum was supposed to have a marriageable daughter—and what a daughter! May I have such a jewel myself! I saw her last year with my own eyes, may I see Paradise just as surely! But when a man has no luck, everything he knows is worth nothing! How was I supposed to know that this beautiful girl was in a hurry, that she had rushed off, and got herself married! She must have been seized by some fever. I didn't know a thing about it, may I know as much about my poverty! Now, let me ask you, whom could I have meant when I started working on this match between Reb Elyokum and Reb Getzl? Reb Elyokum's daughter, of course! His daughter and Reb Getzl's son! It was so clear that people would have laughed at me if I'd said anything about it. Everybody knows that two males don't get married! A male marries a female—that's our custom! How else could it be? All I know is that I did what was right. No one else, as I am a Jew, could have done any better.

"To make a long story short, I had worked fast: the important things—the dowry and living quarters for the couple—were all settled. Don't forget, at a fair with two busy merchants, there's no time for empty talk or nonsense. Each word counts. You have to come right to the point without wasting time. That's my story. Now, let's take Reb Elyokum. When I first brought up the match, he must have been sure that the talk was about his son. How else? He himself wasn't going to marry Reb Getzl! And he'd never imagine that his daughter was meant when he knew very well that he had a son and not a daughter to marry off. So that's his story and you can see that both sides are right. But—nothing! Now, do you understand?"

"*Beh*!" I said, barely able to contain my laughter and straining to keep a straight face.

"*Nu*, thank God for making you understand!" Alter pointed his

190

thumb at me and, with raised eyebrows, drawled a knowing "Aha!" as if my *beh* had hit the nail on the head.

To tell the truth, Alter's explanation did make a certain amount of sense. Why not? Considering the way we Jews arrange our matches, why shouldn't such a thing occur? Unconsciously, I again said, "*Beh*!" and looked at Alter in a most friendly way.

"Aha!" said Alter, pointing his thumb at me again. "Aha, so now you understand! But nothing . . . I'm not finished yet. I still had hopes about patching things up. Once I start something, I don't give up so easily, if you know what I mean."

"Reb Alter, God have mercy on you! What are you talking about?" I actually sat up in amazement, feeling certain that the terrible heat had made Alter lose his mind. "What kind of hope could you have had when both fathers had only sons?"

"Don't get excited," Alter soothed me. "It wasn't as bad as that, Reb Mendele. I had another idea. When God visits a plague on us, He also provides the remedy. You see, I still had Reb Berl Teletse to fall back on. He had plenty of eligible daughters. As a matter of fact, right from the start, those three names danced around in my head—Elyokum, Getzl, Teletse. It was just my luck to pick the wrong pair and leave Teletse out. The best way to patch things up was to bring Teletse into the picture, the honorable Reb Berishl! To make a long story short, I tried to smooth over my blunder with both merchants. Wasn't it everybody's fault—mine a little, theirs a little, and also our luck a little? It was probably not ordained by heaven, not in the cards, you understand! Then I started on the list of praises for Reb Berishl: he was, may the Evil Eye not harm him, wealthy, good-natured, generous to charities, an honored member in many societies. After all, this was Reb Berishl, no less! I didn't have to say anything about what a sage he was: you never have to say anything about a rich man's wisdom—it's understood. But, nothing! My hopes rose like dough with yeast. 'It will all turn out for the best yet,' I said to myself. 'Elyokum's and Getzl's sons have to get married and Teletse's daughters are like made to order! God willing, Reb Berishl is the answer to all my troubles.'

"To make a long story short, I had the runs again back and forth at full steam. The arrangements were going along well enough. Things were looking up. But, nothing! Suddenly, the fair was over. The stores closed, the wagons drove off, the people disappeared, and I was left alone in the empty market square! All my hard work, all my aggravation, was thrown out!

"Now, do you understand?" Alter appealed to me in a plaintive beseeching voice, extending both hands. "Do you see what I mean? When you have no luck, then all the wisdom in the world won't help! *Oy*, the wrath of God has been upon me for a long time. It's a punishment for my sins. And you talk to me about doing business on a cash basis? I don' t even have a groshen to my name, woe is me!"

"*Ai*, just like in the bathhouse!" I said, and moved away.

Alter glared at me with eyes wide open, shaking his head. Highly incensed, he turned and spoke, as though to the world at large:

"What a crooked, false-hearted man! Oh, enemies of Zion, here I am in agony, my troubles are breaking my heart, and he? Nothing! He's just thinking about himself, that's all! I can see right through the whole act! I know the Jewish tricks. I can tell pretty well when a man wants to back out of an offer as soon as he finds out that he doesn't have a cash customer! I can tell when a man doesn't want to do business."

"Really . . ." I exclaimed and tugged at Alter's beard playfully. "How can such thoughts even occur to you, Reb Alter? I meant something entirely different. The way your story ended with the disbanding of the fair reminded me of a very interesting tale which I can't forget to this very day. It's a story about a bathhouse and it ends just like yours. There's not even a hair's breadth difference between them, except the other story is short. It's worth hearing. Oho, you're sweating, Reb Alter! Move over a little, if you please, and we'll be able to lie here with our backs to the sun and talk."

Alter wiped the perspiration from his face with the back of his sleeve. From his bosom pocket, he brought out a meerschaum pipe with a female figure painted on the bowl. He cleaned the mouthpiece and the beaded stem with a short piece of wire which hung from a chain attached to the bowl cover. He lit the pipe, took a peek at the female figure and settled back in all his glory under the tree. I cleared my throat and began my tale.

CHAPTER V

"For a long time, a young fellow lived in the stone bathhouse of Glupsk; his name was Fishke the Lame. Neither I nor anyone else ever thought of inquiring just who Fishke was and where he came from. It didn't matter! Somehow or other a creature, a Fishke, existed in our midst—a creature like so many other wretched souls who appear among us children of Israel, from nowhere, like toadstools after a rainstorm, full-blown, with all their earmarks, without giving the slightest hint that they are budding and about to burst into bloom! Paupers live in their obscure holes and make children quietly. Who cares? They are fruitful and multiply on the face of the earth. The harvest, may the Evil Eye not harm them, is great. And then the young ones suddenly stand on their own feet and a fresh crop of new, quivering little Jews makes its appearance in the world: little Fishkes, little *Khaykes, Khayims, Yosls*—naked, barefoot, clad in rags, cluttering up the houses, the synagogues, the streets, the towns, and getting between everyone's feet.

"It would be hard to call Fishke handsome. He had a big flat head and a large broad mouth with yellow crooked teeth. He lisped, could not pronounce an "r" and limped badly. Fishke was getting on in years. As far as he was concerned, he could have been married for a long time and would have gladly blessed Glupsk with his share of children. But as his foul luck would have it, he had been by-passed and, as we say in our book-peddling business, had become a 'shelf item.' He had even been forgotten during the recruiting of 'cholera grooms,' that is, when the *Kahal* of Glupsk snatched the most hideous cripples, beggars and vagrants and frantically married them off to each other in the cemetery among the tombstones in order to frighten the epidemic away.

"The first time this happened, *Kahal* chose to honor not Fishke but the famous cripple Yontl who had no legs and moved around on his seat by pushing himself with two little wooden blocks. He was mated with a well-known beggar woman who had teeth like spades and no underlip. The cholera epidemic was so terror-stricken by this pair that it wiped out a good part of the population in its fright, after which it took to its heels and fled.

"The second time, Fishke was again by-passed in favor of Nokhemtshe the Village Idiot. Before an assemblage of city nota-

193

bles, all of them fine Jews, at the cemetery, this poor fool placed the bridal crown and cover on the head of a girl whose head had been covered since childhood because of its cankerous sores and about whom it was rumored that she was, pardon the expression, a hermaphrodite. It was said that the assembled crowd made unusually merry at this wedding and that an ocean of brandy was consumed among the tombstones. 'That's fine,' was the general comment. 'Let them multiply, let the children of Israel replenish the earth in the face of the cholera. Let the poor cripples enjoy themselves also . . .' But that's not my point.

"To make a long story short, *Kahal* had forgotten Fishke. Once again the cholera came to Glupsk and still it did not help Fishke. He remained a bachelor as before. Even Auntie Noseless, whose partner scraped away on a sort of a fiddle while she did a jig in the middle of the street and accompanied him in a thin falsetto, even Auntie had forgotten about Fishke—Auntie, who collected alms in a little plate so that the corpses might dance, so that cripples and beggars should have a few groschen with which to get married. Even good-hearted Auntie let Fishke go on without a wife. It certainly was a pity, but such was his luck.

"Fishke usually walked around barefoot, with no coat, in a coarse patched shirt with long greasy tails and pants of coarse linen which hung in many folds. His job was to walk through the streets and cry, 'Gentlemen, to the bathhouse!' on Fridays, and 'Little ladies, to the bathhouse!' on Wednesdays. In the summertime, when garden produce became available, his eel-like voice could be heard throughout the Jewish quarter: 'Everybody here! Young garlic, everybody!' In the bathhouse, he guarded the clothes; or he fetched someone a kettle of water with his dirty shirt sleeve plugged into the spout; or, tossing it from hand to hand with great skill, a red-hot coal with which to light someone's cigar. For this, he might sometimes be thrown two or three kopecks. Because of his job at the bathhouse he was allowed certain privileges which were granted to religious officials, such as: going from house to house with the band of bathhouse employees on *Khanike* and *Purim* to receive the customary few kopecks; to be invited to the circumcision of a rich man's son where he could drink a toast and eat some honey cake; to go to the rich peoples' houses with a basket during Passover and be given broken pieces of *matse*.

"I knew Fishke very well. I used to enjoy getting him into a conversation and listening to his colorful expressions. He was by

194

no means as foolish as he looked. Whenever I come to Glupsk, the first thing I do is to go to the stone bathhouse, have the lice removed from my clothes and stockings, and steam my body through to the bone on the topmost bench. Say what you will, but this is my greatest delight. What can be better than being steamed through and perspiring? I tell you once more, I would even enjoy perspiring right now, if the sun weren't shining into my eyes.

"Move over a bit, Reb Alter! Oho! You're not perspiring so badly yourself, may the Evil Eye not harm you! Move over a little, please, that's the way."

"*Nu*, let's get to the point!" Alter grumbled irritably. "I think you have enough room now. And please, don't drag it out so much. Cut it short."

"Be patient, Reb Alter! The day is still young," I said and continued my narration.

"Several years ago I happened to be in Glupsk walking along a street when I saw Fishke from afar. I almost jumped with surprise. There, indeed, was my old Fishke with his lame legs, but dressed like a dandy in a brand new Circassan overcoat and new shoes and stockings. On his head he wore a big fur cap and under his coat was a new shirt, starched hard as a board, and embroidered with red flowers. What did this mean, I wondered. could it be that *Kahal* had picked him as a cholera groom after all? But there had been no cholera epidemic in Glupsk that year—not because the polluted lake nearby had been drained, or because the piles of stinking mud and the dead cats had been removed from the streets, or because the homeowners had decided to fly in the face of tradition and stop emptying their garbage pails in front of their houses under the noses of passers-by. No, no, God forbid! How could one ever accuse a Jewish community of such action!

"It was simply a miracle, that's all. True it was that even this year Jews complained about stomach pains and many of them died. But this was only a bad run of luck which was ascribed to overconsumption of unripe cucumbers. The poor folk had seized upon the immature greens in a fit of hunger and . . . well, that's not my point.

"While I had thus been gaping in amazement, Fishke disappeared. The rheumatism in my legs was particularly painful at this time, may it not happen today. I had not been cupped nor had I had my blood let, except for some ten tiny leeches, during the preceding few months . . . *Nu*, I decided to visit the bathhouse

195

early the next day. I would spend a few hours there and fish out all sorts of news, not only about Fishke, but also about other important things: local politics, gossip, who received a letter and from whom, what was cooking in so-and-so's pot . . . The only place for Jews to fish out what is going on, to complain about their own troubles and listen to those of others, is the bathhouse. There, one hears many secrets repeated. Many business deals are closed there. The place has more activity than a market place. If you come in on a Friday afternoon, you'll see a pretty scene: in a corner sit two leeches. One of them is busy shaving heads, the other is waving a razor and slashing someone's back with it to let blood. He places fresh cups on one customer's back and snatches spent cups from another's back. Jewish blood flows freely across the floor under bodies on benches, carrying with it shaven hair and leaves from the reeds with which the steam bathers whip each other. The leeches' burning candle with its unraveled wick sputters angrily and casts an evil yellow glare on the scene.

"On the walls and from the ceiling near the stoves hang all sorts of clothes, like in the biggest clothing store: shirts, stockings, sweaters, pants, coats, jackets, and round fur-trimmed hats. From the uppermost benches come tortured screams. Some of the men lie up there in a state of semi-consciousness, sighing and groaning. Others, armed with reeds, whip themselves and scream, *'Gvald*, oh children of Israel! *'Gvald*, have mercy! More steam, *Gvald!'*

"Suddenly, the steam bath becomes cold. Everybody yells, but no one will take the trouble to pour more water on the red-hot stones until finally some wiseacre takes the situation in hand, makes enough steam to fill the chambers of hell and soon everyone is gasping for breath.

"Two soaking Jews quarrel over a pail of water. They tear it from each other's hands and curse each other fearfully. A skinny *melamed* who is wandering about with no equipment at all makes peace between them and soon all three are mopping themselves with their greasy kerchiefs from the one pail.

"Up above, the notables, the fine Jews, the men of good birth, sit, in a little group. Their conversation revolves around business and politics: the kosher meat tax, the troublemakers of this generation, the recruiting of soldiers, the choosing of town councilors, the appointment of a rabbi, about one thing and another and also about the new police chief. A young fortune hunter, with his eye on the job of town councilor, sidles up to this group and, with a sugary smile, invites one of the wealthy men to join him on one of the upper benches. His intention is to steam this man with flattery and win him over to his side. The wealthy man bows winningly to a more powerful man, and soon the three of them are up on a bench together. They are whipping themselves lustily with their reeds. It seems that the deal is progressing satisfactorily.

"For the benefit of the men of good birth, the bath was kept well heated. The big and the small, the old and the young, were whipping and washing themselves with gusto. The crowd groaned and sighed, smacked its lips with pleasure. At that point, I climbed up to the uppermost benches and, lying down in a corner so as to be alone, began to steam my aching bones and body.

"*Oy*, Reb Alter! Move over a bit. A little more into the shade, if you please."

Alter looked at me as at some scourge from the devil and shrugged his shoulders, "*Nu, Nu!*"

"Take your time," I soothed him. "Why the rush? Soon, soon. But let me catch my breath first."

CHAPTER VI

Alter fussed for a while with the mouthpiece of his pipe. It was badly clogged. He finally twisted it out of the bowl, cursing in anger, and set a goose quill in its place. He lit it again—puff, puff, puff—and a dense cloud of smoke poured out like from a chimney. I straightened my old bones a bit and continued my tale.

"I arrived at the bathhouse early the next morning, long before the crowd collected. Berl the Whipper sat on a bench between two stacks of reeds which stood on end like towers. He inspected them carefully, like a woman picking peas, and bound them into brooms. Nearby, at the stove, stood Itsik the Watchman, a man with a broad beard who had been earning his living for thirty years by doing nothing more than keeping his eye on the bundles of clothing with his hands folded over his stomach, and wishing the wealthy gentlemen a "May you prosper" as they left the bathhouse. He stretched his arms up high and yawned out loud. He figured up how much money his wife would want for *shabes*, and discussed with Berl the meager earnings they received, imitated each of the rich men individually and complained that the customers were not what they used to be. In the good old days, even the most god-forsaken miser left no less than six kopecks, and today . . . He spat: 'Today, may they all go to the devil!'

"Berl and Itsik gave me a warm welcome. It was a long time since I had been there last and they considered me to be an honored guest. We talked about many things. Finally, I brought the conversation around to Fishke. 'Where,' I asked, 'is our Fishke?'

" 'Fishke?' repeated Berl and tried out one of the brooms. 'Heh-heh! Fishke is in clover. He's prosperous and very happy.'

" 'Fishke!' Itsik added, shaking his head. 'Fishke lives like a prince today. I wish I had his luck. He never dreamed of living such a life.'

"Finally Berl the Whipper told me all the details:

" 'It was a Thursday night. We had all the ovens going and were dead tired. I lay down on a bench with the other fellows to catch my breath. Aside from us there were a few loafers who are always hanging around here. As we lay smoking and talking, we heard a wagon drive right up to the house. Well, what difference did that make? Before we had time to look around, three big men came in—giants I tell you—men of iron, and said in one voice, "Good evening, gentlemen! Where is Fishke? Give us Fishke!" I was scared when I heard this. What kind of talk was this, and all together, too—"Give us Fishke?" But I soon came to my senses. What was there to be scared about? Fishke was not, God forbid, a thief; nor was he a smuggler. And even if these men should be *khaper's*, what did Fishke have to worry about? With his physique, praise the Lord, he was in no danger of becoming a soldier.

" ' "Is it Fishke you want!" I asked bravely. "He isn't here right now. But tell me, what do you need him for? I'd like to know."

" 'The three men looked at each other and hesitated. Then one of them stepped forward and said to me: 'All right, we'll tell you. Why not? There is nothing to be ashamed of. It's a Jewish thing. This is the story:

" ' "You know the blind orphan girl, don't you? She always sits in front of the Dead Synagogue, near the old cemetery, and begs with that little song that one of the other beggars composed for her. Well, this blind orphan girl became a widow this year. She was in a hurry to remarry, so she engaged herself to a porter. She promised to buy him clothes, to make a respectable man of him, and also to give him money. They were supposed to get married tonight. A good supper has been prepared: brandy, rolls, fish and pot-roast, a golden chicken soup, as is the custom among us children of Israel. And all this costs money, of course. When everything was all ready and the bride all decked out, shining and shimmering, as a Jewish daughter should be, we went to fetch the groom. But this fellow, listen to this, wasn't home. We waited one hour, two hours, and still no sign of him—as if he'd dried up. How did it end? The fellow, may he burn in hell, got cold feet because of his grandmother! She'd been the cook for the richest man in town—may he prosper for many years—so she raised a row. She said the match would dishonor her. It was below her dignity. After all, she'd been a cook in a rich house for so many years and knew many of the town's finest gentlemen. When they came to see her magnate at night they used to slip in through the kitchen door. . . .

" ' "She could make a *kugl* like no one else could, and her *khremzlekh*—there was nothing that compared to them. The cook in a wealthy household is not to be sneezed at: she controls the back door to the house. During *Shevues* the *shames* himself brings her the *esrig* for her blessing, and on *Purim* the assistant cantor comes to read the *megile* to her in the kitchen. And even

Rikl the Sayer comes to drink a cup of chicory with her on *Rosh-Hashone* after the Holy Ark has been opened.

" ' "Why then should her grandchild blacken her face in her old age and ruin the family name? No, sir! He refused to have anything to do with this match or the bride, even if she were covered with gold.

" ' " 'If you don't like it, you can lump it!' he said. 'As far as I'm concerned the comedy is over.'

" ' "We stood there open-mouthed. Actually, we don't care so much about losing the groom as about losing the dinner. What are we going to do with this feast, with such fish and such roasts? We've run ourselves ragged all day getting everything ready. We didn't even get our commission for arranging the match. It's a sin to let all this work go to waste, our effort, our hard work! We thought and thought and finally we got an idea—Fishke! Let him help us out of our trouble! Let him be the groom. What's the difference? Why should he care? And that's why we're here—to lead him to the *khupe* instead of the porter!"

" 'Just as they finished their story, Fishke arrived. Oh, we weren't going to let a bargain like this slip through our fingers. We didn't bother him with long explanations. We just shoved him along: "Go, young man, with your crooked legs. Under the *khupe* with you! You've been single long enough."

" 'It was all done very quickly. Before Fishke had time to look around, the fish and the roasts were gobbled up, the wine and the brandy had disappeared, and everybody was congratulating the newlyweds.

" 'That's why Fishke is strolling around in a brand new Circassian overcoat, meant for the porter, looking like a dandy. Every morning he leads his blind wife to her place at the cemetery and every evening he brings her home. Food and drink are no longer a worry for Fishke. His wife wears the pants. She has a good trade and brings home a steady income. They both love each other, and would be hard put to find, God forbid, fault with each other.' "

"And this, Reb Alter, was what Berl the Whipper told me. Now do you see," I exclaimed, "what miracles can happen in the world?

"Do you see how among us Jews the lame and the blind are paired? How our weddings are arranged! How the fate of couples is decided, and for what purpose? So that the marriage brokers may eat and drink till they burst! That is how it is among the poor and also among the rich, except that when the rich marry, it's a different type of dinner with a different taste. . . . But that's not my point.

"Don't worry, Reb Alter! If you haven't yet succeeded in making a match between two men then you will surely succeed, with God's help, in making some other kind of match. Don't give up! You started your matchmaking like an experienced broker. Just because the young fellow. . . well, *beh!* Upon my word! But once you come across an eligible young lady, things will be different! Whether she's blind, deaf, dumb—'Go, daughter o'mine! Under the *khupeh* with you and my best wishes! The printer needs money. My mare has to eat. My daughter must get married. My wife has just borne me a son, God praise him. Go then, daughter o'mine! Under the *khupeh* with you?'

"Reb Alter! Move over a little more, please. Oh, how you're sweating, may the Evil Eye not harm you! You're as wet as a beaver!"

CHAPTER VII

"Well, I feel low in any case," Alter muttered to himself with a groan. He looked sad and big beads of sweat stood out on his forehead. He raised his eyes and looked at me imploringly—just as an infant looks at its mother when it wants the breast. But poor Alter only meant business with his glance. He yearned to do a little trading with me. After all, how can two Jews with fully grown beards simply lie under a tree at the height of day and do nothing? If two Jews happened to be marooned on a desert island in the middle of the ocean, just the two of them without another living soul, then it is quite certain that with the passing of time one of them would open some sort of little store and the other one—also a little business. They would trade with each other. One would borrow from the other at a certain rate of interest and thus they would both manage to earn their keep.

Alter soon teased, "What does my lordship have in his wagon today?" But to me it sounded like, "Mommy, more . . ."

"Unpack your goods, Reb Mendl, and let's see what you have."

Since I had no choice, there was no point in being lazy. I unpacked my wares, and Alter his. Before long, we were absorbed in a heated session of estimating, bargaining, making exchanges. I tried to sell him some books with uneven print and missing lines: I had been wanting to get rid of them for a long time. But he was no fool and wouldn't even touch them.

"That stuff will never move," Alter said, wrinkling his nose. "It's just trash written by some shabby bench warmers! God knows what they have scribbled there. Who wants it? Nobody can understand a word of it. It must be written in Turkish! Books like that are only dust collectors. It's a waste of space to take them along. *Feh*! Show me something interesting, Reb Mendele!"

I brought out my collection of weekday prayer books, festival prayer books, prayer books for women, *hagodes*—one sort after another. But my Alter was squeamish and found fault with each one. One book did captivate him, though. He looked at it and couldn't tear himself away. It was really quite an antique. The pages were all of different colors and also different sizes. The letters were smudged and unclear and of different types: Rashi type, diamond, pearl, extended and bold-face types. The composition of each page was a marvel to behold. It was laid out in strips—narrow ones with small print on both sides, a broad strip with bigger type in the center, and below this, a belly of tiny type set in like poppy seeds; and, between these patches of print, stretched narrow ribbons of blank space across the page and up and down, like little pathways in the forest. These are some of the qualities that a Jew in our part of the world looks for in a book.

Of course, the pages did not follow in sequence either. In this lay the whole genius of the arrangement: a Jew ought to break his head a bit and figure out the proper sequence. There is no point in dwelling on typographical errors. It stands to reason that there were myriads of them. And who cared? A Jew has a good mind and it wouldn't hurt him to use it to figure out what was meant. But the style made up for all the other faults. The style was delightfully intricate, simply impossible to understand. Just the thing to satisfy the most demanding Jewish taste. Because, when all is said and done, what we Jews appreciate most is something we must break our teeth on and still be unsuccessful in getting it. After all, if you can't understand it, there must be something to it. . . . But that's not my point.

My Alter seized this merchandise with both hands. His health seemed to improve visibly just from handling it. Then we started trading:

> women's books of supplication for the *Tales of Baba*;
> women's homilies for *A Thousand and One Nights;*
> prayer scrolls for good luck charms;
> penitential prayers from Zhitomir for prayer shawls from Berszed;
> lamentations from Vilna for rams' horns;
> *Khanike* candles for wolves'-teeth talismans;
> brass *shabes* candlesticks for children's shiny skullcaps.

Although not a single kopeck passed through our hands, we were both immensely pleased with the trading process itself. After all, we had both been swapping, bartering, trafficking, giving and taking, and keeping very busy.

Alter's melancholy had blown away like smoke. A glance at his face made it clear that his humiliating experiences with matchmaking at the fair in Yarmelinets were now completely forgotten. Quietly he did some calculations on his fingers. His head was cocked to one side, as though some inner bookkeeper sat in it to whose figures Alter paid rapt attention. It seemed that the tally indicated some future profit, with God's help, because his mouth spread from ear to ear under his bushy mustache, and his whole face broke out in a bright smile.

In the meanwhile, evening drew near and it was time to say our prayers. A caressing breeze blew up, and tatters of clouds, which we had awaited like long overdue guests, appeared in the sky. The trees began to rock slowly. They bent their heads toward one another and carried on a whispered conversation after having been silent all day. The breeze awakened the sleeping grain. The stalks woke up noisily like young children and kissed each other again and again. God's creatures were in motion all over: in the fields, in the forest and in the air. One after another the little songbirds stepped forth on the branches of the trees and saplings. They preened their little feathers, wiped their little beaks, cocked their little heads and broke out in sweet song. Butterflies, richly clad in satins and silks, in antique style with precious jewels, danced and whirled in the air; they soared, turned, swooped down and showed off their charms.

Two storks, like guardsmen with long red legs, stood on the grass with beaks raised in the air and glared about in proud defiance. A mischievous little bird flitted from tree to tree calling, "Cuckoo, cuckoo!" as though it were playing hide-and-seek. From the stalks of corn and wheat came an answering call: "Pick-ber-wick! Pick-ber-wick!" as if to say, "You'll never catch me. Shake salt on my tail and see how much good that does. You'll never, never catch me."

In a nearby thicket, the nightingale trilled. Up and down the scale he went, thrilling the soul, putting all the world-famous cantors to shame. Even the frogs in the marshes did their share and croaked hoarsely. Nor were the flies and bees quiet; and the crickets, little thieves, chirped everywhere. For this kind of concert a ticket at any price was cheap. . . . The whole world had come alive and was full of joy. What a pleasure to hear, see and smell the sounds, the sights, the odors all around!

"Reb Alter, it's good! Reb Alter, it's beautiful! It makes your heart leap with joy. God's world is alive! God's world is wonderful! Oh, how I'd like to plunge in, head first . . ."

"Reb Mendele, shame on you!" Reb Alter admonished me. "It's time for our evening prayers. And you'd better remember to start right at the beginning and not let your mind wander."

I pulled up my stockings, tightened my belt and began to recite my prayers lustily in a high-pitched voice. My Alter, may he live long, followed suit and accompanied me in his thick-stringed bass. Thus we both sang our praises to His dear Name, while all the bushes and flowers in the fields and all the birds and beasts in the woods burst into song and gave their thanks to God.

Reb Alter ran through his prayers in a hurry. While I was still only halfway through, he produced a small keg of grease from somewhere under his wagon and busily began to smear his wheels with it.

"Don't dally, Reb Mendele. Hurry it up a bit," he drove me. "Get your wagon ready while I go after the horses. It's time to leave. We can travel a good ways before night falls."

Alter left and I began to do justice to my wagon. I didn't hurry. I smeared the wheels leisurely, without sparing the grease and inspected each axle individually and in detail, This took a while. When I had finished, my Alter had still not returned. The horses must have strayed far into the woods to eat their fill. The sun sank below the horizon. Its last rays climbed down the trees on which they had played with such joy and brilliance only a short while ago—and said, "Good night!" to the forest. . . .

And then I was struck by fear. Maybe Alter had fallen ill? This was no laughing matter after sweating so heavily and fasting all day! Maybe he was lying somewhere in a faint! Or maybe someone had attacked him? After all, it was a forest, an out-of-the-way place! I couldn't sit here doing nothing, I had to go and see. I took heart and entered the forest. I walked and searched but in vain. Alter and the horses had vanished into thin air. I walked further until I came to a long narrow valley which seemed to divide the forest in two. This valley was overgrown with brambles and small thorny bushes. On the one side it led toward the highway and on the other side to God alone knows where. The forest stood in silent slumber, covered from above with a dark quilt. It was quiet all around. Only on occasion, two tall trees, close neighbors, whispered to each other with heads bent close, tickling each other from behind with their branches. Or a few leaves flapped, moved as though they were upset and could not rest. This was the forest talking in its sleep. It was dreaming of the day that had just ended, with all its joys and sorrows. The murmur of the reeds—that was the forest dreaming of the poor trees which had been chopped down before their time. The noise of something falling—that was a dream of a nest of innocent little birds which the murderous hawk had destroyed, and this was also why the leaves were restless. They were flapping over the dead mother and her murdered young. A cloud of melancholy descended upon the forest and enveloped me too.

Fantasy, that terrible prankster and notorious liar, began to play havoc with my thoughts. He shipped me a supply of wild and terrifying images and my mental factory reworked this raw material and made it even more fantastic. In this shipment I found a corpse, the murdered Alter Yaknehoz, and the bones of our horses. My mind refined upon this and developed it into a fiery red monster and a wolf of tremendous size with huge frightening teeth. . . .

I was about to descend into the valley when the thought occurred to me that I had left the two wagons standing unattended in the middle of the field. Neither sight nor smell of our small fortunes would remain. It would be wisest to go back and check before doing anything else. It was also possible that Alter had returned with the horses long ago and was now beginning to worry about me. This thought settled in my mind and gave me renewed strength. My hopes grew and grew until they tore to shreds the clouds of melancholy and allowed a few rays of peace to shine upon my troubled heart.

I hastened back to the wagons.

CHAPTER VIII

With God's help I arrived in one piece without broken limbs although, in my haste, I had walked into a tree more than once. Rising from a fall in the forest is by no means as embarrassing as in town where people gather around and laugh. Therefore, each time I raised myself from the ground, I did it with pleasure and thanked the Lord for being able to do so with dignity. And since God, in His mercy, was so generous to me, I felt I had reason to believe that when I arrived I would find my Alter and the horses. But I had not deserved that much charity from His beloved Name.

Alter was not there.

I was petrified. God alone knew what had happened to Alter and where his remains lay now. This time his dismal luck had really shown what it could do. And what was I to do? What would happen to me? That was a problem. My plan had been to unload my wares in Glupsk, stock up there with as many copies of the *Book of Lamentations* as possible and distribute them in surrounding towns and villages, as I did every year at this time. The "Three Weeks" were almost upon us. I couldn't afford to lose an hour. If I lost time on the road, the Jews in the towns and villages would be without their *Book of Lamentations* . This was no laughing matter—Jews without *Books of Lamentations!*

I could just imagine what would happen on *Tishe Bov:* Jews would gobble up their *milkhike* noodles, fill their bellies with hard-boiled eggs dipped in ash, and would seat themselves sullenly on the ground in their stocking feet showing their worn-out heels. The young mischief-makers would be ready to throw their stockpiles of burrs at a moment's notice. Everyone would wait for the beginning, for the good word, and suddenly—no *Book of Lamentations* ! The black plague must have taken Mendele, he didn't bring the *Lamentations* ! Ten men to one Book. What shoving and crowding! What a confusion of Lice! What a tangling of beards! And side curls full of burrs! And the stench of eggs and noodles rising into everyone's nostrils. . . . The women would not be nearly as badly off. To them it mattered little whether it was the *Lamentations.* Anything would do so long as it was in print: *Tkhines, Festival prayer books, Hagodes*—it was all the same! They'd wail over them in their high-pitched voices. What difference did it make, if only they could have a good cry? Yes, it was a nasty situation any way you looked at it . . . but that's beside the point.

I had to do something. I could not just sit idly by with folded hands. The search had to continue. I looked at the stars and remembered that it was time to eat. Out came my little satchel. I took a few gulps from the bottle, bul- bul-bul, to ease my troubles, snatched a few bites to eat, only for appearance's sake, bid farewell to the bottle, bul-bul-bul again, and set off in haste.

Once again I was in the forest, once again near the valley, and soon in the valley itself. But to tell the truth, I was not alone, nor was my heart as heavy as before. Yes, this time I had company. We talked about my troubles and I was cheered.

When I took my hurried snack after fasting all day, I must have spent too much time with the bottle. An extra sip on an empty stomach and I was over the limit. Besides, I had hardly eaten anything. With all the excitement and fright, I had lost my appetite. I couldn't force anything down my throat. Well, this extra sip stood by me in this time of need like a father. It gave me courage and made me very talkative, may I be protected from this today. I've always been that way—an extra lick of brandy on Purim or *Simkhes-Toyre* and the words began to flow like from a sack full of holes. I could talk to a wall and smile ever so sweetly. I became so good and soft—you could use me for a compress on a boil. My body stretched and became light and thin as weak tea. Jumbled little pieces of Mendele bounced around—hard to tell which was the most important one. At that point, it used to seem as though I turned into two Mendeles, one pulling east and the other west. The pair of feet that they shared tripped over each other not knowing which one to follow. One Mendele asks, the other one answers. My words came back at me from afar, like an echo, not like my voice at all. The tone had the ring of an empty barrel. Nevertheless, I did not lose my head completely. A trace of sense remained, as in a dream.

"Good evening!" I bowed. "And where are you off to this time of night?"

"*Ta* . . . addle-heads, asses!" answered the other Mendele with a good-natured little smile. "They decided to get lost. A farce, upon my word!"

"There's a hole there, Reb Mendele. Take care!"

"Yes, as I am Jew, there's a hole! This must be at least the twentieth time I've fallen, I'm sure!"

"Get up then, if you please. It's not respectable to lie there stretched out like that."

"Thanks for the advice, uncle! Well, I'm up again. I'll try feeling my way with the whip. It's a comedy, upon my word! The trees are walking! Here's to your health, let's walk together! *Feh*, don't scratch like that! *Ai*, another scratch! Almost took my eye out that time, *tfu!*"

"Spit on them, Reb Mendele! It's the only way to get rid of them. Here, follow this little path, if you please, and you'll come out in the open field."

"Good, I'm here already. Oh, what a moon! Like a hunk of dough! A real moon, like in Odessa, with a nose and eyes. *Sha*, should I say the prayer to the moon? Peace unto you!"

"And unto you, peace!"

"Peace unto you!"

"And unto you, peace! Just as I spring toward you and cannot reach you. . . . Then jump, uncle!"

"Hup, hup, hup! Just so shall my enemies be unable to reach me. . . . What is it that they want from us anyway!" I sobbed suddenly. "Is it my fault that I'm alive and must eat? Here, look at my body! You call that a body? It's as thin as a rail! Always sick! Always in pain. I had a mother once, she petted me and kissed me. Woe is me, I'm an orphan, an orphan!" I wept in earnest.

"*Sha, sha!*" came the encouraging reply. "You know it can't be helped. How is it that an elderly Jew with a beard, with a wife and horde of children, isn't ashamed to weep out in the open with the moon watching! It just shows a lack of respect! Stop crying, the devil won't take you. Better keep your eyes open, here's a fence."

"Yes, as I am a Jew, a fence indeed. I've walked right into it, as a matter of fact. What shall I do now!"

"Why, just climb over it. That's the way."

"Thanks for the advice, uncle. Now I've got both my feet in the garden."

"Well, congratulations, cousin! Now, march on, if you please."

"Be calm. I'm going. My, what a crop! Chick-peas, beans, and cucumbers without end!"

"Bless the fruits of the earth, then, and don't wait for a second invitation."

"What delicious cucumbers! May they multiply! Hah, what hit me? Who's that?"

The blows came from a sturdy peasant who had come up behind me and was letting me know that it's impolite to prowl around in other people's gardens. The point he was getting at was that it is wrong to steal fresh cucumbers at night. The blows on the one hand and the fresh cucumbers on the other made me sober up. For a moment I stood befuddled, as though I had just awakened from sleep. Naturally, the first words out of my mouth were, "*Gvald!*" Help! But I reconsidered this approach and decided to act unconcerned. I turned to the peasant and asked him winningly, in coarse Ukrainian: "You didn't happen to see a little Jew with a couple of horses passing by here by any chance, did you?"

But the peasant's mind was made up. He wouldn't be swayed, nor would he listen. He pulled me along by the sleeve, he shoved me from behind and just kept on repeating, "Move along! Move along!" It was no use. I stumbled along until at last we arrived at a house with lit-up windows. In front of it stood a *britshke* harnessed to four good horses.

On entering the house, the peasant shoved me ahead while he doffed his cap and took up a position near the door. Not knowing what else to do, I took my cap off also. I scratched my head and felt terribly out of place.

At a desk sat a little clerk busily scribbling with a scraping pen which begged for ink every few minutes. No sooner was its mouth filled than it would spit it all out on the paper. The little clerk was impatient with the pen. He winced and cursed at every dip. It was obvious that this was torture for both of them, poor things. They were both unhappy: the pen with his heavy hand and shameful mistakes; he with the maddening blots. He—a squeeze; the pen—a blot. In the middle of the room stood a red collar with brass buttons, a big belly, and a puffy, glistening face, with small bloodshot eyes. This creature twisted his mustaches. His voice, booming out of his double chin, spoke harshly to two men with hanging heads who stood to a side of the door. The first one was tall, with a powerful body, a shaven neck and a silver earring in his left earlobe. The other one was thin with a pointed little beard, a tin badge on his chest, and a long stick which he held with both hands, squinting continually and bowing every few minutes. The red collar was furious. He roared at the first one: "Some village

210

elder you are! To Siberia in chains with you!" And to the second one: "I'll slice you into thin strips, you sot! You so-and-so, the devil take your mother!"

Each of my limbs died separately. I shook as though in high fever. There was a buzzing in my head and a ringing in my ears. I couldn't hear, I couldn't see what was happening. I did not even hear properly what charges the peasant made against me. But when the red collar hiccoughed and turned to me with his harsh Russian speech, I suddenly woke up and heard everything. Before my eyes a fist waved and terrible words assaulted my ears:

"Thief, contraband, smuggler, pickpocket, chains, prison, the knout, Siberia . . ." Suddenly he seized one of my prayer curls and, angrily imitating my grimace of pain, he snatched a scissors from the desk and, in a rage, snipped off the entire curl!

Seeing my prayer curl on the floor, I burst into tears—my old, gray prayer curl which had been with me from childhood until now; my prayer curl which had shared the joys and pains of an entire lifetime! Why, my mother had fondled it, combed it, and took pride in its shiny black waves when I was a boy. It was an adornment on my face in days gone by, when I was young and fresh. The poor thing became prematurely gray from troubles and worry, and I was not, God forfend, one bit ashamed of its grayness. We had both aged early from poverty, loneliness, afflictions, threats, uncalled-for enmity and persecution from the rest of the world. Oh whom, good Lord, had it offended? Whom, I ask, had my gray hairs harmed?

My heart wept within me, "*Gvald*," silently. I stared mutely like—a lamb at shearing time and from my eyes—drip, drip, drip, big tears like chick-peas . . . My cheek smarted in its newly acquired nakedness. My appearance must have changed terribly. It must have been a pitiful sight indeed, because the red collar lost his power of speech and softened, putting his hands on both my shoulders. It seems that a human heart beat under those brass buttons. My gray hairs and my whole appearance convinced him of my honesty. As if in apology to me, he fell angrily upon the peasant, demanding why, for a cucumber, he dragged a poor old man around. With a hiccough, he drove the peasant out. Then, taking his cap, he mumbled a few words and, after turning aimlessly around the room, left. Soon the *britshke* was heard driving off.

211

Everyone in the room came to life. The clerk flung the pen away with an oath. The village elder and the other man both straightened out, raised their heads and waved their hands at the street as if to say: "Good riddance and don't bother coming back!" The village elder caught his breath and, combing his hair with his five fingers, exclaimed, "Well, there's a chief of police for you!"

After I told them of my misfortunes, the gentiles advised me to go to the village inn not far from there. There would be a crowd of people there on their way home from the market. Maybe one of them would be able to help me. I picked up my curl, hid it in my pocket, covered my naked cheek with a kerchief and bid them all a good night.

CHAPTER IX

The inn was surrounded by wagons and carts of all sorts. Some were empty except for straw. Others were full of wares and stuff which had been bought at or left over from the market that day. On one cart a pig lay in a sack, his handsome snout poked through a hole, and squealed so shrilly that my skin crawled. Behind a wagon full of new puttees and new clay tubs and pots, a onehorned spotted cow was struggling with all her might to free herself from her rope. She wanted to rejoin her girl friends in the barn with the good tidings, "It's not so easy to get rid of me, praise the Great Wild Bull! I'm back again and in the best of health!"

A pair of gray, broad-boned oxen stood in their yoke and chewed their cud earnestly—they didn't waste a moment. It almost looked like they were thinking deep thoughts and arriving at important conclusions. The inn keeper's goat was on top of a wagon. He poked his head into a sack and pulled it out with a full mouth. He snorted, swished his tail, and swiftly glanced in all directions with a quivering beard. An old, scrawny village hound with a lame leg and clump of matted hair dangling at the end of his tail edged his way toward the wagon, looked up with great respect, came a bit closer, sniffed and smelled until his nose found a dried-up bone. Seizing the bargain, he limped away a few paces and lay down to crack the bone, resting his head on its side as he held the bone in his paws.

A horse hitched to another wagon, bored with standing in one place with nothing to do except to nap and wiggle his ears, decided to pay a visit to a pair of young oxen in a yoke, who were doing themselves proud over an open sack of grain, and decided to be their guest for supper. On the way, however, a wheel hub from his wagon caught the wheel of another wagon and almost upset it. The other horse, in fright, jumped out of his traces and kicked a neighboring horse who reared on his hind legs with a whinny. The terrified goat jumped off the wagon and landed on the old dog's tail. The poor old dog ran off on three legs howling at the top of his lungs.

With much effort, I fought my way through the maze of vehicles and, after looking around carefully to see if our two horses were here, I entered the inn.

I became conscious of what was going on inside only piece-meal—not all at once, but rather in successive waves. The first greeting I received was directed at my nose. As soon as I entered, that poor organ was assaulted by a sharp, bitter, overpowering stench of brandy, tobacco smoke and sweat all mixed into one. My nose promptly returned the greeting with a resounding sneeze while my ears awaited their turn. They were welcomed by a din of shrill and piping, deep and hoarse, blaring and bellowing voices which rolled in on them with deafening effect. My nose and ears having been duly saluted, the next in order were my eyes. At first they wandered about aimlessly in the murk. Later, a dense crowd of people emerged, but individual features could not yet be distinguished. And last, at the far end of the room, on a long wooden table, a wax candle in a clay pot became visible. It burned with a glaring red flame encircled by halos of yellow, green and blue which danced in the clouds of steam and columns of smoke which filled the room. Only now did beards, goatees, stubbles, whole faces and features of males and females come swimming out of the murk. Little groups of people came into view. Those who were still on their feet were only on their fourth or fifth drink.

Off to a side, two drunks were hugging each other and calling each other foul names from sheer love. Near them stood a barefoot woman in a short skirt and patched low-cut blouse. She enjoyed the scene and good-naturedly slapped each one on the back alternately, laughing, "Enough, enough, go home!" And the pair of them simply melted from love and, hugging each other even more tightly, collapsed in a heap.

Some of the customers sat on long benches at tables with bottles of brandy and food. Two fat peasants drank to each other's health and were, as the saying goes, mellow and merry. Another one, a lover of the bitter drop, who had found himself a home in the inn, puffed on his little pipe and called to the first peasant and then to the second and then to anyone at random: "To your health! To your health!" But nobody paid any attention to him.

The last figure to swim out of the fog was that of a woman, lively, strong, with fuzzy beauty marks on her face and some sort of kerchief over her head—the innkeeper's wife, in all her glory! She flitted among the barrels, bottles, baskets, glasses, rings of bagels, boiled eggs, lean, dry fish and pieces of hard liver. Her mouth did not close for a moment. Her hands did not rest for an instant. She complained without cease. She took cash from one, security from

214

another, and kept accounts for others by marking crosses and circles on a board with a piece of chalk.

I wandered about in this crowd like a lost soul. I tried talking to various people but the result was, as Alter used to say, "In short, nothing!"

Finally, the crowd began to thin out. Folks began to leave for home. I made my way toward the innkeeper's wife, with my whip under my arm and pointed directly at her. I did this on purpose, for I had an ulterior motive: innkeepers in general like coach drivers, and will bribe them with brandy and food so that they will bring their passengers to the inn. My whip was to be my guardian angel and endow me with grace and charm in this lady's eyes. A conversation sprung up between us:

"Good evening!"

"A good year to you!"

"Tell me, please, where is your husband?"

"What do you need him for?"

"Just like that. No particular reason."

"Tell me. Maybe I can help you."

"*Ta*. . . . Well, all right."

And so, a word here and a word there, and I told her my troubles and about the ugly situation in which I now found myself. She supported her head on her hand with two fingers extended along her cheek and sighed in sympathy as she listened: "Oh my! How terrible!"

To please her, I told her about myself: who I was, what I did for a living. She, in turn, drowned me in a torrent of talk. She told me her troubles in great detail—about her ne'er-do-well husband, her children, and the inn. A close acquaintance quickly sprang up between us. It even turned out that we were distant relatives! She was called *Khaye-Treyne* after a grandaunt of mine on my grandmother's side. What a joy, what happiness! She asked about my wife, my children and each of my relatives. When her husband arrived, she quickly informed him:

"We have a guest . . . a dear guest, Reb Mendele Moykher Sforim! A relative of mine!" Then, she placed her hands on her hips, and talked condescendingly to him:

"So! You thought you took me out of a barn, did you? Don't you worry! I don't have to be ashamed, praise the Lord, before anyone. You might begin to appreciate what a family I come from!"

215

"*Ta!* Lord of Nations!" I said to myself. "Saul went forth to seek his asses and found himself a kingdom. I went forth to seek my horses and found myself a Khaye-Treyne . . . !"

Khaye-Treyne's husband was a man with a long nose; his thin beard, his side curls and eyebrows—blond as flax. When he wasn't talking, he chewed his tongue. When he was readying himself to talk, he first licked his lips thoroughly, looking, for all the world, as clever as a sheep. Upon giving me his hand by way of greeting, he mumbled unintelligibly and his whole appearance bespoke the fact that he lay firmly under his wife's heel, that he trembled at the sight of her. I later found out that in these parts he was known as Khayim-Khene Khaye Treyne's, and Khaye-Treyne herself was called Khaye-Treyne the Cossack.

"Where have you been loafing till now?" Khaye-Treyne began to cross-examine him. "Where did the devil carry you off to, *shlimazl*!? Who ever heard of such a thing? To neglect house and home and to disappear. Don't worry! Reb Mendele is a relative. He ought to know what a scourge you are, a plague that his Holy Name has saddled on me. Just look at him! Stands there like a clay statue and chews his tongue!"

"Didn't you yourself send me to Gavrilo for a sack of potatoes, didn't you?" Khayim-Khene defended himself, first licking his lips thoroughly.

"And the *rebbe*, that handsome *rebbe*, what's the matter with him? Is he too weak to bring the sack of potatoes? He's not too weak to eat enough for ten!"

"The *rebbe* took the cows and the calf out to pasture, the *rebbe* did," Khayim-Khene tried to explain to his wife.

"Oh, keep quiet! Better keep quiet and chew your tongue!" Khaye-Treyne said impatiently, glaring angrily at her husband. Then she turned to me and complained about the troubles she had with each and every member of her family. Were it not for her, everything would have gone to pot long ago. She repeatedly interrupted herself with, "I don't mind if you know, Reb Mendele! To you I can talk like to a father, you're a relative."

I attempted to make peace in the family and to raise Khayim-Khene in his wife's esteem. To accomplish this, I lied a little, decried all men in general, myself included, and praised and extolled women and Khaye-Treyne in particular. If, God forbid, they did not exist, life just wouldn't be worth living. Khaye-Treyne softened.

216

"May your health prosper, Reb Mendele!" She beamed at me with a glowing face. Then she turned to her husband and spoke to him more gently.

"Enough of that tongue chewing, Khayim-Khene! Why don't you wipe the dishes and the glasses which *Esau* used instead? Reb Mendele is probably very hungry," she said, turning to me and rising from her seat at the bar.

"I'm hungry myself. We always have supper late on a market day. There's never any time. Come, please. We'd like you to come into our house."

Two dark little rooms led from the bar-room to a rather large room with a low ceiling, no floor and tiny windows. Some of the panes were cracked, some patched with pieces of greased paper, and some were missing almost entirely, with only a triangle of glass left in a corner like the last tooth of an old woman. The slightest breeze made it rattle and hum a sad little tune—zim, zim, zim. In a corner of the room stood a table with long, narrow, unpainted benches next to it. The bed in the opposite corner was piled high with bedding, may the Evil Eye not harm it: pillows—large, middling, small and tiny—in a tower which reached to the ceiling. Next to the stove stood a broad bench which was used as a bed at night. On the walls hung portraits covered with cobwebs, dead flies, dried cockroach eggs, and flyspecks. From underneath the covering of filth, peculiar figures peered out: a wailing wall with rabbits and fantastic animals which looked like half goat and half deer or half lion and half donkey or half leopard and half bird. A tall Haman, in a Russian Army officer's uniform, hung on a noose which barely reached his shoulders so that it looked more like the noose hung on him! Nearby stood Mordecai in a fur cap and threadbare capote tied around his waist with a rope. With his shoes, stockings and prayer curls he looked like a Jew from any small Russian town. Napoleon was there, too. He had also fallen into Jewish hands, poor man, Lord have mercy on his sad condition! His portrait hung between a small, greasy, warped mirror, on one side and Potiphar's wife on the other, a hideous creature who was flirting with Joseph and tugging at his coattails.

A broad, chubby, hard-working girl, with a pair of cheeks like dumplings, moved about the room. She had little hair on her head and two short pigtails behind. She kept her elbows pressed close to her sides. Both her forearms were thrust forward like two wagon shafts be tween which she moved. She glided along without lifting

217

her feet, her head leading the way. She brought out a tablecloth and dishes, and began to set the table quickly. Khaye-Treyne whispered something in her ear. She turned the shafts around, thrust her head forward, her body following directly behind it, and disappeared from the room.

In a corner, four children were quarreling over a little pug dog which pierced the air with its shrill cries. Khaye-Treyne fell on them without warning, silently pinched one, tweaked another, and flung the puppy out of the room. The children thumbed their noses at each other and separated into different corners.

Khayim-Khene arrived with a big jug of sour cream. His wife took it and, after fussing with it for a while, asked us to wash.

A barefoot boy, in a sweater and a pair of tattered trousers, dashed in; the *rebbe* had caught a little sparrow in the barn! The children craned their necks and gaped. Before they had a chance to recover, a young man with a somewhat swollen nose and thick lips stepped in, washed himself quickly over the pail of slops, sat down at the table, shoved a big piece of bread into his mouth and began chewing in haste, without looking around at anyone, as though fearing that the food would be gone before he could get at it. In the meanwhile, the chubby girl, the one with the dumpling cheeks, glided in again decked out in her best *shabes* clothes and also sat down at the table.

Khaye-Treyne advised me, pointing a finger at the girl: "That's my oldest daughter, Khasye-Grune!"

The company ate, mannerly at first—ladling out the soup and laying down the spoon each time—but soon the tempo increased and the din grew louder. Ten spoons dipped industriously into one bowl and flew swiftly back into ten mouths which sucked up the contents, each in its own fashion. The spoons hurried and scurried, the mouths sipped and sucked: "Whoof-hoof, hoof-foof!" My newly found relatives urged me on: "Eat! Don't wait for invitations!" And I: "Wiff-hiff!" in my own style.

The young man with the swollen nose didn't have a moment to lose; he worked for ten until he ladled his way down to the bird which was painted on the bottom of the bowl. Having finished his labors, he sighed from the depths of his belly and turned a pair of glassy eyes on the rest of the company. Then, suddenly, rising slightly from his seat, his hand shot forth toward me, accompanied by: "*Sholem aleykhem*! You look familiar to me. . . . What is your name?"

218

I told him and he actually jumped up in surprise.

"Reb Mendele! Reb Mendele Moykher Sforim! Pish! What do you mean, who hasn't heard of Reb Mendele? Why, I had the privilege of buying a little prayer book from you in Glupsk some time ago."

"Reb Mendele is my relative," said Khaye-Treyne haughtily, ready to burst with pride. Then, pointing at the young man, she informed me: "That's our *rebbe!*" Turning to the barefoot boy in tattered trousers, she said, "Now, Sheekele, Reb Mendele will hear you say your lessons. Don't be ashamed, he won't eat you!"

Sheekele, with a finger in his nose, looked away and mumbled, "I'm assamed to, I'm assamed to. . . ."

"How old is your Sheekele, may he live long?" I asked the mother.

"My Sheekele, may he live long, was *bar mitsved* this past spring," answered the beaming mother.

"Well now, Sheekele," I said, gently pinching the boy's cheek, "tell me, and don't be ashamed, which *sidra* is being read in the synagogue this week?"

"Go ahead, go ahead!" Sheekele was urged from all sides.

He stared blankly and said nothing.

"B . . . b . . . b. . ." The *rebbe* hinted with his thick lips.

"B . . . b . . . bull!" exclaimed Sheekele looking to the *rebbe*.

"Well, Balak, Balak . . ." I prompted him and questioned him further: "And what did Balak say to the elders?"

The *rebbe* licked his finger in order to give his pupil a hint.

"To lick!" shouted Sheekele with enthusiasm.

"Who, who?" the *rebbe* urged him on, believing that his pupil was on the right track. "Who, eh?"

"The *rebbe!*" Sheekele cried.

"Oh, you clogged head!" the angry *rebbe* exclaimed with heat. "Who, did Balak say, will lick?"

"The Jews!" answered Sheekele quickly with a shriek.

"The Jews, the Jews . . . Sheekele!" I said, patting his cheek. "Very good. You know your lessons."

The mother did not know what to do with herself for joy. She folded her hands over her belly and said with a face all aglow: "Blessed be the belly that bore such a gem!" The father chewed his tongue and was immensely pleased.

After supper, Khaye-Treyne suggested the following plan to me: "In a couple of hours, my worker Yanko will arrive with the horses. You, Reb Mendele, will ride one and my husband the other and you will bring the wagons and the wares here. And then we will decide what else to do. In the meanwhile, lie down and rest. Here is a freshly made bed for you."

"Thank you kindly!" I said. "But I'm afraid that if I crawl into that soft bed, it will be hard to get me out. God knows how long I can sleep there, and every moment is dear to me now. Some other time, God willing, I'll come to visit with my wife and children. Then, you will see, I will place myself in His hands and plunge into that pile of softness and stay there for a long, long time!"

"We want you to come, we do!" Khaye-Treyne said winningly. "And remember to bring all the children. And bring Yakhne-Sose too! But don't refuse to take a little pillow, at least, into the little room with you. Sleep well," she said. "Don't worry about a thing. I'll wake you early, at the crack of dawn."

CHAPTER X

Khaye-Treyne was indeed a pious Jewess and a good woman, but the bedbugs in her house were positive villains. They attacked as soon as I lay down on the sofa in the little room, and war broke out between us. Both sides were determined and fought valiantly; they with their mouths, I with my hands. They advanced, and I jumped up; they bit and I scratched; they drove ahead, and I retreated into the pillow. Finally I flung the pillow aside—the devil take it—but it struck a three-legged stool which toppled over smashing the clay water pitcher with a crash. Frightened cockroaches scurried over the floor in confusion. Feathers from the torn pillow flew about, into my nose and into my eyes. The sofa under me creaked and squeaked. The biting did not cease for a moment, nor did my twisting and turning. The stench of bedbugs was overpowering. At last, disgusted by the whole business, I decided to give it up. I sprang off the sofa and made for the window to catch a breath of fresh air.

God's world spread out before me. The golden moon sailed calmly across the dark blue sky. Her bright face was deep in thought. All was quiet around and about. . . . Her thoughtfulness cast a spell of sweet melancholy over me. Somehow she spoke directly to my heart and each glance of hers pierced my very soul. She stirred up a sea of emotions within me. My thoughts were inclined to dwell on myself—thoughts about my bitter life with its fill of illness, humiliations, insults and injuries, both old and new. I whimpered like a weak child before its mother: "*Oy*, Mama! My heart is black and blue. Haven't I had my share of headaches and bellyaches? Why, then, am I in everyone's way? Haven't I had wounds enough already? Then why do they begrudge me a little peace and quiet? *Oy*, it burns! *Oy*, it hurts!"

The moon's shining face gazed down on me earnestly, intently. She looked so comforting: "*Sha*, poor child, *sha!* It can't be helped. . . . " My heart wept even more. My eyes filled with tears. I lay my head down on my arm, the side with the shorn side curl facing the moon: "Here, look! See what they've done to me!" A well of pent-up feelings opened within me, roared into my heart and flooded my mind. I stared blankly into the void with my swollen eyes and begged: "*Gvald!* Help me! Have mercy! It hurts so. . . ." That's how a sick child wakes up at night, wailing to itself, seeking help with its poor little eyes. And there is nobody! Nobody! No one hears a thing. Everyone is asleep, quiet. . . . Only a dog down the street, with his tail between his legs and his head thrown back, was awake and howled gloomily at the moon. But she sailed her course placidly, rapt in thought. There was no reason to get excited over a dog's yelping.

The weight lifted from my heart. Something warm stirred within me, a wordless feeling of hope and cheer. Just such a feeling enters a Jew's soul after he has laid his troubles before God and has cried his eyes out over them! It is a feeling which makes a man soft as dough, good without limit, glad to do anything for anybody, ready to embrace the entire world and kiss it—so overwhelming are his feelings of love.

And the little bedbugs, aren't they God's creatures?

Is it their fault, poor things, that they stink? Can they help it if it is their nature to bite? They don't do so out of spite or evil intent. It is only their way of earning a living—to drink, to fill themselves with someone else's blood. Goodness! This was not the first time in my life that I'd had to deal with bedbugs! Where is the Jew who can't count his dealings with them in the hundreds, nay, in the thousands?

It was with great effort that I rose the next morning. Every bone in my body ached. But Necessity drove me and raised me from my place of rest. A Jew lives in haste. It is Necessity that drives him to it, forces him to run and chase about, to hustle and bustle. He only has to slow down a trifle and he collapses like a sack of flour. It is during holidays that a Jew becomes aware of all his aches and pains. Only then does he have enough time to be sick.

Necessity raised me from my berth; Necessity kept me on my feet; Necessity sat me on a horse and gave me a jolt that sent me off at a gallop together with Khayim Khene, Khaye-Treyne's husband. It is only the first move that is hard for a Jew. Once he is in motion, the spring needs very little winding to keep him bobbing up and down as long as need be. As a matter of fact, he may continue his motions even after he should have stopped, even after—but that's not my point. I soon regained my strength and felt hale and hearty again.

There is reason in the popular saying: "A Jewish soul cannot be fathomed." I had been under the impression all along that Khaye-Treyne was so pleased with me simply because she had discovered a relative, and one, no less, who was associated with books! Being associated with anything or anyone in itself carries much weight with Jews. Take our respectable bigwigs, for example. Whenever they have any business to transact in the government offices, they start first with the janitor of the building. After all, being associated with officials, as he is, some of their grandeur rubs off on him. So they talk matters over with him and go away happy. "That should do for the time being," they say to themselves. "After all, the janitor isn't a bad fellow."

Hence a janitor of a government school for Jews is known as "the inspector"; a Jew who delivers letters is a "post office official"; and a Jew who works in the post office proper is a "postmaster." Small wonder, then, that we have a saying: "The Rabbi's gentile scrub woman can also interpret the *Toyre*."

While we were having supper, I noticed that the broad, chubby girl was all dressed up—obviously a girl for whom it was high time to get married—and I began to suspect that Khaye-Treyne's joy meant that I would be of use to her in making a match for her daughter. I suspected further that she had her eye on me proper. That was why the girl had her best clothes on, My suspicions were confirmed by Khayim-Khene's conversation as we rode along. He was far too interested in my son:

"So! Your boy was *bar mitsved*, was he, and he isn't engaged to anyone, is he? When I was his age, I was married already, I was . . . my Khaye-Treyne doesn't let me sleep at night, she doesn't: '*Gvald*, find her a husband! How can you sleep there like that? What kind of father are you!' You saw my girl, didn't you? A good house-keeper, she is. Maybe it's time for her to be married, maybe. You're a scholarly man. Tell me, is it time? My wife talked to me about it last night. She thinks very highly of you, she does. . . . Things always happen unexpectedly. It just had to happen that you should wander into our house. So your son was *bar mitsved*, your son was?"

While we were conversing this way, we arrived at the field where the two wagons stood. First, I made sure that my wagon was intact. Then I looked at Alter's wagon. It stood in the same place and seemed to be in order. I lifted the canvas cover of the wagon to check the contents. But hardly had I put my hand in, when I froze in horror. Something was moving inside. I jumped away in fright. The canvas lifted, and sitting bolt upright before me with a bandaged head was—Alter Yaknehoz.

CHAPTER XI

What had happened to Alter, where he had been, how he had returned, why his head was bandaged—all these questions were soon answered for us by Alter in his own way:

"Well, I started out after the horses. In short, no horses! I thought to myself that they must have wandered a good way off. The grass in the woods is very good and there is plenty of shade there, so why not! A human being, forgive the comparison, would also wander a good way off in search of something good. Well, I walked further and further, if you know what I mean. But there was neither sight nor sound of them. I didn't know what to do. A nasty situation! Suddenly, I thought I heard something on the other side of the valley. Without a second thought, I went down one side and up the other. I looked here, I looked there, in short—nothing. Meanwhile it was getting late. It was dark in the woods—a bad business! Again I thought I heard a sound. I started off after it, wandered around, looked, searched—again, nothing. I was getting annoyed. What was going on here? Again a sound and something like steps.

" 'Now I've got them, the fine fellows! May they break their bones!' I cursed in anger and worked my way toward the sounds. After much effort, I finally came to a forsaken spot with thick, tangled branches. Aha! Here it is! And what do you think it was? A red cow, the devil take her—a cow that must have strayed from the herd and got herself lost in the forest.

"What next? I didn't know where I was and there was no point in standing here. Well, I put myself in God's hands and started walking again. I stumbled along until I came across the smoldering remains of a campfire. Potatoes were still smoking in the ashes. Many feet must have walked on the grass around the fire. All around were bread crusts, eggshells, skins of cucumbers, onions and garlic, and shreds of cloth and rags. There must have been quite a company here, probably gypsies. Not a good sign at all—gypsies like to steal.

"Suddenly, I thought I heard someone calling. The first thought in my mind was, 'Maybe it's Reb Mendele!' and I hurried toward the voice. The closer I got to it, the more terrible it sounded, as if someone were crying, 'Help! *Gvald!*' I was scared, but in short— nothing! I wasn't going to stop now. I took good care to look around in case there should be trouble. In short, a little inn appeared—a hovel on shaky legs. There was something I didn't like about the whole business. I hid off to a side among some bushes. My hand found a stick. I grabbed it, if you know what I mean. It might come in handy as a weapon. I sat there and waited to see what would happen. Horrible thoughts occurred to me; I remembered tales about the Glupsk bandits and robbers.

"Suddenly, another scream, a bitter cry from someone in great distress. And it came right from the hovel! My heart leaped. Before I knew what I was up to, I was out of the bushes and standing next to the little inn. I don't even know how I got there. A thought pecked away at me: 'Maybe it's Reb Mendele who is in trouble?' I had no idea where I was, but I had to find out what was going on in there if it was the last thing I did. You know, I'm sort of a stubborn mule myself.

"In short, I moved slowly and listened carefully. I could hear a muffled cry. I came upon a crumbling stone wall which could barely stand up, it was so old. I slipped in on tiptoe and looked, trying to see in the darkness. There was a deadly silence. I took a pack of matches out of my pocket. I rubbed and rubbed; but it was no use. My hand shook and they wouldn't light. Finally the last one flared up for a minute, long enough for me to hear the cry again from a corner of the room. Then the match went out. I felt my way in the darkness and stumbled on a body. I tell you, my hair stood on end.

"In short, the light of the rising moon came in through a broken window and showed a moldy little room without a door, with someone lying, tied like a sheep—both hands and feet—half dead, white as a sheet, and barely breathing.

" 'God himself must have sent you here!' he exclaimed. 'Cut me loose right away, or I'm done for. The rope has cut into my hands and I feel like I'm on fire. I need a drink!'

" 'Who tied you up like that?' I asked and, taking out my knife, cut the ropes.

" 'The devil take his father's fathers!' he swore and straightened out. 'The bastard! Notke the Thief!'

" 'What, a thief?' I cried and looked sharply at the fellow.

" 'Yes, yes! A thief! He just stole two horses today.'

"I almost jumped when I heard this. In short, I questioned him about the details. I described our horses and soon it was all clear as day. It turned out that a whole band of tramps had camped at that fire in the woods. One of them went for a walk in the woods and came back with our horses. As soon as I found out which road they had taken, I wanted to go after them without wasting any time. The fellow tried to talk me out of it. He threw cold water on my plan. He knew this bastard. He was a murderer and was traveling with several vans full of tramps no better than he. But I couldn't rest. I couldn't be without a horse. No, no! I had to catch them, come what may. No one was going to make a fool of me! Every second was dear now.

" 'You wait here for me,' I told him. 'Rest up. When I come back with the horses, with God's help, we'll both go away from here together.' That's what I told him. He attracted me for some strange reason. Then I set out after them as fast as I could.

"That ruined old inn in the woods was near the cross road on the highway. The road to the left went to Glupsk, to the Volhynia; to the right, the towns of Podolya. In short, I didn't walk, I ran. I was so angry that it hurt. I could have torn that thief to pieces like a herring. I needed only this to round out my luck—to be stuck in a field without a horse and without a groschen in my pocket. But nothing! Soon my feet began to complain. I was walking too fast. Then my stomach began to demand food—it just wouldn't listen to reason. This was no laughing matter!

We had fasted all day.

"One thought plagued me: that this was thrown-out work, that my running was in vain! Those fine creatures had a head start. Besides, they were riding and I was on foot. My only hope was that a wagon going my way would overtake me. Luckily, the moon was full so that it was almost as bright as day. In short, I kept right on, not as fast as before, not as eagerly as before, but onward I went anyway. There wasn't a living soul in sight. But, nothing! I kept at it, and walked on and on. When I decide to do something, I don't quit so easily, if you know what I mean. In short, I thought I heard the sound of wheels. . . . Damn it! They were coming toward me, instead of going my way! *Ai*, what luck, what miserable luck!

"I appealed to one driver and to another. They were all as drunk as Lot. I was bursting with anger, if you know what I mean! I started of again at double speed. I had already walked a long way and it was very late. I still hoped that a wagon going my way would catch up with me and help me. Up ahead, I thought I saw some wagons, but the devil take it! Again the wrong way! 'No,' I thought, 'this time I won't let them pass so easily. I'll give them whatever I have and make them take me my way.' I walked toward them, feeling brave, but it seemed that they weren't moving. They were standing still.

"What a heartache! What cursed luck! But, nothing. In short, coming closer, I saw that they were vans. It occurred to me immediately that maybe this was just what I was looking for. I slowed down, walked quietly, cautiously, and thought, 'What shall I do now?' A little wood stood at the side of the road. I ducked in and hid among the trees. From there I could look the vans over closely. Yes, they fitted the description in all details. It was they! One van lay on its side surrounded by a crowd: men, women— young and old—children, in rags and tatters. One was chopping, another was banging, a third one was offering advice, and still another was swearing and cursing. Women were screaming and children whining. It was a cursing, a growling, a slapping, a groaning, a crying and a laughing all mixed into one.

"Shouts pierced the air: 'It's all because of that new horse, he should burn in the fires of hell!' or 'What a cripple! He kept on pulling to one side all the way, as if for spite. He should drop dead!' One of them, a redheaded broad-shouldered thief, cried, 'It's another one of Notke's bargains, the cholera take him! He only brings us mouths to feed, stink pots, bundles of straw without feet, without eyes, without anything—just bellies to stuff!' and he stomped around waving his fist at everybody.

"I looked around and what do you think I saw, Reb Mendele? Your horse! Behind the last van, he stood unharnessed, with traces trailing on the ground. They gave him the honor of riding free, without a load. 'Ah, my sage.' I was overjoyed. 'You've created a real commotion here! Good boy! And where is my wretched beast? There she is, tied up behind the same van.' Taking out my knife, I tiptoed to the van, quiet as a kitten, while the whole company was busy at the axle of the other van. I swiftly cut the ropes, leaped up on mine bareback, and without any farewells rode off with both horses. But, nothing! One of the bunch, the devil take him, had to see me and give the alarm. The redheaded thief rushed after me pell-mell and tried to overtake me. But I didn't spare the whip and drove the horses as fast as I could. This time they did not wait for invitations and galloped for all they were worth. I left the redhead far behind. But, you need luck, if you know what I mean. My mare tripped in the traces dangling behind your horse—I was in such a hurry that I didn't remove them. She fell, and in no time at all the redhead was on top of me and flung himself at me like a wild

227

animal. We wrestled in silence with all our might. We were both in such a rage we couldn't talk. We tried to throw each other down but we both fell. We held each other in such a tight grip that our bones cracked. In short, we both worked hard. One minute I was on top of him and he squeezed so hard I thought the devil would take him. The next minute, the tables turned; he was on top of me and I was underneath. But, nothing! I gave it to him good, if you know what I mean. He twitched and lay there like dead. This was only a feint. I let go but, that was just what he was waiting for. He fussed quietly and pulled a knife out of his pocket.

" 'Ha! So that's the kind you are!' I shouted and gave him a crack on the hand so that the knife flew far away. With all his strength, he leaped at me, nimble as a cat, and grabbed my throat. He might have choked me, but just then the tinkling of a bell could be heard in the distance. He was frightened. After all, he was a thief. 'It's your filthy luck!' he growled like a bear. 'Here's a present from me!' He gave me a wallop on the head and disappeared. I got up, jumped on the horse and was off again. Later I began to feel the pain. I touched my head—*beh*, a big bump on my forehead! But, nothing. I did what I'd set out to do, if you know what I mean. I had the horses!"

"Praise the Lord that you got away alive!" I exclaimed and hugged Alter for joy.

"That's nothing," said Alter. "Let that redhead praise the Lord that he came upon me after I'd been fasting for twenty-four hours straight and was all tired out. But our horses are here."

"Where are they, our lions?" I inquired, looking all around.

"Take your time, Reb Mendele," Alter answered. "The fellow I came back with is watering them. I came back myself just a little while ago. I was tired and aching, may it not happen to you, so I lay down in the van to take a nap and covered myself with the canvas. I had just closed my eyes when you arrived, Reb Mendele, and praise God, you are well. Why is your cheek bound, Reb Mendele? A toothache, eh?"

"Your head is bound, Reb Alter, because you have a bump, and mine—because I'm missing a side curl. You brought your fellow and I brought Reb Khayim-Khene Khaye-Treyne's husband!" I introduced him for the second time with his complete title.

Alter stared at me inquiringly.

"What do you mean;" I asked in wonder. "You don't know Khaye-Treyne?"

"Well, Khaye-Treyne is Khaye-Treyne," Alter wondered in turn, "but the side curl, what does that have to do with the side curl!"

"A relative. My wife is a relative," Khayim-Khene explained doltishly.

As we conversed, sitting there on the grass, our lions appeared in the distance, bumping up and down and acting as if they were galloping. They looked different to me, somehow, since yesterday. Their heads were thrown back proudly, as if to say: "Go ahead, laugh at the way we gallop! Still, there was someone who wanted us, who wanted us badly enough to steal us. Yes! Even with one leg bandaged in rags and a festering eye! Yet, we still know how to run free behind a wagon. And when it comes to breaking axles, we know how to do that too—as well as anyone else. It's our misfortune that we are Jewish! You, Reb Jews, know how to promise food to your horses, but who can live on promises?"

I slapped my horse's chin lovingly as he came up to me and chuckled to him, "You rascal, you."

Right behind the horses came the fellow Alter had brought. I took one look, clapped my hands, and shouted: "Fishke! Speak of the devil and there he is!"

"The same Fishke? The one you were telling me about?" asked Reb Alter with great wonder.

"Yes, the very one. The one from the bathhouse. Well, *sholem aleykhem*, Fishke!"

"And I recognized you too, Reb Mendele," said Fishke and shook my hand.

"We owe thanks to your Fishke, Reb Mendele," said Alter to me. "If not for him, we would have seen our horses again like we'll see our ears."

"And if not for Reb Alter"—Fishke turned to me also —"Fishke would have been a dead duck by now."

"So I heard," I said. "But tell me, Fishke, how do you come to be here at all?"

"That's a long story," answered Fishke turning his head away.

I stood there a moment and looked closely at Fishke. The poor fellow was in rags. His bloody swollen feet were bare. He was sunburned and thin as a rail—a bag of bones. My heart wept at the sight of him. He must have had a bellyful of troubles. I took him by the hand and said:

"We'll hear your story later, Fishke. There's time enough for that. Meanwhile, rest here with us a little."

229

CHAPTER XII

Had a talented writer seen us out that fine morning, he would have found ample material for a poem. This would have been a poem about four married Jews and how they lay unbuttoned on the grass, enjoying the day in silence. Also included would be a sun and its warm rays, a sky, nature, dewdrops, songbirds and horses, each prettier than the last. Such a writer should, of course, be generous enough to add some products of his own imagination too: a flock of sheep grazing in the meadow, a clear running brook at which "Jews do break their thirst." He would doubtless place flutes in our mouths on which we would trill a song of praise to the beloved bride in the Song of Songs, just like the shepherds of yore. We had our own baskets of food, thank God, so that we would not have to impose upon the writer for refreshments. This far you may go, Reb Writer, but no further! You shall not delve into my soul or palm off your little wisdoms by putting them in my mouth—that is not for you. You'd better find yourself another victim. . . . I can express my thoughts better myself.

Nothing simpler. I lay there with my eyes open and had a wonderful time. Why? No particular reason. I just felt good all over. And I started humming out loud, not for the purpose, God forbid, of giving a concert or exercising my voice, but just so—just to *brim-brim brim-trim*. . . . Really, you can hear any Jew brim-brimming away without words, when the worry of making a living has left him in peace for a while and he has nothing on his mind. Isn't that why Jews brim-trim, each to himself and in his own style, when they go strolling on a holiday, or on *Shabbes* after they've eaten their heavy *kugl*—twirling the ends of their coat belts, or twisting the tips of their beards, or clasping their hands behind their backs?

My Khayim-Khene, with beaming countenance, brimmed and trimmed also. Then, suddenly, he stood up, grasped his beard, licked his lips, and spoke:

'*Nu*, Reb Mendele! It's time, I think, time to go, eh!"

"You want to go home?" I responded and got up too. "*Nu*, then! Go, and in the best of health!"

"What do you mean!" Khayim-Khene stared at me in astonishment. "And you, Reb Mendele, aren't you coming with me? We talked about something, didn't we?"

"How can I?" I answered, pointing at my companions.

"We invite them all, all!" Khayim-Khene exclaimed. "Let them come too. My Khaye-Treyne is making *varenikes* today. There will be plenty for everybody, plenty."

"Thank you kindly." I bowed. "There really isn't time enough. There's the problem of earning a living. Give my best regards to your wife."

"God have mercy on us, Reb Mendele! My wife will murd—" Khayim-Khene wanted to say "murder me" but he caught himself and exclaimed, greatly disturbed: "My wife won't let me into the house without you. She talked the whole business over with me last night . . . you understand? You can't imagine how she is expecting you. And my daughter Khasye-Grune, too. You understand?"

"I understand, I understand. But you must have patience. My wife will also murd—not let me into the house if I make a decision like this without talking it over with her first . . . you understand? What can I do, Reb Khayim-Khene?"

Khayim-Khene stood there as though he had been slapped. I could see that the poor man was in agony. His whole appearance showed it.

"Do me a favor and come!" he urged. "And if you really can't, then at least give me a letter, something in writing. She won't believe me alone. She'll tell me I'm a good-for-noth . . . a good-for-noth . . . she will . . . she will! Understand? Just write a few words. The *rebbe* will read it to her. I beg you!"

I had no choice. It was a mission of mercy, a question of saving a soul. Although such a husband deserved to meet his fate, let me not be the agent—let him not be punished because of me. Out of my little satchel, I brought a pencil. I tore the flyleaf out of a book and sat down. Leaning back against a wagon wheel, I wrote the following words:

> To the wealthy, renowned and pious lady, Khaye-Treyne, may she be healthy and well, Amen!
>
> Be it known unto you, that thanks to His Blessed Name, I am in a state of excellent health which penetrates into each and every limb of mine. May God not turn His face from us also in the future, that we may soon hear from each other, tidings of help and hope and that these tidings may find us proud, wealthy and honored, *Amen Selah*, thus be it forever. To your little children, may they live long and have many years, I send my most cordial

regards, and, in particular, to your daughter, the virgin bride Khayse-Grune, please convey my most special greetings without fail.

Further, I hereby inform you that, praise be given to His Blessed Name, the wares and the vans were found intact and in their proper place. Secondly I beg to inform you that the horses also were found. Reb Alter Yaknehoz liberated them from the hands of thieves. The blessings of our forefathers stood him in good stead in his quest. Undoubtedly, we have witnessed the occurrence of great miracles. Only we are not worthy of such benevolence from His hands. Your husband, may his light shine, will describe to you each and every detail in its particulars. Such events are indeed worthy of inscription in the Chronicles.

I beg your pardon, Khaye-Treyne, as I would from my own mother, for venturing to act as a protector for your husband who, poor man, has great fright and sickness of soul because I am not returning to you today as had been agreed upon. Have mercy on him; let him not suffer a decrease in his alotted years nor any other form of punishment because I am breaking my promise and not returning with him according to agreement. It is a question of showing mercy to a living creature. He practically swooned before me; on his part, he did whatever was humanly possible. He sang praises to you and to your daughter, the bride with all possible virtue, to whom I send my most cordial regards. In brief, on his part, he did all that a husband and devoted father could possibly do . . . do you understand? And once again, do you really understand? He even tempted me with jelly dumplings and many other good things. But earning a living comes before all other things. Because one must earn his living, one must, on occasion even forego dumplings. Secondly, don't I have a spouse also? You understand what I mean, don't you? You are well versed in such matters. . . After all, what is a man without his better half? I pray to Him that lives eternally that we shall see each other again without fail and be able to partake of jelly dumplings in a joyous mood, and maybe of *lekekh* too . . . you understand? In the meanwhile, your husband must not suffer, poor man. It is a pity.

I herewith send you a gift with your husband: a new *tkhine* on the subject of earning a living; a *tkhine* for the lighting of candles; a *tkhine* with prayers to greet each new month; a *tkhine* about our ancestral mothers Sarah, Rebecca, Rachel and Leah; a brand-new *tkhine* for *Yom Kippur*. In addition, I am sending you a copy of the *Fountain of Clarity*, a book whose laws and precepts should be mastered and followed by each and every female. You will derive great pleasure therefrom. Your daughter, the virgin bride, will also enjoy it immensely.

Khaye-Treyne! I have a request to make of you. When your bedbugs, may it not happen today, attacked and tortured me yesterday, I, in my misery, removed my woolen stockings, the ones made in Breslau, and, in my confusion, forgot them on your sofa. Find them, if you please, and let your husband wear them in good health. They are a gift from me.

Be well. Once more, convey my best regards to your little children and, in particular, to your daughter, the future bride. Do not neglect, under any conditions, to encourage and support your husband. Your husband, poor man, has a dejected and bitter look.

My whip, which I left in your little room, I leave as a gift for the *rebbe*. He will know how to use it. Your humble servant who greets you and your little children and, in particular, your daughter, the future bride,

Mendele Moykher-Sforim.

When I had read this letter aloud to Khaye-Treyne's husband, he was a different man and licked his lips in delight over each new sweet turn of phrase. At several points, he slapped his forehead for sheer wonder that a person could write so well and exclaimed, "What sweet talk! Like honey, upon my word as a Jew!"

We parted in a most friendly fashion and he left with a light heart.

CHAPTER XIII

Since both Alter and I were very tired from the previous night, we decided we would sleep for a few hours. Then we would start out fresh and travel until late at night if need be. Fishke took it upon himself to watch the horses and prepare lunch.

"After what happened to me last night," he said, "I slept soundly—like after a bath. Reb Alter had a hard time waking me when he came back."

At my request, Alter lay his head on my lap. I took my knife and squeezed out the bump on his forehead with the flat of the blade. We yawned, stretched, and lay down in the shade of a tree.

Were it not for the sun which roasted us with its burning rays, we would have slept until well past noon. When we opened our eyes, we found a cheerful fire blazing nearby. On it, a pot of potatoes, with an onion and a lean Jewish *kishke*, was boiling. We each took a sip of brandy and sat down with hearty appetites. We praised Fishke's cooking to the very heavens: it had the real Jewish flavor; his potatoes were fit for a king. Fishke was in ecstasy.

"Eat in good health!" he wished us. "I hope you enjoy it!"

"Where, Fishke," we asked him, "did you manage to dig up a lean Jewish *kishke*? Certainly, not in either of our baskets."

"You ask where the lean Jewish *kishke* came from?" he answered. "From my basket! It so happens I was lucky enough to hide it from that redheaded bastard, he should drop dead!"

"Tell us what happened to you, Fishke," we asked him. "*Ett..*" he sighed. "There's a lot to tell. It's a long story."

"The day is long. We have enough time, thank God, to hear your tale. Come, let's hitch up the horses," I said to Alter. "We'll start on our way and Fishke will talk to us while we ride."

When the vans were hitched up, I invited them to ride on my wagon. But Alter invited us to ride on his. "Mine is roomier," he said. "It's not so packed with goods."

"Well, then! Out with it, Fishke!" we said to him after we had settled down and managed to convince our horses to start moving. Fishke, however, was reluctant. He lowered his eyes and cracked his knuckles.

"What can I say? I'm ashamed to, somehow. I can't just start telling! It makes me feel funny."

I encouraged him, and Alter prodded him along, in the following fashion:

"It's only the beginning that's hard, my boy. Just say the first word and the rest will follow by itself. I know it from my own experience. Well, to make it short, what's the difference? Later, you'll see yourself that it isn't so hard. Well then, you married this blind orphan girl. Nu, nothing! We know about that already. In short, what happened after that?"

"After that? The devil take her father and his father together!" Fishke shot out in anger. "Oh, how they took me in!"

"*Nu, Nu,* go on!" we prodded Fishke, who came to a halt after this explosion. Fishke's mouth opened again and he continued, but with less heat than before.

"Oh, she was a wifey, she was! After we got married, we lived all right—like a Jewish couple should. I went out of my way for her. Honest, my lips should dry up if I'm lying! Every morning, I took her out to her spot at the Old Cemetery where she used to sit. She sat there and begged from the passers-by, singing a sad tune from the *Book of Lamentations.* It would have touched your heart to hear it.

"A few times a day I brought her food—something cooked or a hot bun, a sour pickle, sour milk. 'Eat, you'll feel better!' After all, she sat there all day busy making a living. Sometimes, I'd go out there just to see how she was getting along and to help out a bit. I'd give change. I'd keep track of the passers who made promises and remind her to collect from them when they came by again. Or I'd chase away cows and goats that wandered over to her and tried to eat the straw she sat on. In the month of *Elul,* I used to take her to the big fair on the outskirts of the city. She did as well as the charity hounds from the synagogue (the cantors, the sayers, the watchmen, the psalm singers, the Cabbalists, the collectors, the wick twisters, the field measurers, the weepers and the moaners). Oh, children of Israel, how they milked the crowd! It wasn't hard to make a living. But once you have it good, you want it even better. When you've tasted bread, you'd like some cake.

" 'Do you know,' my wife once said to me, 'people like us will always make a living, wherever we are. In our business, to be crippled like we are is a blessing. Others with such blessings would have made a fortune by now.

"But we are both *shlimazls* and don't do what we ought to. Listen to your wife, Fishke. I'm a little older and more experienced

235

than you. Take me out into the great, big world, Fishke, to far-off places. You'll see! You'll see—we'll be swimming in gold! There's nothing to do here any more. Lots of times I have to sit for a long time until someone breaks down and gives me a groschen. Everybody is talking about Lekish, the cholera groom, and his wife Pearl and how lucky they are. After they got married, they went away. Their luck, may the Evil Eye not harm them, followed right in their footsteps! Motl the Mystic met them in Kishinev begging from house to house. Their baskets, he said, were stuffed full of all sorts of good things—hunks of khale, hominy, smoked sheep's-meat, lean *kishke*, and roast. Pearlie shines like the bright sun itself. She is fat and has a double chin, like a duchess. She won't have anything to do with Glupsk, even if they give her the whole town free.

" 'And people coming back from Odessa just can't get over the good luck that *Yontl*, the other cholera groom, has had there. They saw him riding along the main streets on his butt and God provides for him. He's doing very well there. Folks can't see enough of him! And, mind you, Odessa has enough cripples of its own, because wherever cripples are born, by and by they head for Odessa. But how can any of them compare to the cripples of Glupsk? You couldn't find cripples like the ones from Glupsk even in England! Folks say that Glupsk has a name all over the world. People come running to look at a Jew from Glupsk! I'm sure that God won't forsake us either. Let's go away, while it's still summertime. And don't dilly-dally. It's a sin to waste another day here.'

"I gave in to my wife's wheedling and we went away.

"To tell the truth, we did very well. No matter what village or town we came to, we were a success. Everyone stared at us, no one turned us away. The poorhouse was always open to us for a night's rest. And houses—as many as our hearts desired. All we had to do was go from one house to another and fill our pockets, our bosoms, our baskets! For a few groschen, the *shames* at the Synagogue would find a place for us to stay for *shabes*.

My wife taught me the art of begging. I was very green and didn't know any of the tricks of the trade. My wife was a past master at it. She knew every trick in the books. She showed me how to come into a house, how to moan and cough and look pitiful. I learned how to beg or even demand, how to stick like a leech and bargain for more, how to bless the giver, or to swear and curse with deadly oaths. Did you think that you can just start begging from house to house? Oh, no! There's a whole science!

"To be wealthy, all a Jew needs in the beginning is luck. Later his heart becomes hard and his eyes become blind. That's to be expected. But for a Jew to be a beggar, a successful beggar, he needs more than luck. There are many things he must learn. He has to know all the tricks. He has to be able to get under someone's skin in such a way that the other fellow must give simply to get away!

"We were foot beggars, my wife and I. I see from the way you're looking at me that you don't understand. Be patient and I'll try to make it a little clearer. Beggars are divided into kinds, like soldiers. The first kind is the infantry. . . . but wait a minute, wait! There are so many kinds, hundreds of them. And I can't remember all the names. Beggars that crawl and limp and drag their feet—the devil knows what else! Beggars like flies—tramps and idlers from everywhere, loafers, Cabbalists, plate lickers. All sorts. Let me get straightened out."

But all his thinking didn't help. Fishke was so enmeshed and entangled in his armies of beggars that he couldn't free himself. From his words, however, I made some order of the groups into which our beggars are divided. The two main ones are the *infantry*, or *foot beggars*, and the *cavalry*, or *van beggars*. The first travel on foot; the second in vans or wagons. These are further subdivided into branches: *city beggars*, those who were simply born in a city, usually in Lithuania, and *field beggars*, those who were simply born on a van in a field. Their parents and their parents' parents as far back as anyone remembers have been wandering. These are the Jewish gypsies. They wander forever from one end of the land to the other. They are born, grow up and marry, they multiply and die—all on the road. They are free people, relieved of being Temple slaves, of paying the kosher meat tax and the like. They are also rid of praying and Jewishness—they have neither Lord nor Master.

The branch of *city beggars* is further broken down into many types. There are the simple *starvelings*—men, women, girls and boys who go from house to house with their baskets on *Rosh-Khoydesh* and also in the middle of the month and beg groschens and crusts of bread. Many of the boys and girls run after you in the streets and catch at your coattails until you ransom yourself by giving them something. Then, there are the *synagogue official*

237

starvelings—the Cabbalists and the loungers who mouth the traditional saws and who say *kadish* for the dead at the Holy Resting Place. To their number may be added the *shoyfer* blowers, the *mezuze* inspectors and their ilk. Then, there are the *Toyre* and *good-deed starvelings*—the Pharisees who desert wife and children and bury themselves in a far-off prayer house to study the tractate *Betsa* at public expense. To this type belong the *Yeshive* students who wander about in a bedraggled state, sit at the stove scratching themselves and eat in a different house every day. Also, those Jews who tramp about with a kerchief in hand, so-called collectors, supposedly collecting donations for this or that charity. There are *secret starvelings*, wealthy proprietors who quietly accept support and alms. There are also *semi-starvelings* such as, for example, the *Talmud-Toyre* teachers in many cities who are semi-beggars. In this class may be included synagogue attendants, judges, and rabbis. Each of them is half—half what he is supposed to be and half what all Jews with baskets are. Then there are the *holiday starvelings*. They play the part on holidays like Purim, when Jews go from house to house in groups to celebrate the festivities. But the *holiday starvelings* claim to be collecting money for charitable purposes. And finally, there are the *loan-of-honor starvelings*, who accept alms all their lives under the pretext that it's a loan of honor. They swear that they'll return it tomorrow or the day after with thanks.

"Reb Alter," I said after I had succeeded in arranging our beggars in the above order from Fishke's description. "Reb Alter, remind me, I beg you, if you remember any other sorts of beggars whom I've forgotten, God forbid, to include in my list."

"What difference would it make?" Alter answered and looked at me like a grown man looks at a boy who is making a fool of himself. "*O-vah,* he has, God forbid, forgotten! Such an important list! And if you're not included in the list, you can't be a beggar?"

"Don't say that, Reb Alter!" I defended myself. "Our paupers are very conscious of their dignity. They seek honor with all their might. Insult a pauper and he will remind you of it to the end of your days! *Sha!* You see? While we've been talking, I reminded myself of a whole catalog of beggars, may the Evil Eye not harm them: pilgrims to Jerusalem, Jews on their way back from Jerusalem, Jews who were burned out, sick Jews, Jews with hemorrhoids and doctors' letters to prove it, deserted wives, widows of all sorts, writers, and—the devil won't take us, Reb Alter—we might as well

238

include book peddlers. And if that be the case, why not count in our printers and editors and all their workers, the typesetters, the proofreaders, the correspondents-let them all join the ranks of the paupers! And now, Reb Alter, we really ought to sort them all into their proper places on the list. I didn't forget anyone, did I?"

"*Ay! feh*, Reb Mendele!" Alter exclaimed irritably and began to scratch himself. "Enough of your beggars! I'm itching all over. I feel as if I'm being eaten alive by an army of fleas. As far as I'm concerned, you can cut the whole story short: all of Israel—one big pauper! And an end to this nonsense. Let Fishke finish his story and stop interrupting him. If he gets stuck and you help him out. . . that's all right, but no interruptions!"

Right from the start, Fishke was our cantor. He opened his mouth, puckered his lips and came forth with halting and choppy notes. And I? I was his understudy. I helped him in time of need and extracted the words which jammed his throat. Without my aid, it would be almost impossible to understand him. Alter simply urged him on with a "*Nu*, in short . . ." or "In short—nothing!" as one prods the cantor in the synagogue on *Shabbes* when there is a good soup and *kugl* waiting at home after the services.

239

CHAPTER XIV

"My wife and me, we bewonged to the infantwy so you can guess how swowwy we cwawwed awong, me with my sick feet—just like cwabs," Fishke began again in his manner, unable to pronounce an "l" or an "r." His tale, with my corrections, continues:

"Little by little my wife began to scold and swear at me. She called me names and harped on my lame feet. She complained about what a complete disappointment I turned out to be, from head to toe. She had made a man of me, showed me what the world was like, earned a living for me, put me on my feet, but I didn't appreciate it and did everything I could to spite her. She acted like this rarely, so I didn't answer back. I swallowed it all and thought: 'But that is the way a wife is supposed to be. That's the way they are. A woman honors her husband with a few curses and sometimes even with a blow.' When her anger died down, we lived in peace again; once again Fishke was a good husband. She laid her hand on my shoulder and: 'Off we go, Fishke!' I walked ahead, she followed behind, and somehow we both felt good. And that's how we crept and crawled from town to town.

"It took us such a long time to reach Balta that we missed the famous fair which is known all over the world. My wife was beside herself. She acted as if she had lost a vast sum of money. I cheered her up by telling her that the houses of Balta were all still there, thank God. Wasn't that enough for us, so many houses, such a city? We shouldn't be such sinners! Before I could catch my breath, she shot out: 'Burn up, you and your houses! What's the good of a city, a mudhole, like this? Who wants it? Not I, do you hear! I'll have nothing to do with it! Drown in the mud here and choke on your city, your bloody Balta!' "

"Reb Alter, I've got it!" I shouted. "I just remembered another type of pauper: Bankers!"

"A real bargain!" said Alter and clicked his tongue. "As far as I'm concerned they're not worth a second thought!"

"I know one of them in Glupsk very well—Simkhele the Merry. He carries with him a special book listing of all the houses on which he holds mortgages and how much income he gets from each. 'The houses,' he says, 'are mine. They pay duty to me! All of Glupsk belongs to me.' Every day he goes to a different block of houses.

He breezes into a house with a loud greeting. If he receives his alms promptly, then all is well. If not, he says, 'Good day! Don't you worry, I'll keep track of your debts!' and off he runs. Maybe you have heard about the beggar from Glupsk who made a match with another one from Teterivke and, as dowry, threw in half the houses of Glupsk? That was Simkhele the Merry! Or, perhaps you have heard tell how, at a meal for paupers given by a wealthy man in honor of his child's marriage, a beggar who was invited arrived dragging with him another one who wasn't? When they asked, 'Uncle, how is it that you brought along another mouth to feed?' he answered, 'Oh, that's my son-in-law. I give him his room and board!' That, too, was Simkhele the Merry! In short, Simkhele looks upon Glupsk as his city and all its houses belong to him."

"For my part, your Simkhele can drop dead," Alter commented briefly and asked Fishke to continue his story.

Fishke began again after his fashion and I helped him along after mine.

"We didn't follow any straight path. We just wandered along from city to city. Finally we came to the city of A—. *Oy*, how much better off I would've been if I'd never laid eyes on the place! It's not that I have anything against the city itself. Just the opposite—it is a good city. I went from door to door to my heart's content. But it was there that I met my Executioner, he should be slaughtered with a dull knife! May his bones rot! This is how it happened.

"The cavalry was stationed in that city—the field beggars with their vans. A revolution had just taken place there. The richer young men of the town had just started something new. They decided that it wouldn't hurt the beggars to work for their daily bread—except for the old and sick and crippled. There was no reason for healthy young men and women to live on alms and charity. The foolish Jewish spirit of charity causes only trouble, they claimed. That's why, they said, there are so many lazy loafers among the Jews—who suck other people's blood like bedbugs. The rich young men set up a sort of factory where the beggars were put to work making ropes and sewing sacks and, in return, were given food. Beggars began to turn up much less often in the town.

"The field beggars that we met there were up in arms against this new custom. '*Gvald!*' they cried. 'What's happening to the world? Where is Jewish charity? Jewishness is dead!' One of them— a redhead and strong as an ox may his bones rot!—was the ringleader and shouted louder than anyone else. 'It's Sodom, that's what it is! Sodom all over again! Why should the rich sit around like princes, doing nothing, while others work for them?

" 'Doesn't everything they own come from other people's toil, other people's tears and sweat? They think they're fine folks. They take care of themselves and want others to work. A rich man, the fatter he is and the bigger his belly, the more honor and respect he gets. With us it's just the opposite. A healthy beggar has to be ashamed and hide like a thief. Otherwise people raise a hue and cry and demand why such a healthy fellow isn't working. It's time for a change—let the rich try to work a bit! What's wrong with them? They're not sick.'

" 'Right, Faybushke! We are also children of Israel and just as good as they are!' The other beggars stood up for the redheaded bastard. Then, little by little, they began to walk away from the poorhouse.

"That evening, it was my luck to be walking by the courtyard of the synagogue. It was dark and there were many people, may the Evil Eye not harm them, milling around. Off to a side, I heard someone crying so bitterly it would have moved a stone. I stopped. Not far from me stood a broken man. A little pillow lay on his two outstretched arms. A tiny baby on the pillow squealed and lost its breath in a fit of sobs. The poor father didn't know what to do. He rocked it, bounced it, tried to quiet it with a weeping voice and miserable groans: '*Oy*, woe is me! Black is my lot! My wife is dying and leaving this tiny infant on my hands! *Oy*, woe is to you, poor little orphan! Black will be your lot without a mother! A-a-a-ah,' *sha, sha!* What can I do for you, poor baby?'

"Everyone who passed by put something in his hand. The women tried to comfort him but he didn't stop moaning for a minute: 'Woe is me, black is your lot,' rocking the pillow and turning hopelessly with it in all directions. My heart was torn with pity for the poor father and his unlucky orphan still in diapers. I took three groschens out of my pocket and went up to the poor man. I stretched my hand over the pillow to give him the money when he suddenly pinched me and cried in his wailing voice, 'Oy, woe is to *you*,' accenting the 'you' as if he meant me. I jumped aside in fear and rubbed my hand in pain. The miserable father turned to me and pushed the pillow into my hands, saying, 'That's enough for today. Come here. Hold the child a while!' I stared and couldn't believe my eyes. The little orphan, I saw, was a doll wrapped in rags, and the unfortunate father—the redheaded bastard Faybushke, may his bones rot! He did the job like a real actor! He cried and screamed and lost his breath just like a little baby.

" 'That's the way to do business with the foolish children of Israel,' he explained. 'If they won't give you alms with good will, you have to get it out of them with tricks. That's the only way. What does the rabbi, or the judge, or any of that pack of officials do? They all disguise themselves and perform tricks. They have their tricks and I, woe is me, have my little orphan. There's more than one way to milk a cow! Say amen to that, Fishke!'

"While we were staying at the poorhouse, the red headed bastard began to sidle up to my wife. Somehow, he was very much attracted to her. Whenever she wanted something, he rushed to get it for her. He enjoyed serving her. He stayed so close to her that little by little they both became great pals. He would sit with her for hours on end talking about nothing and telling her smutty little jokes. My wife would stop her ears and act as if she didn't want to listen. And when he flattered her and told her that she was a juicy, plump, meaty woman—just the way he liked them—she scolded him and even slapped him and laughed. I also laughed, although sometimes it was a bitter little laugh, and thought, 'Why should I worry about that bag of wind? Tomorrow or the day after, we'll be rid of him. He'll go his way, we'll go ours, and I'll never have to look at his ugly mug again. Besides, when we go begging, she goes from house to house with me, praise the One Above. When he, the bastard, takes her hand and wants to lead her, she pushes him away angrily and tells him to go away: she is a married woman and has someone, thank God, to go begging with.'

"The morning after the unfortunate father act, I went begging by myself. When we got up, my wife complained that she wasn't feeling well. She yawned and stretched again and again—a good omen—so she stayed home. I felt bad myself. I had a heartburn. It was lonely going from house to house all alone that day. I was worried, too. I have to admit that after the redheaded bastard started sidling up to my wife and telling her his little jokes, she became dearer to me. Sometimes I was very angry, burning mad but at the same time, I don't know why, I was drawn to her. It was like magic. It was like—how can I explain it—like scratching one of those itching sores that I get sometimes. It was pain and pleasure, both together. My begging somehow had a different taste that day than on other days. I made a short shrift of it and got done quickly.

"When I came back to the poorhouse, I found my wife sitting with the bastard. Both of them were whispering together. Her face was flushed. She bent her head toward him and listened to his talk with a sweet smile on her lips. When I came up to her and asked how she felt, she was caught off guard. She sat speechless for a minute and didn't know what to do. Then she stretched out her hand to touch me, as she usually did, and said, 'Do you know why I'm sick, Fishke? It's because of an Evil Eye. It's because of our dragging along on foot. The woman leech came in to see me and sent me down to the bathhouse. She told me to whip myself well and let them cup me. Then, before I go to sleep, she said I should rub myself down and work up a sweat during the night. No, Fishke! I can't go on foot any longer. Reb Faybushke here has invited us to ride with him in his van. What shall we do, Fishke? What do you say?'

"The bastard, may his bones rot, grinned at me with a look in his eye that went right through me. It cut me to the quick. I felt like a little boy when the *rebbe* tells him to lie down on the bench for a whipping. I hemmed and hawed and couldn't put two words together.

" 'Why are you silent? Why don't you answer?' my wife shouted angrily. 'I know that you don't care a bit about my health. You want to be rid of me as soon as you can. You want to drive me to an early grave. But wait, you viper! Wait! You'll go first, you'll meet your end before me. Do you hear, Fishke with your crooked legs, I'll sweep the floor with you! You won't have a hair left on your head. I'll knock every one of your teeth out!' Whenever my wife opened her mouth like that, my blood froze in my veins. I stood there, angry, disgusted and beaten. God alone knows how I felt then. What could I do? I bent my head toward my wife and said, '*Sha!* Don't scream and don't get so upset. If you want to ride, we'll ride. Why not?'

" 'That's the way to talk!' my wife replied a little more softly. 'Why don't you answer when people talk to you? Why do you stand there like a clay statue? This man is kind enough to take us along free—and you don't even say thanks! Shame on you, you low-life you!'

"What could I do? I had to say thanks to the bastard, too."

"Reb Alter, another one!" I cried out.

"What is it, Reb Mendele? Another bargain?" Alter twitted me.
"Reminded yourself of another kind of pauper maybe? It's time that
God granted you bigger bargains. We have enough paupers!"

"No, Reb Alter! What I mean is that we have here another
Khayim-Khene who quakes and quivers before his wife. Our
Fishke, I'm afraid, has probably been beaten more than once by
his wife."

CHAPTER XV

Fishke began again in his fashion, I worked and helped him along in mine, Alter drove us both along in his, and the story continues as follows:

"The next day, the cavalry moved out of Sodom. That's what they called the town. They left with a clang and a clatter, with a swearing and scolding, with a creaking and scraping of wheels. Deadly oaths rained down on the town: 'It should burn to the ground! The rich should die from hunger ten times a day! They should have to wander around the world barefoot and bareback. . . .'

"Three vans were packed to the rafters with all sorts of creatures: men, women, young women, boys, girls, big and small, and among them my wife and myself. Congratulations! We were promoted! We were now serving with the cavalry.

"I must tell you, dear people, a whole new world opened for me. At first, it was very gay to be with this band. I saw and heard such new and wonderful things! I couldn't even begin to tell you. They made fun of the whole world. They would mimic and laugh at anyone who rubbed them the wrong way. One of them would describe in thieves' language the tricks he played or the traps he laid: how he had 'borrowed a bead' (stolen a bread), or 'racked up some ringers' (stolen money), or 'lectured a lamb' (beaten a child of a rich family). They cursed the rich at the drop of a hat, for no particular reason, but just so. I swear by my *tales* and *tfiln* that they hate the rich far more than the rich hate them. What wouldn't they call a rich man: a bloodsucker, a bursting belly, a clogged head, a stone heart, a stiff neck, and the devil alone knows what other names! They considered it a *mitzve* to swindle a rich man— and the oftener, the better. Whenever they had troubles, they cursed the rich; they wished them aches and pains, cramps and convulsions, anguish and agony, and the worst kinds of disease.

"Sometimes they jokingly called me 'The Magnate' because I often defended the rich and stood up for their honor. I had lived all my life in the bathhouse. In a way, I was brought up among the rich and, after all, I'd had dealings, with them: I had watched their clothing, brought them kettles of water or hot coals and other bathhouse needs.

"The van beggars set great store on the knack of putting on an act. They needed it for their business. Whenever it paid, these fine folks would become hunchbacked, blind, deaf or dumb, or lame. But they set even greater store on the genuine article, on undisguised cripples like my wife or me. They often said that handicaps like ours were treasures for a beggar—blessings in disguise. Handicaps like ours could bring in a lot of money. They thought even more highly of my wife's than of mine. But it was her tongue that fascinated them; it ran like a machine. When she opened her mouth, it was enough to make your hair stand on end.

"The redheaded bastard hovered over my wife. He actually clung to her. He smiled to her, he pampered her, he would have brought her birds' milk. Whenever he laid his hands on something good to eat—like cooked chick peas, plums, apples—he brought it to her. I said to myself: 'A plague on you! Why should I care? Go ahead, pet her, pamper her. What good will it do you? Nothing! She's a married woman. There's no danger. . . . If it's her blindness you're after, if you're figuring that you can make a lot of money with a blind woman, then eat your heart out, you dog, because my wife goes begging with me. What can you expect to accomplish by sticking to her when the main thing is that she goes from house to house with me?'

"Since this was how my thoughts ran, I decided to learn the ways of a beggar down to the last wrinkle so that my wife would be more pleased with me. I already knew how to walk into a house. The trick was to enter in a huff, to be angry, to demand the alms as if it were coming to you, to hunt down the owner of the house or his wife even if it meant going upstairs and walking into the bedroom! The next thing was to bargain with him. As far as bargaining went, I was a past master. The whole trick was to grumble about anything they gave. If they gave a piece of bread, I asked for a shirt or underwear or stockings. The trick was aways to find fault and complain. You must never thank the giver. You must scowl and sometimes even curse.

"But the redheaded bastard wasn't asleep either, may his bones rot! He was thinking up ways to get rid of me. He must have said to himself: 'Fishke, in the art of being a beggar, you're not even fit to wash my feet. I know the tricks of the trade eighty thousand times better than you. And, once I've taken it into my head that I'm going to work with your blind wife, that's the way it's going to be. Don't worry, with God's help I'll know how to take care of you too.'

"He hounded me until I looked worse than a stray cat. I fell terribly in my wife's estimation. She only laughed at me now. All I heard from her was: 'Split a gut! Break your neck! May worms eat you! You scoundrel, you glutton, you so-and-so!'

"The redheaded bastard, may he never rise on Judgment Day, kept on baiting me and doing me dirt until I became the laughing-stock of the whole company. All the vans were picking on me now. Every minute they played another trick on me. Every instant they called me another name. They did whatever they wanted to me. I was everybody's scapegoat. When I got angry they were offended: 'Look how worked up The Magnate is! He'll have a fit in a minute!'

"Or, if I couldn't hold back my bitter tears because the blows and insults I got were more than I could stand, they would say, 'What's the occasion, Fishke? You're laughing so hard you're showing your teeth. Lookee here, folks! See how Fishke is laughing.' And then the bastard's voice would rise above the others: 'Help the poor fellow, children of Israel! Give it to him in the ribs or fix his shoulders for him—that's a sure cure for laughing. And, if that doesn't work, get hold of his hair or his ear! That will put tears in his eyes as sure as an onion. You've got to help him. You just can't let a Jew suffer like that!'

"Sometimes they threw me out of the van, and when I limped after the wagon as fast as I could and had to wiggle my hips, they clapped their hands and shouted, 'Bravo, Fishke! That's the way, Fishke, dance a little, dance! Come on, folks, look at Fishke! Look at him dance, may the Evil Eye not harm him! Look at him lifting his legs! May he dance like that at all our weddings!'

"Once someone cried out—it was the redheaded bastard, may his bones rot! 'Folks! Fishke isn't lame at all! He is only acting lame and putting us all to shame, the faker! Let's try to make him stand straight. Give him a smack in the back there and you'll see how straight he'll stretch his legs!' Well, they tortured me and made my life miserable. *Oy*, how I longed for those good old days when I sat in the bathhouse like a king and lived like God in France!"

"Well, then why didn't you divorce her?" Alter interrupted Fishke's tale. "That's what divorces are for! "

"You're right," answered Fishke with a sigh. "I wish I had done it then. I would be much better off today and maybe someone else would be too. . . . I don't know what was the matter with me then. It was like being under a spell. It's shameful to admit it, but my heart was somehow attracted to my wife. No matter how much I suffered, and I went through hell, the devil himself drove me to her. Maybe I was just plain stubborn: 'If you, you bastard, want to break up my marriage and get rid of me, then, just to spite you, I'll cling to her more tightly than before.' Or, maybe it was—what's a good way to say it—just because it was that way . . . I was under a spell. I was charmed by her looks. She was healthy, chubby and firm, with a full face, not pretty but charming. There were times when I didn't know where to put myself because of all my troubles and heartaches, and I wished I were dead together with her. 'Today, today,' I would say to myself, 'it must take an end. Today I will tell her—a divorce! But as soon as I would come over to her, she would start talking to me, put her hand on my shoulder and say, 'Lead me, Fishke!' My tongue would freeze, my heart would melt a little, and I was bewitched again.

"One fine day, when I was going from house to house with my wife, I felt rather good and said to her, 'Basya, dear soul, what is the point to this endless wandering? It's not for us. In Glupsk, we both had, thank God, something of a reputation. You took me out of the bathhouse there. It's nothing to sneeze at, the stone bathhouse of Glupsk; through its doors such lions passed each week, such fine gentlemen! And you, too, were well known and respected. And now, we're wandering from town to town with these beggars. And what kind of respectability do we have, tell me!'

" 'Maybe you want to go back to Glupsk!' she flared up. 'You can go back there if you want to, Fishke. But I won't under any conditions! There are plenty of paupers in Glupsk today without me. Every day new paupers pop up there, and brand-new alms takers. Why, even the rich go begging there today.'

" 'It doesn't have to be Glupsk,' I answered. 'Dear soul, pick any city you like and let's settle down there. Our own town and our own rich people will bring us blessings and fortune. No wonder people say: "Every dog to his own bone." ' "

" 'Soon, Fishke, soon,' my wife said, slapping my back in a very friendly way. 'Let's travel just a little longer. Let's live a little and see some more of the world. It's so good and lively. Be patient with your city, Fishke. Soon!'

"This 'soon' of hers was long—no end in sight. During that time, we stopped in countless cities and I went through endless torture and agony. And all because of him, that redheaded bastard, may his bones rot. . . ." Fishke sighed from the depths of his heart and closed his eyes. We let him catch his breath and then he continued his tale.

CHAPTER XVI

Not only did they gall me 'the magnate,' but they began calling me 'The Cabbalist' also. The bastard gave me this new title, may he drop dead! And so, everyone in the band called me 'Fishke the Cabbalist.' 'Cabbalist' was such an ugly name to them that they spat seven times whenever they said it. The way the merchants, the store keepers, the artisans—men who compete for their daily bread—hate each other is child's play compared to the hatred of the van paupers for the city paupers and especially for the whole tribe of Cabbalists. 'Those wormy Cabbalists, lazy men from good families, trying to look like somebodies in their greasy coats,' they said with gall. 'They're like bedbugs, every house is full of them and there's no getting rid of them. They stuff their bellies every time there is a wedding feast, a circumcision, the naming of a newborn boy, a funeral. They make profits from the dead as well as from the living while we have to break our backs for a crust of bread. Those moth-eaten scholars, those lazy loafers, have taken over King David's little book of psalms and they make a living at it. If King David had known into whose hands his Book of Psalms would fall, and how these moldy maggots with their pasty faces would use it, he would never have written it.'

" 'It's no use, Basya!' the bastard said to my wife. 'We'll never be able to do anything with your Fishke. No, no! He'll never be one of us. He is a Cabbalist from head to toe, to his last hair. Your taking him traveling and trying to show him the world won't help him one bit. He doesn't know the first thing about being a beggar. Poor thing, you'll have only bitterness and heartache from him. *Ai*, what a Basya! If only I had such a Basya! We would make a fortune, so help me, a fortune! '

"The bastard did everything he could to break us up and told her all sorts of cock-and-bull stories and wild tales about me. Finally, he came up with something really juicy. He told her that I was running after a girl in another van and flirting with her a lot. There was a hunch-backed girl with the band that I liked to talk to, it's true—"

"What's this? Who was she?" both Alter and I interrupted Fishke. "Come now, Fishke, out with it!"

"The girl was a total stranger to the band. She had suffered

250

enough in her childhood, poor thing. I really used to like to sit with her and talk. We used to tell each other our troubles and pour out our hearts. More than once she cried for me as well as for herself. *Ai*, if you knew what a girl she is! If you only knew what she's been through, poor thing!" Fishke exclaimed with tears in his eyes. We asked Fishke to tell us who the girl was and what had happened to her.

"If you really want to know," Fishke said after he had wiped his eyes with his sleeve, "and if you're not bored listening to me, I'll oblige you. I'll tell you all I know. But don't hold it against me if it doesn't come out smoothly.

"She was only a little girl when her mother brought her to Glupsk together with a sack of old clothes and bedding. Her mother left the sack with an old woman—an old witch: she must have been an employment agent. The mother used to go away with her for the whole day, leaving the child all alone and without food. The girl told me how she once cried and screamed and begged her mother to take her along. The old witch got very angry and wouldn't hear of it: 'God forbid! No one must know about her. You'll lose your job.'

"A few days later, her mother took her along and quietly kept her in the kitchen of the wealthy house where she worked. But it didn't last long. Her mother and she soon moved to a kitchen in another house and from there to still another kitchen. Every time her mother lost her job, she treated her worse and worse.

"She knew very little about her father. Before she came to Glupsk with her mother, he was hardly ever home. He was always on the road and here, in the kitchens, she never saw him at all. She would have forgotten that she ever had a father except that her mother cursed him fifty times a day. 'May he break his head somewhere, your fine father!' she would curse. 'After all the years of hardship and heartache I had with him, he leaves me in the lurch with a ball and chain, a child, hanging around my neck—may he hang himself!—and now I can't keep a job and have to choke myself and keep her in hiding. Who needs a cook with a child?'

"More than once the mistress of the house would come running into the kitchen when the meal was not just so and make a scene about the cook who skims the cream from the milk to give to her dear little daughter. But the truth was that the dear little daughter starved and wasted away with nothing to eat but her own little heart. Her mother used to stow her away, like smuggled goods,

251

on top of the stove and there she sat in a corner all day, hunched over, not daring to move or make a sound. Her mouth watered from the kitchen smells—the roast goose and the fried livers—but she? *Sha*, not a word!

"She suffered in silence, poor thing, until someone remembered to push a dry crust of bread into her hand, or a gnawed bone or some other leftovers. But many times no one remembered to give her anything. When she couldn't stand it any more and finally made a sound, a rolling pin or a broomstick would appear on top of the stove and beat her—on the head, on the hands, on the feet, wherever it happened to strike—while deadly oaths and curses rained down upon her father and her father's fathers all the way down to Abraham, our Father. That's how she spent her childhood in sickness and suffering on top of kitchen stoves. Because she always had to sit humped over in one position, she became hunchbacked, poor thing.

"Looking down from her perch on the stove, she used to see a young man. He often came to visit her mother in the kitchen. Her mother beamed whenever he came and looked after him like the apple of her eye. She filled his pockets with good things to eat and sometimes gave him money too. He used to often come late and spend the night in the kitchen. Sometimes her mother dressed herself very carefully, looking into her little mirror, and then disappeared for the whole night. Her mother must have been getting ready to remarry and was very busy with the bride-groom. . . .

"Once, toward evening, a stranger came and took her mother's things from the kitchen. Then her mother thanked the lady of the house for the bread and salt, took her almost naked little daughter off the stove and left with her. She led her far, far away to a side street. 'Sit down here and wait. People will take pity,' her mother told her and vanished.

"The poor little castaway sat quietly on the street and was afraid to move, just as before on top of the stove. A cold autumn drizzle soaked her to the bone. She sat there, huddled up, in her thin little dress, shivering and shaking. When a passerby asked her: 'Who are you, little girl?' she answered: 'I'm my mother's little girl . . . she told me to sit still here. . . I mustn't cry. . . a rolling pin or a broomstick will beat me.' She sat there until late at night, when some woman coaxed her home with sweet talk, way out, to the edge of town, to a little hut that was ready to fall down.

"She lived with this woman for a long time. It was no land of milk and honey for her. The woman said she was an aunt of hers and that's what she told the girl to call her. This Auntie was a market woman; she sold roasted potatoes, hot babkas, tiny wild pears, and little apples from Palestine. She used to go to the market early in the morning. The hunchbacked little girl stayed behind to rock Auntie's baby daughter, to pick up slivers of wood from the street to burn in the stove, to gather the eggs from under the chickens' roost, to scrub the dried *kasha* from the pots, to soak the baby's dirty shirts in the pail of slops, to watch the wooden *milkhike* spoon drying in the sun together with the baby's pillow, and to do other similar chores. In the evening, when Auntie came home, she sent her little servant begging for crusts of bread from house to house. These crumbs that she gathered were her food, and what was left went to Auntie.

"One summer evening, while begging from house to house, in a coarse blouse and skirt, she strayed far to the other end of town and couldn't find her way back. The sun had set a long time ago. A black cloud covered the sky. Soon the storm broke with flashes of lightning and peals of thunder. Suddenly some vans appeared, packed full of people, on their way out of the city. 'Look! There's a hunchbacked little girl! She's crying. She must be lost!' came a cry from one of the vans. Soon, a redheaded man jumped down— the same redheaded bastard, may his bones rot—and asked her who she was. 'I want to go home, home to Auntie!' sobbed the little girl. '*Sha!* Don't cry,' the bastard said to her. 'I'll take you home to your aunt.' He swept her into the van and rode off with her.

"Since then the hunchbacked girl, poor thing, has been roaming the countryside with these van beggars. They made a living from her hump. Whenever they came into a city, they sat her out on the main street barefoot and half naked. She was supposed to sob and beg for alms, whining and pulling peoples' coattails as they passed by. Sometimes she didn't play the part with her whole heart and came back with very little. But she certainly received plenty of beatings in her van. They beat her without mercy and threw her out of the wagon, poor thing, hungry and naked, so that she had to whine and cry in earnest.

"She told me how once, during a terrible cold spell, they threw her out on the street in the middle of the night. The cold made her double up like a *bagel*; it pinched and pricked. She thought she'd go out of her mind. Light and dark flashed before her eyes. In a

253

minute she'd die, she thought. She couldn't stand it any longer and began to cry bitterly, asking them to let her back into the house. She shivered and begged for mercy: 'Open up, Auntie, open up, Uncle!' she called to some of the band. She screamed: 'Uncle, I'll beg in earnest from now on! *Gvald!* I'll really beg well!' But it was like talking to the wall. They wouldn't answer.

"She lay down quietly. She didn't feel the cold or pain any more, and fell into a deep sleep. It seemed to her that she was being hugged and kissed. It was so good and warm, a pleasure! And they carried her away half dead. She was sick for a long time after that.

"Another practice of theirs was to drop her off the wagon as soon as the carriage of a wealthy nobleman or a merchant appeared in the distance. She had to go through the whole performance: she had to run after the horses or alongside the carriage, with outstretched hands, and sob and whine through her nose and look pitiful. She had to come back with money if it was the last thing she did. Sometimes the coachman lashed her but she swallowed it without a sound and kept up the performance. A lash from the coachman was nothing compared to what she would get if she came back to the wagon empty-handed.

"I can't even begin to tell you what she's been through. And it's still going on todayl Even in hell things can't be as bad. Oh, my blood boils when I remember how she lives! *Oy vey,* I'd give my life to free her. Listen to me, there is no one in the whole world as good and as sweet as she!"

CHAPTER XVII

Fishke's story cast both Alter and me into a deep melancholy. Alter rubbed his forehead with his fist, as if he had an itch, and groaned to himself.

"Do you hear, Reb Alter?" I said with a little smile.

"Our Fishke is really head over heels in love with the hunchbacked girl. It's strange. . . ."

"Why should I deny it?" said Fishke. "I pitied her with all my heart. I was drawn to her more and more. It did me good just to sit with her. What did we do? Nothing! We just sat and talked or looked at each other without talking. Goodness was written all over her face. She looked at me as only a devoted sister looks at her brother when he's in misery. And when the tears stood in her eyes after listening to my troubles, a warm feeling spread all over my body and I felt good. Something was happening inside me. What it was, I didn't know. But I began to understand: 'Fishke, you're no longer all alone in the world. You're not lone as a stone any more!' And my eyes were wet with big hot tears.

"And my wife? What a surprise! I didn't care much whether she carried on with the bastard or not. I made faces, of course, but without spirit—I didn't feel as hurt as I used to. Sometimes I even worried about what I would do if my wife suddenly said to me: 'Fishke! Enough of this wandering. Come, let's pick out a city and settle down!' I tried not to think about it, and my thoughts turned to her again—what would happen to my poor hunchback?

"But listen to this! The more I cooled toward my wife, the more she warmed up to me. More and more often she would have a good hour and be kind to me—soft as dough—and hang around my neck. But I paid for it later. She tormented me a thousand times worse than before, so that I wished I were dead. I had it from her—hot and cold. I couldn't figure out what was the matter with her. Was she crazy or just plain out of her mind? But a little later, something happened which broke the blister open. I finally understood what was eating her and what was behind her madness. It's a disgrace to talk about it."

Fishke thought for a moment. Then he scratched himself and continued his tale.

"We once arrived in some small town and, as usual, drove right

255

to the poorhouse to set up for the night. Well, let me tell you, I've seen plenty of poorhouses in my time and know what to expect, but this one was different. Even today; whenever I think of it, I start itching all over and I have to scratch myself. This poorhouse was a very old inn, a ruin with crooked walls and a roof like a crumpled cap, turned up in front and very low in the back, almost down to the ground. This tired old poorhouse looked ready to faint. The poor building wanted to collapse and lie down to rest on the ground in a pile of dust and rubble. But the townspeople had talked it out of such nonsense. They propped it up with sticks, tied it up with string, and begged it to last for another hundred twenty years.

"What used to be a gate led into a large house. You could see daylight through the cracks in the crumbling walls. The ground was full of holes and puddles. Some of them were filled with dirty rain water that had come in through the rotten roof. Others were full of stinking garbage that had been dumped there. Pieces of rotten straw lay all over mixed with all sorts of rags and junk: pieces of baskets, chopped-up matting, dried-out uppers of shoes, old heels and soles with rusted nails, pieces of pottery, broken barrel hoops, spokes from wheels, hair, bones, broom reeds and other trash. All this rotted on the ground and made the air so thick and stinking you could faint.

"On the left side of the house was a greasy old door. It opened with a creak into a room with small, narrow windows that didn' t set right. Most of the panes were missing; the holes were covered with fish paper, or stuffed with rags. The whole panes were very dirty and had thick layers of mold in the corners. Some were so old that they were covered with glaring yellowish-green film whose sharp reflections hurt your eyes just as scraping on glass hurts your ears. Long benches—boards lying on wooden blocks and stumps—stood along the crumbling walls and around the big stove. Wooden hooks were knocked into the walls over the benches. From the black ceiling hung several nooses with wooden rods through them. On these hooks and rods hung the greasy old coats, dresses, baskets of all the beggars who caine there, some on foot, some by van. Young and old, male and female—all stayed together.

"The poorhouse was also the charity hospital. This was the place where the town's sickest beggars died. The doctor did everything he could: he cupped them, he bled them, he physicked them at the expense of *Kahal*, until their kosher souls fled from his treatment. Then the poorhouse keeper, who was also the town grave digger, buried them free.

"The poorhouse keeper and his family lived there too in a little alcove which was an excuse for a room. Aside from being poorhouse keeper, grave digger, official in the Burial Society, inspector of the charity hospital, Queen Vashti in the *Purim* play, a bear during *Simkhes-Toyre*, a waiter, a punster at all weddings and circumcisions, he had another business: he made wax candles. All the rich families and all the synagogues in the town bought their candles from him. And when he made a batch, there was a stink for miles around.

"When we arrived, the poorhouse keeper had more than enough guests already. He drove them along: 'You've sat here long enough. It's time to move on to some other town.' Since it was late Thursday, they had a good reason to beg for more time: 'At least until after *shabes!* That night the ground, the benches, the stove were swarming with droves of people. They pushed, shoved, cursed and fought for a place to sit. It was a war between cavalry and infantry. Each tried to show the other who was stronger. During the whole uproar, a sick old man, who had been brought in the day before, was groaning in a corner. A little baby, whose foot someone had stepped on during the shoving, screamed to make you deaf.

"Later, when things quieted down a little, I found myself a corner and lay down to rest a bit. I'd hardly stretched out when I was attacked by armies of roaches, bedbugs, and fleas like bears. They wanted to eat me alive. To this day, I start itching all over when I think of that night, and I have to scratch myself. I soon saw that it's hard to fight roaches—a roach is a creature that creeps, and his partner, the bedbug, is one that stinks—and I gave up my corner to them, let them choke on it! Then I went into the front part of the house to find a place there to spend the night.

"It was very dark out there. A cold wind was blowing, howling like a pack of wolves, and whistling in through the cracks in the walls. Wisps of straw from the roof and other pieces of trash danced around like devils. Big drops of rain came in through the holes in the roof. I crawled into a corner and lay down shivering with cold. '*Ai*, my bathhouse!, my bathhouse!' I groaned and moaned. 'How can I get back to my old bathhouse? It was so warm there, a real Garden of Eden, a Paradise! Oh, how happy I used to

257

be in my Garden of Eden. I couldn't have wanted anything better, but the devil had to thrust a wife on me that I might be driven out by her to spend the rest of my years wandering over the face of the earth. That's the only thing women bring—trouble! That's all they're good for. What else can you have from them?'

"But then I remembered my hunchbacked girl and felt ashamed. She was a kind, gentle soul. It felt so good, so sunny and bright, just to sit with her and talk. Why, her little toenail was worth a thousand bathhouses! A look of hers warmed all my bones, like the sun. 'Shame on you, Fishke!' I lectured myself. 'You sin when you talk like that. Why, women make our lives sweet. A woman can make a man very happy. She can even make a heaven out of hell!'

"These sweet thoughts drove all my troubles away. I felt very good in my little corner. It wasn't cold any more. I began to read my prayers with feeling. But my eyes wouldn't stay open and I soon fell asleep. Suddenly I was awakened by a terrible scream.

" 'Just look at that creature!' someone shouted at the door and, with all his strength, threw something heavy into my part of the house. It fell to the ground like a stone with a thud. 'Look at her! Thinks she's a princess, she does! It won't kill you to lie out there, you filthy princess.'

"I recognized the bastard's voice, may his bones rot! He yelled some more, cursed 'the princess,' spat and slammed the door shut.

"The moon came out from behind the tattered clouds and, through the holes in the roof, threw some light on the ground. A body lay there like a sack of flour without moving. I got up to see who this 'princess' was. I took one look—and my hair stood on end. I saw spots before my eyes and felt faint. It was my hunch-backed girl! She was stretched out on her back like a corpse. I tried to revive her as well as I could. Finally, with God's help, she began to move. I lifted her with a power that was not mine and carried her to my corner. I could swear that at that moment I walked straight, like other people, without a sign of limping! Slowly, slowly, she opened her eyes and sighed softly. The whole world belonged to me. I felt like the beggar in the fairy tale when his hovel suddenly turns into a huge palace and he finds himself sitting with his queen at a table loaded with food. I took my coat off and quickly wrapped it around my queen, who was shivering with cold.

" '*Oy!*' my poor hunchback sighed. She rubbed her eyes and looked around, as if to find out in which world she was.

" 'Why are you staring like that?' I asked. 'It's me, Fishke! Praise and thanks to God that you're alive.'

" 'Oh, woe! Oh, woe is me!' she sighed from the depths of her heart. 'What's the good of my living? It's better to be dead than to live this way. God is so kind, so merciful—why did He create people like me, who only suffer in this world?'

" 'Silly girl!' I said to her. 'Surely, God knows what He's about. It must give Him pleasure that people like us live in this world. God is a father; He sees, hears and knows all. Do you think, silly girl, that He doesn't know all about our troubles? God knows, don't you worry! See how His moon shines in, even here, right from heaven? See? Don't sin with talk like that.'

"She looked at me with a pair of fiery eyes, filled with big tears that sparkled in the moonlight like jewels. I'll never forget her eyes and the way she looked at me that night.

"When I awoke early the next morning, my little hunchback lay in the corner, nestled in my capote, and slept like a little bird. Her face was pale and looked so gentle, so pitifully gentle. . . . Her lips trembled from time to time and moved as if she was praying. She was begging for mercy in her sleep, poor thing: 'Don't torture me! What have I done to you? What do you want from me? Don't ruin my life! What have I done to you?' It tore my heart to pieces. My eyes filled with tears, and I cried. . . .

"The first one to come into this part of the house in the morning was the bastard, may his bones rot! He looked at me and my hunchback with his thievish little eyes and went back into the room with a prickly little laugh."

CHAPTER XVIII

Suddenly Fishke was silent. He turned his face away as if he were ashamed. No matter how Alter coaxed him, it was no use.

"*Ett* . . . Really!" Fishke muttered and blushed, reluctant to open his mouth again.

Fishke was ashamed of what he'd said, it seemed. At first, spurred on by the heat of anger, he burst into flame and talked like a man with a high fever. He poured out his bitter heart in words that were far beyond his intellect. These words came to him by themselves, welling up from his soul. He forgot the world around him and talked and talked, hardly hearing what he was saying, until, suddenly, he awoke, somehow heard his own words, wondered at himself . . . and became embarrassed.

Who among us has not experienced, at least once in his lifetime, a brilliant hour of inspiration, when his mouth gave utterance to pure, true, human feelings which burst forth like clouds of seething and steaming gases from a fire-spouting volcano? Even upon Balaam's ass* a blessed hour descended during which he opened his mouth and delivered a fine speech. It also happens sometimes that even a preacher, pardon the comparison, who is forever chewing his cud and talking nonsense enough to make you sick, is suddenly struck with inspiration and, without thinking, comes forth with an idea that leaves both him and his audience gasping with wonder.

As soon as the moment of inspiration evaporates, the ass remains an ass and the preacher, pardon the comparison, a bag of wind and . . . but that's not my point.

I used to know two men who turned the presses in a Jewish printing house. Their job consisted of turning the wheels of the press, one on each side, like two oxen; turning and turning forever, without stopping, standing in one place, day after day. Then, one day, the two of them, as though bewitched, began to crank the wheels with great ardor, full of enthusiasm. Sparks shot from their eyes and they cranked with such rapture that you might have thought they were in seventh heaven and that each turn gave birth to a thought, or an idea, which had been agitating them. A while

---

* Numbers XXII, 28-30.

later, when the inspiration evaporated, they looked at each other with glassy eyes in dull amazement, spat, turned their heads away, and cranked the wheels in the usual manner looking again, for all the world, like two oxen.

I glanced at Fishke, who sat speechless, and sought a means to make him talk again. Suddenly, I thought of the Golem of Reb Leyb-Sarah's* and how he used to rise after Reb Leyb said the magic word and do everything he was commanded to do. "A good idea! Welcome!" I thought. But instead of the magic words used in bygone days to waken that Golem, may he rest in peace, the magic words I was going to use to waken my Golem, may he live long, would be about the hunchbacked girl.

I fed coal to the fire and warmed him up with a conversation about his girl. In the meanwhile, I became excited myself and ended up speaking with heat:

"How many innocent children there must be who suffer because of their parents' sins! Parents who think only of themselves, who divorce each other and leave the children, their own flesh ,and blood, to the winds! What do they care about children? They only care about their own little pleasure, their own little selves. Some of these fine parents even remarry—"

These last few words stuck in my throat, for I chanced to glance at my Reb Alter. He was very excited and could hardly sit still. My heart sank: *Ai*, how shamefully tactless I had been to make such remarks in Alter's presence! They fitted his position all too well. I had probably cut him to the quick! I felt terrible and took myself to task quietly:

"*Gvald*, Mendl, Mendl! It's high time you had more sense and did not blabber to others everything that comes to mind like a schoolboy! After all, you are, thank God, a Jew with a full-grown beard. It's time to come to your senses and realize when and when not to hold your tongue. *Oy*, that tongue of yours, that tongue! "

I promised myself to be more careful in the future, to think twice before speaking once, to do as many of our clever and successful people do—to see and hear only what it pays to notice. From now on, I would utter only words of praise so as to be more popular among the people. Visions of our do-gooders swam up before my eye, droves of those little uncles with glowing faces. They are boon companions of each and all, they dance at all the weddings, they

---

* Refers to the Golem of Rabbi Judah Löw of Prague (1513-1609).

261

are always having a good time. They kiss the fellow on top; they simply bubble over with joy when they talk to him about his successes; they wish him the best with tears in their eyes and sweet little smiles on their lips. They tell the whole world how good-natured he is. They always circulate pleasant rumors. Wherever there's a party or a celebration, there they are with their bright beady eyes, their moist foreheads shining, their cheeks glowing in the light. They are always pleased and happy and full of good cheer. How well off you are, uncles! I, too, will be an uncle from now on. Something about the name intrigued me and soon I was repeating it to myself with delight: "Uncle! Uncle Mendele! Uncle Reb Mendele!"

In order to make amends for my tactlessness, I began to worry about Reb Alter's comfort and tried to take him in with sweet words: "Reb Alter, you can't be comfortable sitting like that all the time. You're almost off the edge of the wagon, poor man. Your bones must be aching from sitting in one position. Listen to me, let's go and sit in my wagon. I'll fix you a good place to lie down. We'll have a sip of brandy and we'll be refreshed."

My Alter did not have to be begged. We all climbed down from his wagon and informed my horse of the honor that had befallen him: he was to lead the procession and Reb Alter's nag would bring up the rear. We walked a while to limber up our legs, then climbed up on my wagon and had a few sips. I was as sweet as honey and wished Reb Alter the best of everything: There were tears of joy in my eyes, just so—like a real uncle. I warmed up to Fishke too and tempted his Evil Genius so that his tongue began to wag once more.

Fishke began in his fashion; I worked and helped him along in my fashion. Alter was impatient and drove us both along in his fashion and the story continues:

"The next day was Friday and the little prayer house in the town was terribly crowded with beggars. They were shoving and pushing to get closer to the *shames*. Each one wanted to be up front, to be sure of getting a good *shabes* assignment to eat with a rich man or just a well-off merchant who serves a fat *kugl*.

The best assignment was the one to the tax collector; the worst ones were to the synagogue and *Kahal* officials. These gentlemen took good care of themselves, but they'd hand only a few crumbs to anyone else. These charity collectors always sighed about how badly off the poor folks were, but when they had one as a *shabes* guest, they hardly let him come close to the food. Beggars always feel that it's bad luck to have to be a guest of theirs for *shabes*. They avoid them like the plague. If someone is assigned to one of these officials, the other beggars laugh at him.

"The *shames* was very angry. He shouted that there were more paupers that day than usual. 'Paupers!' he yelled. 'Why have you descended on our town like a swarm of locusts? It's impossible to take care of all of you! It's a punishment from God—a plague!' He yelled, he screamed, but the beggars pressed closer and closer. They only cared about one thing: 'Me! Give one to me!' They all shouted together. Some of them forced a few coins into the *shames'* hand. What could the poor man do? He took the money and handed out the assignments.

"My little hunchback and I stood off to a side and watched from afar. We weren't strong enough or nervy enough to force our way in among these bears, these aristocrats of ours. Oh yes, there are aristocrats even among the poor. They're a thousand times worse than the rich.

"The bastard, of course, was way up front. He got two good assignments—one for himself and one for my wife. She didn't even have to bother shoving. He pointed to her, saying to the *shames*: 'Just look at her, please. There she is—blind, the poor thing!'

"When the crowd broke up, each one with his meal ticket, my hunchback and I went up to the *shames*, for better or worse, and asked for assignments for ourselves.

With a sort of sweet-sour little smile he glanced at us an didn't say a word.

" 'Take pity,' I said to him, 'on two unfortunate creatures, cripples. All week long we don't even taste a spoonful of cooked food.'

" 'There are no more assignments' the *shames* answered. 'You saw what just happened here. Where can I send you?'

" 'Here, take this,' I said and folded six groschen into his palm. 'It's for you. Have pity. Take care of us and it will be a *mitsve* for you!'

" 'Look here, you . . .' The *shames* spoke more softly. 'I don't need your money. I have one assignment left and can give it to one of you only. You can toss a coin for it if you want to.'

" 'Give it to her, to her!' I begged and pointed to my hunchback.

263

" 'No, no! Give it to him!' she begged, pointing to me. 'I won't take it myself.'

"We tried to talk each other into taking it. We each swore several times that under no circumstances would we take it alone. The *shames* was moved by all this. He smoothed his beard and looked at us in a very friendly way.

" 'I'll tell you what I'll do,' he said. 'If you'll both wait at the synagogue door after the evening prayers, I'll ask for you while the people are leaving.'

"And so it was. After the evening prayers, while the congregation was leaving the synagogue, he went up to two proprietors and, pointing to us, asked them to accept us as guests for *shabes*. 'I really didn't have the heart to send you any guests this week,' he apologized.

'I almost never leave you out. But if you don't mind, please take these two paupers.'

" 'With pleasure!' they both exclaimed. 'Where is the Jew who will refuse to accept a guest for *shabes*? It is the one day in the week when a Jew can catch his breath. Why shouldn't he, on this holy day, take in the needy and poor and share with them God's gifts! We beg you, *shames*! Send us needy guests each week and don't forget us.'

"Both proprietors walked ahead followed by their sons, all neatly dressed and freshly washed. Their faces shone and they all chattered happily. It was plain that in each of them their second soul—the Jew's Sabbath soul—was in command. My little hunchback and I walked quietly behind them and felt very happy.

" 'Good *shabes*!' my host greeted his wife when we came into the house. She sat on a chair, neat and clean, and shone like a princess. She kissed the baby on her lap. At her side played two pretty little girls, all dressed up.

" 'God has granted me a guest for *shabes*, my dear, else you might not let me into the house,' he said with a smile and began to greet the members of his household with a hearty '*sholem aleykhem!*' During the prayer 'Valiant Woman,' he placed himself before his wife and, still chanting the words, took the baby into his arms and kissed and petted it, while the other children joyfully gathered around him. It almost seemed as if the house were full of angels . . . I'm telling you all this because just then I thought of my little hunchback and wished she were there with me . . .

"My host was fairly well off. The Sabbath candles burned in

264

highly polished candlesticks made of, I don't know which, real silver or Warsaw silver. The table was set with porcelain dishes and the *khales* were covered with a cloth napkin. A bottle of wine sparkled on the table; we each poured from it when we said *kidesh*. During the meal, the hostess served me with an open hand and begged me not to feel ashamed to eat my fill. It was wonderful. The only thing that bothered me was the thought of my poor hunchback. With each bite of fish, with each spoonful of soup and noodles, with each piece of meat, I wondered whether she was being treated as well as I.

"After the meal, they asked me to spend the night. 'Let him sleep here,' the hostess said quietly to her husband. 'Where will he go? To that stable of a poorhouse? Here, at least, he can rest for a night.'

"How I would have liked to spend the night here in this warm house in a soft bed and straighten my bones out a bit! It was just what I needed, especially after what had happened the previous night. But I thought of her. I thanked them warmly but declined to spend the night. She was having her *shabes* meal in a nearby house. I went there and soon we both left together.

"It was beautiful outside. The moon shone brightly and it was a pleasure to walk.

" 'Come!' I said to her. 'Let's go for a walk. There's nothing to rush back to the poorhouse for.'

"The thought of the poorhouse made a cold chill go down my back. The sick old man, who was groaning all last night, began his last fight for life in the morning and died after the evening prayer. They lay him, over the Sabbath, in that part of the house where I was going to sleep.

"We walked along and found ourselves wandering down a street of gardens and trees which filled the air with delicious odors. It was quiet all around—not a sound. Everybody had gone to bed long ago as Jews usually do after supper on Friday night. We sat down on the grass near a fence.

"For a while we just looked and didn't say a word. We were both busy with our own thoughts. Then my hunchback sighed from the depths of her heart and began to hum the sad familiar tune to herself:

> 'My father used to beat me,
> My mother used to hate me . . .'

"I looked at her. Tears were rolling down her cheeks. Her face was aflame. She looked at me and smiled sadly. That look of hers took the strength out of me. My heart stopped beating and there was a pounding in my temples. I didn't know what happened to me and . . . before I knew what I was saying, the words escaped from my mouth: 'My dear soul!'

" '*Ai*, Fishke,' she said quietly, choking on her tears, 'I can't stand it much longer. How he tortures me. How he tortures me! '

" 'Who?' I exclaimed in a rage. 'He? The bastard? May his bones rot!'

" '*Ai*, if you knew, Fishke. If you knew!'

"I took her hand and, with tears in my eyes, begged her to empty her bitter heart. She covered her face with both hands and bent over to me. With a trembling voice she hinted at such things, such things! May that bastard drop dead, not to arise even on Judgment Day!"

CHAPTER XIX

Again Fishke was silent. He was somehow angry and sad at the same time. To make him talk again, I decided to tease him a little and said:

"You know, Fishke, you haven't even told us whether your hunchback is a pretty girl or not. Really, what can a hunchbacked girl have that makes her so attractive?"

"What do you mean?" Fishke asked hotly. "Since when does a Jewish girl have to be pretty? If she's pretty, she is pretty for herself and it's no one else's business. It's true, my hunchback is not bad-looking at all—she has a charming face, a beautiful head of hair, a pair of eyes like jewels—but that's none of my business! What am I, a skirt chaser, to start running after pretty girls? Nonsense! I liked her because she was good, warm, and she pitied me like a sister. In turn, I pitied her like a brother in a time of need. That's what it was!"

"Well, what's the difference!" Alter spoke up. "Pretty or not, you said that she told you something strange. What was it? *Nu, nu,* tell us!"

Alter urged him on in his fashion, Fishke started in his, I helped him out and corrected him in mine, and the story continues as follows:

"He used to pinch her, the bastard, may his bones rot! I'd noticed for a long time that he used to sidle up to my poor hunchback and pinch her. At first, I thought that he pinched her because he was a brute and enjoyed torturing and hurting other people. But, from what she told me, these were pinches of a different sort. They had a completely different taste, *tfu!* These were the pinches of sin, inspired by the devil. The bastard used to pester her. He gave her no peace. When he caught her alone, he laid it on thick with all kinds of sweet talk. He talked himself out of breath promising her mountains of gold. When he saw that promises were getting him nowhere, he began to bully her. He threatened her—he'd make her life miserable, he'd ruin her reputation, he'd throw her out in the middle of the road—and at the same time he tried to grab her by force. She usually had to tear herself out of his hands, sometimes by hitting him in the stomach and leaving him breathless. But he paid her back later with interest. He gave her the dirtiest jobs and tore pieces of flesh from her. Later on, the whole business started all over again—first sweet words, then threats. The more she avoided him, the more he followed her. When other people were present, he used to bump into her accidentally and pinch her, just so, for no reason at all.

"Ugly scenes like these took place quite often, but what happened the day before was terrible! *Feh!* I shouldn't even repeat it! After the uproar in the poorhouse, when the whole crowd was asleep and my poor hunchback slept doubled up near the door, she was suddenly awakened by someone whispering in her ear. It was the bastard!

" 'You must be very uncomfortable here, you poor girl,' he said to her with pity. 'Come, I have a good spot for you. You'll be able to get a good rest.'

"She thanked him for being so kind, and told him she was comfortable enough where she was. He began insisting that she should come with him. He told her that he knew all about her and me. He threatened that he would make her life miserable and grind me into the dust. The devil take him, the bastard! He could act like a wolf and an innocent lamb both rolled into one! Again he tried sweet words and threats but he became too bold. She smacked his cheek so that his teeth rattled. He flew into a rage, picked her up like a murderer and flung her out of the door. What happened after that, you already know.

"After my poor hunchback told me this, I sat glumly for a long while. A worm was gnawing away at me. The mere thought of the bastard made me burn with anger. At the same time, I had a warm feeling of pity for her and another feeling, too. I don't know what to call it, but it drew me to her—it made my heart pound. Suddenly, it beat so hard I thought I'd faint. I took her hand, which still covered her face, and spoke to her with a voice that was not my own.

" 'My darling! I'd give my life for your sake!'

" 'Oh, Fishke!' she sighed, moving closer to me and resting her head on my shoulder.

"The whole world seemed so rosy then. My body felt wonderfully warm and light. I comforted her and spoke to her like to a dear sister. I cheered her and told her not to worry: 'With God's help all will be well.' I swore I would be like a brother to her forever. She gazed into my eyes and smiled sweetly. Then she lowered her eyes and said:

268

" 'I don't know why it is, Fishke, but I feel so good now! I really want to live.'

"We talked for a while lightheartedly about how, with God's help, the future would be kind to us both and grant all our wishes.

"Suddenly we heard a tapping not far from us. I got up and walked in the shadow of the fence. On the other side of the alley, a man was fumbling with a cellar door. Something urged me, drove me forward a few more paces. I looked closely and . . . aha! May his bones rot, it was the bastard! He finally forced the lock open and disappeared into the cellar. He probably wanted to steal the things that were stored there for *shabes*. Like a lightning flash, the thought struck me: 'Fishke! This is your chance to avenge your poor hunchback. Now, while there is time, lock the cellar door and let him lie there like a bear in a trap! Tomorrow they'll find him and he'll get his proper reward!'

"For the first time, I knew the sweet taste of revenge! How good, how delicious it was! My blood was on fire in my veins. I was drunk with power! It took only a minute to dash up to the door and slam it shut. 'Lie there, you dog!' I laughed to myself. I seized the hasp and tried to force it over the staple, but it was bent! I pulled, but it was no use! It wouldn't give. I grasped it with both hands and took a deep breath for a last try. I was just about to force it on when a strong tug from inside pulled the door open and I flew into the cellar, banging into the bastard on the threshold.

" 'So, Reb Fish!' said the bastard after we had stared at each other in silence for a moment. 'It is on my account that you were puttering with the cellar door and violating the Sabbath! I surely appreciate it. Come, my kitten. Since you're visiting, come, let me entertain you. . . .' He shoved me down the stairs. I almost broke my neck and stretched out flat on the ground. 'And now, my dear guest, take this as an advance!' And he gave me a resounding blow in the back. 'And you won't mind waiting here until I fetch the roast chicken and the plate of fish that I was going to leave behind because you frightened me when you were fooling with the door.' He struck me again.

" 'Count, Fishke!' he exclaimed. 'Here's one, and two, and three, four, five . . . that's to settle my account. And now for the hunchback's! Count, Fishke! Here's nine, and ten! Aren't you ashamed to be dragging around at night with a girl in secret places? Here's twelve, and thirteen! I saw you before, ah yes I did, prowling

269

around the back alleys with her. There's sixteen, if I'm not mistaken, and seventeen!'

"My blood boiled up at his last words.

" 'You bastard!' I shouted. 'Don't you dare to mention her name!' I jumped up swiftly and sank my teeth into him. It was quite a fight; I with my teeth and he with his hands. He tore me away with brute force. Then he held me with both hands and squeezed. It was terrible! Then he threw me away like a ball.

"Thank your lucky star that you're getting off so easy. I don't feel like continuing this conversation with you. Stay here, Fishke, and rest up for tomorrow. Instead of *gefillte* fish they'll have a live fish tomorrow. Good night! Any message for your wife? I'll give her your regards as soon as I get back.'

"With these words, he shut the door and left.

"When I came to, the first thing I did was run to the door and try it. I tugged and pulled, but it was no use! He had locked it well from outside. I didn't know what to do next. I was afraid to make any noise because the owners might hear me. But to stay here was also dangerous. I was dizzy with fear, with anger and with aches from the bastard's blows. I went back down the stairs and threw myself down on the ground. But the thought of what would happen when they found me here tomorrow, of how they would hang out the welcome sign for me, of how the whole town would come running to see the thief—these thoughts tortured me and didn't let me rest. Everyone who believed in God would beat me and no excuse would be good enough. While I was imagining these things, I thought I felt something crawling over me. I put out my hand and grabbed a rat which quickly slid through my fingers with a squeal. I jumped up in terror. I felt nauseous and broke out in a cold sweat.

"In the darkness, I groped around—I could hardly stand on my feet—until I felt a cold, damp wall. I leaned against it and thought bitterly: 'Lord of Nations, what kind of life is this? Why do you punish me like this? Wouldn't it have been better, for me and for the world, if I'd never been born? Why do I always . . . always have to be despised?' This last thought broke my heart and I burst into tears. 'Oh, God, where are you?'

"I stood there like a statue without moving. What would happen to me? Suddenly, the door creaked and a thin band of light cut the darkness before my eyes. I could hear soft steps coming down the stairs. My hair stood on end from fright. Here, right now, they

270

would seize me and punish me like a thief. I stood there with hanging head and knocking knees, when I heard someone call my name cautiously: 'Fishke, Fishke!' And, in a moment, I saw her at my side—my hunchback. I came to life and shouted for joy.

" '*Sha,*' she whispered and took my hand. 'Come quickly, let's get out of here.'

" 'My darling! You saved my life!' I shouted, forgetting the danger, I was so confused. For the first time, I must confess, I kissed her there in the cellar.

"I asked her how she came there, but she reminded me that we were in someone's cellar at night. 'Come quickly. I'll tell you everything later,' she said and led me out into the street. While we were walking along, she told me what had happened.

"A few minutes after I was gone, she had a feeling that something was wrong, that she ought to go and see where I was. She walked to the end of the fence, looked around, and saw someone on the other side of the street bending over a door and fumbling with the lock. Thinking it was me, she decided to go across. But when she came close, she heard these words: 'And now, Reb Fish! You can lie there and rot like a dog. I've locked it carefully, never fear!' Before she had time to get over her fright, the bastard stood before her. He pinched her and snickered, 'Good *shabes*, it's the *rebitsin* herself! What a girl! Drags around in the middle of the night and makes pious faces! Humph! Get home, you slut!' And shoving her along with his knee, he forced her to go his way. All the way back, he kept on looking around and shifting the loaded basket from one shoulder to the other. At the same time, he didn't forget for a minute to use sweet words and threats on her. She went along glumly. She knew I was in trouble and there was no way for her to help me because the bastard made her stay within reach.

"Suddenly, a company of Jews appeared on their way from a *ben zokher*. They were happy and talked and laughed at the top of their lungs as is the custom among the children of Israel. The bastard hopped to a side quickly and ran down a narrow alley. My hunchback also jumped aside and ran the other way.

"Her first thought was to get back and help me. But, imagine her anguish when she got lost in the crooked alleys and side streets. She knew I was in great danger, that she had to get to me as soon as possible, that every moment was precious. And here she was, lost and unable to find her way back. She wandered around for a good while until, with God's help, she found the cellar and set me free.

"We walked along and talked happily. I to her: 'My darling! You stood by me in a time of need.' And she to me: 'Fishke! Yesterday, you were like a brother to me. Remember? Back there in the poorhouse?' But when we came close to the poorhouse, we both fell under a spell of gloom and our tongues froze. Our hearts told us that we could expect only trouble and that this night would not pass smoothly.

"Half of the gate to the poorhouse was closed. The other half was partly open so that part of the house was lit up by the street lamp. When we came up to the door, we both stopped with dread in our hearts. I went in first. The first thing I saw when I poked my head through the door was the bastard sitting with my wife. The two of them were stuffing themselves with the food he had stolen. The bastard whispered into her ear and soon disappeared. She got up in a rage and fell upon me, screaming:

" 'You so-and-so! The devil take your father's father! Do you think you can drag around all night with that slut of yours, that harlot? Do you think I don't know what you're up to? I've known all about it for a long time. I've been choking it down in my poor heart. Is this the thanks I get for my kindness, for taking you into the world among people, for making a somebody out of you? Do you think, you cur of curs, that you'll get away with it? Oh, no! I'll show you, the devil take your father's father, and your slut, the devil take her father's mother and her mother's father! I'll show you both. You'll learn not to fool with me. Here, take that, and that!' And she began to beat me. 'Here's for today and there's for yesterday and there's for before. There, there, there—may you drop dead!'

"I barely managed to get out of her clutches alive and ran out into the street. She stood outside for a while, shouting and screaming. Then she went back in again, screaming, 'Lie out there like a dog!' She slammed the door shut and locked it.

"My poor hunchback and I stood outside and looked at each other. We both felt miserable. Our hearts were heavy from this latest misfortune. Our troubles wouldn't let us stand idle very long. We started off and followed our noses. We walked along in silence, each thinking his own thoughts. When I finally looked up, I saw that we had wandered into the yard of the synagogue. My heart wept when I saw how tired my hunchback looked. This was her second night without rest. Where could we find a place to spend the night? Just then, I got an idea—the women's gallery in the synagogue!

"With God's help, we managed to get to the top of the rickety stairs which swung and swayed beneath our feet. We pushed open the door at the head of the stairs and tripped on something warm and soft in the dark. Suddenly, something was running and hopping all around us, on top of us, and over us in the darkness. We were hit in front, in back, in the sides—we couldn't tell where we would be hit next. I thrashed about wildly and finally seized a beard! What do you think it was? It was the beard of a goat! The town goats, as is the custom, had been sleeping in the women's gallery with the billy goat!

" 'Where are you?' I called my hunchback. 'Don't be afraid. The place is full of goats, may the Evil Eye not harm them! A town with this many goats can't be poor!'

I rounded up the goats and herded them out the door.' They would have to swallow their pride and spend this night outside. I said good night to my hunchback and soon left myself, closing the door behind me.

"When I got down to the last step, the billy goat was waiting for me with his head and long horns lowered. He was in a rage because I had insulted his wives by chasing them out. I wrestled with him for a while, but I couldn't get rid of him. He dodged my kicks. Finally, I managed to slip inside the door to the men's synagogue.

"There, on the tables and benches, Cabbalists lay stretched out like princes and whistled to each other through their noses in all the tones of the scale. It was a pleasure to see, may the Evil Eye not harm them, how soundly they slept. Cabbalists really have it soft in the world, I thought, and in my heart I envied them. They are an altogether different type of beggar—somehow they're respectable. I found a place for myself near the stove, threw myself on a bench and fell soundly asleep. But it was not my lot to have any pleasure in life. It seemed like only a few minutes later that someone shook me, saying: 'Get up, young man! Up, up, please!'

"I rubbed my eyes and saw a group of Jews looking at me very seriously. This was the Society of Psalm Sayers. It was their custom to come to the synagogue early on *shabes* morning to recite

273

psalms. There was nothing else for me to do. I had to get up. I washed my hands and sat down, barely able to keep my eyes open. I yawned, stretched and recited psalms together with them.

CHAPTER XX

"After my wife beat me that Friday night, I understood why she'd been acting so crazily for the last few weeks. She was steamed up over my friendship with the hunchbacked girl. The bastard had built up quite a story for her by telling her a pack of lies. He thought that she wouldn't want to know me any more now, that she would spit at me, and—finished! But he had figured wrong. Instead of letting me go my own way in cold blood and so separate from me forever, a hellish fire flared up inside her. That her husband should do such a thing to her! That a hunchbacked girl should attract her Fishke more than she! She wouldn't stand for such an insult! Oh no! She wouldn't allow it!"

"*Ai*, but the question is, why could she—your wife I mean—run around with the bastard?" Alter couldn't restrain himself and interrupted with the singsong used in studying *Gemore*.

"You're right," answered Fishke. "But, this much I learned in the Glupsk bathhouse: such a question makes no sense. Where do people talk about each other more than in the bathhouse? And who does most of the talking? Just the ones who ought to keep their mouths shut. A man who never yet said a true word laughs at others for being liars; or, another man, who can't be trusted with a groschen calls someone else a thief; a miser, who would sell his own eyes for a pfennig, accuses another man of being stingy; a spiteful man with a heart of stone says that someone else is a brute.

"Sometimes, when we bathhouse workers talked about this, Berl the Whipper held his head with both hands and said: '*Ai, ai!* I don't understand it! How can a man's tongue let itself slander others when it knows that its owner is a thief himself, or a liar, a miser, or some other kind of scoundrel!'

" 'Don't you see, my sage,' Itsik the Watchman would answer him; 'that's the whole trouble. The owner himself doesn't know it! A man won't notice a boil on his own nose, but he won't be able to take his eyes off a little freckle on someone else's face!'

"Shmerl, one of the loafers who made his home in the bathhouse, smiled, grasping his little beard. 'Take it easy, Reb Berl! Take it easy, Reb Itsik! You're both wrong. The truth is simply this: each one thinks that he has the right to do what others may not do.' "

"You're right, Shmerl!" I shouted, jumping from my seat. Shmerl's words awakened the little devil who sleeps in the breast of each of us sinners. The little devil in mine awoke with a biting laugh, pricked my heart, confused my mind, stirring up old insults and injuries which were buried there and gathering dust. He whipped them up inside me and my mind became a market place filled with characters who sprang full-blown out of nowhere. The devil pointed at them and made faces:

"There they are, those fine gentlemen! They do anything they want to—anything, anything, anything. . . They have their say in everything: in trade, in town politics, in charity societies, in deciding what is Jewishness and what is good conduct." There are old and young women in my market place too. "*Sholem aleykhem*, all of you!" I said, as if to myself. "God knows, I'd be only too glad never to see your faces or hear your names again. That's how sick you make me now. But what can I do? Since the devil himself has brought you to life again, I can't just ignore you, but being something of a writer, I'll have to please him and say a word about each of you!"

"Wait a bit, Fishke! If you please, Reb Alter!" I exclaimed. "There's something I have to tell you, but I have to think about it a little." And while I was thinking about it' I winked at one of my characters from a charity society. "Come on, now! Up on the stage with you!" He twisted and turned, kicked his legs, like a bound rooster to be sacrificed on *Yon Kiper*. The other characters looked at me angrily, motioning me to keep quiet. "Fools!" I thought to myself. "I'll pay no more attention to you than to last year's snow. You won't frighten me by putting a bearskin on your head and crying, 'Boo!' You're monkeys, not bears . . ." The devil in me became excited and urged me on: "That's it, that's the way! Get them up on the witness stand, one and all of them, those fine gentlemen!"

"Listen, please, Reb Alter! It's quite a story. In a Jewish town, the wealthier gentlemen, as their custom was, decided to . . ." Thus I began to tell my tale and stopped in the middle of a sentence as if the words were choking me. The women winked at me beseechingly: "Good, sweet, dear Reb Mendele! Have mercy, don't tell the tale!" Their feminine charm made me soft as dough. Each sweet glance from their burning eyes made me softer until I almost melted altogether. And then I remembered my vow to buy my way into the Society of Good Uncles, "The devil take the lot of you!" I said to myself with a smile, and, turning to Alter, I continued: "They, I mean those fine gentlemen in that town . . . Somehow, I don't feel like telling that story today. They can all go to the devil. I hope you won't mind, Reb Alter!"

"On the contrary! I'm in full agreement. For my part, too, they can all go to the devil. But, what kind of manners is it to interrupt someone, to break into his story, to tell your own?" Thus spoke Alter, and glared at me a while, shrugging his shoulders as if to say: "The man's like a sieve. Words pour from him like water! Who needs his stories? What good are they, can you tell me?" And, waving his hand hopelessly, he turned to Fishke and said: *"Nu,* what's next? Let's get to the point." Fishke began in his fashion, I helped him along in mine, and Alter urged him on in his fashion, and the story continues as follows:

"Time passed and my wife and I drifted further and further apart. She became even more attached to the bastard; they were a real pair of pals by now. They went begging together, like a prince and a princess, from house to house. It didn't make any difference to me any more. My head was troubled by my poor hunchback. She never left my mind for a minute. 'Go ahead, both of you,' I said to myself. 'For my part the two of you can go to hell!" When I met the pair of them by accident, the bastard sneered at me, as if to say: 'Well, I sure fixed your wagon, didn't I?' I usually spat and went my way, thinking: 'And even if you do drag around with her from house to house, what's the good of it to you? She is a married woman, heh-heh! She's nailed down. I've fixed your wagon too, haven't I? Eat your heart out.'

"I was now begging from house to house with a little old man, one of the bastard's bunch, as mean as they come, and just as crooked as the bastard himself. He made good use of me; everybody gave him alms. He walked in with such a piteous look, heaved such a sad sigh from the depths of his heart when he pointed to me, that you would have sworn that here was a heartbroken father with his crippled child.

" 'Limp, Fishke! Limp well, my boy!' he would say and poke me from behind when we entered a house. 'Make faces, and sigh! Sigh, you dog! They pay me well for every one of your sighs.'

"On our way, he used to teach me how to act my part better. He cursed the rich, pinched and poked me, and called me names— 'The devil take you!' or 'Drop dead!'—all with a smile or a grin. Once, for a joke, he gave me such a blow in my chest, right here

277

under my heart, that I almost passed out. He kept the money. It was hard for me to tear even a groschen out of him. 'What do you need money for, Fishke?' he used to tease. 'You're a treasure yourself. May your limping get worse and may you look sicker and sicker until you bite the dust, my fine fellow!'

"Once I demanded my share hotly and refused to take no for an answer. Necessity forced me to this. When he saw that I wouldn't give up so easily, he unleashed his nasty tongue: 'Shut your mouth, you lame dog! Do you think you're going to ride for nothing in my wagon? Do you think I'm going to carry a piece of carrion like you around for free? You worm! I'll tell your wife about this. I don't know you and I don't have to argue with you. I know only your wife! She gave you to me. It's from her that I got a piece of goods like you and it's with her that I'll settle my accounts.'

"Things were bad. I saw now that I was to the band what a bear is to a gypsy. They led me around by the nose and made money from me. They took my wife from me. They tricked her and now she was helping them against me. She handed me over to this band of thieves and robbers like a piece of goods for sale! Things were really bitter!

"I also saw that it was all over between my wife and me. We'd never live together again. Then why, I asked myself, should I stay here? I should run away right now, if I could. To spend an extra day with these thieves was a sin in the eyes of God. After all, these people had no God. They wouldn't dip their fingers into cold water, if it meant work! They had thrown off their yoke. They wouldn't touch anything resembling honest work. They only sponged on others and sucked Jewish blood. Why, they were the blood enemies of all other Jews!

"Then I took a close look at myself: the time I had spent with this pack of wicked people left its mark on me. I wasn't the same as before. Many of their nasty ways had rubbed off on me. The best way to be rid of all the pain and wickedress was to tear myself away from them and avoid them like the plague. But what about her? How could I leave her, my poor hunchback, with them? I felt as though I stood on the edge of a deep pit—dark and black, like hell itself. In one ear, a voice cried: 'Don't gamble with your soul, Fishke! For God's sake, run away!' In the other ear, I heard my hunchback calling: 'Fishke, Fishke!' '

"I had to choose one or the other: either the bright world, away from sin, pain and evil—or this hell, but together with her. I cried my eyes out and, may God forgive my sins, I stayed with the band of thieves.

"Later on I got the idea of running away together with my hunchback. But there was no point to this unless I could first get a divorce from my wife. After all, what would be the sense in my wandering around with an unmarried girl! Everyone would wonder and think ugly thoughts about us. There was only one remedy—a divorce! But would my wife give me a divorce? If I asked for one she would refuse just for spite! Her greatest pleasure lately was to hurt me and do me dirt. But I wasn't going to be frightened off. I decided to get what I wanted by hook or crook. Maybe God would have mercy. In the meanwhile, I kept my secret to myself and didn't breathe a word about it to anyone.

"Ever since my argument with the old man, I refused to beg with anyone from the band. This caused me all sorts of trouble. But I stuck to it. If it was the last thing I ever did, I would not be a bear for these gypsies any more. The bastard and his pack were very angry about this and showed me how they felt, with their hands and fists, whenever they could. While they were beating me once, they cried. 'Why should we let you ride along for nothing, you useless garbage, if you refuse to work, if you refuse to earn anything? Get out and go to hell!'

" 'This very minute!' I answered. 'But first give me back my wife!'

"They looked at each other and broke into loud laughter. Of course, when I said, 'Give me back my wife!' that was only an excuse. What I really meant was: 'Keep her, keep your bargain and make her give me a divorce.' I ached all over from the beatings they gave me for my stubbornness, but at least I had the pleasure of thinking: 'This will help me get what I'm after. They'll see that I am stubborn and useless to them. They'll want to get rid of me and this will be useful in getting my divorce.'

279

CHAPTER XXI

" 'Basya!' I once called to my wife and went up to her gently. We were alone. I thought I'd try to get what I was after through kindness. I wanted to sound her out about a divorce. 'Basya, what do you have against me?'

" 'Drop dead, Fishke!' she said.

" 'There you go again!' I grumbled as if in anger. 'I talk gently to her. I try to please her, but she tells me to drop dead! Why?'

" 'Then, have a stroke!' she said, her face twisted with anger, and moved away.

" 'May you live long, Basya!' I answered gently. 'Forget this foolishness and let's live together as God has commanded.'

" 'Drop dead, Fishke my dear, together with your harlot!'

" 'A-a-a-h! Better you should drop dead together with your bastard!' I said to myself. But aloud I said: 'Listen to me, Basya! If you don't want to live a decent life together, there's a simple way out, that's why Jews have a divorce. Once and for all, red or dead!'

" 'Aha, he's hankering after his harlot! He wants to get rid of his wife and hop-skip after that hussy! You'll never live to see the day! You'll sooner bite the dust! She won't get it so easily, that slut of yours. She'll plow the ground with her nose for me first. Do you hear me, Fishele? The devil take your father's fathers!'

"And my wife let loose with such wild cries that I showed her a clean pair of heels and was gone.

"I saw no way out. Things were bad any way I looked at them. I didn't have it easy myself—the band really gave it to me. But they rode all over my poor hunchback. My wife treated her like a servant. If she didn't like something, she took it out on the poor girl. The bastard, of course, tortured her in his own way. Our lives were pitiful. The only time we could catch our breaths in peace was late at night, when everybody else was asleep. Then we both stole away for a few minutes to talk and pour our bitter hearts out to each other.

"One night we were both sitting together near the Big Synagogue. The sky was covered with stars. There wasn't a living soul in sight. She sat hunched over on a stone near me and wept. With tears streaming down her cheeks, she sadly hummed the familiar words of her song:

> 'My father used to beat me,
> My mother used to hate me . . .'

"Each word cut into my heart like a knife. I tried to cheer her, I tried to give her hope: 'It won't be long, God willing, and we'll be free.' I wanted to make her see how we would live later, after we'd been released from our torment, with the help of the One Above. I tried to make each detail stand out like it really would be. I told her about the stone bathhouse of Glupsk with its cracks and crannies. I would get to be watchman after a while. She might also be able to find some work there. Maybe she could do mending or darning. And if this didn't work out, there were all sorts of other ways to make a living in Glupsk. For beggars, Glupsk is the Promised Land. The city is big, and the houses are many, like dust in a heap.

"The people there are plain folk, with no fancy ceremonies. They all do as they please and nobody cares. For example, well-to-do merchants walk around in rags, dirty and unwashed, and—nothing! Or they go strolling in bright day light in greasy coats, unbuttoned, with coattails flying, and—nothing! Or, on the other hand, you'll sometimes see beggars in velvets or silks and, again—nothing! In short, in Glupsk it's hard to tell the beggars from the rich, either by their dress or their actions. It often happens that the men who collect money for charity are beggars themselves, and together with the rich make a nice living from the contributions. One hand washes the other and it's a good life. It's no shame to be poor. With a little luck, a man can do very well for himself. There are many men who only a short time ago were unknown, low-down lackeys or beggars and now they're the bigwigs, the leaders, the wheels of the town!

" 'Even I, as you see me sitting here, can become a somebody, a director or a manager of some sort, and God willing, things will be good. We will live in riches and honor. Don't laugh, dear soul! I'm not out of my mind. Things like that happen often in Glupsk; you just have to believe in God and in yourself. And you must be a good Jew . . . with humility. *Akh*, Glupsk, Glupsk! How long will it be before I can tear myself free from this dirty pack of thieves and fly back to you, Mother!'

" '*Oy*, Fishke! I don't have the strength to stand it much longer,' my hunchback said, sighing from the depths of her heart. She rested her head on my shoulder while her face pleaded for mercy. I smoothed her hair, cheered her and tried to give her hope. She became happier, looked straight into my eyes and laughed.

" 'Fishke,' she said softly, 'you're the only one I have in the whole world. You're my father, my brother, my friend, everything! Fishke, be faithful to me and don't forget me. Swear it here, at the synagogue, where the risen dead are praying now—my father may even be among them, my father whom I hardly knew. He is my witness. Swear to me that you'll always be faithful.'

"I started working for a divorce in real earnest. I argued with my wife until I was blue in the face. Finally, we made an agreement:

"I would turn over to her the little money I had saved during the time I had been working by myself. I would also play the bear for the band for all of the coming winter. They could take me from house to house and all the alms they collected would go to my wife. This would be her payment for the return of the marriage contract. When the bastard heard this, he smiled and beat me to within an inch of my life. Then he congratulated me on my wisdom. Once more, I played the bear. Again I was a valued piece of goods. Again, I went from house to house with the little old man. I had to limp, sigh, make faces and play the game as he directed.

"After Passover we stopped in a little town in the province of Kherson.* At first, I kept on working according to my promise. But one day I declared: 'Enough! I've done my share.' My wife was surprised and wanted a few days to think it over. Finally, she replied: 'Fine! Tomorrow we'll be divorced.'

"I couldn't sit still or stand in one place, I was so happy! I felt like being out in the fresh air. I walked the streets for a long time. I even begged with spirit, thinking to myself that it wouldn't hurt me to have a few spare groschens at hand now that I was leaving the band. My begging went very well—it was a long time since I'd had such a good day. Money poured in hand over fist. When God wants to help a man, He takes care of everything! Wherever I walked in, I did not leave emptyhanded. I was even lucky enough to walk into a house where a *bris* was taking place. The guests had all had a few drinks and were happy and generous. I was given

* Kherson—a city on the Dnieper River near the Black Sea, not far from Odessa.

282

a whole *kidesh*-glass full of brandy, a big piece of sponge cake, money, and a roll shaped like a rose.

"I controlled myself and didn't even touch a crumb. I hid all the good things deep in my bosom so as to have a present for my hunchback when I came back. You should have seen how happy I was on the way back, thinking all along:

" 'Tonight, when the whole band is asleep, I'll give her the goodies. Let her have some pleasure too, poor thing. She is so miserable, so wretched. In her whole life she has never had a sweet moment. Now she'll know that Fishke is her brother and guards her like the apple of his eye. He won't even eat unless he can share the best things with her.'

"I pictured the two of us sitting near the Big Synagogue and enjoying ourselves. She was eating the cake with great pleasure. I was saying to her: 'My dear soul! May it do you good! May it be a good sign. God grant that we shall soon eat sponge cake to celebrate our own happiness!' And then I would tell her the good news that tomorrow I would be free; my wife was giving me a divorce. And she, my poor dear, would shine and beam like the sun. The two of us would plan how we'd run away from the band of thieves unseen and be free again. With God's help, all would be well.

"With these thoughts I walked back, dreaming about my happy future. I even saw a water carrier with full pails along the road—a sure sign of good luck. But how did it all end?

"The outcome, oh, woe is me, was disaster! When a man has no luck, even the best of good omens is of no use! When I came back to the poorhouse that evening, the whole band had vanished! While I was strolling around so happily, they skipped off with my wife and, alas, with my poor hunchback, too. This must have been the bastard's idea, a typical trick of his. May he wonder where his life will lead him as I wondered then what would become of me! May his stomach, O Lord of Our People, turn inside out as my mind did then! I was dizzy and nauseous! Black and bleak was the world to me. My one ray of hope, my one star of light, had vanished. Gone, woe is me, was my hope. Gone my poor hunchback. Again I was deserted, lone as a stone, all by myself in the whole wide world. And she? Where was she, and what was she doing now, poor thing? To whom would she now cry about her bitter life and open her troubled heart? *Oy*, gentlemen! It was a double blow to me.

"Later, I remembered the cake I had saved and took it out of my bosom pocket. The wounds in my heart opened again. I held it in both hands and soaked it with my tears, as if it were a relic of some dear beloved child who had died. 'It was not destined that you should taste it and enjoy something for once in your life, my poor dear unfortunate soul!' I stared and stared at the piece of cake, kissed it, and, wrapping it up like a jewel, hid it in my bosom again, pressing it to my heart from time to time. God alone knows how I felt then!"

CHAPTER XXII

With these words, Fishke covered his face with both hands and turned aside with a sob. We felt his anguish and left him in peace. A feeling of melancholy descended upon Alter and me, and we sat quietly, each thinking his own thoughts. Alter scratched his side curls and nervously passed his hands over his face, starting with his forehead and ending with his beard, which he grasped with all five fingers, muttering. It was clear that something had upset him badly and he was disturbed. Nor was I at ease. Fishke's tale distressed me. One thought ran through my mind: "Lord of nations! What is this? Is this what it means to be lovesick? I have heard of such things happening, but I have never really been able to understand them." In my town, people talked about such things in the following manner: "It's witchcraft, that's what it is. There's a little bottle of ointment and some herbs from some old peasant witch at the bottom of all this! Old witches love to play tricks like this. They love to go riding on their broomsticks with husbands who desert their wives and ruin their lives. They've been seen doing this by many witnesses, good kosher Jews with respectable beards. It's as clear as day." To be smitten by love was to us the same as being sick, as having a fever, as being possessed by a *dibek*, as being in delirium, as having melancholia or epilepsy. When we talked about love, we used to hold our eyebrows, spit seven times and make a pious face, saying: "May it not happen here! May Jewish children be protected from it!" We laughed at someone in love just as we laughed at the village idiot. But, I also remember that whenever this disease struck, it was either among the very wealthy or the very poor. The respectable folks in between were immune, they never caught it.

I often used to think that there was something remarkable in this. What did it all mean? The stories of old peasant women with their love potions and herbs—those were all nonsense—I was never satisfied with them. Many folks considered me somewhat of a heretic because of this. That was just as bad as not believing in witchcraft, in evil spirits, or in the *Tatar* who can cure all ills with his magic powders! I had long sought a better explanation and, at last, I thought I had found one.

The very wealthy have it very good in this world. They have

everything: food, the best of drink, the most expensive things, all with no worries and no headaches. Really, what do they lack except, maybe, a good fever? Having nothing better to do they play lovey-dovey. Do they do so in earnest or just for entertainment? That's their secret. On the other hand, the beggars also have it good in their own way. Aside from a good fever, they have nothing to lose. They have no headaches or worries either, since they sponge on the rest of the people. So they, too, can afford to take up such nonsense. Love affairs and marriages for love are customary only among the upper and lower classes. The rest of us, folks of a middling sort, have our minds in a bowl of *borshtsh!* We're too busy earning our daily bread, trying to make a living. Our first worry is business. Everything is business; even marriage is a business. We procure a wife for ourselves: first, we haggle over the price, over the dowry, over each and every little detail to our heart's content. All this is carefully written into the engagement contract. Even the fur cap or the *shabes* capote which goes into the dowry is listed in the contract. When all conditions are properly fulfilled, as stated in writing, "Then come, dear bride, let's go under the *khupe* together with the matchmaker, the master of ceremonies, and the whole pack of synagogue officials who all expect some commission. Be a wife, bear children, suffer and get wrinkled and gray together with me until we both reach one hundred and twenty; that is, if you can stand living that long and don't wish to die before your time. Whether you are pretty or ugly, clever or stupid, that's your affair—it's all the same to me, for a wife is a wife. We are not lords or noblemen. We have no time to pay attention to such foolishness. We are Jews, merchants, traders, storekeepers, busy with our business."

There's many a Jew in my class who hardly ever talks to his wife, never eats at the same table with her, rarely looks at her, and thinks that this is as it should be. Husband and wife are both pleased with this arrangement and, should the subject come up, they wish such a life for all good people and for their children, too. When the wife dies, the man sits in mourning like a good Jew for the prescribed seven days and soon procures himself a second wife, sometimes even before the prescribed thirty-day waiting period has run out. And, in the same way, his third, fourth and fifth wife is procured, and so on until the last old woman whom he marries in his old age, usually under the pretext that he will go to Jerusalem with her to die.

Among Jews, this whole procedure goes under the name of fulfilling a *mitsve*, of doing God's bidding. The same holds true when Jews speak of the way they eat on *shabes*: they never say that they are simply gorging themselves, for every sinner must eat. They say they are fulfilling a *mitsve*, the three Feasts. Or, take the little glass of wine at the Passover *seyder*. Will a Jew admit that he gulps it down simply because it tastes good and makes him feel good, especially after the soup and *kneydlekh*? God forbid! He says a little prayer with a pious face: "*Hareyni mookhen umzumen* (I am ready and able . . . ready to fulfill the *mitsve* of drinking wine)," and thus he gulps down the first glass and then the second, third, fourth. . . . We never eat, drink or get married, except to glorify His Holy Name and for the sake of the Holy Spirit.

But none of this applies to Fishke. In his unfortunate situation, the hunchbacked girl was a good thing for him. She was his hope, his all and everything. A drowning man grasps at a straw. Is it any wonder then that Fishke held on to the hunchbacked girl as though his life depended on it and became so attached to her? When the soul is wounded, it is the heart that cries; it weeps the same way for all people. The language of the heart is universal; it is the same for young and old, for the scholar and the simpleton. Why then should anyone wonder that such warm feelings gushed from Fishke's heart, such purely human words? That is why I was so moved by his words. They softened me like the notes of a little violin which speaks when it plays a sorrowful tune. None of the preachers or moralists I have ever heard—put them all together— ever moved or softened me, or made me so good and gentle, as a groan from a broken heart or a pure note from a little fiddle.

Well, as I said before, Fishke's tale moved me deeply. That is why I've been sitting here sunk in thought. "But you, horse o'mine, what are you thinking about?" That's quite a pace he's set himself! Why, he's hardly moving. What does he care if *Tishe Bov* is almost upon us and we must hurry to provide many little towns with the *Books of Lamentations!* He isn't even walking in the road! He's off to a side where the grain grows. He stops every now and then for a nibble. And that pretty mare of Alter's, is she any better? She imitates him and also takes a mouthful. Just as in *kheyder:* when the *melamed* looks aside, either to rock his child or to quarrel with his wife, the pupils also look aside and cheat at their lessons. I used the same remedy as the *melamed*. I took my whip and showed it to my *shlimazl* and accompanied it with a lecture on the difference

287

between right and wrong. He pricked up his ears, stretched his neck, stuck out the point of his tongue, tapped the ground with a rear hoof and flicked his tail at me. "*Ai*, so you want to be fresh!" I exclaimed and warmed his hide with the whip. He didn't like this at all. He reared up on his hind legs. Then, for a minute, I thought he'd stretch out on the ground, but he reconsidered and, pulling himself together, gave the wagon a hefty tug so that we started moving again.

By this time we had all recovered. Alter began to urge Fishke on in his fashion, Fishke began his tale again in his fashion, and I am correcting it in mine. It continues as follows: "I started out all alone toward Odessa. I was hoping that maybe I would come across the band or at least hear some news about them. But it was no use. It was as though they had sunk into the earth. I began to hate this endless wandering. I was dying for a rest. I wanted to be able to sit in one place, as I had been accustomed to all my life. With God's help I finally dragged myself into Odessa.

"For the first few days there, I was more dead than alive. I roamed around all alone, a stranger in the big city, and didn't know what to do with myself. Everything was new to me, new and strange. I couldn't find a poorhouse like in other Jewish towns. There were no houses to go into either. In our Jewish cities, there are houses—plain houses, nothing fancy, one-story, with the entrance off the street. Push the door, just crack it open, and you're smack in the middle of the house. No big ceremonies, everything you need is right there. Do you want to eat or sleep? Do you need water? Here it is. The pail of slops? Right there. Go ahead, wash your hands to your heart's content, but say your prayers first. Why, here are the people who live here—man, wife and children! Say: 'Help a poor man, in the name of the Lord!' Put out your hand and you'll get something. Kiss the *mezuze* on the way out, and go your way in peace. Also, in our cities, it's easy to tell a Jewish house from the outside. There's a little pile of garbage, a little puddle of dirty water, and the windows, the walls, the roof all shout together: 'This is a Jewish house!' The smell alone tells you that a Jew lives here. . . .

"But in Odessa, the houses are crazy. They're so high! First, you go through a gate into a courtyard. From there you have to climb stairs and look for doors. When you finally find one, it's locked! There's a bell, a knocker, or some other trick. You stand there with a heavy heart. You realize how poor you are, how low you are,

288

that you're a man without a face. Then you work up courage and respectfully ring the bell, just a little ring, almost nothing at all, as if you're ashamed of it. You feel as though you have said a dirty word or sent his father's father's father to the devil, and you run away before the door opens...

"Sometimes the door opens before you can run away and you're at the mercy of an angry cook or butler, or it turns out that a non-Jew lives there! 'How can that be?' you wonder. 'What kind of city is this? And what kind of houses are these? Where are all the beggars with their sacks?'

"I roamed the streets and looked around carefully. I was hoping I would meet another beggar with his sack from whom I could find out the right way to beg here. But, as if for spite, I saw no beggars. As I wandered this way, I saw a young man in the distance, dressed like a German, walking like a man who isn't sure of his way. He looked at all the houses and crossed from one side of the street to the other. 'This fellow,' I said to myself, 'must be a stranger here. I'll follow him and see what he does.' He went into a yard, I right behind him. He went up a flight of stairs, I—also up. He knocked on a door and went into a foyer. I waited just outside the door. Soon a man appeared, with a shaven face. It must have been the owner himself. The young man gave him some sort of book which he pulled out of his pocket, a pocket as broad and deep as a sack! The shaven one looked at the title page and flung the book back at the young man with an angry shout: 'Leave me in peace! What do I need your junk for?' The young man pleaded with him, praised himself to the sky, claiming that he had a real jewel here. But it was no use and the poor fellow went out shamefaced and heartbroken. I went in and simply begged for alms. They gave me a few groschen and I ran out with a joyful heart. 'Now,' I thought, 'I've found the right way. God sends flax to the spinner, beer to the inn-keeper, and a stranger to the beggar as a guide. I must not lose sight of this fellow!' He did very badly. In one place he was told, 'Go your way, young man! We don't need your wares!' In another, the door was simply slammed in his face. He left empty-handed and angry every time. I wasn't doing badly at all, may the Evil Eye not harm me. I took a groschen or two or three each time—whatever they gave me.

" 'What's going on?' I wondered. 'What kind of a beggar is this? I never heard of anything like this in my whole life. It must be a custom here—beggars with books! New fangled beggars, and they're dressed like Germans. What fools! Why beg with books and get a fig for your troubles when you can simply beg for alms and get something! I like our grandfathers' customs better: you go from house to house simply, without tricks. That way I can do better than others with their books. Whatever he was, fool or no, I kept close behind my beggar with the books. I trailed after him and was careful to keep him from seeing me. At first, he didn't, but later he must have felt that some one was dragging after him and he was very annoyed. He began to stop and look around often, seeking a way to get rid of me. I looked the other way, as if I didn't even know he was there, and followed after him. In my heart, I thought, 'Oh, no! You won't get away from me, brother o'mine! Although you don't do anyone any good, especially yourself, still, I need you. You are like a guiding star to me, sage o'mine!'

"Finally, we got into a scrape in one apartment. The owner had just sat down to eat when my beggar walked in. They had a big argument. My beggar tried to sell. One word led to another and the owner became very angry. He showed him the door and finding me there, sent us both off to the devil together. Our common lot naturally led us to get to know each other better. As we started down the stairs, my partner looked at me angrily. I turned my eyes away and didn't know what to do. I waited for him to go first. We stood there like that for a few minutes and both felt bad. Then my partner said to me:

" 'Just what do you want, Mister?'

" 'Me? Nothing!' I answered. 'The same as you.'

" 'The same as I?' asked my partner, looking me up and down from head to toe with great wonder. 'Are you also an author?'

"I didn't know what 'author' meant. I thought it was the German word for what we, in plain Yiddish, call 'beggar.' So I answered him in his own language:

" 'Yes, an author.'

" 'And what have you done?'

" 'Oh, I've done quite well,' I answered, thinking to myself that I had done a sight better than he had. 'About forty groschen.'

" 'And what's the name of your opus?' he asked.

" 'He's talking German to me again,' I thought. What he meant to say was: 'And what's your name, partner?'

" 'Fishke!' I answered to the point.

" 'May I have the honor of becoming acquainted with *Fishke*?' he" asked with a sugary smile.

" '*Akh!* By all means! It's my pleasure, upon my word,' I answered warmly, and gave him a big grin.

" 'Well? Where is this opus?'

" 'Why, here I am standing right before you, may you prosper!'

" 'Go to hell!' he exploded and ran off in a rage.

"When I came out of the yard, I saw my partner running like a madman. He was already halfway down the street. Then he ducked into a side alley and vanished. I stood there as though I had been slapped and wondered what was the matter with him. He must have gone mad! One minute he was nice and friendly and the next minute he is in a rage. What did I say to him? I even answered him with his own German words—'author' and 'opus'! In plain Yiddish, all they mean is 'beggar' and 'sack'!

"For my part, he can go to the devil, too!

CHAPTER XXIII

"It wasn't long before I became familiar with Odessa. I got to know all its side streets and alleys. I had figured the city out and now knew where to open doors. Odessa is like one of those tricky little snuff boxes—you have to find the catch. Once you know that it opens easily, you can stick your fingers in and take a pinch whenever you want to. I discovered a whole new world of houses, the kind I needed, just like back home in Glupsk. I found all the beggars I wanted! Armies of them, and of all different kinds—beggars with sacks and beggars without sacks—types you could find only in Odessa and nowhere else. There were Jerusalem Jews and Frankish, Turkish and Persian Jews who babbled away in the Holy Tongue; there were old paupers with their wives, and also without their wives, who claimed they were on their way to Jerusalem to die, but, in the meanwhile, stayed on in Odessa, had more children, and thought the world owed them a living; there were wives whose husbands had deserted them; there were women with spasms and men with fits who came here for a cure at the shore; there were Cabbalists of the old homey sort who used to loaf in the Houses of Study; then there were the new-fangled Cabbalists with shaven faces who used to loaf in the cafés and taverns together with the Galicians and Frenchmen; there were refined beggars without a groschen to their name who dressed like rich men; and there were others who even owned their own houses but dressed in rags and tatters like the poorest of the poor.

"The beggars that I met there from Glupsk all praised Odessa to the sky, but I could never see in what way they were better off. One of them explained to me that the difference between a beggar in Glupsk and in Odessa was this: in Glupsk, a beggar eats his dry crust of bread in dreariness and weariness; in Odessa, he eats the same dry crust of bread to the accompaniment of a hurdy-gurdy. There's a hurdy-gurdy in the street, in the houses, in the taverns, in the theaters. Even in the synagogue—forgive the comparison, *feh!*—there's a hurdy-gurdy. There is always excitement in Odessa; something is always happening! The air whistles and screeches. Walk by a tavern, and there's always a drunkard at the open door, groaning and singing 'Pretty Maiden'—that's a song of theirs there.

Across the table from him, happy, tipsy Jews sing psalms and prayers to merry marching tunes!

"One day I was walking at the side of the street when I felt a sharp blow in my back. I decided not to make a fuss, thinking that someone in the crowd had accidentally bumped into me. But soon I felt another blow, like with a piece of wood. I turned around— and there was Yontl, the cholera groom from Glupsk, sitting on a little wooden platform with wheels and two wooden pushers, one in each hand! He leaned on one pusher and held the other one up in the air with a grin. He was glad that he had run into me. I was also very glad to find Yontl. He and I used to be good friends in Glupsk. I was at his wedding in the cemetery during the cholera epidemic, may we be saved from such a calamity today!

" 'Well, Fishke!' he greeted me. 'So you're here in our Odessa too? Quite a city, my Odessa, isn't she!'

"Seeing that I shrugged my shoulders and wasn't impressed, he looked offended, as though I'd insulted his dignity.

" 'You think your Glupsk is a city? A worm in a sour apple has no idea that there are sweet ones! Wait, I'll show you my Odessa, then we'll hear what you say!'

"Yontl told me how well liked he was in Odessa. Everybody enjoyed watching him ride around on his butt. He was something of an honored guest in many stores. They gave him alms willingly, without any complaints! He was doing very well, may the Evil Eye not harm him. When I asked about his wife, he answered with a little smile:

" '*Oy*, did Glupsk give me a fine wife! Did you ever hear of a cholera wife that turned out to be good? She should have died from the cholera before she became my wife. Her lower lip was missing, but that didn't keep her mouth from working, screaming, making noise all day long, grinding away like a mill, worse than a woman with two healthy lips.'

"I said to myself, 'There's no defense against a wife. If she is a scourge, she will scream even if she is missing a lip or a nose. She will fall upon you blindly even if she has no eyes.' I told Yontl about my wife and what I had to put up with.

" 'Don't be a fool!' he said. 'Do what I did. Spit at her and let it end at that. Let her go to the devil!'

" 'What do you mean, Yontl, spit at her? What about a divorce? I am a Jew and must be married.'

" 'Oho! You must be married?' Yontl looked at me with a laugh.

'You're really from Glupsk, upon my word! Fishke, listen to me. Stay here in Odessa a while and then we'll see.'

"After this, I used to meet Yontl often. I went all over Odessa with him, he on his butt and I on my lame legs. Yontl took it into his head to make me admire his Odessa. He showed me the beautiful streets and boasted about the beautiful houses, as if they belonged to him and gave him profit. Every time he showed me something, he looked at me with pride and snorted with pleasure, as though this wealthy house or that pretty street made him more important in my eyes. He would poke me and say, '*Nu*, Fishke! What do you say about my Odessa? Maybe in your Glupsk you have something like this, eh?'

" 'Listen to me, Yontl!' I said to him one day when my sides were sore from his poking. He was showing me the Boulevard in the distance. Great crowds were strolling along and I saw that he was unwilling to go up any closer. 'What do you want me to say, Yontl? Odessa is a beautiful city, but it's a pity that there are no *mentshn* here! Tell me yourself, Yontl, are those people out there on the Boulevard *mentshn?* Just look at the men holding the ladies' hands! It's a sin just to look! Jews with shaven faces! Jewish women with their own hair—sweeping the street with their long trailing dresses which are cut so low in front that you can see their bosoms. *Feh*, it's disgusting, as I am a Jew! *Akh*, if we could bring our Jews from Glupsk here! Then this would be a city, a Jewish city, with Jewish customs, and things would be as they should be.'

"Yontl moved along with me and said nothing. What could he say? On the way, two well-dressed gentlemen came toward us, Frenchmen, and Yontl stretched out his hand. One of them stopped to talk to him for a minute and gave him some money.

" 'Do you know, Fishke, who they are?' Yontl asked with pride his eyes shining with pleasure. 'The one who gave me money is the chief *melamed* in our *Talmud-Toyre* here. An acquaintance of mine, do you understand? He cuts quite a figure, doesn't he?'

" 'May all my enemies look like that!' I spat. 'From the looks of my handsome *melamed*, I can imagine your so-called *Talmud-Toyre* here. I ask you, Yontl, aren't you ashamed of yourself to say that this is good? No, no, Yontl! They've spoiled you here! You're just like them! Some *melamed!* Look at him and look at our Reb Hertzele Mazik in Glupsk, God forgive the comparison. There is a Jew for you! Why, all of Glupsk is full of Reb Hertzele Mazik. Who extols the dead at a funeral? He! Who makes the final arrangements

for a wedding? He! Who recites psalms for the dead at the cemetery? He, again! When he goes from house to house every week to
collect his fee for teaching the children, folks carry the money
toward him! On *Simkhes-Toyre* he runs to the wealthy houses with
the little boys from the *Talmud-Toyre* to say prayers in honor
of the rich. When he cries, 'Holy sheep!' the little boys answer, 'Baa,
ba-a-a!' It's something to see. And your Frenchman? What would
he look like with his shaven face reciting psalms? What would he
look like extolling the dead at a funeral or saying prayers in honor
of the rich?'

" 'But you're making a terrible mistake!' Yontl broke in. 'This
melamed never does any such things and doesn' t even know the
first thing about them.'

" 'What do you mean, he doesn't do such things?' I asked in
wonder.

" '*Sha, sha,* Fishke!' Yontl tried to calm me. 'He buries them, but
in a different way. It's all right, the gentlemen here are satisfied—'

"'*Feh, feh, feh!*' I cried, stopping my ears. But Yontl wouldn't
leave off and asked:

" 'And do you know who the second gentleman is? He is quite
a man, a politician here in the city just like Aaron-Yossl Stillwhistler
back in Glupsk!'

" '*Feh, feh!*" I shouted so angrily that several passers turned and
looked. 'You call him a man, Yontl? Like our Reb Aaron-Yossl? At
least you should add: forgive the comparison! Reb Aaron-Yossl is
a Jew with a beard and with prayer curls! Jewishness is written all
over him. He keeps Jewish money in trust: money willed for
philanthropy, money belonging to the societies, and all sorts of
other moneys. No one even asks him for a receipt, his word is good
enough. When he takes money, he knows he is taking it and
probably knows what to do with it. You can rely on him for that!
And your man here? Who would want to trust him and for what?
For his Jewishness? For his shaven prayer curls?'

" 'Just for his word, Fishke! Believe me!' Yontl insisted. 'With or
without prayer curls, it makes no difference, as I am a Jew.'

" '*Ett!*' I said. 'What are you trying to prove to me? All right, I'll
grant you that maybe his word can be trusted. But could you let a
person like that be a *sandek?* Oh, he would do a fine job, I'm sure!
Feh! It would be a joke! No wonder people say that you can see
the flames of hell forty versts around Odessa! There must be some
truth to it.'

" 'Still,' Yontl answered bitingly, 'I'd rather be here in hell than back in that Garden of Eden of your Glupsk!'

"Yontl seemed altogether different to me now. Odessa had spoiled him and we argued very often. What he thought was good, I thought was bad, and what I thought was good, he thought was bad. We couldn't agree, for example, about the Big Synagogue in Odessa, or about the rabbi or the cantor there. A cantor, indeed! He sat in a booth while a chorus sang the prayers! He did nothing at all. You wouldn't catch him sticking his finger down his throat or pulling on his cheek like our Reb Yerekhmil Weepsister, who shouted in low register, then skipped to a few piercing notes like pistol shots, then back to the thick strings again, shifting the words up and down the scale, breaking into a thin falsetto for a sweet little Rumanian shepherd song with which he tried to soften the Lord of Nations: '*Oy, tatenyoo*, dear Father! *Oy vey*, woe is me, woe!' Reb Yerekhmil put his heart and soul into his singing and was soaking wet by the time he reached 'Who is Blessed.' But the cantor here? Did he work like that? God forbid! He hardly did a thing. As soon as he sang a note, the chorus caught up the cue and dished it out on a little platter, carried it up and down, mixed it with *kasha* and poppy seeds! That's what they called 'services' here! And where was the Rumanian shepherd song? And where was the appeal to the Lord of Nations? Instead they made a fuss over an unimportant little prayer, 'There are none like unto Thee.' They worked it to death—a joke, as I'm a Jew! And what else? They held up the *Toyre* and danced around the synagogue with it! Did you ever hear of anyone dancing with the *Toyre* on *Shabes* just like on *Simkhes-Toyre*? Who ever heard of anything like that?

"Then you might ask, 'And where was the rabbi? How could he permit such things to go on?' That was the whole trouble! The rabbi himself led the dance in a French suit with a trimmed beard! *Feh!* And Yontl didn't mind at all!

" '*Gvald*, Yontl!' I exclaimed. 'Yontl, what have they done to you? Have you gone out of your mind or did you lose your senses? How can you stand such shamelessness? *Gvald*, the devil take your father's father!'

"And he grinned at me! He beamed with pride and said: 'Fishke, you're a fool! You can't even tell the difference between good and bad. How can anyone argue with you?'

"I saw that it was a lost cause. Yontl was stubborn. I knew that I couldn't get anywhere with him, so I promised myself not to talk about it any more. From now on people could stand on their heads in Odessa and I wouldn't care a fig!

" 'Listen,' I said to Yontl one day. 'I'm not going to argue with you any more about Odessa and its ways. You're a stubborn mule and I won't get anywhere with you. Let's talk about more important things! I need your advice—what's going to become of me? I'm sick of this begging from door to door. There are plenty of beggars without me. They cover this place like a horde of locusts and will soon cover the whole world. It would be better if I had some business or a trade. Tell me, what should I do?'

" 'Running an office is not for you,' answered Yontl. 'A store or shop is also no good. I don't know, why don't you tell me?'

" 'Don't laugh, Yontl,' I said. 'Talk sense. Jews do lots of other things besides running offices or stores or shops.'

" 'Oh, of course!' Yontl agreed. 'Like collecting the meat tax, for example, or keeping the treasury of a charity society, or collecting funds for Meyer Bel-Hannes' *Talmud-Toyre*, or messing with city politics and rubbing shoulders with the politicians—these are all high-class businesses. But they're not for you. Let's go over the list of little Jewish businesses. How about being an old clothes dealer? Many Jews make a good living from old clothes . . .'

" 'No!' I explained to Yontl: 'Old clothes have to be bought and patched. For that you need money and some know-how. That would be hard for me. If it was used Glupsk underwear, I wouldn't worry about it. Who would care if it was a little torn or patched so and so? But here in Odessa, it's enough to scare you out of your wits! Underwear, excuse the expression, in Odessa is worn with great ceremony and pomp! I'd be too scared to touch a pair!"

" 'If you're so scared of Odessa underwear,' said Yontl, 'then sell onions, garlic, rotten lemons and oranges and that sort of thing. But you have to remember that the right way to do it here is to get a cart and pull it through the streets and shout out your wares with the right sing-song.'

" 'I can shout beautifully,' I answered. 'I'm a past master at that, but I can't hitch myself to a cart like a horse. I don't have the strength! Then there's the other question: where am I going to get money? I have to buy wares to get started!'

" 'Listen, Fishke,' Yontl said very seriously. 'The only business I know of where you don't have to work hard or invest money are the high-class ones, the ones I told you about before. I don't know of any others. Why don't you tell me?'

" 'What I would like best of all,' I told Yontl, 'is to work in a bathhouse. Everybody liked me when I lived in the stone bathhouse in Glupsk. I was made for that job and, if not for that marriage of mine, I'd be a somebody today! Oh, I would have made my way up in the world! Sweet, good Yontele, if you really have any connections at all in Odessa, try to get me a job in a steam bath. Be a brother to me, Yontl, and show me what you can do here!'

" 'I won't promise you a thing right now, Fishke,' said Yontl with a little smile. 'First, look over the bathhouses in this city with your own eyes and then we'll talk.'

"I followed Yontl's advice and went first to one and then another bathhouse. I never saw anything like it! Who ever heard of steam baths like these? They were bright and clean like the inside of a house. The benches were strong and solid, as I am a Jew! God help anyone caught lousing himself there! There wasn't a single shirt hanging there! This was a joke, not a steam bath. 'No!' I thought. 'I can't work in this kind of steam bath. It's not for me. It won't be the same as in Glupsk. There, the whole feeling was different: people used to stretch out on the benches in a company. They talked about things, told each other stories, settled the affairs of the world. There was something so good, so warm, so homey about it!' I went to see other steam baths, many of them. There wasn't one like ours in Glupsk. They simply didn't have the same smell as our stone bathhouse. And the water they used in their bathing pool . . . ! In the Glupsk bathhouse, the water in the pool had a different taste, a different color, and was somehow soupier than other water. You knew right away that this was a Jewish bath house. But here in Odessa? The water was fresh and clear, just plain water, like water should be—drinking water.

" 'Nu, Fishke?' Yontl asked with a little smile when I returned. 'Did you see any of the bathhouses here?'

" 'Ett,' I answered without enthusiasm. 'There's nothing to talk about, really. Everything here is topsy-turvy. It's as if they were trying to make fun of the world. Your Odessa is not for me.'

CHAPTER XXIV

"I was not happy in Odessa, but I had to remain there through the winter. I couldn't have started out on the road barefoot and naked in the middle of the winter all alone in a strange part of the country. But as soon as the bright sun made her warmth felt and the odors of summer filled the air, something started pecking at me and wouldn't let me sit still. There was a time when summer made no difference to me. Just summer. Nothing special! It was warm; the days were long and clear; it was green all around. It felt good. The cows went to pasture. There was more milk and a little sour cream. Also, I could eat my bread with a green onion, some garlic, a fresh radish or a cucumber. For a poor Jew, this changed a meal into a feast.

"But this time summer was something special for me. I don't know how to say it, but this summer spoke to me with real words and filled my heart with desire. Everything reminded me of her, my dear hunchback. Each little blade of grass, each little green tree, each trill of a songbird—they all spoke to me and brought me regards from her. I could see it all so clearly: how she had sat with me, how she had looked, how she had laughed and cried and poured out her bitter heart. My blood bubbled. I fell into a sweet melancholy and something drew me, drew me yonder, far away. Was it this particular summer? Did I catch some disease, some fever which made me weak? I don't know. All I know is that I seemed to be melting away like a candle. I was not the same as before.

" 'Fishke, are you sick?' Yontl asked me once after looking at me. 'Your face looks so thin. Does something hurt you?'

" '*Ett*, it's nothing,' I answered while I pressed my hands against my chest.

" 'Oh, it's your heart?' Yontl asked. 'There's a good medicine for that. Dip a piece of bread in salt and eat it on an empty stomach.'

" 'I have enough salt on my wounds already,' I answered with a sigh. 'I feel as if something is pressing on my heart. It presses and doesn't let me sit still.'

" 'Now I understand,' Yontl said with a little smile. 'It's your Glupsk that's doing it; Glupsk is calling you back. Back to where the stinkweed blooms, where poverty whistles in through the

299

windows and garlic and onions perfume the air. Don't be ashamed, Fishke. Go back to where you'll feel at home again.'

"A few days later, I parted with Yontl and set out for home on foot.

"I had one thought on my mind and one feeling in my heart: she! Where was she, where could she be now? How was she getting along, poor dear, without me? And my feet moved along, by themselves somehow, slowly but surely on the road to Glupsk. I passed through towns and villages, and everywhere I went my eyes searched and searched—maybe I would meet her. I don't know how many Jewish towns I passed through, but the closer I came to Glupsk, the lighter my heart felt. It was a pleasure to be among our kind of Jews again. Their way of talking, the way they lived, their customs did my heart good. I felt that I was really back home among my own people. The Jews in our part of the country are so down to earth! No ceremonies, no fuss or bother, they just don't care about all the new-fangled ideas. If you feel like it, you can talk loud, shout at the top of your lungs, do as you please, just as God commanded. Whose affair is it if it's in place or out of place, if it's proper or not? If some one doesn't like it, let him close his eyes and stop his ears! I began to feel stronger. I calmed down, thought about Glupsk, about the stone bathhouse, and hoped that His Blessed Name would provide for me.

"One beautiful morning, I happened to be walking in wheatfields and cornfields and came to a dense forest. I walked into it a ways, threw down my pack and took off my coat. I stretched out under a tree among some tall bushes whose big broad leaves hid me from sight. Well, what was there to worry about? It was a forest like any other forest with trees like any other trees and bushes like any other bushes. The songbirds were songbirds and I—I was Fishke and might just as well take a little nap and rest up from my journey. I stretched, yawned, closed my eyes—but listen to this dream. . . .

"I imagined I heard noises: footsteps and the snapping of dry branches. I pricked up my ears and listened with closed eyes. The rustling became louder and the footsteps nearer. I began to worry and wanted to open my eyes, but I couldn't. I lay like a log and couldn't move, I was so tired. The footsteps seemed to move away. I calmed down and fell asleep. It felt so sweet, so good. I heard a soft, sad tune. There was something familiar about it. The tune went through my whole body and made me dizzy. I felt like crying

300

and laughing at the same time. Just like a bride and groom laugh and cry before they go under the *Khupe*—at one and 'the same time—like a summer shower while the sun is shining.

"Suddenly, someone pulled my hair and screamed. I jumped up quickly and spread the broad leaves apart. I saw a pot full of big red berries lying on its side near me. Not far away a woman sat on the ground looking around fearfully. I soon understood what had happened. She must have been gathering berries here. Her mind was occupied with her search and she had been humming busily to herself. She must have touched my hair and that scared her. I picked up the pot and called to her in a friendly way: 'Everything's all right!' But as soon as I came closer, the pot slid out of my hands, a shout escaped from my lips and my feet froze in their tracks. A minute later, we were squeezing each other's hands and looking into each other's eyes, my dear hunchback and I.

"This was no dream! I was awake. I looked around. I was in a thick forest of big trees. Way up on the highest branches, little birds hopped up and down. They trilled and whistled and shared our happiness. We were both so happy. We laughed through our tears. We marveled at finding each other here and couldn't stop talking and telling each other about what we had been through during the last year.

"She told me about the torments she had had to suffer since the band had abandoned me last year. It was all the bastard's doing. He did not want my wife to divorce me. He was afraid that she might insist that he marry her. He wanted a blind woman but not a blind wife. He was glad to make love to her and make money with her, but let someone else take care of her. He also wanted to get even with me by keeping me from being free. My friendship with the hunchbacked girl was like a knife in his breast. He was ready to do anything to keep it from going any further. As soon as he was rid of me, he took my wife in hand and began to teach her who was master. He knew that it was impossible for her to escape his clutches now. What could a blind woman do by herself? He finally became sick and tired of her and gave her to the little old man. She had to play the part and go begging with him from house to house like I used to do. The bastard ground her under his heel. He beat her without mercy, while the little old man had his own methods of teaching her. In a short time, she began to look like an old woman.

"The band had been roaming the countryside all year and visited many towns. This morning, they had stopped here in the forest to rest. She had an urge to go picking berries and suddenly—she said with a little smile—she stumbled on a very good one: me.

"I told her in turn where I had been during the year and how I had chanced to stop there that morning on my way to Glupsk. We decided never to part again. We would do everything we could to talk my wife into giving me a divorce. If, God forbid, she refused, we would run away from the band anyway and hope for the best. As we sat there, enjoying each other's company, we heard someone shout 'A-ha!' somewhere deep in the woods.

" 'That's one of them calling,' my hunchback explained. 'They're looking for me.'

"A little later, one of them came by. I recognized him. He looked at me crookedly and, laughing, rushed back in a hurry to announce the good news. We got up also and, taking our time, slowly set off for the camp. Behind a little inn, a crumbling ruin, I recognized a line of familiar looking vans stretching back into the woods. Beyond the vans, in a clearing, burned a merry fire. The whole band was gathered around it.

"My first *sholem-aleykhem* came from the bastard, who sounded off in a loud voice: 'A-a-a-h! A dear guest, indeed! How do you do? I was beginning to miss you, Reb Fish!'

"And soon the air was filled with shouts: 'Look who's here! Come, let's welcome the Magnate!' And from all sides, wild greetings came down on me together with blows and pinches, so that I lost my cap. I covered my head with the hem of my coat and bent down to find it while they beat me without stopping. Just then, my wife came running all out of breath and full of joy.

" 'Where is he, my dear one? Where, where's my Fishke?!'

"Her joy hurt more than all the pinches and blows put together. 'Her joy won't help me get a divorce from her,' I thought. 'I'd be better off if she hated me like the others here do!' But she hung around my neck and called to her own dear Fishke. I felt very bad to see her looking this way—a blind, dried-up, weak, old woman! Where was her plumpness, her health, her chubby cheeks and mouth? I had to force myself to ask her, for old times' sake, 'How are you, Basya?'

" 'Oh, you were right, Fishke, when you used to say that in Glupsk we both, blessed be His Name, had a reputation. People knew me there and respected me!' my wife declared in a loud voice

302

so that everybody would hear. She looked around proudly, like a fallen magnate talking about the wealth he had had years ago. She sighed deeply and continued: 'We've wandered long enough. Let's go home, lead me home! Fishke, back to our city, to our houses, to our rich folks!'

"Her talk made me feel nauseous. I didn't expect such a greeting from her and I made a face. The bastard made an ugly face too, thinking that I wanted to rob him of his goods and ruin his trade. But my thoughts were quite different : 'She's all yours, if you want her. I forgive you with all my heart—take her!'

"He must have been raging with fury. He glared at me until his eyes became bloodshot. Then he got up with a growl and marched away angrily.

"The women and girls of this fine crowd were busy around the fire, pushing pots in, pulling them out, baking potatoes. Some of the younger fellows hung around, fooling with them and teasing them, sneaking in a slap here and there, or stealing a quiet pinch—all accompanied by wisecracks. The women acted angry. They scolded and cursed but giggled and laughed at the same time. They let themselves be caught like hens by the barnyard rooster when he spreads his wings and lovingly pecks their heads.

"The other beggars were spread all over the woods. One lay on his belly snoring for all he was worth. Another one was busy patching an old robe. A third one was scratching himself with such a serious expression on his face that it looked like he was hunting for gold. Still others were wrestling, trying to see who was stronger. Life went on at its merry pace here!

"My wife clung to me and wouldn't let go—one body and one soul. She talked a blue streak, lamented her bitter lot, told me how she had suffered. She wanted only one thing now—that I should take her away from here and live with her, as God had commanded, to the end of our ordained years. I said one word for every ten of hers and looked for a way to get out of her clutches. When she finally ran out of talk, I managed to squirm out of her grip and catch my breath. I looked for my dear hunchback and quietly went off with her. Things looked bad for us. There was no sense in bringing up the subject of a divorce. My wife wouldn't even listen. She would snort and toss her head. I couldn't stay here with the band of thieves either. It meant selling myself to the devil again. It meant playing the bear for them again. What could I do?

"We puzzled over this for a while. Finally we decided that the only choice was to run away. Since the band was going to spend the night here, this night here in the woods was the time and place to do it. As we sat together thinking over our plan, the bastard appeared in the distance with a pair of horses. 'Let's not wait,' said my hunchback, 'until he comes closer. It won't do any good for him to see us sitting together. Let's separate while there is still time.'

"She went off to one side and I to the other.

"The bastard was very busy and whispered all the while to the little old man, his right-hand man. I stayed out of the bastard's sight. While the other beggars worked and fooled with each other, my hunchback came up to me and whispered in my ear that the bastard wanted to move on before sundown. That pair of horses was stolen and he was in a hurry to get out of this neighborhood. All our work, our whole plan, collapsed like a house of cards. I stood helpless and didn't know what to do next. My heart felt as if it was pressed in a vise. My head spun so that I could hardly stand on my feet. My hunchback looked at me with great pity. Her eyes burned like coals of fire and her face was aflame. She thought for a while and said to me with a quivering voice:

" 'Fishke! A little later, try to be in that little ruined inn, in the attic. Do you understand?'

" 'I understand, I understand!' I almost shouted. 'And you'll come there later?'

" 'Yes, *sha!* she said, nodding. 'But it must be done quietly. Do you hear?'

"I didn't think it necessary to say good-bye to my wife. I pitied her, but it was her own fault. She was the first to make a crack in our marriage and the crack grew wider and wider. Now it was all over. What could I do? Just as the sky and the earth will never meet, so she and I couldn't think of ever coming together again. That's why I didn't bother saying good-bye to her, and quietly slipped away to the little inn.

"You can imagine how I felt when I went into the ruined little inn. After so much trouble, so many heart aches, God was going to unite me with my dear hunchback in a crumbling hut. Here our lot would be changed. From now on we would lead a new life! I had no trouble climbing—into the attic. The hut was low and the rear wall so fallen to pieces that the roof almost touched the ground. The ceiling was full of cracks so that I could look down from the attic into the room below. I sat down in a corner and waited. My heart pounded like a hammer. Each minute seemed like a year to me. I froze stiff at every sound: the least motion of a straw and I thought it was a step, that she was coming; the softest breeze, and I thought it was she calling my name. Suddenly I heard a voice in the room below. The thought that it was she, that she was here, that soon, soon we would both be free made me shake like a leaf. I felt hot and cold at the same time. I would have called out but my voice choked and my tongue wouldn't move. At this moment I heard someone call my name very clearly. I looked through a crack and whom did I see? The bastard and the little old man! " 'You take care of your piece of goods,' said the bastard. 'Make sure that the blind witch doesn't slip. You understand?'

" 'Don't worry!' answered the little old man. 'I've done my part. I just hope she doesn't die on me. The old nag is lying there like dead and doesn't move, I gave her such a beating!'

" 'And that lame good-for-nothing,' said the bastard, 'belongs to me! I can't stand the sight of his ugly mug—that's how much I hate him. I'll fix him, don't you worry! I've got an old score to settle with him.'

"My blood froze in my veins when I heard these terrible words.

" 'It seems,' the old man commented, 'that your stolen horses belong to Jews. They're dried up, beaten, sick, with crooked spines, and thin necks like birds, and piles too. Fine creatures indeed, just like their owners.'

" 'May your tongue rot, you old buzzard!' the bastard cursed. 'You'd better look around, you old dog, and see if you can't sniff out some old clothes that we can use. There might be some up in the attic. After all, this was an inn once upon a time.'

"I broke out in a cold sweat. I felt so sick, I thought I'd die. My lame leg began to tremble badly and knocked against the floor. The two fine gentlemen looked up and gaped at the ceiling for a while. Then they both exclaimed together:

" 'There's dust falling from the ceiling! We'd better take a look.'

"My head spun, my ears rang, I saw spots before my eyes and felt as though I was flying through the air.

"Yes, through the air. A pair of iron hands grabbed me and flung me down from the attic to the floor below. Someone greeted me with a loud 'Welcome!' and a sneer: 'Well, if it isn't Reb Fish!' I looked up and saw the bastard glaring down at me. His face was terrible to see—it was the face of a cat ready to choke a captured mouse. The little old man wasn't there any more. He had disappeared, leaving me to face the bastard alone.

" '*Nu*, confess your sins, you carrion!' said the bastard. 'What I should have done to you back there in the cellar, I'll do now. Don't you worry, Faybushke doesn't forget!'

"I fell at his feet and begged him, as I would have begged a murderer, to grant me my life. It was no use.' He took out a knife, held it before my eyes, and watched gleefully how I shivered and shook. I tried to convince him that if he let me go, he would go to heaven after he died. I even offered him my share of Paradise. I tried everything possible. He glared at me and said nothing. I began to threaten him with God's vengeance, with the fires of hell, with the price he'd pay for shedding innocent blood. He bit his lip, raised the knife—and just as the blade was at my throat, someone behind him snatched it from his hand with a cry that wasn't human: 'No, no! You won't dare!'

"He looked around, frightened. It was the hunchbacked girl! 'Get out of here, you tramp!' he shouted wildly as soon as he had recovered. 'Get out, or—'

" 'No, no! I will not get out of here! I'd rather die here together with him,' my hunchback shouted back hotly and fell down before him, crying bitter tears, begging for mercy, caressing him so that he would let me go. She too promised him her share of Paradise. The bastard flung her away from himself like a little ball. He cursed and swore for all he was worth. When he finally calmed down a little, he turned to me and said:

" 'It's too bad that I don't have you here alone, you hunk of garbage. You can thank your filthy luck, you stinking carrion, that I haven't crushed you like a mouse between my fingers! But I won't let you off so easy!'

"He took the rope from around his waist and tied my hands and feet, saying: 'Lie here quietly, you dog! Don't even let me hear a whimper from you! Lie here until you croak! But remember, you good-for-nothing, if, by some miracle, you get out of this, if some mother's mother of yours should rise from her grave to help you, keep out of my way forever. Don't let me ever lay an eye on you again, because if I do . . . kh—kh—kh—k!' And he passed his finger across his throat to show me what he meant.

"When he was done with me, he turned to my hunchback, who was sobbing on the floor.

" 'Ah, you tramp, you!' the bastard growled, shoving her, poor thing, with his foot. 'I understand everything, don't you worry! You two had a private arrangement—a wedding without musicians, up there in the attic. A fine little girl you are. I know all about it. But with me she acts as pure as a rabbi's wife. From now on, I'll know better how to deal with you, you tramp!'

"He seized her and turned to me: Remember what I said, you dog!' Then he disappeared with her.

"Can I tell you how I suffered? The torments of hell can't be worse! I was not in hell—hell was in me. A wild, hellish fire burned within me. My hair stood on end. My scalp felt as though red-hot pins were pricking it, yet I couldn't cry out or even breathe too loud.

"A little later, I heard noises far away: the creaking of wheels, people shouting, the sounds of moving. The band was leaving— the whole crowd of them, and with them, my heart, my dear, good, unfortunate hunchback, poor thing.

"For a long time I lay like a stupid sheep with all four legs tied. My eyes were filled with hot tears. The rope burned my skin and felt like a knife cutting me every time I moved. My throat was dry and I was dying for a drink. I thought I would pass out at any moment. Everything hurt so much that I began to scream in case someone was passing by. I figured that the band must be quite far away now. I shouted, I screamed, but it was no use. I might as well have shouted to the wall. My throat was raw and I was aching all over. It was harder and harder to yell. I had to rest more and more. I hardly had any strength left to cry out. I clung to life by a thin thread, and the Angel of Death, I was sure, had come to break that thread. It was my lot to die young, to leave my years unfulfilled. I collected the little strength left in me and shouted—one last time—my last cry to the world about my unfortunate life.

"But God brought you to the rescue, Reb Alter! You came in a time of need and saved my life."

CHAPTER XXV

As Fishke finished his sad tale, night fell and our horses arrived at the green hill just outside of Glupsk. The green hill of Glupsk is known almost all over the world. There is an ancient folk song, sung by young and old, about it. Mothers and wet-nurses soothe their crying babes and rock them to sleep with it. My own mother, may she thrive in Paradise, also used to sing me this song when I was still in diapers:

> "Way up yon green hill
>   Where the grass grows tall,
>   A pair of Germans stand
>   Their long whips in hand.
>   Tall men two are they,
>   But their pants are short,
>   Our Father, our King . . ."

This used to be my favorite song. Somehow, my childish mind imagined the green hill to be wondrously beautiful. I used to think that it was not made of common soil like the other hills around my town, but of some indescribably rare and delightful stuff—like Mount Olive or Mount Lebanon—of the soil of the Land of Israel.

And the Germans! I imagined them to be a sort of outlandish creature, may they pardon me, something in the nature of cattle or oxen, like the legendary Wild Bull. Their long whips whistled through the air and guarded the approaches to Glupsk like the River *Sambatyon* guards the approach to the home of the Little Red Jews. Anyone entering Glupsk must receive the lash. And, to tell the truth, everyone in Glupsk did have a beaten look.

In later years, when I had outgrown my children's shoes and had seen something of the world, I looked at things with different eyes and understood the true meaning of the little ditty. The green hill was really nothing more than an ordinary hill—not green, but muddy, full of ruts. And the Germans, tall men two, they were merely a hint at those gentlemen with long hands and sticky fingers who robbed the wagons and stole the goods of travelers to Glupsk. People who came to Glupsk for the first time generally took no special precautions. But the second time, they would become uneasy several versts before reaching the city. Their eyes began to

308

search all around them to make sure that there were no strangers in their vans. Their fingers patted their bosom pockets and buttoned their coats from top to bottom to make sure that everything inside would remain there. All I am trying to say is that upon reaching the green hill each of our senses, including our noses, became aware of the nearness of Glupsk. A little later, after we had looked around in all directions and checked the contents of our wagons, we remembered Fishke and saw him sitting quietly, poor fellow, downcast and drooping.

I began to cheer him up. I tried to raise his spirits with brave words. I sang the other half of the previously mentioned ditty, to put him in a good humor:

> "Our Father, our King
> My heart with joy does sing.
> We shall be tickled pink
> And wine by the bottle drink.
> Of *kreplach* shall we eat our fill
> But forget our beloved God?
> That, we never will!"

"Stop worrying, Fishke. We must never forget our beloved God. He can help us."

"I only want to ask you one question, Reb Mendele!" Fishke exclaimed bitterly. "Why did He have to bring us together again, her and me, and then separate us so suddenly? Why did our luck suddenly smile on us only to make things blacker than ever before? It's almost like spite work! Oh, Lord of Nations, whom hast Thou punished? Two unfortunate, miserable cripples, who would have been far better off if they'd never been born! Their lives have been so bleak, so full of pain and torments!"

I made a pious face, shook my head and said: "*Ta, ta, ta!* You mustn't talk like that." I did not say this because it answered Fishke's cry of woe in any way, but rather because it has become a custom in the world. When misery forces someone to start asking embarrassing questions, you must chide him and slow him down with at least a "*Ta, ta, ta!*" Having thus satisfied tradition, I went on to speak like a human being.

"Tell me, Fishke, what is the girl's name? Until now, you've only called her the hunchbacked girl, or 'my dear hunchback.' Now I'd like to know her name."

"What for, Reb Mendele?" Fishke looked at me in wonder. "Why

309

do you want to know, please? Why bandy a girl's name about in vain?"

"Don't you understand, silly fellow," I answered, "that I might be able to help you if I know it? In my travels, it just might happen that I should come across a clue, a hint. Tell me her name. Don't worry about it! It's very possible, you understand, that you may recover your loss. Let me be your emissary!"

"Beyle is her name," Fishke burst out all at once. "Her name is Beyle!"

Suddenly, I heard a loud groan and a thud, as if something had fallen down. I turned around in fright and saw my Reb Alter stretched out in the wagon, gasping for breath and white as a sheet. "What is it, Reb Alter!" I asked. "You don't feel well? Maybe you'd like some brandy?"

"*Beh!*" Alter answered and, with an effort, sat up again.

"Tell me, Fishke!" I continued when I was sure that Alter was in no danger: "do you also know what was her mother's name and where she is from?"

"Yes," Fishke answered. "My hunchback told me that her mother's name was Elke. She remembered that her mother and father were divorced in Tuneyadevke? Her mother used to talk about it whenever she lost her temper with the miserable child."

"Divorced in Tuneyadevke?" I wondered. "Who could have been her husband there—that monster of monsters, with a heart of stone, who cast off his child and made her life miserable? Eh, Reb Alter, it's your town. Who could it have been?"

Alter sat there more dead than alive. His bulging eyes rolled wildly. My heart sank when I saw him gasping for breath.

"His name was . . ." Fishke rubbed his forehead in an effort to recall the name. "His name, his name, I think. . . wait a minute—"

"Alter is his name!" Alter screamed and again fell down in the wagon.

"Yes, yes, that's it!" Fishke exclaimed, looking at Alter without understanding the meaning of his screaming. "And he had another name—Yaknehoz. Her mother used to pinch her cruelly and call her 'Yaknehoz's daughter' or 'Lady Yaknehoz,' especially after she'd had a lot of trouble or lost a job."

By now everything was crystal clear to me and I sat there as if I had been doused with a pail of cold water.

Alter sobbed and beat his breast with his fist, crying, "Verily, I

310

have sinned! I have ruined her life. She was right, poor thing, with her little song:

'My father used to hate me . . .'

"That's why the wrath of God has descended upon me. That's why my luck is bad no matter what I do. Everything is *shlimazl.* ...."

I began to reassure Reb Alter for pity's sake. I tried to soothe him and minimize his sins: he was, after all, no more than flesh and blood. The Evil Genius was very powerful among us sinners. Even great *tsadikim* have succumbed in these matters and have not been able to overcome the Evil Genius in regards to women and marriage. Many of our ancestors, *tsadikim,* lay under their wives' heels, fulfilled their wives' commands and drove away their own children by another marriage.

For Fishke, this whole scene was crazy. He stared at us in surprise, looked first at Alter and then at me and didn't know what to do next. In the meanwhile, night fell. The stars twinkled, winked down to us from the heavens with their shimmering faces, as though they would have liked to take part in our conversation. At the edge of the sky, a big moon, as red as fire, began to rise out of the earth. It almost seemed to be looking directly at us. All the inhabitants of the realms above were watching and waiting for the end of the story. Suddenly, my Alter sat bolt upright, lifted his eyes toward the heavens and spoke with earnestness:

"I swear by Him who lives eternally, that I shall not return home to my wife and children, that I will not marry off my eldest daughter before I find my unfortunate child! Heaven and earth are my witnesses! I am leaving immediately and woe to him who stands in my way."

Fishke fell on Alter's neck, embraced him and kissed him without words. Then, with tears in his voice, he exclaimed: "*Gvald,* save her, save her!"

My Alter swiftly jumped from my wagon, climbed up on his, and waving good-bye to us, turned around, lashed his nag and drove off. Fishke and I watched him for a while without saying a word. Then I glanced up at the sky. The moon and stars were going their way, but they looked different than before. They were not as friendly. They had become distant and haughty. My heart grew sad and heavy.

I lashed my eagle so as to remind him that he still had a job to do pulling the wagon. It was late at night when we rolled into the rutted streets of Glupsk. The roar and rumble of our wheels announced to the inhabitants:

"Attention! Be it known that two new Jews have arrived in the city of Glupsk!"

INTRODUCTION TO

The Mare

The Mare — in Yiddish, *Di Klyatshe,* variously translated as "the nag," "the dobbin," "the hackney," "the dray horse," and subtitled "Pity for Living Creatures"—was first published in 1873 in Vilna. It consisted of sixteen chapters in 119 pages. During the years 1905-1907, Mendele lived in Geneva, having fled there from the pogroms which followed in the wake of the Revolution of 1905. While there, he revised much of his previous writing for a complete edition of his works. The new version of *The Mare* contained twenty-four chapters in 182 pages. In his *Fir Zaynen Mir Gezesn* (Four of Us, We Sat Together), Sholem Aleykhem includes a conversation in which Mendele relates how he happened to write *The Mare:*

Once, on a summer day, I happened to be sitting in the inn in Glupsk and looking out of an open window. I noticed an exhausted, perspiring Jew with the tails of his tattered coat tucked under. He was standing and beating an exhausted, perspiring nag with a tattered hide, harnessed to a wagon full of bricks. He swore deadly oaths at the mare, at himself, and at the world... And the mare? She turned her wretched, careworn head toward him, looked at him... and it seemed to me that she was saying:

'Fool! You curse me for being a nag! You're a nag yourself! Look over there, where I will be taking these bricks, and you'll see that you're all nags— wretched, careworn nags—woe to all of you!'

This is what I thought she was saying, and I looked in the direction she was pointing her chin... I recognized a familiar-looking individual... one of those who managed to have built first one building and then another one on the basis of kosher Jewish blood and sweat... He stood there, this fine creature... his cap pushed back from his perspiring forehead, making grandiose plans, while around him swirled poor little Jews, like slaves, subjugated, looking into his eyes like faithful dogs... For three days afterward, I wandered about Glupsk, distraught like my mad Yisrulik... I came back home to

313

Tuneyadevke, locked myself in my room for sixteen days and wrote all sixteen chapters of *The Mare...**

In *The Mare*, Mendele continues to reflect his *haskole*-derived attitudes toward the plight of the Jews in nineteenth century Eastern-Europe. This time, however, he is motivated by greater sympathy for his people: although Mendele attacks the Jewish people, chastising them for their backwardness and their internal corruption, he also recognizes the malignant outside forces pressing in on them, persecuting them, denying them their humanity, and forcing them to live in poverty. At one point in the novel, he even pokes fun at the impotence and blindness of the *maskilim*, of the *haskole* itself. As Tsinberg puts it (Volume XII, p.140, of his *A History of Jewish Literature*):

"On the threshold of the 1870's, the *maskil*, Abramovitsh [was transformed] into the wrathful breaker of the tablets who stormed the idols of *haskole* and covered them with bitter sarcasm and arrogant contempt in *Di Klyatshe* [*The Mare*]."

There are marvelously "magical" passages in *The Mare*, filled with the devilish spirit Ashmodei, as well as with other imps, witches, and warlocks. Here can be glimpsed the same sources from which a later Yiddish master, I.B. Singer, drew.

The Mare (1889) is an allegorical novel: the mare in the story, of course, stands for the Jewish people—as does the main character "Izzy"**(Israel).

We have excerpted from *The Mare* three whole passages; thus, this selection presents the first fifteen pages of the work (including the "prologue") and its last fourteen pages, as well as eight pages from about the middle of the work.

Although the editors recognize the futility of attempting to convey in only forty pages the entire import of a complete novel, these excerpts were selected as typical and revelatory of the work as a whole.

---

* Quoted by Nakhmen Mayzl in his introduction to Volume II of *Selected Works of Mendele Moykher-Sforim*, YKUF Publishers, New York, 1946. Translated by Gerald Stillman.

**In the original Yiddish, the main character is Yisrolik, the diminutive form of Yisroel (Israel). In the selections here, the main character is aptly called Izzy—in English, also a diminutive of Israel.

314

FROM

The Mare

Translated by Joachim Neugroschel

Introduction by Mendele the Book Dealer

I, Mendele The Book Dealer, say unto you: glory be to the Creator, Who, after making the great universe, took counsel with the angelic hosts and finally fashioned a small world, namely man, who is known as the microcosm for combining within himself—if you take a close look—all manner of creatures and animals. You will find in him all species of wild beasts, and all breeds of cattle. You will find a lizard, a leech, a Spanish fly, a Japanese beetle, and similar creeping and crawling pests. You will even find a demon, a devil, a satan, a fiend, an imp, a Jew-baiter, and similar hell-hounds, hellcats, and freaks. You can also view wonderful sights in him: a cat toying with a mouse; a fox sneaking into a chicken coop and twisting the necks of the poor fowls; monkeys aping everything and everybody; a dog prancing and wagging its tail for anyone who throws it a crust of bread; a spider inveigling a fly, entangling, enmeshing it, and then sucking it dry; gadflies hounding you and buzzing your ears off; and similar wondrous things. But that's neither here nor there. Praised be the Good Lord, Who silently contemplates everything taking place in this microcosm and yet never makes mincemeat out of him; Who keeps His temper, endures the transgressions, and shows great benevolence to sinful man. In short, what I am leading up to is to tell you about the vast grace that God bestowed upon me, a poor sinner, after punishing me a bit.

Dear Reader, my equine hauler had trotted on to greener pastures! My horse kicked the bucket! My loyal nag, who had been in service since time immemorial, laboring with devotion and know-ing nothing more than our books; who had been a renowned

315

expert in all roads, with an unfailing memory for all taverns; who had traveled about with me to nearly every corner of the Jewish globe and was well known in all our Jewish communities. This equine being, this horse, had met with a dreadful demise in Dumbsville, during spring, on the Jewish holiday of Lag b'Omer! It wrenches my heart to talk about it, but poverty is no disgrace—the poor thing died of hunger! Its usual fodder was chaff, with occasional crusts of dry bread that I purchased from beggars. Ah, woe betide the poor dobbin that winds up with a Jewish book-peddler! It hauls and hauls, laboring perhaps even harder than the beasts dragging heavier goods. But all that the poor things gets to eat is garbage, and all that a Jewish book-peddler gets to eat is garbage, so that he and his wife and children starve to death a dozen times a day!

But that's neither here nor there.

God punished me and I was left without a horse. I didn't even have the wherewithal to buy another, and yet I had to get to the county fairs. I felt awful!

And as I sat there, down in the mouth, along came a friend of mine. He walked straight up and said:

"Mr. Mendele, would you like to buy a mare?"

"Of course I would," I moaned, "but what am I going to do for money?"

"Bah!" he said. "Don't worry! You won't have to lay out a kopek! Maybe they'll even advance you something. Why, everyone knows how honest you are."

"If that's the case," I said, "I'd be delighted to buy the mare. Right now! C'mon, let's go and have a look at it!"

"You can save yourself the trouble of going anywhere," he replied. "I have the mare right here, on me!"

"What do you mean, right here?" I asked him in surprise.

"Right here, under my coat," he smiled.

"You're pulling my leg!" I said, exasperated. "Get yourself another victim. I'm in no mood for jokes."

"Me pull your leg? God forbid!" bundle of paper from inside his coat. Look, Mr. Mendele, the whole thing belongs to a friend of mine. You'll find his name right here on the manuscripts. And one of these pieces, you see, is entitled *The Mare*. The author himself is... (may you be spared) sort of, well... confused... not quite all there. And his friends are very anxious to have his stories printed and distributed. Now who else could we have chosen for the task if not you, Mr. Mendele, who are so famed among Jews. We would like you to look over these papers and put each story in the right shape—we'll trust to your judgment. And the first story we want you to print is *The Mare*. We'll discuss the terms later. I'm sure you'll be satisfied. If you need any money now, we can give you some on account. Well, what do you say, Mr. Mendele?"

"What do I say?! With all my heart and soul!" I exclaimed, practically jigging for joy.

After attending to all my business matters, I eagerly tackled the mare—put her into shape, divided her into chapters, and gave each chapter a fitting title—a drudgery for which some people would affix their names to a manuscript and call themselves authors... In short, I spared no pains, I did my duty faithfully.

And now, my friends, a few words about the mare.

The Mare is written in a lofty manner, the style of the ancients. Each reader will comprehend it in accordance with his intelligence and on his own level. For people on a surface level, it will simply be a lovely tale, and they will enjoy the plot. But those on a deeper level will also find an allusion, an application, to us sinful human creatures. I, for example, on my level, found in it nearly all Jewish souls, all our beings, and the secret of what we are doing in this world. I am convinced that during your perusal, a number of you, each according to his nature, will be unable to help himself and will ardently call out: "Why, that's an allusion to Mr. Yosl!" Or: "Oh! That's a reference to Mr. Nathan! Mr. Zalman-Jacob! Mr. Hershke!" Or else: "Hey! I've discovered the secret behind our kosher-meat tax, our philanthropists, and all our behavior!" And so on.

I submitted a question to the rabbinical judiciary in Dumbsville, and the local bigwigs. Since I had promised my readers that I would put out a sequel to my play The Kosher-Meat Tax, I was virtually under oath and as good as committed.

"Now what does the law say, gentlemen?" I asked them. If I put out my 'Mare' now, would that count as fulfilling my promise?"

They mulled and mulled, the poor men, scratching and scratching their heads, and at last they pronounced their verdict.

"Yes, indeed, Mr. Mendele, having had a sniff, a whiff, of the essence of your *Meat Tax*, we would be most willing to release you from your oath. May your equine surrogate be reckoned in all due value as an equivalent of your having fulfilled your promise in all good faith and published an additional section to *The Meat*

Tax, with all the particulars. By all means: *The Mare,* according to all opinions, will be an excellent way of keeping your word!"

How grateful am I to God! If I had gotten the mare without any advance, just to buy myself a horse, that would have sufficed. If I had gotten her with an advance and she had not had something of the essence of the *Meat Tax,* that would have sufficed. If she had had something of the *Meat Tax* and the rabbinical judiciary had not released me from my vow, that would have sufficed. If the rabbinical judiciary had released me from my vow and not scratched their heads so much, that would have sufficed. If they had scratched their heads so much and I would not have known the reason, that would have sufficed. If I had known the reason and not comprehended that the mare was something to scratch one's head about, that would have sufficed.

How much more then am I grateful to the Lord that I found the mare, and with an advance to buy a horse, and that she had something of the essence of the *Meat Tax,* and the rabbinical judiciary released me from my vow, and scratched their heads so much, and I know the reason, and comprehend that the mare is evidently something to scratch one's head about, an atonement for our sins.

That, my dear readers, is what I was after in my brief introduction. Out of the abundance of the heart, the mouth runneth over!

On the 29th day of Elul, on the bookwagon, between Dumbsville and Yawnstown.

Yours truly,

Mendele Moykher-Sforim
(*Mendele the Book Dealer*)

1. IZZY WANTS TO BECOME A HUMAN BEING

Just as Noah, in his ark, was the only survivor of all the creatures in the world, who were drowned in the Deluge, so I too, Israel the son of Tsippe, was the only survivor in my little town, the only bachelor among all my friends, who, because of that pestilential nuisance known as marriage-brokers, had become boy-husbands before their time and were up to their ears in poverty and squalor. That scourge of God—the marriage-brokers—beat a path to my mother's door, proposing matches for me. My mother, a simple woman, but with a good head on her shoulders, was a widow, not what you would call wealthy, but then not quite poor either. She made a living off her haberdashery, wore a few strings of pearls, and did rather well. I was her only child, her pride and joy. She indulged me in everything. I put my foot down about not marrying young and I got my way. At first, she did try to make me change my mind:

"Izzy! How often have I prayed to God to let me live long enough to see you getting offers from matchmakers! You're the apple of my eye, I'm only thinking of you, please do what I say and get married! It's high time, Izzy, just look at yourself! You're a grown man (may no evil befall you!)—you've got a beard! All your friends married by the time they were bar-mitzvahed. Listen to your mother. Do what God has ordained so that you can still bring me some joy!"

But when she saw that she was wasting her breath, that no matter how much she talked I stuck to my guns—No! No! And no!—she finally relented and dropped the subject. I simply told her the plain truth. I was resolved to bone up on everything taught in the Russian schools, take the examinations, and enter the university to study medicine so that later on I might be of use to myself and the world.

"Mama," I said to her. "The world's different today. It's time we opened our eyes to that great happiness of early marriage, the grandeur and glory of our young householders! Parents used to marry off their children in the faith that 'God sent us enough to live on, He'll probably send them enough to live on too, they certainly won't starve.'

"Back then, that sort of faith may have been useful, but today it

319

can only cause suffering. In our time, it's hard, very hard, to live by the sweat of your brow. You can't turn dross into gold. A man should make every effort as early as possible to make sure all his major needs are covered, for always, for all his life. Particularly we Jews, who live in such awful conditions, hemmed in and stifled on all sides. There's no other way for us to heave ourselves out of our misery than by means of some scholarly or scientific pursuit, say, medicine, or a similar profession. If I don't plan my future now, while I'm still young, then what's going to become of me, for heaven's sake! The same thing that's happened to so many young men from our background. Supposedly, they made good matches and landed in a goldmine. But the gold turned out to be fool's gold, and they were shafted! Some of them are scattered now, some are Hebrew teachers, and some can't even do that! But if I become a doctor, the world will open up for me, I'll make something of myself, become a human being, and have no trouble earning my living."

My mother had no choice, she had to let me have my way again. I could study, but I had to promise her I would remain a good Jew.

I had a sharp mind. Nothing in the Talmud had been too difficult for me, and people used to say that some day I would become a great rabbi. Leaving such aspirations to others, I locked myself in my room and sat up day and night, eagerly studying all the subjects required for the university entrance examinations. Mathematics, plus physics, Russian grammar, as well as languages—all easy as pie. The only thing I had any problems with was history, and what the Russians call "literature." I had to cram it all, word for word— inane stories and battles, descriptions of how people have been killing, murdering, and slaughtering one another since time began, inflicting heartache and mayhem on each other, and in every case I had to memorize the exact year and place! This and similar stuff was known as history . . . . In addition, I had to learn all kinds of wild fables, fairytales about transmigrations, about witches and warlocks; stories of living waters and dead waters, golden apples and golden horses.

Furthermore, I had to be able to chatter like a parrot about some writer's fancy words and phrases, and find all kinds of subtleties, niceties, and hidden meanings that neither I, nor the author himself, nor my tutor ever saw. You were supposed to be all excited, ablaze, shouting, flailing your arms and legs, talking full blast, as if these things were occult mysteries or cabbalistic formulas. You had to clear the way, so to speak, with long preambles, in order to make the whole affair more complicated, more confused, so that others would understand it in a different way and not just straightforwardly. All this rigamarole, all this mumbo-jumbo, all this twisting and turning, was known as "literature."

You can say what you like. Once you're past boyhood, it's very hard to store up things like that in your head, especially if you've got a good mind and a passion for learning more useful things. Yes indeed. I found all that stuff very difficult.

The constant grind numbed my brain. It robbed me of my health, my vital strength, it turned me into a zombie. At times, I felt dazed, I reeled about more dead than alive. My head buzzed, it whirled like a windmill, driving me crazy. I would start doubting whether my plan of going to the university would ever work. Who could tell what might happen? At the examination, I might forget some stupid tale or trip over some author's gibberish and fall flat on my face. And so much for all my efforts, my studies, my medical ambitions, which I was so anxious to realize. My hopes would be a shambles, and so would I! What would I do, and what would I look like? I would be left a downtrodden little Jew. I would completely lose face and, like all other Jews, have to put up with insults and injuries from the rest of the world. I would remain a *luftmentsh*; up in the air for the rest of my life, force without fuel. I would feel the energy to do something, but have no way of activating my energy, applying it to something useful. I would be like so many pitiful failures among us Jews . . . . I would be a Jew and not a human being . . . . An enigma! A hobgoblin who sweeps up, cleans out, but lives in dirt, off in a corner somewhere. A hobgoblin who is up and about and yet doesn't exist in this world. Flesh and blood and yet nothing to anyone! . . . I knew one of the three hobgoblins from my studies—a broom—and the other two . . . . But what difference does it make! Who cares if I knew or didn't know! I was what I was but I wouldn't be a human being!

Cooped up all the time, cramming and reviewing, constantly fearing it was all a wild-goose chase—perish forbid!—I finally broke down. I lost weight, became as skinny as a beanpole, feeble, highstrung, and so anxious and depressed that people almost didn't recognize me. At times, I walked around dazed and bewildered, my actions, my behavior, were very peculiar. When a depression overtook me, I would curse all the witches, Baba Yaha, that old shrew, and that wizard Kashtsey. To hell with them all!

321

When I felt better, I made up with them. Back to Baba Yaha, back to Kashtsey, and the whole pack of them. My mother would cry when she saw me and started calling in doctors and healers. They gave me vials, poured serums down my throat, and strongly urged me to take long walks in the summertime, for goodness' sake and for heaven's sake—to get some fresh air outside of town, and don't think so much.

Ah, if the doctors had only been more understanding and freed me of the nonsense that made me so sick and confused!

2. IZZY EXPLODES WHEN HE SEES WHAT'S HAPPENING

One lovely summer morning, in Tamuz [early July], when the heat was unbearable, I walked out of town and into the open fields. I was very gloomy that day, my head was spinning, my temples were pounding, my heart was boiling like a kettle. I was very bewildered, worse than ever. For a long while, I rambled about, not quite knowing where my feet were taking me. I trudged and trudged, until I collapsed under a tree by some ditch and stretched out full length.

When I plopped down the whole world seemed to collapse with me. Everything turned black. My ears were banging and bursting as if rockets were zooming through them. I felt as if I were sinking in a bottomless pit, deeper and deeper, through an awful din. I wanted to clutch at something, grab hold of something. But I didn't seem to have any arms or legs. I was beside myself, out of my skin, a mere Izzy, or Izne, an airy thing, with no body, no limbs, nothing left of me, only my bare, naked soul.

Suddenly, I rose upward, I was swept higher and higher until I touched the ground and lay there with the sun roasting my back. I felt like a new man, completely reborn; completely transformed. Everything around me, the earth, the sky, the trees, and the grass, looked newly hatched. They sprang and rocked and greeted one another, unable to stay put, motioning to me: "C'mon and join the hop, cousin, grab a dance!" Two crickets leaped and jigged out of the grass, peered at me with big, foolish eyes, waving their feelers.

322

And now they seemed to be climbing into me. And then they really jumped, one, two—oh, my head! My head! . . .

I waved them away and turned my head, and as I lay there, I looked around, gazing, musing, mulling.

In the field, I saw some animals pasturing, aristocratic rams, donkeys, whole troops of horses, not coarsened by any labor, pedigree horses with patents of nobility attesting to the pure blood of their parents. One steed's grandsire was an English stallion who, anciently, while passing through the land of Canaan, had wed an Arab mare. Another horse's granddam came from a renowned dynasty, which had smelled its share of gunpowder. And still another horse's great-grandmother had enjoyed a fine upbringing, an education, on a famous breeding farm. She had been very learned and, in her time, together with many other educated and well-trained horses, she had given recitals of dancing and cantering.

For you must know that pedigree is very important in horses. Blue blood is greatly in demand, and scions from a good stud farm are known as blood horses or thoroughbreds. This nobility was dining unmolested, working mischief, destroying the grain that poor peasants had sown in the sweat of their brows. And the onlookers turned the other way and said nothing disrespectful to them. The horses capered, neighed, and stamped their hooves. Their strength, their power, their fierceness were extraordinary.

And lying there so angry, I suddenly heard a dreadful scream in the distance, men were yelling and dogs barking. At first I thought it was the peasants running together with a shout, to drive out the noble rams and horses from their grain. But I was wrong. The hubbub kept receding and shifting. What was going on? I stood up and followed the turmoil, until I came to a large grassy meadow, where I witnessed a terrible scene. Young, wild bullies were harassing a skinny, haggard mare on all sides, pelting her with stones, sicking whole packs of dogs on her. Some of the dogs were doing no more than barking, grinding their teeth, some of them were pouncing on her and biting as much as they were able.

I couldn't simply stand there as a silent observer to such misdeeds. For one thing, compassion and decency won't put up with such barbarism. And besides, disregarding compassion, the mare actually had a right to my assistance, what with my being a member in good standing of the Society for the Prevention of Cruelty to Animals, which prohibits tormenting or hurting any living creatures, for they are flesh and blood and have the same right to live

323

in God's world as we do. I don't want to launch into that venerable and profound discussion about human beings vs. beasts. Let us grant, as some maintain, that I, Homo sapiens, am the crown, the ornament, the apex of creation; that all other creatures live on this earth only for my sake, for my needs and my pleasure, for me the acme. Let us even grant that I, the acme, am the king, the overlord, of all animals, and that they are meant to serve me, wear the yoke, and sacrifice their lives for me. Nevertheless, I felt that the mare, such an ordinary drudge, had a right to my assistance. I would have to fulfill my duty toward her, if not by law than at least out of humanity . . . .

"Savages!" I said, making straight for this pepper of the earth. "What do you have against that poor horse!"

Some of the bullies didn't ever hear me, others did catch something and guffawed arrogantly. A few of the dogs looked at me in surprise, several of them barked at a distance, others glared, ready to leap at me from behind and tear me to shreds.

"Savages!" I repeated. "Why are you harassing and tormenting a poor creature of God?"

"Poor, my eye!" they sneered. "Why is she pasturing here? Why is this fine mare pasturing over here?"

"Why not!?" I exclaimed. "This *is* a meadow, the town's livestock have been pasturing here for ages!"

"The town's livestock," they replied, "are different. They can but she can't!"

"Why can't she?" I said. "Doesn't she have a soul like the town's livestock!"

"Maybe she doesn't!" they said.

"Bullies!" I said. "But she must have an owner who pays taxes in town and all the other duties. She's a town animal too!"

"Says who!" they answered derisively. "We'll have to find out whether she really is!"

"Be that as it may," I said, "the mare is hungry now, the poor thing wants to feed!"

"Let her eat worms, garbage, dirt," they replied. "What are we supposed to do? ! Why should a brute like her eat our own cattle out of house and home!"

"Cutthroats!" I couldn't contain myself any longer, I screamed in anger. "Why don't you look over there at the aristocratic rams, the herds of horses in the grain, gobbling up the sweat and blood of poor peasants! You begrudge a broken-down mare a heap of grass

324

and yet you don't mind those horses wreaking immense havoc and bringing unhappiness to a lot of people. The grain that they're trampling and destroying without a second thought would be enough to feed generations of mares until her children's children's children. Bullies, you haven't a shred of justice in you, no loyalty to anyone but yourselves. And yet you have the colossal nerve to defend the town's animals!"

"Hahaha!" replied the bullies. "My-oh-my! Isn't he angry! And isn't he asking questions! C'mon guys! Why argue! Let's go!"

One of them whistled and the whole gang and their dogs chased after the mare and fell upon her again. They hounded her and harassed her, ripping and biting, until they finally drove her into a deep mudhole.

3. BLESSED IS HE WHO TRANSFORMS HIS CREATURES

The evening was silent and beautiful. the sky was pure, starry, and very near. At its lowest point, the moon, blood red, arose as if from the earth. The town cows, well milked as usual and having eaten their normal supper from the troughs, were sleeping peacefully in the byres. I procured a bundle of fresh hay to bring to the unfortunate mare in her ditch, just as a decent member of the Society for the Prevention of Cruelty to Animals ought to do. The poor creature was lying in the mud, exhausted. If she hadn't been panting and writhing in pain, you would surely have taken her for a carcass—she was so haggard, all skin and bones.

"Neighhhh, neighhhh!" I said in horse language, going over to her. I stroked her neck and put down the sheaf of hay.

The mare lifted her head and gazed at me in surprise. To think that a man like me was paying my respect to a common horse, visiting her mudhole in the middle of the night.

"Neighhhh, neighhhh!" I said in horse language. It meant: 'Good evening, mare! . . . . Neighhhh, neighhhh! Here's some supper for you, some hay, if you've got a tooth left in your mouth. Neighhhh, neighhhh! May God pity your soul, you poor creature. Neighhhh!" I caressed her and put the hay right against her nose. "Welcome!" came a muffled voice.

I froze at that "Welcome!" Where could it be coming from, I wondered. Who was talking? There wasn't a trace of a human being for miles around.

"Don't be afraid, young man!" the voice reassured me. "Don't be afraid. It's me, the mare, talking to you."

"The mare!" I screamed in a horrified voice. A hot stream of ants scurried over my limbs, making my blood seethe. I could make out a cricket chirping in my head. That does sound like the good mare, I thought to myself. And then I realized it was Wednesday night, the time when the demons come out.

"Don't mull over it," the voice continued. "It's really quite simple. I, the mare, am talking to you."

"What?! How can a mare be talking?!" I said in astonishment.

"There's nothing extraordinary about it," she replied. "Such things have happened before. The chronicles mention any number of speeches by jackasses and sermons by horses, from Balaam's ass till the present."

"Ha! Maybe it's really so!" I said to her, scratching my head. I remembered the stories I was studying for my examinations. "Yes indeed, I do know of talking horses—but a mare?"

"Why not a mare? On the contrary, if anyone talks, it's usually the female. Balaam's ass was a mare. But calm down, it's not really a mare talking to you."

"What do you mean? First you're a mare, then you're not a mare!" I said, amazed, and then bent over to have a closer look at the matter. "Why, you must be—"

"A demon?" she broke in. "No, no, my friend, you're wrong. I'm no demon, I tell you, and no mare either. My shape and appearance are those of a mare, but I'm really something entirely different. If you knew what's happened to me in the world, you would understand and you wouldn't be surprised any longer."

And suddenly, two eyes were gazing at me, expressing sorrow and weariness, as well as an entreaty and an infinite kindness, the eyes of a sick, downtrodden, browbeaten person, who gazes at everyone in utter silence, and whose every gaze reveals his innermost sufferings; every gaze talks, cries fury, pleads for mercy, and tears out a piece of your heart.

I stared and stared. Was this a horse? I saw a human face before me. How did a human being get here so suddenly, where did he come from! This freak! . . . And as I stared, transfixed, at this

326

creature, it held out a hand from somewhere below, and, taking it courteously, I felt: A hoof!

"Blessed be He Who transforms creatures!" The familiar blessing came to my lips willy-nilly. And a noise hit my ears, something like a bitter wailing, like a mother weeping for her child, like the hustle and bustle of servants around a sick man. I felt as if something had yanked me and thrown me around and dashed icy water over me. It was so cold that my arms and legs were trembling—I huddled against the mare to warm up on her body.

"How long have you been in such a peculiar shape!"

"As long as the Jewish Exile!" she replied with a sigh.

"How did it happen?" I asked, moving a bit closer. The creature rested her eyes on me and stared as though I were mad. Then her expression became earnest and she began to talk in a dismal voice:

"The man who has peered into tomes or listened to the words of his elders knows that people have been said to take on the shapes of all kinds of creatures and cattle, things that creep and crawl, either turning into them while still alive or else as a reincarnation after death. It happens all the time. In the past, such things occurred frequently, and they still keep recurring in our time. Great scholars, including clergymen, have given us oral and written confirmation. The history books tell us that Semiramis, the Queen of Babylon, became a dove in her old age. Daniel, in a prophetic vision, saw the four empires in the guise of lions, leopards, and bears. And he relates that Nebuchadnezzar, King of Babylon, turned into a bear at the end of his days. As for the Greeks—they experienced such things all the time. Their god Zeus, if you'll pardon me for saying so, was quite a ladies' man, and once he changed himself into a bull, and Princess Io, the daughter of King Inachus, into a heifer. The poor girl wandered around in that guise for a good long time. The Greeks also had a species, half-animal, half-human, known as centaurs. One centaur, whose name was Chiron, and who had a beard and sidelocks, and a fur hat, was the teacher of Prince Theseus. Well naturally: Like nation, like teacher: If the people are wild then so are the teachers.... And how many old women and maidens, too many to count, were seen by European scholars and God-fearing men, changing into frogs, dragons, and other venomous reptiles, and riding shovels and brooms through the air. These things were confirmed in black and white, beyond the shadow of a doubt. Conjurors, black-magicians, and illusionists had the time of their lives! They played mischief and did the ghastliest things! A lot of princes and princesses were turned by them into wild beasts . . . . Just read the lore and the written tales of each nation, and you'll see that so many princes, so many kings, were transformed by them into rams, horses, bulls, or the like. And so many princesses and queens were changed into cows, calves, or nanny goats. So many lords, so many earls, were conjured into dogs, wolves, bears. They maimed and mangled people, sucked out their blood, drew the marrow from their bones. Yes indeed, whole villages, whole towns, were bewitched into herds of sheep and suffered the worst troubles, torments, and tortures . . . . These things happened, caused by the powers of illusion, sorcery, and necromancy. Those poor, unhappy people!"

The words boomed out as if from an empty barrel. It wasn't like the speech of lips, it wasn't as if the mare were speaking, but as if some spirit were talking out of her. It tore my brain, roaring and humming, as if a stream of cold water had crashed down on it from the eaves of a house. The mare gazed at me and continued her story.

"In those days, there lived a king's son, a fine, handsome, intelligent prince with all the virtues—a splendid man. In his youth, the prince had wandered a great deal, undertaking many voyages to see the world. And wherever he went, people would sing his praises. A king of Egypt (that famous land of gypsies and conjurors) was very angry at the prince, who had come to visit him. Terrified that the prince might go after him later on and drive him from his country, the king summoned his great sorcerers and said to them: 'Let us deal cunningly with the prince!' Which meant; in plain Yiddish: 'Give it to him, boys!'

"The magicians applied their sorcery and turned the prince into a mare. And then they made the poor creature work like a horse.

"The unfortunate mare had to lug whole mountains of bricks and clay, and she built treasure cities for Pharaoh—Pithom and Raamses. The Egyptians tormented her for years, making her life wretched, until God took pity. There came a great, a renowned man, a Miracle worker, who made fools of all the Egyptians with their sorcery, and performed greater feats with the Holy Name of God. He pronounced an incantation and transformed the mare back into a prince!

"As long as that great Miracle worker and his disciples were alive, the prince retained a human appearance and lived in wealth and honor in his own land. But then, when those friends of his all died out, the prince's enemies turned him into a mare again, and in this form he has heen driven around from one place to another, year after year. The unhappy prince really deserves the name of The Wandering Mare or The Eternal Mare. For the mare wanders about eternally to all corners of the world. Anyone with a merciful heart climbs up on her back. Anyone who believes in God, hits her and kicks her. Anyone who feels like it, dumps his pack and his bundle on her. She roams eternally, in her yoke, dragging about, lugging bricks and clay with great effort, and her blood and sweat have gone to build entire cities! . . ."

At that time, when my head was full of marvelous tales about sorcerers and conjurors; at that time, when, besides perusing such storybooks as *The Arabian Nights*, or *The Book of Bove*, which I had eagerly read in my childhood, I also devoured other tales like dumplings; at that time, when my blood was hot, my heart boiling, and my imagination aflame, when my feelings were gunpowder, kindling, blasting, at the slightest touch; when my eyes were wellsprings, thermal baths, when anyone who suffered could find hot tears in them—it was at that time that the story of the unhappy prince so greatly moved me. I was seething!

"Please tell me," I said. "Tell me, where is he now! Where is the poor fellow, the unfortunate prince!"

"The prince, the unfortunate prince, is lying before your very eyes, in the likeness of a mare!"

I sighed, I wept, I poured scalding tears over my poor unhappy mare.

* * *

7. IZZY STILL WANTS TO BECOME A HUMAN BEING

I was infamous in my town because of three sins: 1: I was over twenty and still unmarried; 2: I had abandoned the study of our sacred Jewish lore and completely forsaken the Talmud; 3: I had given myself over fully to the secular books. The townspeople regarded me as a heretic, glaring at me and keeping out of my way, unwilling to come anywhere near me.

It's hard enough to be solitary abroad, but pity the poor man who

329

who is solitary at home. In a foreign country, the miserable stranger doesn't know anyone, and no one knows him. That's certainly a heartache, and there's no shame in it. But to be a stranger in your own hometown, among your own people—that means both heartache and shame together. Such bitter feelings are known only to a poor man invited to a meeting or a feast but left to sit alone, ignored by everyone, whether purposely or not. He's something like an invisible man, able to see everyone, but with no one able to see him. If he says anything, no one hears him, and his words just come back to his own ears. If someone does occasionally answer him, in a half-hearted mumble, it's as though the man were doing him a favor while thinking to himself: "Take it and go to the devil!"

If I had still been locked up in my room, poring over my books night and day, I wouldn't have been so acutely aware that everyone hated me. But now that my precarious health (God preserve us!) forced me to study less and at times leave off altogether for a while, I could feel how grim and bitter it was to be isolated from both outsiders and my own people, belonging to neither one nor the other.

My mother was deeply hurt that I was acting the way I was, going off in a completely different direction from all the other Jews. But she took care not to say anything unkind, she didn't want to offend her only child. And so my love for her became even greater. And whenever I got despondent, I so strongly felt the need to pour out my bitter sorrows to her.

"Oh, mother, it's so awful!" I once lamented to her, in a dark moment. "It's so awful to be all alone!"

My mother was startled by my words, and then her face lit up:

"How wonderful, my child! We were just talking about it. Speak of the devil—I mean, the Messiah! That's obviously the best sign that what I'm about to tell you comes directly from God. I'm certain that today you'll want to hear everything I have to say. From now on, I hope that your fortune (may God grant it!) will shine like the radiant morning star. Listen, my son! Today, someone proposed a marriage for you, a really marvelous girl . . . beautiful, and rich, too—"

"That's enough, Mama, that's enough!" But my mother didn't hear, she merely continued heaping praises.

"She's got a lot of money, and presents, and jewelry, gold and silver, diamonds, a lovely wardrobe, and you'll live with her father, in the finest style—"

330

"It's always the finest style among Jews!" I screamed, breaking in. "Always the same old story! You start out rich, in the finest style, and you always end up in the poorest style: children, a whole swarm of them, poverty, a grim life, teaching, sitting around and doing nothing, trying to pick up some money by acting as a broker, breaking your back, bowing and scraping and kneeling, 'Why thank you, sir!' and servility, and praising to the skies, praising Goddammit! Praising, praising, praising, praising—"

"Stop it! That's enough!" screamed my mother, jumping back in terror. "Such a deluge of words! May God protect us! It's all right, I'll hold my tongue. If you hadn't started, I wouldn't have said a word. You were the one who said it with your own two lips, that Bible verse: 'It is not good for man to be alone.' That means it is not good for a man to be without a wife."

"Oh, Mama! I said that because I feel so alone and so estranged from people!"

"But Izzy, you're the one who's strange. You don't do the things that other people do. If you wanted to, you could make everything all right."

"Are you telling me to return to the fold, Mama? To become a *luftmentsh*, with all it entails, like any other Jewish *luftmentsh*? To go against my will and my better judgment, and remain a fool for the rest of my life just to please a bunch of fools? No, Mother! I'd only make things worse for myself! A man who acts against his own will and his better judgment—is a nullity, worse than a corpse. That's true of anyone, not just Jews."

My mother kept silent. She gave me a worried stare, shaking her head and sighing. My heart felt so bitter, and I lamented to her in great sorrow:

"Oh, Mother. I curse the day that I was born to be miserable and hated by all the world! My own people, the Jews, are so terrible to me, and so are the 'others,' the Christians! The Jews hate me for not being a Jew after their own hearts, and the Christians despise me for being a Jew—'Ah, that's the trouble! A Jew! ' For this sin with which I and my ancestors were born, and which has been handed down to us from Father Abraham, we are punished with misery, oppression, expulsions, afflictions, sufferings, and every possible torture. I feel it's my foremost obligation to do anything in my power to fight this misfortune. A man who's been expelled from the rest of mankind, in whom God's gift of human dignity has been degraded, who's been crowded into a confining area like

331

a bird in a cage, unable to budge—if that man doesn't give a damn, then it would be better for him not to have been born at all. I'm a human being, Mama! I'm alive and I want to live. I want to get out of this narrow confinement and live on an equal footing with other human beings in God's great world. I have to do my best to keep my being Jewish from harming me and to improve my condition."

"Oh, Izzy, what are you saying!" screamed my mother, turning chalk white as if about to faint. "Don't worry, Mama!" I comforted her. "Your son Israel is still Israel, and he'll be Izzy forever and ever. I want to improve my condition by getting an education. With a university degree I can obtain special privileges, including the right to leave this narrow confinement, the Pale of Settlement, and move about freely anywhere in the world."

"Well, Izzy, so you want to go back to your fairytales, and sweat over your books day and night!" said my mother, anxious about my physical health and my peace of mind. "Oh, your books, your books! They won't bring us anything but sorrow and misery! I'm only a simple woman, and I don't understand what that outside world of yours is all about, the world you keep talking about all the time and find so attractive. Stay here with your mother, you've got everything you need right here at home—thank goodness! Who am I laboring for and working my fingers to the bone for? No one but you, my darling child!"

"The very thought of never doing anything and being a burden on my mother for the rest of my life makes me sick! A grown man like me, hanging on to his mother's apron strings, eating and not working! It would have been better for me and you and the whole world if I'd never been born! I don't want to be a daydreamer. There are enough Jewish daydreamers as it is!"

"Please, Izzy, do me a favor and put your books away, those books of yours . . . . Israel . . . . There's a way of getting the right to live in the forbidden areas. All you need is money and an artisan's license."

"What do you mean 'money'?"

"Well, you just buy a business license from whatever guild you like, and that gives a Jew a right to settle in the world, which you find so attractive."

"Ah, Mother, pity the poor man who depends on money and not on himself. A privilege that's gotten with money is a disgrace to both the man who sells it and the man who buys it. Damnit! I don't want it, and I hate commerce anyway. I hate it because of the businessmen! Most of them, from the ragpickers to the shop-keepers and bankers, are devoted followers of that great thief Laban.... And I hate them because of their competitiveness, and that enormous chaos in the business world, which rubs off on them, whether they like it or not. There are enough Jewish rag-pickers and shopkeepers as it is! And that thing you talked about, Mama,—the artisan's license! What connection do I have with a craft?! I haven't the foggiest notion about any craft whatsoever!"

"The craft isn't so important," murmured my mother. "The main thing is the license, don't you see?"

My reply was a grimace. Her words made my gorge rise. Actually a rabbinical permission may be obtained in a matter of life or death, to hit upon some stratagem, say, a wire strung on the circumfer-ence of a town to classify it as enclosed private property so that Jews can carry things on the Sabbath. A rabbi can also give a dispensation to charge interest, and so on. But a craft license?

I kept silent for quite a while, just curling my nose. And then I spoke again briefly, and to the point: "The only thing I'm interested in is a university degree, and I'll do anything I can to get it. I won't rest until it's mine. Once and for all, I want to study at the university!"

"Study? You call that studying?! Oh my goodness! Your studies are devouring all your strength, Israel."

"Loafing weakens your strength even more, and it wipes you out!"

What could my poor mother do? She let me have my way. But only on condition that I budget a time for studying, a time for going on walks, for sleeping, and the like, to safeguard my health. A sound mind in a sound body!

And so, in a happy moment, I went back to my books, studying hard and systematically, just as before, until the time came for my examinations.

8. MOTHER KNOWS BEST

One lovely spring morning, a wagon stopped in front of our house to bring me to Dnieprovitz, where I was to take my exam-inations. My mother was very mournful, she couldn't hold back her tears. She kept crying and looking at me, looking at me and then crying again.

"Don't cry, Mama!" I begged her and burst into tears. My heart felt so heavy.

"Please don't cry, Mama dear! I'm not going to some God-forsaken place. I just have to get it over with. I've studied and worked so hard. God will help me get my wish. I'll be able to earn my living respectably, and I'll be a free man. And then you'll be so proud of me, Mama. Oh, please don't cry, Mama, please don't cry!"

"Oh Izzy!" she replied. "That's easy for you to say. When a mother's heart cries, you can't just calm it down like a child. It's got its reasons for crying. It senses something. It knows something that no mind can grasp. Please, Izzy, think it over and don't go! Why should you work so hard at your age, you poor baby! How can you tell whether it will be worth all the trouble and drudgery? How many educated Jews are there among us, without even a pair of boots to their name? How many scholars come to nothing and suffer terribly all their lives? Israel, all the Gentile schools and education are just some new-fangled nonsense. Our ancestors didn't even know there was such a thing. I hope to God it doesn't bring trouble to us and the Jewish people, and tear children away from their parents. Please, Izzy dear, stay home! It's so hard for me to say goodbye to you, so hard!"

The driver came into the house and took my things, thereby ending the conversation. My mother and I tearfully kissed and said goodbye. I climbed into the wagon, and away we drove.

Laugh all you like, you modern, enlightened Jews. Laugh at anything you like. But please don't deride the notion that a mother's heart has its reasons for crying! As long as you remain silent and fail to tell us what life is, how all our thoughts and feelings arise and flourish inside our brains, how marvelous dreams are spun and woven within us from a stuff, a thread, that, for now at least, doesn't exist in the world and won't be developed till later on. As long as you remain silent and without the least shimmer of understanding, I just won't let you guffaw at the notion that a mother's heart feels and divines! You musn't laugh, you don't have the right to laugh when I say that my mother's heart had its reasons for crying!

I flunked!

It doesn't hurt to know how and why. On the day of the examination, I felt plucky, and to bolster my courage I had a drink, though I usually never touch the stuff. Don't worry, I thought to myself, God will help! Why should I be scared? The examiners are fine, educated people. They're sure to treat me gently, decently, like gentlemen and scholars, and raise my spirits.

But, oh God! When I stood before them, I quickly learned the error of my ways. The teachers sat there, dressed in uniforms with brass buttons. They glared at me, as grim and severe as if I had robbed or killed someone. They scowled like a police official who welcomes you with: "Where you from! Why, I'll . . . . Show me your passport!"

Now why should teachers, whose job is to make us and our children sensible and sensitive, whose job requires them to be decent, straightforward, and accessible to everyone, so that all hearts will open to them and let them sow and plant the seeds of decency and virtue—why should teachers have brass buttons and glare like police officers! Say what you will, I just can't imagine Socrates, Plato, Aristotle, and the others with such brass buttons, sour faces, and grim looks . . . .

Naturally, their welcome unmanned me. I no longer knew what was happening. If that was their goal, then they certainly achieved it—with a vengeance. My head began spinning. One teacher addressed me with a look that seemed to say: "Get a load of him! I'm the one with a great mind, an open mind. I'm asking the questions! Do you get me! I'm asking! Respect, do you hear!" He turned to me with that look and treated me to one question after another, a line from here, a verse from there, until we came to a fairytale, to Baba Yaha of all people! I was befuddled, lost my bearings, and went completely adrift. The teachers did me the honor of laughing their heads off, with cheerier expressions!

And thus ended my examination, thus ended my great efforts, thus ended all my hopes!

I felt so awful that I couldn't stay in my room. I wandered around the city, up and down the streets and the lovely surrounding hills. I only stopped at my hotel to have a bite and to sleep! But actually, sleeping became impossible, and I spent terrible nights, tossing and turning. The moment I closed my eyes, wild creatures would loom up, glare at me with sour expressions—and a spectacle began, a fine spectacle. There was a comedy, and I played the sacrificial rooster. But I had nothing to crow about! I felt myself soaring through the air, whirling around and around. My hands and feet were tied. I was being spun around as a sacrificial rooster on the Day of Atonement. Up against a stone wall.

Once, during such a spectacle, I crowed at the top of my lungs, so loudly that I was terror-stricken. I tumbled from my bed more dead than alive, and raced out in a dreadful turmoil. I thought some person was at my heels, yelling: "Where is he! Stop him!" Dashing helter-skelter, I cannoned into someone. I felt a clammy hand clutching me with an iron grip. An old hag stood in front of me, scrawny, scraggy, not an ounce of flesh on her frame, all skin and bones. Instead of eyes, she had two yawning holes lined with a dirty, wrinkled, leathery skin of a disgusting color. Her mouth gaped from ear to ear, toothless, hollow, empty, except for the tongue flicking around inside, writhing, twisting, like a worm in a pit. From her arm dangled a basket of huge live crabs, crawling, lumbering over one another, waving their nippers. She glared at me in silence, her mouth widening even more, as though laughing, if you could call it that—a mirth that casts a dark shadow of melancholy on the soul and freezes your guts. I thought of Baba Yaha, my nemesis of the past few years, obstructing my path, preventing me from getting ahead. A cold sweat covered my body. I felt so sick I nearly fainted. I pulled myself together, tore myself away from where I was standing, and ran like a madman.

Baba Yaha had kindled such a panic in me that as I ran I kept looking around every which way to make sure I wouldn't meet up with her again. I had heard long ago that she lived in Dnieprovitz, keeping people with long noses in constant terror. If one of them ever crossed her path, she would grab his nose and whistle—and then her gang came, the demons and devils. She would pull on his nose and the others would push him from behind—and the longnosed would come to rest. From that time on, I kept touching my nose and hid it from danger as well as I could.

*   *   *

23. ISRAEL IS CROWNED AS A BENEFACTOR AND PUT ASTRIDE THE MARE

If you've never ridden a poker through the air, as I have, then no words can possibly make you feel what it's like. You have to experience it yourself. And that was why I prayed fervently during my flight:

"O Lord! What did I, poor sinner, do to deserve this more than all other human beings, the children of Adam and Eve? What did I do to deserve this elevation and this flight under Your heavens, the way a bird doth fly through the air? O, Almighty God, make them, too, fly through the air, the people of this world, if not all, at least some of them, for the sake of Your truth and justice, O Father in heaven! If You have not graced them with wings, then let the devil take them and carry them on his wings, and let all of them fly through the air, old and young, men, women, and children. Let them know what it's like to soar through space."

I can't say for sure how long my air voyage lasted. All I know is that we flew and flew until at last we came to a huge and deep valley, far, far, away, between mountains that towered to the very clouds. I still shudder at the memory of that wild and deserted valley. There wasn't a sign of grass or trees. At every step of the way, there were only brambles and heaps of stones, with serpents, vipers, and lizards, darting and scuttling among them. There were ear-splitting shrieks from wild beasts and birds in their lairs, all kinds of dismal and weeping screams. Everything stank of sulphur and devil's dung. Here and there, clouds of smoke arose from the ground and spread everywhere like a fog. This was the valley that the devils had chosen for themselves, this was their home!

A gorge between rocks led to an enormous cavern, and words couldn't even begin to describe how dreadful it was. A river of black ink flowed through it. Forests of pens grew along its shores, teeming with hobgoblins, apelike creatures resembling humans. In the distance, I could see some of them ducking my poor mare, bathing and dunking her, until she emerged as black as a devil.

"This is my office!" said Ashmedai. "This river and the forests, which you see over there—I've prepared them for your brethren. My clerks will write and write about you people as long as there's ink in the wells and pens in the forests. Look! There are channels running from the inkhorns, inkducts leading to so many places—newspapers and offices. Pipe number nine hundred and ninety-nine thousand, nine hundred and ninety-nine, the one you're looking at now, runs into the inkwell of a journalist in Dnieprovitz. There's a sea of ink and pens, and there are as many writers as grains of sand on the beach."

He whistled, and the hobgoblins came swarming from the

woods like flies. They lined up, each with a pen in his hand and a foolscap helmet on his head.

"These are my writers!" he exclaimed, smirking at me. He saluted his regiment of scribblers like a general. They cheered: "Hurray! Hurray!"

When they quieted down, he began drilling them. Their exercises consisted of sticking out their tongues, giving the finger, and guffawing. Next, he commanded in a loud voice:

"Present pens! Dunk!"

Then he let out a long, drawn-out call:

"Wriiiiiiiiiiiite!"

The regiment set about scribbling, almost all of them using the same topics and the same words. My hair stood on end when I read. Their words were barbed and pointed, they cut like spears. Hands were trembling, hearts pounding. These, as I found out later, belonged to recruits who had only just joined the regiment. They were still having a thorny time of it . . . . Others were working like firemen and simply slinging mud.

After this inspection, Ashmedai whistled again—and some devil walked in, a giant of a fellow, in full regalia. His head was hung with plumes, pens, and dusters.

"What have you done while I was gone? How's our business?" Ashmedai asked him. He also introduced us to one another: 'This is my secretary Duke Lucifer, and this is Mr. Israel!"

Lucifer, the secretary, made a wry face and didn't even deign to glare at me. He took out his report and read:

"Your Ashmedaian Darkness! King of all devils and demons! Prince of all the hobgoblins, Duke of the seven chambers of Hell, Count of Sodom and Gomorrah, Archpastor of all scapegoats, etc., etc.

"Our agents, the do-gooders in all towns, have reported that thanks to their ubiquitous efforts in the proper places, the tax on kosher meat has not been abolished."

Ashmedai was radiant with delight. "Thank you," he told his secretary. "I am grateful to Your Blackness, Duke Lucifer, for starting your report with this crucial matter." Then he said to me:

"Now that's what I call news! First of all, your brothers are going to eat crap instead of meat and be sickly all the time. They'll be ill, they'll fester and—to hell with them! Secondly, I need the kosher-meat tax for my business. That's how I can form my whole gang of do-gooders, who lead you around by the nose and never let you raise your heads. They provide my agents with salaries and a

338

decent livelihood. And that's how all your hollow men get their hands on large sums of money to waste on unmentionable things. It's the best proof that with all your necessary community expenses, you're different from the Gentiles. That makes it impossible for you to join them in their feelings for the country. And so bad people will always have a rationale for attacking you.

"Your condition will be confused and chaotic. If I could only keep all other people on the same level as you! . . . Now do you see why that's good news for me! If, heaven forfend, the tax were abolished, then you'd be rid of all your troubles—may you live so long! Well, my agents know their politics. They deserve a bonus for their hard work.

"According to reliable intelligence," Lucifer went on, "a great many poor people have died. And generally, they're very badly off because of the benefits they get from the philanthropists."

"Great!" said Ashmedai. "Wonderful! The tax always shows what strength it has among the poor in a cholera epidemic. Just the other day, in some town, I read a notice on a house wall. It was signed in Hebrew: 'Those who wish the very best to our brethren, the nation of Israel.' The poster announced that because of the cholera epidemic it was absolutely essential for the Jews to eat meat, even on holidays when it was forbidden.

"I simply had to laugh when I read it. They advise eating meat 'for the good of our brethren, the good of our brethren!' And all the while, they've raised the prices!"

"Candidates for the office of philanthropist," Lucifer kept reading, "are to be found among people from all walks of life. There aren't even enough positions available, unless we give every assistant of a chief philanthropist a hundred subassistants, and they, in turn, will take care of tapping new sources for their salaries. A few of them have already submitted excellent projects on this score. I have turned the proposals over to a special committee consisting of Shenkhasai, Azael, Ahriman, Acheron, Typhon, Shiva, and Beelzebub.

"In the Dumbsville Hospital, things are going tolerably well, thanks to our agents. We've gotten quite a way with Dumbsville!

"As for recruits, three thousand, three hundred and thirty-three have come into the clerical regiments. They're still not properly trained, but Beelzebub is in charge of drilling them.

"In regard to ink, seven thousand, five hundred and ninety-nine buckets and one and a half quarts have been used since my last report."

"Is that all?" said Ashmedai, his face showing discontent.

Lucifer was about to explain, but just as he opened his mouth, a demon flew in with dispatches. Ashmedai motioned Lucifer to take the telegrams and read them.

"This wire is from Rumania," announced Lucifer. "They're frantic for ink. They promise to send us copies of everything they write, for our library. This other wire is from Austria. Congratulations on some good news, great Ashmedai!" said Lucifer, cheerily smiling and baring his sharp, canine fangs. "Cardinal Schwarzenberg is ordering a huge amount of ink for his gazette. He wants to do business with us. Aside from his own needs, he wants the concession for all the Catholic priests in Bohemia and Moravia who've started writing, some of them even at an advanced age."

"Long live my faithful disciples," said Ashmedai, his spirits soaring. "As long as their pulses keep throbbing, I don't have a thing to worry about. Lucifer! You'll have to add some of these substances to the ink to make it really effective: blood, venom, gall, scorpions, devil's dung, and so on."

"I've already done it on my own!" said Lucifer and began reading the rest of the telegrams. He perused the request from the editor of the *National Inquirer* in Galicia. Then, with a pitying expression, he waved his hand, saying: "Oh, this is from our man in Dnieprovitz! The poor guy's complaining that his inkhorn is almost dry. He has nothing to write, but he has to keep putting out issues on schedule. Isn't that sad?"

"Hurry! Open the spigots!" yelled Ashmedai.

A whole company of demons stormed the taps. The ink gushed through the conduits to various places.

All at once, a naked soul came flying in, fluttering up and down like a butterfly, beating its wings on the ground. Its wings were as blue as the flame of an alchohol lamp. It looked like a very thin, huge soap bubble, glittering with all sorts of lovely, attractive colors. Taking a close look, I could make out a shape of pure gas.

"Ahh!" screamed Ashmedai, grabbing his head when he saw it. "A noble philanthropist has passed away! A distinguished benefactor, one of my best agents! That's his soul. After death, it's come to me to live with the souls of all the other philanthropists."

I peered hard at the soul and recognized who it was. It was an enormously important benefactor in my home town.

340

"Weep and wail, Izzy!" said Ashmedai with a dismal voice. "Your native town has lost a great treasure, your community is bereft of a truly merciful human being, a rare gem! Oh, sob and lament, you devils, you demons! I, your king, have lost my finest counselor, my most devoted adviser. Without him, I am deprived of my right hand."

Throughout the cavern, throughout the valley, there was a hideous keening, a mixture of all kinds of wild sounds. There was a dreadful howling, like the nocturnal baying of a dog. There was a meowing, a caterwauling, like cats in heat. There was a melancholy dirge of owls, a cawing of ravens, a croaking of frogs. There was a hissing of serpents, a squeaking of rats, a bellowing of bulls, a growling of bears, a snarling of leopards. As though all the beasts were sobbing and grieving for such a fine philanthropist, such a pure soul. I nearly fainted, I practically turned deaf from that terrible mourning.

Ashmedai barely managed to restore peace and quiet. He caught the soul like a fly, and buried it deep in the earth, with these words:

"What's the use of weeping? Man is mortal ! Sooner or later, the devil has to take you! So lie down six feet under and go to hell! I'll have to get along without you, somehow, and find another wretch to take your place . . . .

"Izzy, dear boy!" he turned to me after his eulogy. "You have no choice. You'll have to take his place as a benefactor in your home town."

"I won't, I can't!" I yelled in a fearful voice. "Have pity. Send someone else. There are so many people interested in the job, there are so many candidates. Send anyone you like, but please don't appoint me!"

"Now, now! Spare me your advice!" he replied. "I know what I'm doing."

"What do you see in me anyway?" I cried. "I'm all thumbs. I'm no good for that sort of thing. I can recommend people who are smarter, better, more experienced. Send Leybele, or Moyshe, or Treytl, or Fishke, or any one of their crowd. They all know what they're doing, and they do it so well. How can you compare me to them?"

"All these people are busy. They've all got jobs. It won't help, Izzy. I, Ashmedai, tell you again. Just hold your tongue, and don't be so stubborn if you want to keep living and if you don't want me to drive out your stubbornness forcibly. Don't say another word. Shush! Or else, I'll—"

He put on a horrid expression and shook his finger at me so hard that I felt goosebumps all over and fell as silent as the grave.

"That's how I like you, Izzy—silent," he said, with a mellow smirk, and he patted my cheek. "Ah, you're really nobody's fool, Izzy! I have to keep on my toes with you. I just know you'll do well, and in time you'll be a man of parts. But before I give you such an important office, I have to break you in a little and instruct you on how to act.

"Listen, my dear Izzy! *The town is—I!* The meaning of this is very simple. Do anything you like, and then say: 'That's what the people want.' There's no such thing as the community. You're all that exists. That's my first commandment.

"My second commandment is: *A God-fearing face!* Piety is a good cow for a smart man. You can milk her for all she's worth, like the best dairy cow. Such a marvelous animal has to be treated with kid gloves. You have to give her a bundle of ritual garments every so often, feed her on phylacteries, offer her a good sack with a prayer shawl, pages from the Bible and the Talmud, so that she'll spend several hours a day at the trough. You have to let her lick mezuzahs, suck the blood at a circumcision, water her with memorial drinks, a nip at the burial society, and so on and so forth. That's piety for you among my agents of the pious sort. My more secular agents also put on a devout face, but it's a different kind. They usually play the fool, try to get on well with everyone, smile pleasantly, turn their tongues this way and that, wear clothes that are neither new-fangeledly short nor old-fashionedly long. Their beards aren't quite all there, but they're not clean-shaven either. They turn every which way and try to get along with everyone.

"A few of them aren't all that pious. Their wisdom is in their strength, their power, their fists . . . . But there are very few. And these arrogant few are far from typical. Not every human being can attain this level.

"My third commandment is: *Compassion!* This means you can do any vile thing you like. You can fleece the living and the dead and always say: 'What a pity!' In secret, you can pinch and bite and squeeze. But in front of others, you show concern, you moan, you pretend to be acting for the community.

"My fourth commandment is: *The common good!* This means, always make common cause with the stronger. Stick with the tax collector, for he is the Primal Cause, the source of all good, he is goodness in the flesh. Flesh of your flesh and bone of your bone.

342

Therefore you shall leave father and mother and cleave unto the tax collector, and be of one body and soul with him. Let your will give way to his will, so that sometimes his will can give way to your will, so that you both shall rejoice and be glad.

"My fifth commandment is: *Demands!* This means: No matter how much you take on the sly, no matter how much you fleece and earn, keep complaining to people, grumble and grouse, make demands upon the town, say that you're losing money, that you're adding money of your own, that it's simply not worth running yourself ragged for the community.

"My sixth commandment is: *Lull!* It's as easy as pie. Just rock people to sleep, sing lullabies. People are such infants. All you have to do is sing them a lullaby, tell them a fairytale, and they'll shut their eyes and go to sleep. Just growl, and they'll think you're a bear. Whip them, and they'll kiss the lash. The best lullaby to cradle them to sleep is the old ditty about the little cash box. Then comes the song: 'Torah is the Highest Good.' Next the old story 'The Rabbi and His Wife,' the tale of the scamps, the wonder workers, and so on and so forth.

"My seventh commandment is: *My-oh-my!* The plain meaning of these noises is: In case the public, that silly little child, ever starts yelling and carrying on—then don't do a thing. The poor baby's probably got a bellyache, just let it suffer. My-oh-my! And don't say another word. Don't worry, the child will bawl its lungs out and then doze off again, and it will sleep even more soundly than before.

"My eighth commandment is: *Belittle!* This means: If someone starts asking questions, and says that this doesn't make sense or that doesn't make sense, then just belittle him. Say he's a heretic, a hooligan, a nobody, he's not worth talking to.

"My ninth commandment is: *Backbiting!* This means: If some poor wretch starts weeping and yelling bloody murder, 'They're squeezing me, they're fleecing me'—all you have to do is sic the gang on him: 'Ugh! What a crybaby! Tattletale, tattletale!'

"My tenth commandment is: *Home remedies!* When the child falls ill, gets in a wretched state, and is about to give up its soul, don't send for a doctor. It's better to resort to tried and tested home remedies. Go to charmers, gypsies, conjurors.

"And you shall keep these ten commandments. And thereby, you will please me, you will live in happiness and prosperity, you and your wife, and your children, and you will thus purchase the afterlife. And you will pay off others with the afterlife. Promise them meat and wine in the world to come, after they die. But you will eat meat and drink wine in this world, while you live."

I gaped, I gazed, I stared, like a golem, at hearing this decalogue.

"You've got to get going, Izzy!" said Ashmedai. "Your town is bereft of a benefactor. No good can come of that for me. I'll give you the mare. You can ride her."

"Oh, no!" I exclaimed at the word *mare*. "I can't. I don't know how to ride!"

"Nonsense!" he said. "You'll get the hang of it in no time! We'll teach you! The mare is very submissive. She's easy to ride. So what if she doesn't look so good! She's got other qualities. She comes from a fine background! You'll be satisfied with her, don't worry. In the end, you'll never want to let her go. Take my word for it!"

At his command, they dragged over the unhappy mare. She was heartbreaking to look at, wretched, lamentable. God only knew what the poor thing had endured from the hobgoblins. I hung my head in shame like a thief, I just couldn't look her in the eye. I burst into tears at the thought of having to ride her and get on her back like a massive load. I saw no way of getting out of it.

"Let's crown Izzy!" said Ashmedai. "Let's see what Izzy looks like dressed as a benefactor and riding the mare. C'mon gang, get to work!"

In the twinkling of an eye, his servants brought in a mass of clothes, all cuts and sizes. One of the servants, in charge of wardrobe and Ashmedai's valet de cham', took me in hand and dressed me. He arranged a lock on my head, smeared a pomade in my hair, cunningly did my beard, put a chemisette on me with mother-of-pearl buttons, a sateen cloth at my throat, then a pair of solid hobnailed boots, my goodness, a pair of woolen trousers that hung down like bags, a camlet jacket, an overcoat that reached down past my knees, and an artistically sewn cap on my head.

"Now what do we have here?" said Ashmedai, looking me over from head to foot. "This is the uniform of a community scribe! It's not the right thing for Izzy. Find something else."

The valet de cham' quickly changed my coiffure, trimmed my hair, straightened out my whiskers, put a different vest on me, satin I think, and buttoned up to my Adam's apple, a cotton overcoat with a split in the back and a hem reaching down much farther than the previous one, so that barely an inch or two of the trousers stuck out. And on my head, a worthy and dignified hat.

"Well, how do you look now?" said Ashmedai, inspecting me. "Ah, the uniform of a community deputy! The devil take them with their splits in back and their cavernous pockets. No. Izzy needs a different uniform entirely. Just look at his lamentable expression, and you'll understand what he ought to have."

The valet tried all sorts of uniforms on me. And while dressing me and combing me over and over again every minute, he tweaked and yanked and pulled my hair, bringing tears to my eyes. At long last, he cropped my hair, leaving me a pair of fine earlocks, stuck a skullcap on my pate, with a high fur hat over it, put a shirt on me with a huge turn-down collar, tied with ribbons and without a necktie, a long ritual four-colored garment, velvet breeches, shoes and stockings, a long satin gabardine with a belt, and a sheepskin overcoat. The valet looked me over, made a sour face, and stuck out his tongue.

"You're gorgeous, Izzy!" Ashmedai laughed joyously. "I'm absolutely delighted to see you in these clothes! Your face is as red as a carrot stew, you're sweating in that fur, and you're shining from underneath your fur hat like the radiant morning star. Sweat, sweat, Izzy. It's good for you! . . . But there's something missing to make the uniform perfect," he went on, turning to the valet. "Do you remember how Yossel-Dintshes used to receive a new governor?"

"Right! Right!" the valet answered. "I completely forgot. Oh, yes! I'll do it in a jiffy!"

He shaved a pair of round spots on the back of my head, and stuck on cupping-glasses for a few minutes, for beauty's sake.

"Now Izzy's in full regalia," said Ashmedai. "And he can mount the mare."

With great pageantry, I was dragged over to the mare. "Ride, Izzy. Ride!" the devils sang. "How lucky you are that you're privileged to ride on such a mare, the mare of the world! Just climb up with your hands and feet, and ride on her, like a lord, ride till the end of your life, till the devil gets you and someone else takes your place!"

"Please forgive me, poor mare!" I begged, astride her back, my eyes weeping and my heart sorrowing. "What can I do, what can I say? The devils made me do it.... It's hideous for both of us! It's horrible for you because you're a mare and you have to carry me. And it's horrible for me, your friend, because I have to get on your back! What can we poor wretches do! We're in the same boat, and there's no way out!"

The devils lashed the mare so hard that she scurried off. There was a yelling and screaming! *Hurray! Hurray!* As she galloped, a deep sigh came from her heart. A sigh that cut me to the quick. I was so bewildered that I tumbled to the ground.

"Now, just don't let it get you down, Izzy! You'll make it!" Ashmedai laughed and plopped me back on the mare. "Don't delay, it's time to get going. Just repeat my ten commandments. Put your hands under my loins and swear you'll abide by them."

I sat there like a clay golem, not knowing what was happening.

"Don't dilly! Don't dally, Izzy!" said Ashmedai. "Do what you're told. Quick! Quick! Time's awasting!"

Willy-nilly, I reached out and put my hands under Ashmedai's loins. He motioned to his secretary, and Lucifer began reading a terrible oath.

"Cat's got your tongue, Izzy?" Ashmedai grumbled. "Why aren't you repeating the oath, word for word? Do you think I'll put up with tricks, qualms, and betrayals, the way you fine human beings do? No! I tell you. No reservations! Don't play the clown. It won't help! Just swear!"

"I can't swear," I replied in a trembling voice.

"What?!" Ashmedai screamed in rage, and the earth quaked beneath us.

The mare nodded her head as though to say: "Stick to your guns! Say, no, no, and no!"

"I can't swear!" I repeated, with greater courage.

"Swear!" yelled Ashmedai, angrier. Sparks flew from his eyes and smoke curled from his mouth.

My poor mare heaved a sigh. Her sigh reminded me of all she had gone through in her life. "Oh my!" I thought to myself. "The wretched creature suffers enough from others. Why should I add to her misery! Let come what may! I won't do such a thing! I have to resist temptation like a decent man."

"Absolutely not! I absolutely refuse to swear!" I answered Ashmedai coolly and pulled back my hand from under his loins. As I did so, I had the devilish misfortune to scratch him.

All hell broke loose! Ashmedai was terrifying to look at. With a fearful scream, he leaped into the sir, stretched out terribly high, planted one foot on the earth, the other in the sky, grabbed me by my hair, and flung me away like a piece of wood.

346

I plunged like a bolt from the blue! As I plummeted, I heard taunts and laughter from all the demons at once. I saw the mare whooshing through the air, whirling and tumbling after me.

"We're falling, we're falling!" I barely managed to scream.

"Don't worry!" the mare yelled back. "When I fall, I either land on my feet, or else I get right back up again. I never bite the dust. I've had my share of falls, but none has ever spelled my downfall!"

I plunged and plunged, until at last I landed on my head, screaming in pain.

I felt hands taking hold of me. It was as if someone were weeping over me and hot tears were pouring onto my face.

24. GODDAMN THEIR MOTHERS!

Opening my eyes, I saw that I was lying on the floor next to my bed in my own room. My mother, in tears, was helping some people heave me up.

As I lay in bed, I began wondering what had happened. How had I suddenly ended up here? I felt my body all over and inspected it. I caught sight of the wonder worker again and the old witch, who were doing something and mumbling their spells. My mother touched my head and wept.

"Why are you crying, Mama?" I asked, and gave her a loving kiss.

"Oh, Izzy, Izzy!" she sobbed. "Oh what awful troubles I've had with you! Thank the Lord that you've opened your eyes. You really had a hard fall from your bed."

"Mama," I said. "What happened?"

"Oh, please don't ask, please don't ask! It's all because of your books."

"What do you mean my books?"

"Those silly stories you crammed into your head." My mother waved her hand. "Well, you absolutely insisted on studying medicine. What could I do? I had no choice. But what good are all those books, those tales, those nonsensical things? What do they have to do with medicine? If you want to be a doctor, well then study to your heart's content and learn anything you have to. You can get a diploma saying you can cure people, even if you don't know

347

a word of those stories. They can't help you in the least. It seems to me that that's how it ought to be, at least according to my female way of thinking. But what did they say? What did they reply, when I ran to each one of them? They said: No! You might have a great mind! You might even become a great man, and a renowned physician. But if you're not well-versed in those tales, in . . . what they call 'histories,' then nothing can come of you. Oh, what suffering all those tales and stories brought me! Oh, Good Lord, if only the devil had taken them all, I would have been spared a lot of trouble!"

"What kind of trouble, Mama?"

"What kind of trouble! Izzy! Oh, what they did to me!"

And this is what my mother told me, weeping and wailing:

"You wrote me from Dnieprovitz, saying you hadn't done so well in the examinations on those stories, and that you had to give up studying medicine. I figured you'd soon be coming home. And then you'd throw over all your silly plans, and get married, as God commanded, and as Jews have to live.

"I waited for a week, but there was no sign of you. I waited another week, and still you didn't show up, and you didn't even write. I was worried sick, wondering what it was all about. I couldn't sleep. I couldn't find a moment's peace. I couldn't eat. You're my only child, after all, the apple of my eye. How can I go on living without you? Meanwhile, there was a lot of talk in town. Some people said you had died. Others—may their tongues rot— said you had converted to Christianity. And goodness only knows what else our enemies made up. I couldn't stand it any longer, so I went to Dnieprovitz.

"When I arrived, it was so awful. I found you in a wretched state! Your face was dark gray, you were all skin and bones, there wasn't an ounce of flesh on you. I asked you how you felt. And you gibbered something about castles in Spain. I tried to talk rationally to you, but you merely jabbered all sorts of nonsense.

"My heart bled for you. I felt like dying. People advised me to go to the teachers and beg them to overlook your mistakes.

Perhaps the good news would bring you to your senses. So I went, of course. I cried, I pleaded, but it was no use! They replied: No! Impossible!

"I hired a wagon and brought you home. Every day you got more and more despondent, you were always lost in thought. But the moment you started talking, you went on and on, a blue streak, cursing all the decent people, all the fine and upright men in town. It was a good thing—a miracle!—that I let no one in except for close friends. So people didn't hear the terrible things you were saying about them. You got sicker and sicker, and finally you took to your bed. You lay there in a coma, for about two weeks, never opening your eyes, practically without a sign of life, except that at times you ranted feverishly, raving about wild things.

"Oh, Izzy! My darling Izzy! What awful things your stories and books have done to us! Put an end to them! For goodness' sake! If only you had listened to your mother and gotten married. It's the way of the world. It's customary and traditional for us Jews. You would have spared us so much sorrow! Oh, Izzy! Your stories, your stories. Your histories, your histories! . . ."

"It all comes from *them*, from *them*, the evil spirits!" said the wonder worker. "Just the other day, I had the same sort of business with them. Our Christian friend here knows about it. Well, wasn't it a fine thing?" he asked the peasant woman.

"A fine thing indeed!" she replied with a yawn, absorbed in her spells. "He's right, he is. This is *their* doing. Goddamn their mothers!

קיצור

מסעות בנימין השלישי

דאס הייסט

דיא נסיעה אָדער אַ רייזע־בעשרייבונג פון בנימין
דעם דריטען :

וואס ער איז אויף זיינע נסיעות פערנאנגען האט וייט אזש
אונטער דיא הרי חושך , אונ האט זיך גענוג אנגעזעהען
אונ אָנגעהערט חדושים שיינע זאכען , וואס זיא זיינען
צרות געמעבטן נעוואירן אין אלע שבעים לשונות אונ היינט
אויך אין אונזער לשון .

ארויס גענעבען בהשתדלות

מענדעלי מוכר ספרים

ספר ראשון

ווילנא

בדפוס והוצאות האלמנה והאחים ראם

שנת תרל״ט לפ״ק

КИЦУРЪ МАСООТЪ БИНЯМИНЪ ГАШЛИШИ.
т. е.
Краткое описаніе путешествія Бенямина III.
Книга I.
Сочиненіе С. Абрамовича.

ВИЛЬНА,
Типографія Вдовы и бр. Роммъ.
Жмудскій переулокъ дома №№ 327 и 328.
1878.

Title page of the first edition of Benjamin the Third *(1878).*

INTRODUCTION TO

The Travels of Benjamin III

According to Leo Wiener (*The History of Yiddish Literature in the XIX Century*, 1899), Abramovitsh based the character of Benjamin on "a real fellow, named Tsharny, who had been employed by some French society to undertake a scientific journey into the Caucasus, but who was entirely unfit for the work, as he had a very superficial knowledge of geography."

The *Travels of Benjamin III* (1878) is patterned in some ways after Cervantes' *Don Quixote*, Benjamin being modeled, in Mendele's Jewish fashion, after Don Quixote, and Senderl, his sidekick, after Sancho Panza. Like Don Quixote, Benjamin has allowed his reading of many books to influence him blindly: he sets out to explore the world, to cross the legendary rock-throwing River Sambatyen, and to reach the land of the little Red Jews beyond the dark mountains.

Mendele calls him "Benjamin the Third" because there were two renowned Jewish explorers before him named Benjamin: Benjamin of Tudela, a Spanish-Jewish traveler of the twelfth century; and Joseph Israel Benjamin, a Romanian Jew who traveled widely in the Near East, Asia, Africa, and North America in the middle of the nineteenth century and who, calling himself "Benjamin II," wanted to "examine the position of Jews and to discover the lost ten tribes."

As in *Dos Kleyne Mentshele* or *Fishke the Lame*, Mendele concentrates on the perceived narrowness, provincialism, and ignorance of his Jewish world—but renders it with ironic humor and warmth, rather than with his usual biting satire and bitter irony.

Theodore Steinberg in *Mendele Moykher Seforim* writes of the novel in this way:

Benjamin both is and is not a fool: the Jewish world both is and is not practical and level-headed. Both, to a certain extent, can only be defined in relation

351

to the hostile outside world, which leaves us with Benjamin's questions: "What harm did I ever do them! Good God, what do they want of me?" Beneath the poverty, the foolishness, the superstition, and the paralysis lies nobility, just as the external form of the nag [in *The Mare*] conceals a king's son. At the end of *Benjamin the Third* we get a glimpse of that nobility (107).

The following selection is all of a piece, representing the prologue and the first three chapters of *The Travels of Benjamin III*.

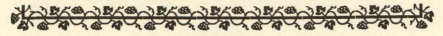

The Travels of Benjamin III

Translated by Joachim Neugroschel

Mendele Moykher-Sforim (the Book Peddler) says: "Praised be the Creator who marks the course of the spheres in the heavens above and the course of all His creatures on the earth below. Not even a blade of grass can creep out from the ground unless an angel strike it and say: 'Grow now! Come forth?' And how much more so a human being, he most certainly has an angel who strikes him and says: 'Come, come, come forth!' And even more so, our fine people, our praiseworthy little Jews. No fool can blurt out a word among us Jews, no moron can give advice, no ignoramus can become a Hassid, no ruffian an enlightened gentleman—unless he be struck by his angel, who thereby goads him to become what he becomes. The angels also strike our paupers, saying: 'Grow, ye paupers, beggars, schnorrers, ragpickers, native poor, nouveau poor, open, hidden: Sprout, grow, like grass, like nettles! Go, ye sons of Israel, go—go a-begging!...'"

But that's all neither here nor there. The point is, gentlemen, I want to tell you about one of our brethren, who traveled to faraway climes, thereby becoming famous.

A year ago, all the English and German gazettes were bursting with the wonderful journey that Benjamin, a Polish Jew, had taken to the Eastern lands: "Just imagine," they exclaimed in wonder, "just imagine, a Jew, a Polish Jew, without weapons, without machines, with only a bag over his shoulder and a sack of prayer paraphernalia under his arm—managing to get to those regions, which world-famous English travelers were unable to reach! One can only assume that non-human forces were at work here, the human mind cannot grasp such matters, for such matters are simply mindless. But in any event, and in any case, mankind is indebted to Benjamin for the great marvels and miracles which he has revealed and which have utterly revised the map of the world.

Benjamin rightfully deserves the medal awarded to him by the Geographical Society..."

The Jewish newspapers eagerly swooped upon these testimonials and couldn't stop talking about them all last summer, as anyone who follows those papers knows so well. They added up all the sages who have ever appeared among Jews, from Adam down to the present, in order to demonstrate what intelligent people the Jews are. They also drew up a list of Jewish travelers in all ages from Benjamin the First, seven hundred years ago, and Benjamin the Second, down to the whole crew of globetrotters wandering about in our climes today. And in order to magnify the importance of our present-day Benjamin, the newspapers thumbed their noses and snapped their fingers, as Jews are wont to do, at all those other journeys, saying that the whole gang of modern travelers were nothing but common panhandlers who didn't know a mountain from a molehill, and all their so-called travels were nothing but door-to-door begging: They all looked like monkeys compared with the present-day Benjamin, Benjamin the Third, the true and authentic traveler. In regard to him and the tomes indited about him, they quoted that well-known biblical verse: "There is something new under the sun." Which means, in our plain Yiddish, that the sun is shining upon a new Jewish hero. "Blessed and showered with diamonds," they all unanimously exulted, "be he who takes this precious treasure, Benjamin's travels, now available in all foreign languages, and translated it into the Holy Tongue as well, so that Jews, poor things, may also taste the honey dripping from the Jewish beehive and may delight and rejoice therein."

And I, Mendele, whose intention has always been to be as useful as I can to our Jews, I could not restrain myself, and I said: "Before the Jewish authors, whose little finger is thicker than my loins, before the Jewish authors get around to publishing their tomes on Benjamin's voyage in Hebrew, I will, in the meantime, try to put out at least a digest in plain Yiddish. I have girded my loins like a hero and, old and weak as I am—may you be spared—I have made every effort to pull forth from the great treasure trove such gems as would be of interest to the Children of Israel, and to retell them freely, in my own style."

And I felt someone striking me from above with these words:

"Awake, Mendele, and creep out from behind the stove! Go forth and take up handfuls of fragrant herbs from Benjamin's treasure trove and prepare succulent dishes for thy brethren, to their liking."

And so, with God's help, I crept forth and prepared a tasty repast, which I will now set down before you. Eat, gentlemen, and hearty appetites!

WHO BENJAMIN IS, WHERE HE'S FROM, AND HOW HE WAS SUDDENLY OVERCOME BY WANDERLUST

"*All my days*," writes Benjamin the Third (he starts his book off in Hebrew but is kind enough to explain everything in Yiddish), "*All my days did I dwell in Moochville,* I mean, I spent my whole life in Moochville until my great voyage. I was born there, I was raised there, and there I married *the wife of my bosom,* my missus, *that pious spouse,* Zelda—*long may she live!*"

Moochville is a tiny, jerkwater shtetl, far from the highway, and so cut off from the rest of the world that if ever anyone happens to come driving in, the townsfolk open their doors and windows to gawk and gape at the newcomer. Neighbors, peering through open windows, ask one another: "Ha! Now just who could that be? Now just where did he pop up from out of a clear blue sky? What's he after anyway? Doesn't he have something up his sleeve? It just doesn't look kosher. You don't just up and come like that. There's more here than meets the eye, we'll have to get to the bottom of this...."

And they all want to show how smart they are, how worldly, and they spout conjectures off the tops of their heads, as rich as rubbish. Old folks tell tales and fables about wayfarers who arrived here in such and such a year. Comedians crack jokes, not quite on-color. The men stroke their beards and smirk, the older women scold the comedians just for fun, rebuking and laughing at once. Young wives peep up askance from their lowered eyes, holding their hands on their mouths and choking with mirth. The discussion about this issue rolls from home to home like a snowball, growing bigger and bigger until it rolls into the synagogue and behind the stove, the place to which all discussions about all issues come rolling—domestic secrets, the politics of Istanbul, the Sultan, the Austrian Kaiser, high finance, Rothschild's fortune compared

355

with the wealth of the great aristocrats and the other magnates, as well as rumors about persecutions and about the Red Jews (the Ten Lost Tribes of Israel), and so on and so forth. And all these things are taken up in due order by a special committee of honorable and venerable Jews, who sit there all the livelong day until the wee hours of the night, abandoning wives and children and devoting themselves to all these matters, completely dedicating themselves, simply out of pure idealism, charging nothing for their efforts, not asking one kopek for their toil.

The issues often proceed from this committee, on to the bath-house, up to the top bench, where they are resolved once and for all at a plenary meeting of the town burghers, and their decisions are so firm and abiding that all the kings of East and West could stand on their heads and wave their feet—and they wouldn't accomplish a thing. The Turk has had quite a few close shaves at top-bench plenary sessions. If several worthy householders hadn't stood up for him, then goodness knows where he'd be today. Once, poor Rothschild nearly lost about ten or fifteen million rubles here. But God came to his rescue a couple of weeks later. Everybody on the top bench was, well "high," the place was jumping, the whisk brooms were going full swing—and all at once they granted him a clear profit of some one hundred fifty million rubles!

Most of the townspeople here in Moochville are terribly poor and horribly needy (may you be spared), but it must be said that they are cheerful paupers and merry beggars, bursting with faith and hope, if not charity. Should you, for instance, happen to ask a Moochville Jew how he earns his living, he'll stand there flustered, unable to answer. But then, a little later, he'll gather his wits and reply in all innocence: "Me, earn a living? Me? Why, there is a God, you know, and he doesn't abandon his creatures, he helps, and he's sure to keep on helping, you know."

"But just what do you do? Do you have some kind of a trade or a business?"

"Praise the Lord, Blessed Be His Name! As you see me here, I have a gift from God, a precious instrument, a singing voice, I'm a cantor on high holidays in this area, I perform circumcisions, and I do occasional work rolling holes in matzos—I'm a whiz at it—and every so often I arrange a marriage, yes indeed! As you see me here, I have a seat in the synagogue. Furthermore—but this is strictly between you, me, and the lamp post—I have a little shop,

356

where I can skim off a bit of cream, I own a goat that gives a lot of milk (knock on wood), and then not too far from here I've got a rich relative, whom I can also squeeze in bad times. And besides all these things, you know, the Good Lord watches over us like a father, and Jews are the merciful and the sons of the merciful, you know (knock on wood)...."

Furthermore, you have to credit the Moochvillers for being content with what God gives them and not being very fussy, Heaven forfend, when it comes to clothes and food. If the Sabbath kaftan, for instance, is shabby, grimy, sleazy, a little muddy and not so tidy, who cares, so long as it's satin and it shines. Now here and there the naked skin peeps out as through a sieve. But so what? What's the difference? Who's going to look? What about heels? Is that any worse than worn-out heels? Aren't heels human skin and flesh?...

A hunk of bread and potato soup—if you can get some—make a fine lunch. Not to mention a roll and pot roast on Friday—if only you can afford them—why, that's a royal treat, there's probably nothing better in the whole wide world. If these Jews were told about other dishes besides fish soup, roast, and carrot-or parsnip-stew, they'd think it highly peculiar and they would crack jokes and crack up, and split their sides as though the men telling them this were stupid and cracked and trying to make fools of them, to pull their legs and the wool over their eyes, claiming a cow had jumped over the moon and laid an egg.

A piece of carob on the Fifteenth of Shebat (Arbor Day)—now there's a fruit for you, sheer bliss! The sight of it conjures up the Holy Land. The Moochvillers turn their eyes to heaven and moan: "Oh...Lead us erect into our land, Merciful Father, our very own land, where the goats eat carob!..."

Once, somebody happened to bring a date into town—can you imagine—and you should have seen the way they came running to feast their eyes. Somebody else opened a Bible and demonstrated that tamar (date), was to be found in Scriptures: "Just think, the date, this very date, right here, comes from the Holy Land!..." Looking at the date, they were whisked away to the Holy Land. There they crossed the Jordan: There was the cave where our Patriarchs and Matriarchs are buried, there was Mother Rachel's tomb, there was the Wailing Wall. Now they were bathing in the hot springs of Tiberias, climbing up the Mount of Olives, gorging themselves on carob and dates, stuffing their pockets with Holy

Land soil. "Ahhh!" they moaned, and tears welled up in everybody's eyes.

"At that time," says Benjamin, "all of Moochville, big as it is, was in the Holy Land. People spoke fervently about the Messiah, it was already afternoon on God's Friday. The new police commissioner, who had only arrived a short while back, was running things with an iron hand. He had torn the skullcaps off a few heads, shorn an earlock, seized a couple of poor men without passports in a side street one night, and arrested a goat for eating a newly thatched roof. And he was the reason why the committee behind the stove kept talking about the 'Turkish Sultan,' by which of course they meant the Tsar. How much longer would the guardian angel of 'Ishmael' stay in power? They launched into their usual discussion about the Ten Lost Tribes and how happily they lived in those faraway lands, in glory, grandeur, and wealth. They pulled out the Red Jews, the Sons of Moses, with tall tales about their strength and what not. Naturally, Eldad the Danite also danced in their midst. Those days were mainly responsible for the voyage I undertook afterwards."

Benjamin used to be like a chick in its egg, or a worm in horse radish, or a pig in a poke. He thought that the world ended on the other side of Moochville. Life couldn't be sweeter or better than here.

"I believed," says Benjamin at some point, "that no one could be richer than our tenant farmer. What a house, and what furnishings: four brass candle-holders, a six-armed chandelier topped by an eagle, two pareve copper pots and about five copper pans, a cupboard full of pewter plates, and, of course, about a dozen spoons of German silver, two goblets of real silver, a spice box, a menorah, a turnip clock in a double case, and a heavy string of artificial pearls, no less than two cows, plus a heifer about to calve, two Sabbath gaberdines, and so many other wonderful things.

"I believed there was no sage like Ayzik-Dovid the son of Aaron-Yossel. Just think, people say that when he was young he actually dabbled in *fractions*. With a little more luck, he could have become a minister of state. Who, I wondered, could possible look more majestic or speak more gracefully than our Khaykl the Stutterer? Or who could be so skilled in healing, a physician making the dead come alive, as our barber-surgeon, who, according to rumor, mastered the art of medicine from a Gypsy descendant of the Egyptian sorcerers."

358

In short, life in his little shtetl was fine and dandy for Benjamin. He did live in poverty, he and his wife and children wore rags and tatters, to be sure. But did Adam and his wife in paradise know anything like shame for going naked and barefoot?

However, the wondrous fables about the Red Jews and the Ten Lost Tribes went deep into his heart, and from that time on he felt too confined in the town, he was drawn far, far, to distant places. He felt his heart pulling away, just as little children clutch out for the moon. At first blush, you may wonder what all those things had to do with it: a date, a police commissioner, a skullcap, an earlock, a poor Jew arrested in a side street late at night, a goat and a thatched roof. Yet the whole kit and kaboodle spawned a great change in Benjamin so that ultimately he blessed mankind with his renowned voyage. In the world, one often sees how big things come from little things—very big things at that! Thus, the farmer sowed his wheat and rye, which the miller ground, and some of it went into the distillery and became liquor, and some of the flour got into the hands of Gitl, the tavernkeeper, and she leavened it, kneaded it, rolled it, and made knishes, in addition to which the Phoenicians discovered how to make glass thousands of years ago, and thus came cups and beakers. Now all these little things led to those carousers in a lot of towns, those infamous, those fine, feathered creatures...

It could be that Benjamin had a spark of a globetrotter in him. But the spark would have died if the circumstances of the day and the tales of olden times had not puffed it up. And even if the spark had not dimmed out fully, Benjamin, but for those circumstances, would have had so little strength, that ultimately he would only have become a water-carrier or, at best, a drayman.

In my time, I've met a lot of draymen and carters who, I swear it, would have been able to become such travelers, like those who wander about today among Jews.... But that's all neither here nor there.

From then on, Benjamin eagerly devoted himself to Rabbah Bar Bar Hannah's sea voyages and desert travels. He also stumbled upon the book *Eldad the Danite,* the opus *The Travels of Benjamin,* by the explorer who journeyed to the ends of the earth seven hundred years ago, and the tome *In Praise of Jerusalem* with appendices, and the volume *Image of the World,* which, in seven tiny pages, contains all the Seven Wisdoms and relates amazing and miraculous things from the four corners of the earth and about its wild and wooly creatures. These books opened Benjamin's eyes and simply transformed him into a different person.

"Those wonderful stories," says Benjamin in his book, "got me so excited, 'Oh my! Oh my!' I so often shouted in my enthusiasm. 'If God would only help me see even one one-hundredth of all that with my own eyes!' My mind traveled far, far away...."

From that time on, Moochville became too narrow for him. He made up his mind to do anything he could to get out, just like a chick starting to peck and creep its way out of the egg into the bright world.

HOW BENJAMIN BECOMES A MARTYR
AND ZELDA AN ABANDONED WIFE

By nature, our Benjamin the Traveler was lily-livered. At night, he was afraid to leave the house, and he wouldn't have slept alone in a room for any amount of money in the world. Going away a bit from the town simply meant risking his life, for who knows what could happen—God forbid! And he was scared to death of even the tiniest puppy.

"Once," Benjamin tells us, "once—I remember it as though it were yesterday—it was a sweltering day in the month of Tammuz (July), and our rabbi, together with one of his disciples, went to have a dip in the creek outside of town. I and a few other boys, friends of mine, followed the rabbi with great respect; we were certain we could rely on the rabbi and not have anything bad happen to us (God willing) and return home safe and sound. Why, that's no small potatoes—a rabbi, whom all the world respects. And who's second to none! And whose honorific titles alone cover an entire page!...

"Now the rabbi, our protector, strode far ahead of us with great dignity, and while he was undressing, along came a peasant and sicked his dog on him. Our protector, half dead with fear, zoomed away, clutching (if you'll pardon me) his unbuttoned trousers in one hand and his round plush hat in the other. We boys were flabbergasted. For if the Leviathan is caught on a fishhook, then what should the poor minnows in the mud do? We girded our loins and, as swift as stags, we ran headlong, screaming for help,

360

shouting woefully, until we reached town, breathless, at top speed, with our hero. There was a tumult, a crowd, a clamor: 'Fire! Murder! Massacre!' No one knew what was happening!"

When Benjamin decided to travel to faraway lands, he resolved, first of all, to grow strong and cast off his fear. He forced himself to walk alone outside the town, even though it told on his health, for the terror made the poor man shed a lot of weight. His new behavior at home and in synagogue, his pale, dreamy face, and his absences outside of town for many hours, came as something of a surprise to everyone. Tongues wagged, and he was soon the talk of the shtetl.

Some people said: "He must be crazy, he's out of his mind. First of all," so they reasoned, "Benjamin was always a bit of a simpleton, he's got a screw loose in his head. Secondly, Moochville hasn't had a town lunatic for years, and we Jews have a tradition—How does it go in Hebrew: *Every town hath its sage and its lunatic....*Especially now, in this great heat! Why it's perfectly clear: He's insane."

Others, however (led by Ayzik-Dovid the son of Aaron-Yossel and Sarah-Zlatte) shrugged, shrugged, and shrugged again: "Now, it's true that Benjamin is something of a simpleton, indeed quite a simpleton at that. Yet that doesn't necessarily lead to the conclusion that he has actually gone insane. For even assuming he *has,* the question remains: Why precisely now and not earlier? After all, two years ago and also last summer, the heat waves were far worse. Now you may argue that, according to the traditional saying, Moochville is no worse than other towns; so then the questions remains: Why haven't we had a lunatic for several years? What do we do with the traditional saying?

"Well, as for that tradition, the answer would appear to be—our river. We have a rule, you know, that since time immemorial, our river has unerringly taken one person every year, and yet nevertheless, it has not taken a victim for several years now! On the contrary, during these past few years it has shrunken so greatly that in some places one can actually cross it without wetting one's toes.... But as for Benjamin?... Well, the question is still moot...."

Most people, however, including the women, said: "He must be carrying on with demons...with the devil.... Why else would he be wandering around in the dead of night, in the darkness? Why else would he be traipsing off for hours at a time? Why else would he be sleeping alone in the pantry?" Even Zelda, his very own wife, said that she could hear a knocking in the pantry at night, a banging, as if someone were walking about in there....

This conversation, as usual, rolled off behind the stove, and from there to the council on the top bench. No conclusion about Benjamin was reached. However, there was general agreement about forming a committee of several pious and prominent men, including the scribe, and they would visit all the homes in proper order, according to the register, and inspect and investigate every mezuzah. And since the council regarded this matter as a community issue, for the benefit of the town, they resolved that to subsidize the expenses that such a committee would entail, they would raise the tax on kosher meat....

There's an old saying in Moochville: "No matter what you talk about, it ends in death, and no matter what you discuss at a meeting, it ends with a higher meat tax." And indeed, that's virtually a law of nature, it can't be anything else. Nor does logic permit us to think otherwise, for it is written: "The end of a man is death, and the end of a Jew is—taxes!" Death and taxes are two laws of nature that we cannot abolish. Thus did the Eternal create the world, and the way He created it is good, this is the way it has to be. Only heretics would question it....

A short time later, Benjamin had an experience that brought him renown.

One hot day in summer, around twelve noon, when the sun was broiling, he walked out of town and came deeper and deeper into a forest, about three or four miles. In his pocket, he had his books, without which he wouldn't move an inch. He sat down in the woods, leaning against a tree, and was lost in thought. He had a great deal to think about. His mind soon drifted off to those lands at the ends of the earth. He trudged over mountains, through valleys, across deserts, and to all the places that were in his books. He followed in the footsteps of Alexander the Great, Eldad the Danite, and others. He saw the terrifying dragon, the lindworm, serpents, lizards, and all kinds of vermin and reptiles. He traveled all the way to the Red Jews and conversed with the Sons of Moses. Then he came to and back, safe and sound, and wondered just how and when he would finally undertake his voyage.

Meanwhile, as he was musing, night fell. He stood up, stretched his legs, and started for home. He walked and walked, but he was still in the woods. He slogged along for an hour, for two, three, four hours, no edge or end in sight. He roamed deeper into the

362

woods, where it was so dark that he couldn't see beyond the tip of his nose. All at once, a stormy wind swept up and a pelting rain came down. There was lightning and thunder, and the trees roared fearfully! Benjamin stopped, drenched to the skin, his teeth chattered with cold, wetness, and great dread. He imagined a bear would pounce on him, a lion, a leopard would tear him to pieces. There was the matool, which, according to *Image of the World,* is a huge towering monster with two long arms that can hurl down an elephant. Benjamin was terrified, poor thing, and he was starving to boot, he had eaten nothing all day but a buckwheat cake. In his great affliction, he began to say his evening prayer, and he prayed fervently, with all his heart.

God helped, and the dawn came. Our Benjamin went on rambling about aimlessly, he plodded and plodded until he finally managed to reach a narrow path. He trudged along this path for an hour or so until he suddenly heard a man's voice in the distance. Instead of feeling joy, he was all a-tremble (it shouldn't happen to our worst enemies). All he could think of was: brigands! He was so scared that he breathlessly doubled back. But then he promplty had second thoughts: "C'mon, Benjamin! You want to wander so far over seas and deserts teeming and crawling with horrible vermin, beasts of prey, and wild savages, and here you're scared at the very thought of bumping into a brigand! Oh my, Benjamin! You should really be ashamed of yourself, I swear! Did Alexander the Great of Macedonia run away like you? Did Alexander despair, like you, when he flew through the air on his eagle's back, and there was no meat left on the tip of the spear, the meat that the eagle nibbled at and flew higher to get at? No! Alexander the Great did not run away! Alexander the Great cut out a chunk of his own flesh and stuck it on the spear! Courage, Benjamin, take heart! God only wants to test you. If you pass the test, you'll do well and fare well! You'll be a valiant man and you'll deserve the privilege of having His Holy Name make your wish come true about reaching the Sons of Moses and talking to them about the Jews here at home. You can tell them every last detail about our Jews here, what they do and how they live. If you just overcome this ordeal and go back to where the voice came from, you'll conquer all fears and terrors. You'll be a wonderful person, a blessing, a paragon among the Children of Israel, and you'll bring honor upon all Moochville. Moochville and Macedonia—both cities will be equally famous throughout the world because of Alexander of Moochville and Benjamin of Macedonia!..."

Our Benjamin really did turn back, and he strode as courageously and confidently as a hero, until he saw before him: the brigand! It was a farmer riding on a wagon, which was filled with sacks and drawn by a pair of oxen.

"*Dobry dyen*! Good day!" said Benjamin in Ukrainian, as he drew nearer, his voice, suddenly changing—it had everything in it, wailing and pleading, as if to say: "Okay, do whatever you like with me!" And imploring: "Help, have pity on me, on my wife and children, the poor things!"

After speaking, or rather shouting and weeping his *dobry dyen,* Benjamin remained speechless, as if strangled. His head whirled, his eyes darkened, his legs buckled, and he fell down lifeless.

When he opened his eyes and came to, he found himself sprawling on a big sack of potatoes in the wagon and covered with a thick, coarse coat. At his head lay a trussed-up rooster, who glared at him askance with one eye and scratched him with his claws. At his feet, there were baskets of young garlic, onions, and other vegetables, and apparently eggs, for the chaff they were buried in kept flying into his face and covering his eyes. The farmer sat there, calmly smoking his pipe and calling "sop, heita, sop!" to the oxen every moment. The oxen barely stirred, and the wheels creaked wildly, each in a different voice.

Together, they melded into an ear-shattering creak-concert. The rooster didn't seem to care much for the creaking either, because every time the wheels turned, letting out a long, shrill squeal, the rooster dug his nails into Benjamin and emitted such a quick, angry cockadoodledoo that a muffled rattling came from the throat for a few seconds afterwards. Benjamin felt numb in every limb and he lay there dazed for a long, long time. He had gone through so much: terror, hunger, rain, and cold! He imagined a Turk had captured him in the desert and was carrying him off somewhere to sell him into slavery. "If only," thought Benjamin, "if only he sells me to a Jew, then at least there'll be some hope for me. But if I end up with a Gentile prince or even, God forbid, a princess, then I'll be doomed forever." The story of Joseph and Potiphar's wife flashed through his mind, and he felt so miserable that he let out a heavy groan.

Upon hearing Benjamin's groan, the farmer turned around, then shifted closer to him, and asked in Ukrainian:

"Well, my li'l Jew, how are ya? Feelin' better?"

Benjamin's head had cleared a bit and he remembered everything that had happened to him. But still, he found his predicament very serious. He didn't know a word of the farmer's language, so what could he do? How could he answer him? How could he inquire and find out exactly where the man was taking him?

Benjamin tried to sit up. But it was no use. His legs ached horribly.

"Ya feelin' better?" the farmer asked again, and in the same breath he shouted at his oxen: "Sop, heita, sop!"

"Betta, yes, legs, legs, oh, oh!" poor Benjamin tried to speak the goyish language as best he could and pointed at his legs.

"Where ya from, my little Jew?"

"Wheyafrom?!" Benjamin repeated in a cantorial warble. "Me, Ben, Benjamin, from Moochville."

"Oh, so you're from Moochville? Then why did you glare at me like I was crazy?! Well, maybe *you're* crazy, goddamn it! Sop, heita, sop!"

"Me, you see, tell you at start, me Benjamin, from Moochville!" answered Benjamin with a woebegone face, raising his arms and pleading: "In Moochville, wife, give schnapps, shabbes roll, and thank you good."

The farmer apparently got Benjamin's drift.

"Okay, little Jew!" he cried, sat down in his seat facing the oxen and called: "Sop, heita!"

A couple of hours later, the wagon rumbled into the marketplace of Moochville. Women and men crowded around with various questions.

One man yelled: "Hey, whattaya want for the rooster? For the onions?"

Another asked: "Ya got eggs, potatoes?"

A question shot out of the crowd: "Listen, did you see a Jew on the way here? One of our people, Benjamin, has been missing since yesterday!"

And before the farmer even had a chance to reply, the women swarmed all over his wagon like locusts, pulled away the coat, and then shouted in unison:

"Benjamin!...He's here! Tsippe-Kroina, Bathsheba-Braindl, run straight over to Zelda, tell her the good news! Her lost husband's been found! She's not abandoned after all!"

There was a tumult, more people came running, all Moochville was on the move, everybody and his uncle dashed over to look at Benjamin. They showered him with comments, questions, jokes, they said they'd been hunting for him, searching for him all day and night, they'd already decided that he was martyred and his wife abandoned.

Suddenly, in the midst of the hubbub, his wife came running up, weeping. She wrung her hands at the sight of her one and only sprawling there pale and lifeless, unable to move a limb. The poor woman didn't know what to do: Should she curse him, pour out her heavy, bitter heart to him, or should she show him her joy, her delight that God had assisted her, her, the abandoned wife?

A few minutes later, Benjamin, lying on the sack of potatoes, was taken home across the marketplace in a grand parade. All the people of Moochville, young and old, paid homage to him, no one needed to be asked twice, and they escorted him, shouting and yelling: "Martyr! Martyr! Martyr!"

From that moment on, the name "Martyr" remained with Benjamin forever. He was known as Benjamin the Martyr and his wife as Zelda the Widow.

The town healer visited Benjamin that very same day and helped with all possible remedies. He applied leeches and cupping glasses, shaved the patient's head, and told him, upon leaving, that after all these remedies he would recover, God willing, and would be able to go to synagogue the very next day—if he had the strength—and thank the Good Lord for escaping death.

HOW BENJAMIN HITCHED UP WITH
SENDER THE HOUSEWIFE

This ordeal, which was so harrowing for Benjamin, which caused so much grief for his wife and so much gossip in town, behind the stove, and on the top bench, should—one might think—have forever dislodged Benjamin's plan of traveling to distant places. But far from it! In a pig's eye! The plan was lodged more firmly than ever before. From that point on, Benjamin felt great esteem for himself as an experienced man who has gone through a great deal in his life. He appreciated himself tenfold for his strength and bravery in enduring so many trials and vanquishing his cowardice. He began seeing himself as a hero, a philosopher, an initiate in all the Seven Wisdoms (or as much of them as is contained in *Image of the World*), a wise man who had read more than his fill of such books and knew what was happening all over the earth. He began to understand himself now and pity himself—that he, a man like him, poor thing, should be like a rose among thorns. Where? In Moochville, some backwater town, among ignorant people, who grasp nothing, know nothing about their own lives! The jokes and rumors circulating about him were what really egged him on to travel. He yearned to get out of Moochville as quickly as possible. "If only I can do it," he kept thinking, "If only I can travel there, far away, and come back safe and sound with salvations and consolations for Jews, respected and renowned throughout the world, then all Moochville will realize who Benjamin is, and what a great man he is!..."

Meanwhile, only minor obstacles kept Benjamin from his journey. First of all, where could he get the money? He never had a kopek in his pocket. He always sat idly in synagogue, and his missus was a "woman of valor," the breadwinner, for she owned a little stand, which she had put up soon after they had moved from her parents' home. But, I ask you, how much was the little shop really worth? If she hadn't knitted socks, if she hadn't plucked feathers in winter till late at night, if she hadn't rendered fat to sell at Passover, if she hadn't gotten occasional bargains on market days from friendly peasants—then they wouldn't have had enough to keep body and soul together.

Should Benjamin pawn any of the household belongings? But

367

what was there really? A couple of brass candlesticks, which Zelda had inherited from her parents. She used them for the Sabbath candles, was forever polishing them, and enjoyed them so much. She had no jewelry except for a silver ring set with a pearl from her mother's headband, and she kept the ring locked up, wearing it only for major celebrations and on congratulatory visits. Should Benjamin sell any of his own clothes? But all he owned was a satin gaberdine for the Sabbath, which he still had from his wedding; it was worn and tattered in front and in back, and the yellow lining showed through in places. True, he also had a sheepskin over-coat—if one could call it that, for want of a better name! The collar wasn't even lined. At the wedding, his father (long may he live!) had said don't spare the collar, make it long and generous, and line it for now on top with a piece of lining left over from the overcoat; and he had promised that once the rest of the dowry was paid, he would line the entire coat and trim the collar with squirrel fur. But the rest of the dowry had never come, and so the coat and the collar remained as they were to this very day....

In addition to the money problem, Benjamin just didn't know how to get away from his home.

Could he discuss the journey with his wife and tell her every-thing in detail? God forbid and heaven forfend? She would scream and rage and weep and plead and she would certainly think he'd lost his mind, for how can a woman be smart enough to under-stand such matters? A wife may be a "woman of valor," but she's still a mere woman for all that. The lowliest man has more intelli-gence in his little finger than the finest and smartest female could ever possibly have in her head....

Should he sneak off without saying good-bye? That would be slightly unpleasant, the kind of thing a Litvak Jew might do. Then again, should he just remain home and forget about traveling? That was absolutely impossible. It was nothing less than suicide.

The journey had become second nature for Benjamin, like praying three times daily. And so he had to keep thinking about the journey at every moment of the day. And he couldn't shake it off even when he slept, he kept dreaming about it all night long. It took root deep in his heart and grabbed hold of his eyes and ears so that he no longer saw or heard the things in front of him; he could see and hear only what was happening far, far away, in those distant lands. Often, while talking with someone, he would suddenly throw in: India, Sambatyon, Antikuda, lindworm, dragon, donkey, mule, carob, manna, Turk, Tartar, brigand, and similar words.

The journey had to be taken, but what about the obstacles? Benjamin was all at sea. He felt he needed someone to talk to about the whole thing.

And there dwelt a man in the city of Moochville and his name was called Sender—he was named after his great-grandfather—*and this Sender was of a simple mind*—that is to say, he was plain, unlearned, sort of ignorant. In the synagogue, his pew was behind the pulpit, and that alone was the best sign that he didn't belong to the Moochville elite, the upper crust, the cream. When the men talked in synagogue or elsewhere, he would usually listen quietly like an outsider. If ever he did put in a word, it would provoke great mirth. Not because it was particularly witty or original, but simply because any word from his lips made people laugh, even though the poor man said it quite naively, not intending to make anyone laugh. On the contrary: When people laughed, his eyes would gape and he wondered why they were laughing. He never resented the mirth, for he was humble and good-natured, like a gentle cow, and he didn't even realize there was anything to resent. If somebody was laughing, well, okay, let him laugh, so long as he enjoyed it.

Still, we have to admit that Sender's comments occasionally harbored a bright idea, even though he didn't realize it and was speaking quite naively. People liked to play jokes on him. On the Ninth of Ab, the fast for the destruction of the Temple, Jews like to throw burrs at each other, and most of the burrs got ensnarled in his earlocks. During the night of the great Hosanna, the seventh day of the feast of Tabernacles, when everyone stays awake, most of the pillows that were thrown around landed on his head. In contrast, he received the smallest share of buckwheat crackers and liquor on religious occasions or liquor simply for no special occasion.

In short, Sender was the scapegoat any place and any time. Now, by nature, Sender wasn't opinionated, like other people. If a man said one thing, that was all right with Sender. He would let the man have his way, not to belittle his own way so that the other man would belittle his own way for Sender's way. Sender just simply went along with him, that was all.

"Why should I care?" he would say. "Why should I worry? If you say so, then it's okay, it's fine with me."

Among boys, Sender was a boy. He would often hang around

with them, talk to them, play with them, and enjoy himself. When he was with them, Sender was truly a docile animal, he allowed the children to come up and ride him and scratch him under the chin. The pranksters would climb on his head and pull his beard. Sometimes passers-by would be annoyed at this and shout:

"Mind your manners, you scoundrels! Have respect for an adult, a man with a beard! Why are you pulling his beard out!?"

"It's all right, it's all right," Sender would say. "I don't mind. I don't care. So let them scratch me."

Poor Sender's home life was no bed of roses. His wife wore the breeches, and he had a terrible, horrible time with her. She ruled with a reign of terror and occasional punches, and the poor wretch had to put up with it. Just before a holiday, she would tie a cloth around his beard and make him whitewash the house. He would peel potatoes for her, roll and slice noodles, stuff the gefilte fish, bring in firewood, put it in the stove, and light the fire—just like a housewife. That was why people nicknamed him Sender the Housewife.

Now it was this man, Sender the Housewife, whom our Benjamin selected to pour out his heart to: Sender would help him figure things out. What was the reason? Why Sender of all people? Well, Benjamin had always been fond of him. There was a lot he liked about him, they felt the same way about a number of things, and Benjamin often had a wonderful time talking to him. Perhaps Benjamin also counted on the fact that Sender never insisted on getting his way: Sender would accept Benjamin's idea and go along with everything he said. And if Sender were ever to dig in his heels on any points, well, then Benjamin would win him over with God's help and with his own glib tongue.

And it came to pass that when Benjamin did come unto Sender, he did find him in the act of removing the exteriors of tubers— Sender was peeling potatoes—on the dairy bench. One cheek was blazing red and his left eye was swollen blue with a scratch underneath as though fingernails had torn his face. He sat there, numb, dismal, gloomy, like a young wife whose husband has deserted her and vanished overseas, or at least slapped her face....

Sender's wife was not at home.

"Good morning, Sender! Why are you so gloomy?" asked Benjamin, entering and pointing at Sender's cheek? "Is she at it again? Where is your lady Cossack?"

"At the market."

"Great!" Benjamin almost shouted for joy. "Put down your

potatoes, old friend, and come into the alcove with me. No one's there, right? I don't need any chaperon with you now, I want to tell you what's on my mind. I can't hold back anymore, I'm seething inside. Hurry, Sender, hurry! She might come and ruin everything before we're done!"

"Fine with me! You want me to hurry, so I'll hurry. It's okay with me!" exclaimed Sender and hurried into the alcove.

"Sender," Benjamin started off, "tell me, do you know what's beyond Moochville?"

"Sure, I know. Pickafite Inn. You can get a good glass of vodka there!"

"Don't be an idiot. I mean further on, a lot further."

"Further than Pickafite Inn?" Sender exclaimed in surprise. "Further? I don't know. Do you know, Benjamin?"

"Do I know? How can you ask! Do I ever know! That's where the world begins," Benjamin said ecstatically, like Columbus discovering America.

"But where is 'there'?"

"There, there," Benjamin was ablaze. "The dragon! The lindworm!"

"The lindworm that Solomon used to cut the stones for the Temple?" Sender asked timidly.

"Yes, Sender, yes, yes. In the Holy Land. In those places.... Would you like to go there?"

"Would you?"

"What a question! I *do* want to go there, and soon I *will* be there!"

"I'm envious, Benjamin. You'll be eating carob and dates to your heart's content. Oh me!"

"You can eat them too, Sender. You have as much right to be in the Holy Land as me."

"I do have the right. But how can we get there? The Turk's in the Holy Land."

"There's a way, Sender, there's a way. Listen, do you know anything about the Red Jews?"

"I've heard enough stories about them behind the stove. But I don't know exactly where they live or how to get to them. If I knew, I'd probably tell you. Why not? It's okay with me."

"Ha! And *I* know, you see," Benjamin said proudly, drawing *In Praise of Jerusalem* out of his pocket. "Just look at what's written here. I'll read it to you:

"'When I arriv'd in Bruti,' that's what it says, 'I found four Jews from Babylon. I spoke with one of them, who understood the Holy Tongue and whose Name was Rabbi Moses, and he told me very true Stories about the River Sambatyon, which he had heard from Ishmaelites who had seen it, and there, he said, dwelt the sons of Moses.'

"And it goes on: 'According to what the Head of the Jewish Community told me: Some thirty years ago, a Man of the Tribe of Simeon had stay'd with him and he told him that there were four Tribes where he dwelt. One of them was the Tribe of Issachar, and they only study the Torah, and a Man of this Tribe is King over all the Tribes!'

"Now listen to what it says in this book, *The Travels of Benjamin*: 'From there it is a Journey of a Score of Days to the Nisbon Mountains, which are on the River Gozan. And in the Nisbon Mountains dwell four Tribes: the Tribe of Dan, the Tribe of Zebulun, the Tribe of Asher, and the Tribe of Naphtali. They have Countries and Cities in the Mountains. On one side, they are encompass'd by the River Gozan. They are not afflicted with the Yoke of the Nations, only a King rules over them, and his Name is Joseph Amarekla ha-Levi. And they have a Covenant with the infidel Turks.' Besides that, there are so many things recorded about the Rachiabites in the land of Tema, they have a Jewish king and they fast and always pray to God for the Exiles of Israel. Well, what do you think, Sender? What would they say, old friend, if they suddenly saw me, their brother Benjamin of Moochville, coming to visit them? Ha, what do you think?"

"They'd be absolutely thrilled, I tell you, Benjamin. What a guest! What a welcome guest! Everyone will invite you home for a meal. Probably even King Amarekla himself. Give them all my best regards. If I could, I swear, I would go along with you myself."

"Ha!" said Benjamin, ablaze with a new thought that popped into his head. "Ha! Sender, my old friend! What if you *did* go with me on the journey? Don't be a fool, I swear, it's the chance of a lifetime. I'm going alone and I'll take you too. It'll be more fun if I have someone with me, Sender. And if I become king there— stranger things have happened—I swear I'll make you viceroy. Let's shake on it.... Why should you sit here, you poor man, and go through the worst sufferings of Exile because of your wife—that shrew. Just take a look at your cheek, Sender. You have a dark and dismal life with her. C'mon, Sender, travel with me. You won't regret it, I promise you."

"Well," said Sender, "if that's what you want, that's what I'll do. And as for her? Why, I'd be an idiot telling her where I'm off to."

"Sender, my dearest friend, let me kiss you," cried Benjamin, overjoyed, and he lovingly threw his arms around Sender the Housewife. "Friend of my bosom, with just one word you've solved a dilemma, a big dilemma. I agree with you: As for her? I mean *my* wife: Who cares! But there's one other problem? Where are we going to get the money?"

"Money? Do you want to buy new clothes or turn your coat? Listen, if you want my opinion, it's really not necessary. In fact, on the road, it's better to wear old clothes. Once we're there, we'll probably get beautiful new coats."

"Yes, that's true. Once I'm there, my worries'll be over. But while we're traveling, we'll need money just for food."

"What do you mean, for food, Benjamin? Are you gonna take along a whole kitchen? What for? Aren't there taverns and homes along the way?"

"I don't understand what you mean, Sender," cried Benjamin puzzled.

"I mean," Sender answered naively, "as long as there are homes, we can go begging. What do all other Jews do? Nowadays, some Jews go begging to other houses, and then those people go begging to still other houses. That's the way it is with Jews.... Just an interest-free loan...."

"Dammit, you're right," said Benjamin joyfully. "You've opened my eyes. If that's the way it is, then, thank the Lord, I'm totally prepared and I've got everything I need. We can leave tomorrow, at the crack of dawn, when the town's still asleep. It's no good wasting time, dammit. Do you agree?"

"If you wanna go tommorrow, then it's okay with me. I don't care."

"So listen, Sender. Tomorrow, at the crack of dawn, I'm going to sneak out of the house, very quietly. I'll wait for you by the abandoned windmill. Don't forget, Sender, tomorrow morning, at the crack of dawn, you're to come out there. Don't forget," Benjamin repeated and started for the door.

"Wait a moment, Benjamin, just wait!" said Sender, rummaging in the breast pocket of his jacket. He finally fished out an old, sweaty piece of leather, bound crisscross with strings and some twenty knots. "Look, Benjamin! I managed to save this money behind my wife's back all the years we've been married. It'll be useful for us at the start, won't it?"

"Sender, you deserve to be hugged and kissed a thousand times!" Benjamin shouted, grabbing hold of Sender the Housewife.

"Goddamn your eyes! Just look at the love birds! Hugging and kissing, and there's a goat in the house eating up the potatoes! May the worms eat your body!" screeched a voice.

The screeching voice was Sender's better half. She stood there, blazing with fury, one hand pointing at the goat and the other hand beckoning to Sender. With his head hanging, Sender very, very slowly inched over to her like a naughty child about to be whipped.

"Be strong, friend of my bosom, this is the last time....Just don't forget tomorrow," Benjamin whispered into Sender's ear and stole out like a kitten.

INTRODUCTION TO

Shem and Japheth on the Train

Published in 1890 as "Shem Veyefet Ba-agole," this story is the only one in this collection which is translated from the Hebrew instead of from the Yiddish. Since there does not as yet exist an English translation of the Yiddish version ("Shem un Yofos in a Vagon"), we made an exception of it because of what seemed to us its unusual interest and worth.

As in almost all the other stories by Abramovitsh, we begin in the presence of Mendele-the-Book-Peddler. This time, however, instead of being perched atop his wagon and urging his nag to pull yet another *vyorst* or so to the next shtetl, Mendele is riding the train, third class, of course, along with other poor Jews of the region.

The story takes place, as Robert Alter tells us *(Modern Hebrew Literature,* 1975), during the time when Bismarck was chancellor of Germany (1871-1890), when both Jews and non-German nationals were being expelled from the newly created German imperial state. It was also a time when, as Alter puts it, "age-old Gentile hostility toward Jews took a new form: a purportedly scientific theory of the relations between races and the inherent characteristics of the different races that went under the name of anti-semitism."

This story, then, is about anti-semitism (as are all the stories in this book, in a way), but it is also about how Jew and Gentile can learn to live together and even love one another.

According to Jewish tradition, the biblical Japheth represents the Greeks, and thus, by extension, all of Christian Europe; Shem (the name is the origin of the word *Semite*), on the other hand, traditionally stands as the ancient ancestor of the Jews.

Again, according to Alter, the title of the story "involves a verse from Genesis (9:27): 'God shall enlarge Japheth and he shall dwell in the tents of Shem.'" This verse contains within it the plot of this story—a story full of irony, bitterness, and hope.

Shem and Japheth on the Train

Translated by Walter Lever

There, in haste and confusion, our brethren press on, with bundles of every size and shape in their hands and on their shoulders; women too, encumbered with pillows and bolsters and wailing infants; all jostling one another as they perilously hoist themselves up the ladder to the third-class compartments, where a fresh battle will be fought for places in the congested train. And I, Mendele the Bookseller, burdened with my goods and chattels, join manfully in the fray. I climb, stoop, and jostle my way through as one of the crowd. Yet, while we Jews hustle and work ourselves into a state of frenzied irritability, lest, Heaven forbid, someone should get ahead of us in the crush, and while we gaze beseechingly upon the railway employees, as if the fact that we are traveling at all indicates an unrequited act of grace on their part—all this while, the Gentile passengers are strolling up and down the hallway in front of the station with their luggage and waiting until the bell rings for a second or even a third time, when they will mount the train at leisure, and each proceed to his appointed place.

After the hubbub outside, there is a renewed scramble for seats. Some lucky ones find places straightaway; others trail up and down in a fruitless quest. A stout, loquacious female is thrust forward, pushing baskets and bags ahead of her. She trips over them and falls headlong. Lying there, she looks for all the world like a goose bought in the market before Passover, after it has been taken home and the strap untied from its legs. It collapses on the floor with its tail and wings outspread, gazing up in terror, and gasping for air. Now, another woman appears in the doorway, clutching her bedding and bits of old clothes, shrilly urging her children to bustle along behind. This is the woman it has pleased the Lord to designate as my traveling companion, together with her husband and her numerous offspring: it is in their compartment that I shall sit, wedged in with the maximum of discomfort between bundles of household goods and bedding that mount up on either side.

All this business of a railway journey is new to me. Never in my life have I experienced it, and I am surprised at everything I see. My place is so cramped that I am unable to stir, but can only sit cooped up and perspiring. Formerly, when I used to travel by coach through all the lands of Jewry, I did not mind being hemmed in by bundles of my own books and—needless to say—it was a special joy to perspire. (Everyone knows this who has chanced to be on the road in the month of Tammuz, when the blessed Lord puts forth such insufferable heat at noon that no bird flies, no ox lows to his fellow in the stall, the forest does not stir, the very leaves on the trees cease their whispering: then, when the world is hushed and mute, one slumps back in the carriage seat and enjoys, as I have done, the most timely sweating of all.) But now it is quite otherwise: perspiration brings no solace, and the constriction only saps my strength. I begin to think that for my sins my innate Jewish character has somehow been transformed, so that I am no longer able to appreciate these same two privileges of the Seed of Abraham.

But the treatment the railway officials accord to the passengers, and the passengers to one another, together with the experiences I have just undergone, combine to persuade me that the change is not in my own disposition, but in this strange mode of travel. For a coach journey in former times was quite unlike today's journeys by train. Then a man was his own master and free to choose for himself. Even if the travelers were crowded in, two facing two with one extra for makeweight, so that their legs were jammed together like herrings in a barrel—well, they could always get out and take a walk, there was nothing to stop them, and they had the world at their feet. Indeed, this very fact that they had a free choice would mitigate their discomfort, so that their afflictions became, as it were, the trials of love. But in the train there is no feeling of independence. One is like a prisoner, without a moment's respite from durance vile. And that, of course, is why this perspiring is so unpleasant: for an imposed sweat is altogether unlike the majestic sweating of a free man. Consider, moreover, that the passengers in a coach are set apart from the common populace; they make up a little colony, a corporate entity of their own. Time flows on for them, evening and morning, one day . . . a second day . . . a

378

third. . . . There is world enough and time to meditate on all things, to satisfy every desire in the course of their travels. The sky is a tent over their heads, the earth spreads its bounty before them, they watch the glorious pageant of God's creation, they rejoice in its variety—yes, and if sometimes the coach is upset, this is not so bad either: for the earth like a kindly mother merely receives her children back into her lap. But in contrast the railway train is like a whole city in motion, with its multitude and its uproar, its population split into classes and sects, who carry with them their hatred and envy, their bickerings and rivalries and petty deals. Such passengers may traverse the whole world without regard to the grandeur of nature, the beauty of mountains and plains, and all the handiwork of God . . . .

The guard blew his whistle and the train started. Our people were now able to relax. They began to take notice of one another, and to make their inquiries as to each man's trade, and his occupation, and whence he came, and whither he was heading; as is right and natural for our people. Strangers fraternized and addressed one another by their first names, as if they had been friends since childhood. And so Khayim opened the goodly treasures of his knapsack and produced a bottle of wine, drank from it and passed it on to Shmuel while Shmuel broke off a piece of his loaf for Khayim, offering it with some cucumber and onion from his bag, and so they feasted together. In the same spirit Shmerl slipped a sum of money to Anshl with the request that he be so good as to pass it on to an in-law whose business was in the town where Anshl would be staying; and Rivn gave documents and bills to Shimen for Levi the produce-dealer; and the whole compartment became a huckster's mart. We of Israel are preoccupied with the problems of making a living; no wonder that the winds of petty commerce raged mightily. My own business instincts awoke too, and I bethought me of trying to sell some books. But I was obliged to abandon this project. My belongings were submerged in a great wave of other people's possessions, and it would have been impossible to salvage them save by very strenuous effort; in fact, cooped up as I was, this was altogether beyond my power. So I continued to sit in idleness perched on the edge of the seat, contemplating without relish the passengers who shared my compartment.

An unattractive-looking woman with a bleak nose faced me, propped up on a large pillow, from which feathers were constantly

379

escaping and floating out into the world. Her eyes were timid, her lips dry and compressed, and her whole countenance shriveled like a baked apple. Since her arrival she had not had a moment's rest from her children, who pestered her continually with their questions and bickerings. The three smaller ones kept exchanging places and disturbing her as they bobbed up and down. In her lap a baby was drowsing now, after having wailed for some time; it snored in its sleep; a tear still stood on its cheek, which seemed utterly bloodless. And beside me sat her husband: a tall, spare man, his back somewhat bowed, with a lean neck, a long nose, and a stunted beard. Sorrow lurked in his eyes, and his lips carried the suggestion of a bitter smile. To the right of him his grown-up daughter sat in a kind of sad trance, with two small girls leaning against her.

I sinned in my heart, I must confess, for I resented these companions from the start of the journey. Their presence irked me, and I silently cursed my ill luck that had placed me in the same compartment with such odd and vexatious folk. But as I considered them more carefully I began to view them in a new light. Their dress, their appearance, their wan expression, testified to extreme poverty and roused my pity. The mother's intermittent sighs moved me; and even more, the excessively humble attempts of the father and children to avoid getting in my way. But what touched me most deeply was the sight of the infant, who had fallen asleep out of sheer weakness, after pouring out his woes on his mother's lap. All this led me to paint in my fancy a grim enough picture of the life of that poor family. My imagination drew me into further speculations as to the many families among our people in a similar plight, who bear in silence their poverty and distress. I was sunk in these reflections when one of the children began to plead with his mother for some thing to eat. To soothe him she answered:

See, Yankele, it's still daylight: now isn't the time for food; you must wait a bit longer!"

"Hush, Yankele," added his father, crooking his lips into a smile, "Bismarck made rules against eating."

"Is your child ill, then?" I asked the father in a gentle, sympathetic tone, for I felt a strong urge now to enter into speech with him.

"I'll? God forbid! He's perfectly sound in wind and limb. I wish I had the weight in gold of the food he can put down at any time of the day!"

"Then who is this Bismarck of yours, who makes rules to keep a healthy boy from eating?" I was all ready for a heated polemic against this man.

"Don't you know who Bismarck is? I'm astonished!"

"And what if I don't? He's some doctor, to be sure; and in Kisalon, my hometown, let me tell you, there are hundreds of smart doctors and bloodletters of his type. We have a common saying, that no man, if he followed the doctor's orders, would live out his year."

I laughed across at this man and his daughters, and they smiled back tolerantly. Taking this as a mark of their approval, and an encouragement to further eloquence, I laughed again in my complacency, and was about to reveal further depths of wisdom and discernment in a series of anecdotes about the physicians of my town, when the ticket inspector, accompanied by other railway employees, entered our compartment, and the conversation came to a halt.

After these had departed without incident, and such folk as had made themselves scarce during the visit had popped up again (in the usual way) from under the benches, the pillows and other paraphernalia were heaped up once more. Suddenly a strange individual appeared from beneath the seat opposite me. He was bareheaded and dressed in outlandish Gentile fashion, with ragged trousers and a Polish cape that fastened with brass hooks across the chest and fell short to the knees. His face was chalk-white, his cheeks sunken, and his moustache formed thin fringes whose ends dropped like lizards' tails from the sides of his mouth. As he stood up on his feet he belched, yawned and stretched himself, like a man who has just come out of his sleep. All my companions, old and young, greeted him in the most friendly fashion, and he in turn gazed smilingly upon them. For my part I was quite amazed, and could not explain to myself the connection between this Pole and the poor family with whom I was traveling, so Jewish in every detail. Many conjectures came into my head, of which the most probable seemed to be that the stranger was that Bismarck of whom my neighbors had already spoken. But at once I found that I was mistaken, for the woman now addressed him by name, in a mixture of Polish and Yiddish:

"Why are you standing, Panie Przecszwinczicki? Sit down here in our Itsik's place, and Itsikl will go over and sit in with his father."

"Please don't put yourselves out for me, Khaye dear," answered the man with the seventeen-lettered name. "I can take Itsik on my knee. Reb Moyshe, I see, has already too many children squeezed in with him on one seat." He spoke the same queer mixture of Polish and Yiddish.

"Did you sleep sweetly under the bench, Panie Japheth?" asked Reb Moyshe with a smile of affection. "You see now, that I gave you good advice, and you followed my instructions perfectly! Lucky fellow! As for me, after the next stop it will be *my* turn to lie under the luggage."

"Take me on your knee too, Reb Japheth!" begged Yankele; and he went over and seated himself together with Itsikl, while the stranger affectionately clasped them both.

I gaped at Reb Moyshe, quite unable to grasp the situation, but he seemed to read my thoughts, and turning to me said:

"This man you see before you is of pure Polish stock, and his birthplace is a little town in Poland."

"Why do you call him Japheth, then?"

"Because his real name, Przecsczwinczicki, is such a jaw-breaker. And besides, the name Japheth fits him perfectly, and nowadays he well deserves it."

"Your explanation, I'm afraid, only confuses me the more. You are like those exegetes who twist their texts to make them the more cryptic to the ordinary man. Tell me your story, please; but let it be a connected account, and not cut up in bits and snippets."

"Not cut up! I am a tailor by trade, and the tailor's way is to stitch the pieces of his cloth together with a needle. But when he has to deal with words, he cuts up the seams of the narrative, patches on digressions, and tears his story into remnants. All the same, I shall try, so far as I am able, to do as you ask . . . . But I have forgotten my manners. Let me say first, in common politeness, *Sholem Aleykhem*, my dear sir, and may I have the pleasure of knowing your name?"

Reb Moyshe greeted me, after the fashion of our people, by rising a little from his seat, and I returned his greeting (doing my best to budge myself likewise) and informed him of my name and occupation.

Moyshe the Tailor was by nature one of those "happy paupers" of whom we have many in our midst. Poverty, it seems, is unable to break their spirits; and its train of afflictions does not lead them to rail, like melancholiacs, at the ways of the world. The notion is fixed in their minds that they have received their deserts, and that it is their inexorable lot to pass their years in squalor and privation: therefore it is not for them to desire, or even to depict in their fancy, those pleasures of life which were created for their more fortunate superiors. They bow their heads submissively before storms, and when they recount their troubles, they spice the story with a touch of humor and seem to deride even themselves.

"I take it," Reb Moyshe began, "that you are not contemplating any marriage negotiations, so there is no need for me to trace my pedigree back to Father Abraham, or to relate the entire history of my life since the day I was born. It is enough to say that my story is a familiar one, and repeats the experience of our race. So I shall pass over many things which may be taken for granted and avoid all needless ornamentation.

"I was born in Lithuania. As a young man I migrated to Prussia, where for many years I supported myself and my wife, who is also a Lithuanian, together with our children, by the work of my trade. All this time I and my family were Jews. I plied my needle and we ate our bread without fear. True it is that the title 'Jew' brought me no great honors, and did not raise me to the rank of princes and peers. Yet it was not exactly held to be a crime, and did not prevent me from earning a living of sorts . . . ."

"What is all this?" I cried in dismay. "Do you mean that now you are *not* a Jew?"

"I am a Jew no longer, for there are no Jews left anymore," answered the tailor with a smile. "It seems you do not know what age we are living in."

"How can I fail to know? Look, here is my calendar, which I have had printed at my own initiative and cost. Today is Wednesday, this week's portion of the Law is about Korah, it is the year five thousand six hundred and forty—by the full reckoning." I recounted the number of years and days back to the creation of the world in a high voice and all in one breath. And taking out one of the little calendars I carry in my breast pocket, I flourished it in front of Reb Moyshe, implying by this that I could sell him a copy.

"But the Germans think otherwise," said Reb Moyshe quietly. "The Germans, who perform miracles of science, have turned the clock back a thousand generations, so that all of us at this day are living in the time of the Flood. Nowadays they call the Jew "Shem," and the Gentile "Japheth." With the return of Shem and Japheth the customs of that far-off age have returned too, and the earth is filled with violence. The non-Semites are hostile toward the Semites; they discover imaginary wrongs, and in particular—do you know what?—in the matter of eating and drinking! For in this the Semites behave like other human beings, and such conduct is regarded as tantamount to treason and theft. Others find fault with the sons of Shem because they reproduce their kind—if you will pardon the phrase—like other men. At first these reactionaries were derided by their neighbors, and held to be madmen, but the madder they became, the more followers they found, until this lunacy struck root in the minds of people and rulers alike, and seemed to be a right and proper attitude. As the animosity spread, many hardships befell us daily, until their great Count Bismarck arose and decreed the expulsion of all the sons of Shem who were not of German nationality. And so thousands of unfortunate people were deprived of their living and turned into a helpless rabble. As for my dear Yankele," he ended with a bitter smile, "this stubborn child refuses to obey the decrees of his rulers. He is hungry, so he will cry for bread. He has a stomach and wants to fill it—the wicked rebel!"

"So now you have come from Prussia?" I asked.

"It is nine months since we left Prussia, just as it is nine months since this child of our old age was born," he replied, pointing to the baby asleep in his mother's lap. "When the police came to expel us, my wife Khaye was brought to bed of our Leyzerke here. They informed me that I was required to leave the state at once. I told them that my wife was in childbirth, and I begged them to grant us three months' stay until she had recovered and the summer season had come round. But the police gave me visible proofs—using the strong arm of the law, not to mention its fists, that the exigency of driving Jews across the frontier is so great that it takes precedence over care for human life, and that even to be naked and barefoot in the rain, to be dangerously ill or on the point of death, does not exempt one from this decree. When I saw that my plea was rejected and they had the law on their side, I took my staff in my hand, slung my knapsack over my shoulder, and we all went forth, on a cold day of falling snow. Thus we left the town I had lived in from the time of my youth until now when I am in the years of decline. The police escorted us with a guard of honor, for we Israelites are, after all, the sons of kings!

"And so," he went on, "Reb Moyshe the Tailor and his family went on their travels, from town to town, through all the lands of the Exile. Our clothes wore out, we were left without money or possessions, there was not a coin in our pockets save what came to us in the way of charity from our own people. But unfortunately our Jewish poor, who wander in search of bread, are all too numerous. They come from all points of the compass, from Prussia and Yemen, from Persia and Morocco, and throng the gates of the charitable, so that there are not enough alms to go round, and the local poor must have priority over strangers. Thus we wandered long, I and my dependents, exhausting ourselves in the search for a resting place but finding none. And at this time I have come from Galicia."

Profoundly affected by this story, I sat staring at the floor and could think of no word to reply. But as I sighed to myself at the fate of our homeless people, the infant Leyzerke awoke from sleep, and raised his voice in loud lament. For me, his weeping made up a dirge on the misfortunes he had brought forth with him from the womb, on the poverty that preceded his birth, and on the world from which he had been exiled even before his eyes had beheld it. His wails mounted into a crescendo of accusation, directed against this world that had embittered his life from the hour when he first saw daylight, and had deprived him even of the allotted period of rest in his mother's body that is the natural right of all creatures. His mother rocked and caressed him, beguiling him with false promises of sweets and all manner of good things in time to come, but he complained the more loudly, as if to prevail over her blandishments, crying, so it seemed to me: *Woe is my lot that you have borne me, O my mother, to see toil and sorrow, and to waste away my days in the vain hope of promises and pledges!* His father, too, in his ironic way, sought to console the child. "Put your finger in your mouth and suck it," he said. "It is not for Jews to complain, my dear Leyzerke, nor to make their voices heard, even if their bellies are empty and their flesh grieves them. If they do, a great bear will come and gather them into his sack." But the little Jew, Leyzerke, only grew more indignant; he kicked out angrily, waved his fists and glared wrathfully at his father, as if to reply: *Wretched beggar and sycophant that you are, father of mine! Why did you beget a luckless soul like me, with as many sorrows as the hours of my life—with as many doors for you and me to knock on in our exile as there are hairs to my head!* Thus Reb Moyshe and the infant Leyzerke answered one another, while the mother sighed, the daughters grieved, and I pondered bitterly until the Pole stood up and took the child in his arms. He caressed him, dandled him, and Leyzerke at last grew quiet.

With mounting curiosity, I turned to Reb Moyshe:

"Tell me please, who is this Pole, and what have you to do with one another?"

"He is an old disciple of mine—not in the tailor's art, for he is a cobbler by trade—but in the art of being a Jew. Have a little patience," he added, noting my surprise, "for I will explain everything.

"This Polish cobbler and I lived for many years in the same town in Prussia. Each of us practiced his trade, and we were at peace with one another. On holidays we used to drink together in the tavern, and ask each other's advice about our problems and those of our fellow workers. In times of need we would help each other, in a brotherly way. True, we used to have our disagreements now and then, as people do, and especially would we dispute about matters of religion. He would take sides for his own faith, I for mine, and each of us would quote chapter and verse for his opinions. He would never allow me to say a word against pigs— naturally, I find them abominable—but he would act as devil's advocate, praising these animals and telling me how good they were to eat. I, for my part, would spit in disgust and retort that they were such ugly, nauseating brutes, that nothing could make them any better, not even the butcher's knife. That is how we used to carry on with each other, but always the argument would end with a 'Well, let's leave it at that,' and we would part as friends.

"He told me once that he thought the Jewish way of cooking fish and making puddings was better than theirs. He also thought that our Jewish girls were prettier and more attractive than those of his own people. And he said quite emphatically, that as far as he was concerned, he saw nothing wrong with the Jews being given a small share of the next world for themselves, to which I answered, just as generously, that I would not put any obstacle in the way of Gentiles eating pork, if they wanted to, and was ready on my side to rail off a corner of the lower paradise for good *goyim*. In fact, since we were both in a mood for concessions, I went so far as to say that I would let them have all *this* world as well—on condition only that they set apart a small share of it for us. So we stayed on good terms, and drank a toast to our friendship, he filling his glass and crossing himself over his heart, and I filling mine and saying the blessing for ale—while we both put the drink down in one draught.

"So it was in those days. But when they brought back the times of the Flood, and chaos returned to the world, human nature changed also. Friends became estranged, and my old comrade's bearing toward me was not as it had been. If he chanced to see me in the marketplace, he would behave like a stranger, neither greeting me nor returning my greeting to him. He no longer drank with me in the tavern, but each of us would choose his own corner. The time came when I saw him there with a set of men who were abusing the Jews in loud voices with the object of baiting me. I let them rage on as if I had heard nothing, and when they realized that I was ignoring them and treating them like the stupid cattle that they were, their anger blazed up. They began aiming personal remarks in my direction, they insulted me in their drinking songs, at last they laid hands on me and shouted at me to clear out. At this point the innkeeper came up and with cunning excuses to save his face, expelled me without too much loss of dignity. So I went out, sick at heart.

"This experience was mental torture for days after, and in my bitterness I would dispute with God. 'God of heaven,' I would say, 'Thou who hast chosen us from all peoples, and cherished us, why have I and Thy people Israel come to this degradation and shame. If such is the portion of those whom Thou lovest, would then that Thou hadst *not* loved us, and hadst *not* desired us above all other nations. It is said, indeed, that the Creator, blessed be He, will reward all mankind according to their deserts. But I find no comfort in this. For what profit is it to me, Moyshe the Tailor—the son of Thy people—whose days are brief and full of sorrow—whose soul is trodden down like dust under the feet of the impious—if, at some date in the far-off future, Thou wilt keep faith with my sons' sons and work their salvation? And what if, at the end of days, the descendants of the impious receive the punishment that their forefathers deserved? Then neither the oppressors nor the oppressed will have received their due. The former will not have been punished, nor the latter rewarded, and what purpose is served by settling accounts, when neither debtor nor creditor remain alive?' Yes, indeed I sinned greatly in these thoughts, and even at the time I feared them, for they were nothing but the promptings of evil, and blasphemy and defiance against the heavens. But all my efforts to suppress them were useless, for they rose up of their own accord, against my conscious will.

"Once I was walking in one of the streets of our town, very low in spirits, for hardships were accumulating, and for lack of customers my livelihood was dwindling away—when suddenly I saw my old companion coming toward me. His head was in the air, his moustache was waxed proudly, and there was a look of scorn on his face. By some impulse, as if the devil had prompted me, I stood in his way, and humbly greeted him, as if nothing had happened.

" 'Nowadays there is no getting away from these nuisances!' he replied provocatively, meaning to insult both me and my people at the same time.

" 'Panie Przecsczwinczicki! ' I said imploringly. 'What harm do you find in me, that you have become a stranger?'

" 'What creature is this?' he cried angrily, and averted his glance. I realized from this curt reply what hatred he nursed in his heart, to the point where he could turn his eyes away from his fellowman and refuse to acknowledge a friend. Nevertheless I made yet another attempt.

" 'Don't you recognize me, your true old friend and comrade? Again I ask you, what harm have I done? How have I sinned?'

" 'You are tainted with the sin of your nation for they are always robbing and plundering people!'

" 'Whom have I robbed? And whom have I oppressed? Don't you know full well that I have no property, and no money, and if you were to search my house from floor to ceiling, what would you find, but a few threadbare bits of bedding, a table, and two or three rickety chairs that still, by some miracle, stand on their legs? You should know better than anyone how poorly I live; how the potatoes cooked by my wife Khaye, God bless her, are the only dish to be seen on my table, and that is as much as I have got from all my labor. Do I have to tell you that I am a workingman, and toil away at my trade by day and night)'

" 'I know that well enough!' he answered scornfully. 'That's exactly the point—that you toil at your trade by day and night! It's your work that takes work away from us. So all your labor is to cause other people loss.'

" 'My trade and yours are completely different,' I said in self-justification. 'I work with a needle and you with an awl, and nobody else has lost anything on my account, either, for I am, thank God, a first-class tailor—you yourself have paid me all sorts of compliments about the trousers I made you. The chief thing is that I don't put up my charges like others in the trade. Now look here,' I said with a friendly smile, 'stop being foolish. Come to my place and we'll have potatoes and fried onions again, as my wife Khaye knows how to cook them . . . . I see that your trousers are torn. They've done you good service for something like three years . . . . And the shoes I'm wearing are down at heel and fairly ask to be mended. Can't you see that we need one another? But if we helped each other, then I would patch your trousers, and you would repair my shoes, so each would be the gainer.'

"Like a man whose objections have all been met, my companion stood silent and bewildered. I could see from his face that he was inwardly considering what to do next, and judging that this was the right moment to win him over, I went on:

" 'Yes indeed, Panie . . . you are not as simple as you look, and in your heart, I'm sure, you think other than what you say aloud. You have been playing the fool too long, brother. Now tomorrow happens to be Friday, so what about your coming over for the Sabbath evening, and enjoying some good fish with us?'

" 'You wouldn't touch my pork, would you? So you can keep your rotten fish!' he retorted, flushing in anger.

" 'So it's the pork you want to pick a quarrel about!' I cried, perceiving what was at the root of his fanatical hatred. 'Just because I won't defile myself with what is forbidden me by my faith, you are ready to persecute me and destroy me! Well, well, I shall only say that I can't understand you, for you are acting like a lunatic. Tell me the truth, Panie: Are you quite sound in body and mind?'

"My companion's only response to this question was to thrust out his hard fist—and in a flash he had slipped away out of sight. "From that time on I did not see him again. But from what I heard, he was one of the rioters in the city of Stettin, when they burned the synagogue there, and he took part in that exploit."

While Reb Moyshe was telling his story, his grown-up daughter would sigh from time to time and tremble convulsively. Suddenly her face turned white. She got up from her seat and went to the door of the compartment for air. Her mother followed her, with tears in her eyes, while the father's face clouded over and he became silent. Sensing after a while that some explanation was called for, he leaned forward and whispered to me. It appeared that his eldest daughter, named Brayndl, was betrothed to an admirable young man who was a carpenter's apprentice in the Prussian town where they used to live. This young man loved her dearly, and she returned his love with all her heart. Accordingly Reb Moyshe in his capacity as father had promised a dowry of two hundred silver marks, to be paid in cash before the nuptials to his future son-in-law, Zelig. The young man would thus have the means to fit up a workshop with the tools of his trade. The date of the wedding was provisionally fixed for such time as his apprenticeship would come to an end, and he would qualify for a diploma from his master. Anxiously these lovers waited for the arrival of their wedding day, and only three months lay between them and their happiness, when the decree of banishment was promulgated. According to its provisions, Reb Moyshe and the members of his household went into exile, and the lovers were parted.

"This is the worst burden I have to bear," the father concluded sadly. "My feelings for my daughter are such that I would give my life for her happiness. What a calamity it is, Reb Mendele, that I must watch her grieving day and night for her lover! The whole world has grown dark for her."

So now I understood why this girl had sighed and trembled while Reb Moyshe was recounting their experiences; and I could have wept, myself, in sheer compassion.

The train stopped at a small station on the way. The Pole took up the jugs that were under the seat, and raced off to draw water from the pump. He quickly returned, and passed the jug round, first to Brayndl, then to Leyzerke, and then to the rest of the children, so that they all were able to refresh themselves. I felt a strong impulse to thank him for this, and was all the more desirous of an explanation to the whole enigma. How came this man to attach himself to Reb Moyshe and his family, after all that had passed between them?

Almost as soon as the train began to move again, the tailor made a gesture dismissing, as it were, the sorrows of his mind, and went on again with his story, telling it in his usual ironic fashion.

"It was once upon a time, in Galicia. I was wandering by night in the street of a small town there when I came upon a tavern, a dim tumble-down place whose lamp did not serve to light up the ends of the room. As I entered, I glimpsed the shapes of men scuffling in a dark corner, and heard the voices of a man and a woman yelling curses and abuse. The person they were insulting

390

lay on the floor, begging for mercy and crying: 'Have pity on me! You are human beings too! Hunger and thirst drove me to it, and that's why I ate your bread and drank your wine, though I haven't a penny in my pocket.' But his enemies kept up their abuse, and threatened to tear the clothes from his back and the cap off his head by way of compensation. I perceived that this cruel pair were the innkeeper and his wife, and that all their rage was because a man had not the money to pay for his meal. Familiar, as a Jew, with every aspect of poverty and hunger, I sympathized with this poor wretch and came forward to rescue him. I entreated the keepers of the tavern to show mercy, speaking fair words and quoting the Bible, which declares that he who commits a crime for the sake of bread has acted under duress and should be dealt with leniently. When this produced no result, I paid them the price of the meal out of my own pocket. They were then silent and slunk away.

"The poor man I had saved was just beginning to thank me fervently, when, coming from the dark corner into the full light of the lamp, we caught sight of one another's face, and each of us started back in dismay. I recognized this humble wretch as—who do you think—Przecsczwinczicki!

"As tailors do, I looked first at his clothes, and found them torn and ragged. His shoes were worn through; the cap on his head was creased like a rag and scarcely improved his appearance. As for his body, it was shrunken to mere skin and bones, while his face had the livid, unnaturally bloated look of starvation. For some moments we stood speechless. At last, moved by pity for my old companion in his misery, I found words.

" 'What has become of you, Panie Przecsczwinczicki?' I asked. 'How do you come to be in such a state?'

"He hung his head, and slowly the answer came, in a still, small voice:

" 'They've issued the same decrees for us Poles as they did for you Jews. So now I have to wander about like you, and beg for my bread.'

" 'I really am sorry for you,' I said, shaking my head at his plight.

" 'How can you possibly be sorry for me?' he answered bitterly. 'Why don't you show how much you hate me? You, especially, after I've treated you like dirt, and plagued you all for nothing!'

" 'Exile atones for sin,' I quoted. 'God will not remember our past iniquities.'

" 'But I cannot forget my own, for it's my fate to stand now in

391

your shoes, I have learned what lies the well-fed tell about the hungry, and the citizens of a country about aliens, and the strong about the weak . . . . It has been a lesson to me, what happened here in this tavern. Oh, if only those pampered fools could have the same experience, they might learn some sense, and then there'd be less trouble in the world. Well, you may forgive me if you wish, but I only feel the more ashamed of myself.'

" 'Be that as it may, you *are forgiven*,' I said to him. 'Say no more about it, for you are not the only one to have done wrong, brother. Many have sinned like you—in every generation. And now, let us sit down together and drink to our old friendship.'

"We made a good evening of it there, and talked our hearts out. It was like the old times we used to have together back in Prussia. We called to mind those days, when we lived in peace and followed our own trades, and then we told one another of all the hardships we had been through since we were driven out of that land. I let him know the troubles that were on my mind, and he told me of his. He had been wandering about for a long time and could not make a living among strangers. There was no work, and no one to give him a helping hand—for such was the competition in every trade nowadays, that each man had only time to think of himself. And so this ex-cobbler had spent all his small savings on the road, and sold his few belongings to buy food, and now had nothing left but the clothes he sat in. It was three days since he had spent the last coin he had, and his position was desperate.

"I cheered him up with glass after glass, for it is written, 'the laborer is worthy of his hire,' or, as I read the text, 'a man in trouble deserves a drink.' And the drink lit him up so that he flung his arm around me lovingly, and we forgot all about the old quarrel and were very happy together, till in the end the innkeeper came round to tell us that it was long past bedtime.

"It was a fine, clear night, and the full moon shone in all its beauty. The marketplace was deserted, the whole town slept, and we walked on in silence, each man thinking his own thoughts. Not a sound could be heard except the tramp of our own footsteps and the occasional barking of dogs in the distance. When we reached the crossroads, and it was time to part from my friend, I took his hand to find it was trembling and cold as ice.

" 'My lodgings are up this lane,' I said to him. 'Which way do you go?'

" 'Wherever my feet take me,' he answered with a sigh.

" 'But have you no place to stay the night?'

It appeared not. "Birds, it is written, have their nest, and foxes their holes—but I, the Son of Man, have nowhere to lay my head."

" 'Are there no wealthy folk among you?' I asked him. 'Does nobody help the poor?'

" 'Our idea of charity is different, and our wealthy folk are different too. A man may be poor and a stranger, but if he is ablebodied, then no one is sorry for him. The houses of the rich are not open to all comers, and there are porters to keep the poor away from the courtyards.'

" 'Listen,' I said to my friend. 'Life in exile—this precious gift from God's store—belongs only to the Jews, His chosen people. It is ours alone, for no other nation or race in the world has the strength to take it and to bear its weight. And since you, my friend, seem to have won a share in this gift, there is no remedy for you but Judaism.'

" 'What!' he cried in terror. 'Are you telling me that I must become a Jew?'

" 'No, you fool! The God of the Hebrews is in no hurry to acquire more souls: He is content with the Jews he already has. In fact, he is sufficiently burdened with His own Jewish paupers, whom He has to care for and sustain by miracles each day and hour. No, I am not trying to convert you. Stay a Christian as you have always been, and keep your religion in your own way, but there is one thing you must do. You must come to master the Jewish art of living, and cleave to that, if you are to preserve yourself and carry the yoke of exile. At first this will be hard for you, but in the course of time you will learn through suffering—for pain begets endurance. Do you believe that the Jews from the beginning of their history were such as I am today? You are wrong, friend! For long ages they went through every kind of affliction and retribution. They tried out many ways of life until they became as they are now. It is exile that has given them special characteristics that mark them off from all other peoples, has taught them special contrivances to gain a living, and has set a special stamp upon their charity, too, from the point of view of both giver and receiver. *Who is like Thy people Israel, a unique nation in the world!* which is skilled in ways of procuring its needs; which must, by the very nature of its being, maintain itself in the teeth of all oppressive laws and decrees that seek to prevent this. What nation in the world has such strange customs as we? Our paupers constantly return to the same doors;

393

they *demand* alms, as if they are collecting a debt that is due to them. And our wealthy benefactors do not scrutinize each case. They give, again and again, freely to all comers, even if these are healthy and able-bodied. Not only this, but of their own accord they invite these paupers as guests to their table, on weekdays, not to mention Sabbaths and festivals, so that the poor are as members of the household. Such is the law of the Exile, with all its six hundred and thirteen prohibitions and exactions. Yes, we know how to keep this law; and we have the strength of rocks to bear the burden of it, and to endure it, and to live by it.'"

"You have spoken the truth, Reb Moyshe," I said in reply. "How many qualities of body and soul are peculiar to us Jews, solely as the result of our dispersion among the nations and our precarious position in the world! Indeed, these very qualities have given us the strength to bear up, to satisfy our needs, and to survive in the Exile. The story goes back to ancient times. Our economic history is one long record of miracles—from the harsh fare of our forty years' wandering in the wilderness, to the bread of affliction in our present exile—wherefore every son of Israel reads in his morning prayers the portion of the law relating to the manna, which is appropriate to all occasions and has its permanent spiritual significance. But let us come back to your own story. Proceed, Reb Moyshe, for I am eager to hear more."

"There is very little left to tell. After I had spoken, my friend, the Pole, stared hard at me, and said:

" 'See now, you say to me: learn to master the Jewish way of living. But you have not told me what I must do. You have talked such a lot, Panie Moyshe, but I can't understand a single word of it all.'

" 'Don't let that trouble you. I shall teach you the rules—the things a man must do if he is to live in the Exile, and which if he neglects, he will certainly perish. From now on you are adopted into my family, and will come with us along the way until we find some resting place. Be brave, my son, to take upon you the afflictions of the Jews, and be faithful to my teaching!'

"From the hour my friend joined us and came under my wing, I have educated him in the ways of poverty, and given him good counsel to ward off evil and to share our kind of life. I have taught him to be content with but little food and drink, to withstand the clamor of the belly, and to punish it at times by fasting. I have revealed to him the mysteries of the art of begging, and have taught him how to bow his head before calamities, as well as how to prevail over obstacles and hindrance in obtaining, by all manner of devices, his essential needs. All these things I have taught him, and, I thank God for it, my labor has not been in vain. At the beginning it was hard for this disciple of mine to face up to such trials, and it seemed preferable to die a speedy death than to draw out his life amid the sufferings and misfortunes of our strange people. But little by little he grew accustomed to them, and made great strides in his studies, until he attained the proficiency standard in penury and endurance, in humility and submission, in mortification of the body and the soul. He became like a real Jew, and is now fully adapted to exile, and trained to welcome its strokes and afflictions.

"Happy man!" concluded Reb Moyshe with a contented smile. "And happy too am I, his teacher, that I am privileged to see this!"

I looked across at the Pole, and observed him playing cheerfully with the infant Leyzerke. He was entertaining him with a series of imitations of animal and bird calls: now he crowed like a cock, now mooed like a cow, neighed like a horse, croaked like a frog, or growled like a bear—and all this as quietly and unobtrusively as possible, lest he disturb the other passengers. The children romped round him merrily, Yankele on one side, Itsikl on the other. Even the unfortunate maiden Brayndl forgot her beloved Zelig sufficiently to smile, and her mother, perceiving it, for the moment seemed transformed into a happy matron. As for Moyshe, he delighted in the whole spectacle, and beaming with pleasure, cried:

"Rejoice, children of mine, for I have lived to see Japheth in the tents of Shem! May you prosper, Panie Japheth, and acquit yourself well in your studies, for your own good as well as for the good of your master, who has taught you to be of such service. So may you flourish and go from strength to strength!"

I had many more questions to put to Reb Moyshe, but there was no time left to ask them, for now the train had stopped at a main junction, where I had to take leave of him and cross to another line.

As I left the compartment carrying my luggage, I saw the Pole standing outside and whispering to one of the train employees in a most humble and ingratiating manner, while he pressed a coin into his hand. I understood at once what this mystery signified, and what the disciple of Reb Moyshe was requesting. . . . And raising my eyes aloft, with a sigh that came from the depths of my heart, I said:

"Lord of the universe! Grant us but a few more such disciples—and Shem and Japheth will be brothers—and peace will come to Israel!"

INTRODUCTION TO

Of Bygone Days

Shloyme Reb Khayim's (Shloyme, the son of Reb Khayim) is the Yiddish title of the last of the important works of Mendele, first published in its entirety in Yiddish in 1911 (sections appeared earlier in 1894 and in 1899). It is the beginning of Sholem [Shloyme] Yankef Abramovitsh's fictionalized autobiography. *Of Bygone Days* is a translation of one of the titles of the Hebrew version.

Like all the other longer works of Abramovitsh, it starts with a preface in which Mendele the bookpeddler (Abramovitsh's *alter ego*) introduces the story. In *Of Bygone Days*, there is an interesting twist in that this is the only such preface in which Mendele meets with and speaks to....Mendele, that is to say, Abramovitsh, now an old man.

Abramovitsh is persuaded in the preface by his old cronies, and Mendele the bookpeddler, to write his autobiography. The story that follows, beginning with Chapter One, is that "autobiography."

An interesting, somewhat confusing characteristic of the novel is that the story begins in *medias res*, at the point after Shloyme's father has died (an important turning point in Abramovitsh's real life), and he is living with his mother and sister at the mill owned and operated by his stepfather. The story then takes us from the mill to Kapulye, Abramovitsh's birthplace, and in "flashback," we see Shloyme's childhood, his education, and his upbringing up to the point, at the end of the novel, where he is thirteen and his father dies. Mendele never finished this "autobiography" (he did write an incomplete "Part II" which has, as of this writing, not yet been translated into English).

The seventeen pages presented here are all of a piece, comprising, in their entirety, the last three chapters of the novella and containing several key episodes: Kapulye, Abramovitsh's birthplace, suffers an economic decline, and, more important, Shloyme's (Mendele's) father dies.

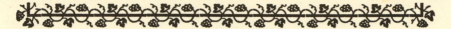

FROM

Of Bygone Days

Translated by Raymond Sheindlin

Shloymele's path up to this time may not have been strewn with roses, but neither was it unduly hard: a straight road at least, without obstacles or pitfalls. But from this point on, the road became ever more crooked and bumpy, and thick with brambles. It led up steep hills, down deep valleys, and across many a dangerous chasm. The first stumbling blocks were communal troubles, a series of disasters that plagued the town of Kapulye.

The economic mainstay of Kapulye, the source of its renown among the Jewish villages of Lithuania, was its "Astrakhan" industry, and particularly its manufacture of cloth for women's kerchiefs. Astrakhan was a heavy material of a dark green color, sold by the *arshin.** It was used mainly for lining, and for making caftans for the poor. The archives of Kapulye nowhere explain how it came to be called Astrakhan. The kerchief material was a thin, bleached linen, in length and breadth about the size of a handkerchief, and it too was produced by the local weavers. The women would wrap this white turban over their hairnet in such a way that two corners fell over the nape of the neck, where they looked like a pair of blintzes, with a second, smaller "fan" alongside each fold. Around their turbaned head a kerchief would then be wound like hoops of a barrel, twisted into a knot on the forehead and the ends drawn back and tucked in on either side near the ears. On the heads of pious old ladies, this knot stood right in the middle of the forehead, like a man's phylactery; younger women wore it modishly off to one side. Wives of well-to-do men wore silk, cashmere, or Turkish kerchiefs on the Sabbath and holidays, and printed wool kerchiefs, known as apple-kerchiefs, on weekdays. A bridegroom's parents would send both kinds of kerchief to the bride before the wedding, while the bride's parents sent the groom a fur hat.

---

* *Arshin*: a Russian measure of length, equal to twenty-eight inches.

Such was the finery of our grandmothers!

The kerchief was always kept starched and ironed. The work of smoothing and ironing a kerchief was performed by two women working together, thus: the women would stand as far apart as the length of the kerchief allowed, holding an edge in each hand so that the kerchief was stretched out lengthwise between them. Into the hollow thus formed, a large, smooth ball of glass or iron was placed. One of the women lifted her arms a bit and the ball rolled down from her side to her partner's; the second woman repeated the motion sending the ball right back. In this way, the ball rolled back and forth until the kerchief was smooth.

It was the greatest fun in the world to watch two women smoothing kerchiefs. They stood so seriously facing one another, raising their arms with a jerk of the shoulders, their stomachs protruding, and their heads cocked to one side; they would make faces and glare, exchange poisonous smiles and sarcastic cracks. Anyone who had the chance to watch them in action had no need of theater.

The kerchiefs were finished by Gentile weavers in their own homes, and local Jewish businessmen would buy them up for cash and spools of new thread, each businessman dealing regularly with his group of weavers. These businessmen were generally young husbands who were still living with their in-laws or who still had some cash left over from the dowry. Reb Khayim's married sons supported themselves in this way. The kerchiefs were then sold to the great merchants, who distributed them throughout the cities of Lithuania. They were very popular and sold well, providing a good income for the many Jews of Kapulye whose livelihood they were.

Business went on in the same way for generations, until a government ordinance, the Clothing Decree, forbade Jewish women to shave their heads, and required that Jews, including Jewish women, dress like Germans.

Mercifully, the decree had not yet come into force in Kapulye, where men still wore sidelocks and fur hats, and women still shaved and covered their heads with kerchiefs as before. But in other towns the situation was shameful. Jewish men were donning hats! Jewish women were replacing their kerchiefs with "Lithuanian bonnets"—a kind of rag, if you will. No kerchiefs meant no business; and no business meant nothing to eat. Kapulye was laid flat by the blow. Spinners, weavers, small and big businessmen—

400

all were hit by the decree. The tavernkeepers suffered, because if the weaver can't afford bread, he can't afford a drink either. And if spinners, weavers, tradesmen and tavernkeepers can't make a living, then the storekeepers, craftsmen and laborers are also in trouble, because who can afford to give them business? A new crop of paupers and beggars came into being. Bankrupt house-holders became *kheyder*-teachers to support their children, and *kheyder*-teachers proliferated like weeds. Soon there were more teachers than pupils. Times were very bad, and when things go badly, people become ill-tempered too, bickering and fighting, each one trying to snatch a morsel out of the other's mouth. The erstwhile peace and quiet of Kapulye was now gone.

Reb Khayim was also affected by the collapse of the kerchief market, for his married sons lost their means of support. Then, a brother-in-law who dealt in linen thread went bankrupt and fled, abandoning wife and child, and leaving Reb Khayim no choice but to support them, though this put a great strain on his resources. His own business fell off too. He had been farming the meat tax, but since the townspeople were now eating much less meat, he suffered enormous losses. His family was no longer as comfortable as it had been, nor as amicable. Shloymele began to taste the bitterness in life. The peacefulness of childhood was at an end.

Once trouble comes, it pours in from all sides. One fine summer day, during the dry season, a terrible fire broke out in Kapulye, destroying over half the houses in town, including the one that belonged to Freydl's family. Heaps of ashes lined the street, and sooty chimneys protruded like gravestones in a cemetery. Hungry, ragged and homeless, people wandered about the streets like living corpses. Some rummaged through the heaps of rubble of their ruined homes looking for mementos of better times. The joy they displayed over a nail or a pot or some roasted potatoes found among the ashes was more depressing than the dumb misery of those other poor souls who merely sat about mournfully, hanging their heads.

Reb Khayim took Freydl's family into his own home. There wasn't enough room for them, and the crowding caused great inconvenience, but in the emergency the change was accepted by everyone, out of pity.

The only one who did not suffer was Shloymele; in fact, the situation rather pleased him. He was together with Freydl under one roof, and the less room there was, the better for him. Each day

401

brought unlimited opportunities of meeting her, of gazing at her face, hearing her sweet voice, watching her bare arms while she worked, and all without any fear of discovery. Shloymele went out of his way to give Freydl's parents a hand however he could, fetching and carrying things simply to curry their favor. In hopes of pleasing them, he went every day with a wheelbarrow to their burnt down house just when Freydl was scavenging there. Silently he dug and searched, putting whatever he found in his wheelbarrow; and whatever Freydl found, he quietly took from her hand and added to the haul. When the wheelbarrow was full he pulled it home, flushed red as a beet and sweating with exertion, while Freydl helped by pushing from behind. In this way he dismantled a whole chimney and oven and carried the bricks home. The joy of a warrior returning triumphant from battle with booty of silver and gold did not surpass Shloymele's joy as he and Freydl reached home, pulling the wheelbarrow laden with bricks, bits of iron, and other odds and ends salvaged from the fire. The truth is bitter, but it must be told: this fire, this terrible affliction that caused suffering to so many people, brought Shloymele a good deal of pleasure. He was like an heir who makes a show of weeping at his father's death, but who secretly feels great satisfaction.

It was only later, when Shloymele himself got burned, so to speak, that he felt the pangs of sorrow. Freydl's parents, who had lost all hope of restoring their fortunes in Kapulye, moved to a distant town, taking their children with them. Shloymele was badly hurt by the separation. His very life seemed ruined.

Like tidal waves, trials and sorrows of all kinds now swept over Kapulye. Luckily, its unlimited experience with all forms of disaster has taught tiny, pliant Israel how to bend like a reed when the great breakers sweep over, and how to raise its head upright once they have passed, Blessed is He who said: "Fear not, Israel . . . when thou passest through rivers, they will not sweep you away, and when thou walkest through fire, thou shalt not be burnt." A decree is enacted prohibiting the wearing of kerchiefs—no one would deny its disastrous consequences. But Jews can adapt to anything.

They pull in their belts a bit, go hungry a bit, eat their hearts out a bit, and make do with a little less. A fire breaks out—true, a terrible misfortune. But God is our Father, and Jews are merciful people. They write letters, send out messengers, wait hopefully, and what happens?—Nothing. The messengers, after all, are also flesh and blood; they too have wives and children; they too have to eat. When autumn comes, bringing cold and rain, making the outdoor life impossible, the homeless slowly move into other people's homes wherever a place can be found. And if there's not enough room for everybody—no matter! At least all are together. An epidemic breaks out and people die—so the rabbis proclaim a fast, and the people recite Psalms. The poverty gets worse—so whoever is able, takes his walking stick and knapsack and leaves. There's plenty of room in God's world, in the region of Volhinia, for example, where teaching is a good business. Jews pick themselves up and move. Does everything then seem to be going well?—A "papers" decree is enacted, prohibiting anyone from teaching Toyre unless he has a government permit, a piece of paper. Terrible! But Jews do what is necessary under the circumstances, and God is merciful, and the teaching goes on.

Thus did the people of Kapulye weather that bitter time.

In those days, rumors of the colonies reached the town, as though carried by the wind: the government was giving Jews land to settle and cultivate. This rumor, as usual, rolled from mouth to mouth like a ball of yarn, and grew entangled in so many versions that in the end it was impossible to unravel. Where were they giving land away? How were they giving it? To whom? It became the town's only topic of conversation. Everywhere—in the market, in the study house and its courtyard, knots of people stood arguing angrily.

"Come now, Reb Zelig," argues Khaykl the Lame, who is committed heart and soul to the colonies. "Tell me, my philosopher, exactly what you mean when you say 'beh-beh'? And what is signified, pray tell, by your 'et-et'? This offer, which is our only hope for survival, can't be pooh-poohed so lightly."

"What should I say to you, Khaykl, what can I argue if you are, with all due respect . . ." Reb Zelig replies with a frown, taking a pinch of snuff, ". . . if you don't understand the true essence of anything. They're giving away colonies! What does it mean, 'giving'? Does anyone come to you for no good reason and say,

'Here you are, Khaykl, go and be a nobleman'!? Et, a thousand times et!"

"I've been telling my Faybish exactly the same thing," interjects a poor Jew of good family, "You think you're going to become a noble, Faybish? Quite the opposite. It smells of peasant. Not only that, but they say that if you don't fulfill your quota of work in the fields, they send you straight to the army or to Siberia. Faybish, I say to him, you are a *kheyder*-teacher, a *kheyder*-teacher you will remain in this world, and in the next. So go back to your teaching, and don't get any wild ideas. The hands of Jacob are not the hands of Esau."

"No!" Someone's voice can be heard from a nearby circle. "We won't try any of the neighboring towns, not for all the money in the world. Better go to the distant provinces, Yakterinoslav or Chersun."

"Right!" other voices are heard chiming in. "But the money, where do we get the money. . . ."

"They're offering money! . . . There is money available! . . . Let's find out what Reb Khayim thinks about it! What does Reb Khayim say? Call a meeting, let's have an assembly!"

And at the meeting the matter of the colonies was explained as follows: Many of the thousands of Jews of White Russia who had been expelled from their villages had, in 1806, been granted their request to be settled on royal lands in the southern district of "New Russia" to work the land autonomously. They were assisted by royal decree and financing. In 1810, the government announced that no more Jews were to be sent to these colonies as the money set aside for that purpose was exhausted. Nine years later, Jews were once again granted permission to settle, but this time at their own expense. Four years later, further Jewish settlement was again forbidden. A law of 1835, renewed in 1847, granted the Jews permission to settle as farmers on royal lands anywhere inside of the Pale of Jewish settlement, especially in the districts of Yakterinoslav and Chersun, their expenses to be paid by the community out of the meat tax. And since it was a matter of community funds, the community had to think it over, and so it was tabled until a later meeting.

This later meeting and those that followed were fruitless, as usual. Money was needed, but the community had none; not only that, but it owed arrears in taxes which the government threatened to collect by force. The entire town fell into a depression. When would the troubles finally end? Behind the stove in the study house people talked about the coming of the Messiah, an event for which a new date had been announced by a certain prominent rabbi on the basis of an obscure Biblical verse. The conversation brightened their spirits for the moment, and their eyes flickered with new hope: "Don't worry! God is God, and he will not let Israel perish!"

The pillars of the community met often to discuss the state of affairs. They talked, weighed the issues back and forth, and concluded, invariably, with a deep sigh, "Dear Lord, help us out of this crisis."

It was a winter evening. Outdoors it was bitter cold, with a moon so dazzling bright, you could string pearls by its light, as the expression goes. In fact there seemed to be pearls shimmering on the street, the reflection of twinkling stars on the silver white snow. It was a lovely night, a glorious night, a night for lovers' walks—but such pleasures were not meant for the Jews of Kapulye: the streets were deserted, not a soul was about. Inside Reb Khayim's house it was warm and bright. A lively flame crackled in the lamp; by the warm oven, Reb Khayim and some of the prominent citizens were sitting around a table, talking about community affairs.

All of a sudden the street door opened, and a cold draft of air rolled in, settling like a cloud of steam over the room. There followed a sound of footsteps, and a squeak, and then, from the cloud of steam, the figure of a man emerged.

"Shimen!" they all exclaimed. "Welcome, Shimen!"

Shimen was a householder in his thirties, a shrewd, witty man, cheerful even when things weren't going too well, and a favorite of all the townspeople. When the rumor of the colonies reached Kapulye, he didn't waste energy on idle speculation like the others, but immediately went to the regional capital and from there to the provincial capital to find out exactly what the story was and what had to be done.

Shimen returned their greetings, shook the bits of ice out of his coat and beard, and stood by the fire to warm himself. The others watched him affectionately, until suddenly they all began to laugh and point at his feet.

"What in the world is that, Shimen!"

"Bast-shoes," replied Shimen earnestly.

"Purim is still a long way off, and already you're masquerading, you clown?" they said, continuing to laugh.

They had good reason to laugh. Bast-shoes—boots made of a

405

soft plant fiber, with long straps that wrapped around pieces of cloth covering the lower leg from heel to knee—were worn by peasants, people of the lowest classes in Lithuania. Even the most wretched pauper of a Jew would no more think of wearing these boots than he would think of eating pork. He would rather have his soles worn through, he would rather go barefoot in the snow. . . . There was no such thing as a Jew in bast-shoes, unless it be a wedding jester, a Purim-player, or a clown of sorts.

"I'm not masquerading," Shimen replied with a shrewd smile on his lips. "I actually am a peasant now. I decided to wear these boots to save myself the trouble of informing every single person in town and having an argument with them one by one. Here they are, my fellow Jews! Take one look! You can see for yourselves what I am, and let me alone."

"So that's it, Shimen—you're a colonist?" they responded, suddenly serious. "Tell us the whole story and give us the details."

Shimen didn't have to be asked twice. He explained every detail about the colonies, and every law thereunto appertaining, in his usual pithy manner. He also related what had happened to him and what he had gone through before finding a congenial group with whom to form a colony in the district of Chersun.

"But who's going to work the land?" one of the group asked.

"Do you think that by putting on peasant boots you've become a peasant, Shimen? You have no experience at that kind of work!"

"Don't worry! Rashi* has provided for this emergency," answered Shimen with a smile, "The government is staffing the colonies with German instructors, who will teach us how it's done."

"Yes, that's all very well," someone else asked, "But what about money to start with? From the meat tax? How are we to raise 170 rubles per colonist from the meat tax? Impossible! The community hasn't got a penny, and its needs are pressing. So much is needed. . . ."

"You don't have to worry about a thing," Shimen cut him off.

"I have a little money saved up; and while I was finding out about the colonies, I managed to pick up a small fee for acting as a marriage broker. I also figure on selling my household furniture;

---

* Rashi, Rabbi Shlomo Yitzkaki (1040-1105), author of the authoritative commentary on the Bible and Talmud, which is called by his name.

and if that doesn't bring in enough, I feel sure that you gentlemen will help out. What do you say, Reb Khayim?"

"I say that you're a fine man, Shimen! We need more like you, people with love of the soil, with courage, and independence—many more!"

Sarah brought refreshments to the table: cracklings, bagels, and wine, and begged them to eat.

"God willing," Shimen said, smiling, "Next year I'll send you a pair of geese from the colony. There, as the song goes,

Food for all, and the bread is free—
*A goat for five pennies, a chicken for three.**

Reb Khayim's business did very poorly that winter, and the expression on his face reflected his concern. Reb Khayim had always been a serious, pensive man; he kept to himself most of the time and rarely exchanged a word with the family. His appearance inspired respect. No matter what racket the children may have been making in the house, the instant their father appeared at the door they would fall silent and no one uttered a peep. Not that the household was kept in fear of him, as with some tyrannical fathers who like to let everyone know who's in charge—far from it! He wore a grave expression, but hardly ever an angry one. The wrinkles on his fine, high forehead were a sign of his deep concentration; the blaze in his eyes reflected only the light of the Toyre on which he meditated. In fact, he was quite soft-hearted; the silence that greeted his appearance in the room pained him. If any member of the family suffered the slightest hurt, it tore his heart out. It was his wife who actually ran the household. Reb Khayim provided what was needed, and had no interest in household affairs beyond that. His only concerns were the business, the community, and his studies, for which certain hours were fixed.

---

* The author was fond of including folk songs and folktales in his writings. The complete text of this song about the colonies can be found in his story, "Di alte mayse" (The Old Story), 1895.

The household understood all this; everyone treasured and loved him, took pride in his wisdom, and accorded him respect.

But that winter, Reb Khayim underwent a great change. His usual calm, thoughtful expression was replaced by an angry one. When he paced back and forth in the room in his usual way, with his hands behind his back, he would stop at intervals, bite his lip, cast an irate glance about him, and tug at his beard, on which many gray hairs had suddenly appeared. Reb Khayim had aged prematurely. He was then no more than forty-two or forty-three years old.

It was the meat tax that aged him. Since the town had gone bankrupt, his business had fallen off, as people ate less and less meat. And on top of that, some people began to evade the tax by smuggling meat into the town from the outside. The ban of excommunication that applies in such cases did no good at all. Need is stronger than iron, as people say, and certainly stronger than a ban of excommunication. Poverty and hunger are serious matters, and after all, the meat tax was not decreed at Mount Sinai. The inspectors, whose job it was to ferret out such smuggled meat and seize it by force, were hardly any help at all. There was continual complaining, dissatisfaction, curses and tears, bringing upon Reb Khayim hatred and resentment. For a while he managed somehow—his Personality still commanded deference. But later, when it came out that Reb Khayim had stopped paying the installments on the meat tax, and had even lost money which he had borrowed for that purpose, his enemies began to talk behind his back and finally to raise an open scandal.

Reb Khayim was not about to give up; he was a shrewd man with a wide reputation, even among the local nobles, as an intelligent businessman, and he might have pulled through. But he was as proud as he was intelligent; he couldn't bear to be gossiped about by people who had once trembled at his glance. He lost his appetite, then his health, and finally his fighting spirit.

Reb Khayim was also deeply troubled by events concerning his daughter Leah, a fine girl, clever about the house, intelligent, and blessed with a strong character. As the eldest child she was second in command after her mother in household affairs, and adored by everyone. Reb Khayim married her off to a boy from a different town, and maintained them in his house. The husband came from good family, as befit Reb Khayim's station; he was a fine and well-mannered boy, and the whole family took a liking to him.

Reb Khayim devoted a few hours a day to giving lessons to him and a few of his friends, also sons-in-law of good families. Among these boys, there were some who came from other, larger cities, and they were conspicuous in their clothing and behavior, so different from the Kapulye manner. This group stuck together and sometimes behaved in "strange ways" which the townspeople viewed askance, giving rise to talk that they were "newfangled." What the people of Kapulye in those days meant by the expression "newfangled" would seem archaic nowadays, even by the standards of old-fashioned people. But the talk went on, and led to scandal, until finally the group broke up. At the same time, tension developed between Reb Khayim and his son-in-law, and mutual antagonism: in town gossip, this meant that Leah was having trouble with her husband. The couple were no longer happy together, and the boy was sent packing back to his parents; that winter Leah was divorced.

Leah's strong character enabled her to act as if nothing had happened. But Reb Khayim could feel she was wounded, heartbroken. He ached with compassion for her, and blamed himself for the sufferings of his daughter, whom he loved as a true father. Had Leah uttered a word of complaint, they would have talked it out, he might have consoled her and felt better for it. But Leah said nothing, and it was her silence that pained him most. Her unfaltering love and devotion were salt to his wounds.

Reb Khayim's health deteriorated, and the family became more and more anxious. They sensed that their mainstay was weakening, that one or two strong waves might topple him and hurl them all into the great abyss.

It was a hard, joyless winter. On Purim night, Reb Khayim sat at the table with his family, making a tremendous effort to look happy and celebrate the holiday in his traditional manner. A purse lay at his side, full of coins for the poor. A few came in, and Reb Khayim gave something to each of them, with a smile and a friendly word. Children of well-to-do families came with handkerchiefs, collecting for others—for a family that had lost its fortune and was suffering in secret, for a respectable pauper, for a widow with small orphans—and Reb Khayim contributed freely, sending along Purim refreshments as well. Religious functionaries came too—sextons, wedding musicians, bath-house workers, Purim-players—Reb Khayim treated them all to a glass of spirits and a donation.

Sarah, for her part, was busy preparing and receiving Purim gifts. Poor yeshive-boys, children, and servant girls were bringing covered dishes from relatives, neighbors, and friends, and under the covers were different kinds of cookies: *homentashn*, poppyseed cakes, sugar cookies in the shape of a fish, or with the name of a Purim character—Queen Esther or Vashti—in iced letters on top. Neatly arranged around these goodies, of which there were only one or two to a platter, was a circle of prunes or almonds or walnuts. Occasionally a platter held a herring pickled in vinegar and honey—this from a neighbor who preferred things simple and substantial.

While Sarah was busy rewarding the messengers for their trouble, and sending her thanks and good wishes to this one and that, the children attacked the food, casting hungry eyes over the little dainties that so teased the appetite. Exercising self-restraint, they rearranged them on the dishes to send them back again: a *homentash* to the family that sent a poppyseed cake, a Zeresh to the one that sent a Vashti, a fig or red apple in exchange for an almond. Naturally, disagreements arose, and fights; slaps and pinches were exchanged, but no one even noticed such minor disturbances at a time of such major rejoicing,

Outwardly it seemed a Purim like any other, but if you looked closely, there was a difference. The poor who came were the same, but the handouts were smaller. In place of the many guests that used to pass a joyous evening at the Purim meal, only a few poor relatives showed up. Reb Khayim sang "The Rose of Jacob,"* and the children chimed in, but the verve of former years was gone. In his singing, you could hear the tears of a suffering soul, and the melody of Lamentations. The "Rose of Jacob" had been plucked: still pretty to look at, colorful as ever, but without the juice of life, and about to wither. Reb Khayim did his best to bring it off. He turned to the poor relations and tried to console them: Don't worry—one must hope, one must not lose spirit. Trust God to help!" But his speeches were forced; care was sucking away at Reb Khayim's heart like a leech. Sorrow and suffering were reflected in his eyes.

Sarah noticed this plainly, and her heart clenched. She went off into a corner, covered her face with her hands, and wept quietly.

Leah, who felt it every bit as strongly, understood her mother's

---

* *Shoshanas Yaakov*, The Rose of Jacob, is a traditional Purim Song.

emotion, but controlled herself and kept her place at the table. She looked pityingly at the children and gave them each some sugar cookies: "Let the poor little ones eat." But at night, in bed, the pillow was wet with her tears.

It was a week after Purim. The sun as it peered down from the sky was friendly and mild, sending a gentle, warm breeze as a first notice to winter that its lease on earth was expired. Winter was acting the bad tenant, postponing its move from day to day with one excuse after another. During the daytime, in the presence of the sun, winter said its teary farewells, sending streams of water into the streets. "I'm going, I'm going. Just let me pack up my things, my poor snow, blackened with toil." But no sooner did the sun shut one eye and go to its nocturnal rest, than winter turned around, thumbing its nose, ice-cold as ever. Ultimately, however, these delaying tactics were of no avail. Winter was as good as gone, and no one had time to pay attention anyway. For the Jews it was the "before Passover" period when closets and cupboards had to be opened, tables and benches taken into the street, and everything scrubbed, washed, and cleansed.

Kapulye was busy as an anthill. Everyone had something to do in preparation for Passover. Children, housewives and husbands were running about the market among the wagons of grain, potatoes, eggs and vegetables that Esau, the man of the fields, brings to his brother Jacob, the man of the town. In the mill, hidden behind the town in the woods, the stones had already been scoured clean, and Jews were bringing their bags of grain to be ground for *matse*, everyone patiently waited his turn, even if he had to stay overnight at the mill, for the rule was first come first served. The *matse* bakers and their helpers were all ready for business: some to knead, others to pour, still others to roll the dough, to make the rows of holes, to put the dough in the oven, to take out the finished product, and to deliver it in huge baskets. Passover was everywhere—in the markets, in the houses, and even in the *kheyder*, where children's voices could be heard

411

studying the Song of Songs in the traditional melody that makes a Jew's heart melt.

In Reb Khayim's house, which had been the hub of activity in former years, the atmosphere was heavy, altogether unlike the eve of a holiday. Reb Khayim lay in his bed fully clothed, pillowing his head on his arms, with a distracted look on his face. He was pale as the wall, and his breath came heavily. Sarah sat, depressed, in the front room doing nothing, her eyes red with weeping. When any of the children made a sound, she motioned, "Quiet! Father is ill, keep quiet!" The children walked on tiptoe, squeezed themselves into corners, and watched gloomily in silence. Only Leah busied herself with housework. But she looked black as death, and avoided meeting anyone's eyes.

The door to the street opened noisily, and there entered ceremoniously a tall, solidly built, impressive-looking nobleman with finely pointed mustaches. Two lackeys followed him, one carrying a bag, the other a pipe with an amber mouthpiece.

The nobleman looked around at everybody in the room and stood a while in silence, with a dark expression on his face.

"Ah, noble sir!" Sarah cried, rising suddenly to greet the nobleman.

"*Pani Rabinowa!*"* the nobleman cried, visibly moved by the sight of tears in Sarah's eyes. "What's the matter?"

Sarah was sobbing too hard to answer. The nobleman left her to collect herself. He sat down at the big, colored table, twisting his mustaches, and his own eyes grew moist.

"Hey, Antosia! My pipe!"

Like arrows from a bow the two lackeys leaped to his service; one brought the long pipe stuffed with tobacco, and the other the fire-tools: a piece of steel, a flint, and a bit of wick. He struck a fire, and lit the tobacco in the pipe. The nobleman sucked at the pipe and ordered the servants to leave.

Jan, the noble of Va—tzitz, was a descendant of a Polish family that owned the towns around Kapulye. This property had been divided among several brothers. On Gentile holidays, and sometimes on Sundays, Jan would drive into town in a carriage at the head of his retinue, as did the other local nobles, and proceed straight to the church, which stood across from the row of houses in the marketplace. Services over, he would cross the marketplace

---

* *Pani Rabinowa*: the Polish greeting, something like "Esteemed rabbi's wife."

on foot to Reb Khayim's house, where he spent some time settling his affairs with artisans and shopkeepers, who would come there to meet him. He had a high regard for Reb Khayim, valued him for his shrewdness and honesty, and loved him as a true friend. Whenever he had a dispute with anyone, his invariable solution was: "To the rabbi!" Jan relied on Reb Khayim completely, confident that he would not deviate from justice by a hairsbreadth. And besides all this, he simply enjoyed chatting with Reb Khayim, who could speak Polish, and even write it tolerably well. He would tell the nobleman proverbs, parables, and Talmudic legends, which Jan enjoyed and praised to the skies. If Reb Khayim was occupied with other visitors, Jan wouldn't interrupt him, but make himself at home, and smoke his pipe while waiting for Reb Khayim to finish. Whatever others may say about friendship between the Poles and the Jews, it is a fact that Jan was a true friend to Reb Khayim. This was evidenced on numerous occasions, as it was now in his gloomy expression and in his moist eyes as Sarah told him how things stood with them, and about her husband's illness.

"Can I visit with him a little while?" Jan asked.

"I'll go and see," Sarah answered, "and if he's up, I'll tell him you're here."

" A moment later Sarah ushered the nobleman into the room.

"What is this, *Pan* Rabbi?" Jan blurted, stopping momentarily by the door as he came in, forcing a smile and shaking his head as if in astonishment. "Pan Rabbi seems to have lost his will to fight! Where is his iron spirit? Where is his wisdom?"

"There are times when human wisdom is of no avail," Reb Khayim answered, managing a weak smile.

"But there is a God, who can always help, in any circumstance. Do I have to tell *Pan* Rabbi things that he knows better than I?" Jan said, taking a seat facing Reb Khayim. "I know—it's a bad business. But such a clever man can't be lost. Are there many Jews like *Pan* Rabbi?"

Jan spent about a quarter of an hour with Reb Khayim. Then he said goodbye, and with a heavy heart went to his carriage, which stood by the church.

The next afternoon a wagon arrived at Reb Khayim's house, and two servants brought in sacks of wheat and potatoes, chickens, and a pair of turkeys,

Reb Khayim's life flickered like a candle. His strength ebbed until he lay weak as a baby, unable to move. The family sank into a black mood. No one ate, drank, or slept. Relatives and close friends came by, each with words of comfort and suggested cures. A certain doctor from the region was brought in. He pronounced the name of the disease, wrote a prescription and accepted his fee, but he was no more effective than the local home remedies.

A week before Passover Reb Khayim spent a terrible night. He lay in a stupor, gasping for breath, his eyes closed, his mouth half open, his lips parched, his pulse weak. From his chest came a rasping sound, like the sound of sawing wood. From time to time he grimaced and heaved a sigh. Sarah bent over and talked to him, but it was like talking to the wall. He was unconscious, unaware of what was going on around him.

Sarah bowed her head and wept silently. Leah sat at his head, choked with tears; from time to time a tremor shook her whole body.

On a long bench by a dimly-burning tallow candle, Shloymele swayed over a miniature edition of the Psalms. A soft, fervent prayer and hot tears poured out to his gracious, merciful Father in Heaven, "O mercy! Have mercy, holy Father! O almighty God, perform a miracle, and spare me and those poor little children that lie there exhausted in the corner. O spare us, our Father! In exchange," he said to God in his heart, "I will do everything you ask, I will be your faithful servant." Shoymele prayed and bargained, and from time to time cast a glance over at his sick father, expecting that any minute God would perform a miracle and heal him. Ceaselessly, he went over the same psalms, and the same thoughts until—with a sudden leap of joy—he saw his mother beckon to Leah. Stroking the patient's feet, she said quietly and joyfully:

"He's sweating!"

"Um-m-m!" Shloymele continued mumbling, exerting himself to the utmost. "O God, dear God!"

It was late by now. The crowing of a neighbor's rooster sounded through the house. The patient lay almost hidden by a huge eiderdown quilt. Sarah moved about on tip-toe tucking him in more soundly to make him sweat. Leah picked up the little children, who had fallen asleep on the hard bench, carried them to their beds, and told Shloymele to go to sleep.

Shloymele was tired, broken from the strain of his long vigil. His head was spinning, his eyelids stuck together. He threw himself, fully clothed, on his bed, and in a moment he was sound asleep.

Reb Khayim recovered his senses toward morning. He sat up suddenly with a tremendous effort, looked at his wife and daughter standing by him, and with a groan, raised his eyes upwards: "Oh God, father of the orphan, judge of the widow!. . ."

Sarah and Leah broke into bitter weeping. Reb Khayim collapsed full length on the bed, his throat rattled, and he died.

Shloymele had gone to bed with an easy mind, confident that his father had been spared. He awoke to find his father stretched out on the floor under a black cloth and himself orphaned. Sounds of weeping filled the house.

BIBLIOGRAPHY

A Chronological List of Abramovitsh's Important Publications

❧

From *A Traveler Disguised* by Dan Miron

1857. "Mikhtav al dvar hakhinukh" ("A Letter Concerning Education"); Abramovitsh's first article, published in the first Hebrew weekly, *Hamagid* (h).*

1860. *Mishpat shalom* ("The Judgment of Peace"; it can also mean "The Judgment of Shalom," i.e., of Shalom Ya'akov Abramovitsh); Abramovitsh's first book, a miscellany including the famous attack on Tsvayfel, which made the author the center of stormy polemics for years. It also includes some articles, juvenile poetry, and biblical commentary (h).

1862. *Limdu hetev* ("Learn to Do Good"); Abramovitsh's first work of fiction (h).

Toldot hateva. ("Natural History"). Vol. I. The first part of Abramovitsh's comprehensive textbook of zoology. Adapted from a German book by H. O. Lenz (h).

1864. *Dos kleyne mentshele* ("The Little Man"); Abramovitsh's second work of fiction and his first Yiddish one; serialized in *Kol-mevaser* (y).

1865. *Dos vintshfingerl* ("The Magic Ring"); first version (y).

1866. *Eyn mishpat* ("The Fountain of Judgment"); a collection of articles (h).

Toldot hateva. Vol. II. Adapted from various authors (h).

1867. The enlarged and complete version of *Limdu hetev*, entitled *Ha'avot vehabanim* ("The Fathers and the Sons"), appears in Russian translation.

1868. *Ha'avot vehabanim* published in its Hebrew original.

---

* Items followed by (y) are written in Yiddish; (h) indicates Hebrew.

417

1869. *Di takse, oder di bande shtot baley-toyves* ("The Tax, Or the Clique of the Benefactors of the Town"); Abramovitsh's first play (y).

Fishke der krumer ("Fishke the Lame"), first version (y).

Der luftbalon ("The Balloon"); adapted with Y. L. Binshtok from Jules Vernes's *Cinq semains en ballons* (y).

1871. "Et ledaber" ("A Time to Speak"); a polemic against M. L. Lilyenblum. Published in *Hamelits* (h).

1872. *Toldot hateva.* Vol. III (h).

1873. *Di klyatshe, oder tsar baley khayim* ("The Nag, Or Against Cruelty to Animals"); Abramovitsh's popular allegory on the persecution of the Jews in czarist Russia (y).

1875. *Dos yidl* ("The Little Jew"); another allegorical work on the situation and history of Jews as an exiled nation; in verse (y).

Zmires yisroel ("The Songs of Israel"); a Yiddish adaptation in verse of the traditional Sabbath songs, with a Hebrew commentary.

Peyrek shire ("A Sequence of Hymns"); a Yiddish adaptation and elaboration on *Perek shire*, added to the hasidic prayer book, in which the whole cosmos praises God in mystical terms. In verse (y).

"Ma anu" ("What Are We?"); an essay on the character and development of the Jewish nation. Serialized in *Hashakhar* (h).

"Yidishe kinder" ("Children of Israel"); a monologue of Yisrolik the Madman, the protagonist of *Di klyatshe*, published in the magazine *Yisrolik* (y).

1878. *Kitser masoes Binyomin hashlishi* ("The Abridged Travels of Benjamin The Third") (y).

"Ahava le'umit vetoldoteha" ("Patriotism and Its Consequences [or, its 'History']"); an essay examining the nature of patriotism and recommending a mild and well-controlled brand of it while warning against chauvinistic excesses; serialized in *Hamelits* (h).

1879. *Dos kleyne mentshele.* A much enlarged and improved version which appears as a first volume in a projected series of "Collected Works" (y). However, subsequent volumes do not appear.

1884. *Der priziv* ("The Draft"); Abramovitsh's second play, and his first publication after five years of silence (y).

Di Takse appears in Russian translation.

1885. *Masoes Binyomin hashlishi* appears in Polish translation.

1886. *Di klyatshe* appears in Polish translation.

"Beseter ra'am" ("In the Secret Place of Thunder"), first chapter; Abramovitsh's first Hebrew story since the publication of *Ha'avot vehabanim*, published in the first Hebrew daily, *Hayom* (h).

1887. "Beseter ra'am," the complete story, published in *Ben-ami* (h).

1888. *Fishke der krumer*, a much enlarged and improved version, published as the first volume of a new "Collected Works" project (y).

Dos vintshfingerl, enlarged version; prologue and Part I appear in the first volume of Sholem Aleichem's *Yidishe folks-biblyotek* (y).

1889. *Di klyatshe* published as a second volume of the "Collected works" (y). Subsequent volumes do not follow.

"Reshimot letoldotay" ("Sketches to My Biography"), published in *Sefer zikaron* (h).

Dos vintshfingerl, Part II; published in the 1889 volume of Sholem Aleichem's almanac (y).

1890. "Shem veyefet ba'agala" ("Shem and Japeth in the Train Compartment"), a short story published in *Kaveret* (h).

1892. "Lo nakhat beya'akov" ("There Is No Good in Jacob"), a short story, published in *Pardes*, Vol. I (h).

1894. "Bymey hara'ash" ("In Days of Tumult"), a short story, published in *Pardes*, Vol. II. With "Ptikhta demendele Mokher-Sfarim" ("Mendele Mokher-Sforim's Prologue"), an introduction to a projected autobiographical novel (h).

"Byshiva shel ma'ala uvyshiva shel mata" ("In the Heavenly Assembly and in the Earthly One"); first section of this discursive, polemic novelette, published in *Lu'akh akhi'asaf*, Vol. II (h).

1895. "Byshiva shel ma'ala uvyshiva shel mata," second section; published in *Lu'akh akhi'asaf*, Vol. III (h),

"Di alte mayse" ("The Old Story"), a Yiddish version of "Lo nakhat beya'akov" published in *Hoyz-fraynt*, Vol. IV (y).

1896. *Mas'ot Binyamin hashlishi*, the Hebrew version, published as a supplement to *Pardes*, Vol. III (h).

"Hanisrafim" ("Pauperized by Fire"), a short story, published ibid. (h).

1897. *Be'emek habakha* ("In the Vale of Tears"), the Hebrew version of *Dos vintshfingerl*, serialized in *Hashilo'akh* (h).

1899. *Shloyme reb Khayims* ("Shloyme the Son of Reb Khayim"), Abramovitsh's autobiographical novel, serialized in *Der yid* (y).

1900. *Sipurim* ("Short Stories"). This collection includes all the Hebrew short stories Abramovitsh had published since 1886 as well as the "Ptikhta levayamim hahem" ("Prologue to Those Old Days"). *Bayamim hahem* is one of the titles of the Hebrew version of *Shloyme reb Khayims* (h).

1901. *Sefer hakabtsanim* ("The Book of Paupers"), a large section of *Fishke der krumer*, serialized in *Hador*. The first draft of this translation was prepared by the poet Byalik. Abramovitsh contributed "the finishing touch" (h).

1902. *Seyfer habeheymes* ("The Book of Cattle"), serialized in *Der yid* (y).

"Yisrolik der meshugener" ("Yisrolik the Madman"), additional chapters to *Di klyatshe*, serialized in *Der yid* (y).

1903. "Di antdekung fun Volin" ("The Discovery of Volhynia"), a "historical" short story, published in *Hilf* (y).

Khayey Shlomo ("The Life of Shlome"), the Hebrew version of *Shloyme reb Khayims*, serialized in *Hazman*, Vols. III-IV (h).

1904. New chapters of *Dos vintshfingerl* published in *Der fraynt* (y).

1905. New chapters of *Dos vintshfingerl* published in *Dos lebn*, as is the short story "Seyfer hagilgulim" ("The Book of Metamorphosis") (y).

1907. Final versions of *Dos kleyne mentshele* and *Fishke der krumer* (y).

1909. The first volume of the "Jubilee edition" of Abramovitsh's collected Hebrew works. It includes the final versions of *Sefer hakabtsanim* and *Be'emek habakha*.

1911. Second volume of the Hebrew "Jubilee edition." Final versions of *Susati* ("The Nag"), *Mas'ot Binyamin hashlishi*, and *Bayamim hahem*.

The 17-volume Yiddish "Jubilee edition" begins to appear.

The series *Mibeyt gnazav shel yisra'el* ("Of the Jewish Treasure"), afterward entitled *Khagim uzmanim* ("Festivals"), begins to appear in *Hashilo'akh* (h).

1912. Third volume of the Hebrew "Jubilee edition." It includes an entirely new adaptation of the early novel *Ha'avot vehabanim* as well as the short stories and a Hebrew version of *Sefer habehemot* ("The Book of Cattle").

New chapters of *Shloyme reb Khayims* appear in *Der fraynt* (y).

1913. *Seyfer bereyshis*, a Yiddish translation of Genesis with Kh. N. Byalik and Y. Kh. Ravnitski.

"Fun mayn seyfer-hazikhroynes" ("From My Memoirs"), first chapter, published in *Di yidishe velt* (y).

The Yiddish "Jubilee edition" completed.

1915. "Fun mayn seyfer hazikhroynes," second chapter, published in *Di yidishe velt* (y). The Hebrew version of the first chapter of these memoirs is published in *Hatsfira*.

1916. "A farbenkenish" ("A Longing"), a further chapter of the memoirs, is published in *Undzer lebn* (y).

Glossary

A scene from the first chapter of Fishke der krumer.

Glossary

ben zokher—a family gathering to celebrate the birth of a boy. The celebration takes place on the first Friday evening after his birth.

betsa—literally, an egg. This is the name of a tractate in the *gemore* which begins by considering the propriety of eating an egg that was laid on a Holy Day.

beys din—the Jewish court of law, having jurisdiction over exclusively Jewish matters.

bris—a contraction of *brismile*—circumcision; literally, *bris = covenant.*

dibek—a ghost or spirit which enters and takes possession of another person's body; sometimes spelled *dybbuk.*

Esau—Jacob's brother—the hunter, the outdoor man, the unrefined man—often used to denote a non-Jew in a derisive manner.

esreg— citrus fruit similar to a lemon; one of the four plants used during the Feast of Weeks (*Shevues*).

farfl—small pieces of dough, either cooked or uncooked.

fleyshiks—Jewish religious dietary laws distinguish between two chief types of food: *milkhiks* (dairy dishes) and *fleyshiks* (meat dishes) which may not be eaten together; two separate sets of dishes, pots, and silverware must be kept for the two types of food.

gemore—the commentaries of the Talmud (sometimes spelled "Gemara").

goylem of reb leyb sore's—Rabbi Leyb Sore's was a Polish khasidic rabbi. His magical power was the subject of many popular legends. Like other *tsadikim* (viz.), he had the power to create a *goylem* (also spelled *golem*), a dead body of clay into which he instilled life by incanting the proper words. Only the *tsadik* could deprive the *goylem* of his life.

425

gvald—a cry of distress.

hagode—the order of the home services at the *seyder* of Passover night (sometimes spelled "haggadah").

haskole—literally, "enlightenment"; movement among the Jews of Eastern Europe in the late eighteenth and nineteenth centuries to acquire modern European culture and secular knowledge; opposed the dominance of rabbinic orthodoxy and khasidism in Jewish life and the restriction of education and culture to talmudic studies. (Sometimes spelled *haskalah*.)

house of study—translation of *beys-hamedresh*, an edifice used both for praying and studying the *toyre* (first five books of the Bible) as distinguished from a *shul* or *beys-akneses* (synagogue), which was used exclusively for praying. Every Jewish town had a house of study near its synagogue. The house of study often served as a meeting house for discussing communal and worldly affairs.

kadish—a memorial prayer recited over the grave of the dead and on the anniversary of death each year.

kahal—the seat of administration of whatever limited autonomy was granted to the Jewish community by the Tsar.

kashe—porridge, frequently made of whole buckwheat.

khale—a twisted white bread eaten on the Sabbath and holidays.

khanike—the feast of the dedication commemorating the liberation of the temple in Jerusalem from the Syrians and Greeks (sometimes spelled "Chanukah").

khapers—snatchers. Men who snatched poor Jewish children and orphans off the street to serve in the Tsar's army in lieu of the children of rich families.

khasidism—a religious and mystical revival movement originating in southern Poland and the Ukraine in the eighteenth century, stressing joy, enthusiasm and communion with God. Its traditionally orthodox opponents (*misnagdim;* sometimes spelled *mitnagdim*) were scandalized by the shouting and ecstatic twisting of the body which often accompanied the prayers of the *khasidim,* their emphasis on inner *kavone* (intent) over learning, and other of their mystical doctrines and practices. (Sometimes spelled *hassidism*.)

kheyder—the religious elementary school conducted by a *melamed*, usually in his own house.

426

khomets—all foods used during the Passover holidays must be prepared under special conditions; anything which does not meet these specifications is considered *khomets.*

khosid—a member of the *khasidic* sect which profoundly influenced the religious and cultural life of Eastern European Jewry (sometimes spelled *hassid).*

khumesh— a volume containing only the Pentateuch, or the first five books of the Bible, used in the synagogue by the congregation in following the reading of the *toyre;* synonymous with *toyre* in the sense of the first division of the Bible, but *toyre* is a much broader term (see *toyre); khumoshim* is the plural form.

khupe—the bridal canopy; the four poles signify the four corners of the world; a blue cloth, signifying the heavens, is supported by the poles.

kidesh—benediction or sanctification of *shabes* and festivals; pronounced over a cup of wine.

kishke—section of intestine stuffed with flour and chicken fat.

kneydlakh— dumplings made of matzo-meal with the addition of melted goose or chicken fat.

kugl—pudding made of flour and fat, often eaten on *shabes.*

lag boymer—a joyous, although minor, holiday, commemorating the end of a dreadful plague during the Bar Kokhba revolt against Rome.

lekekh—a form of honeycake, often served with wine on a festive occasion.

mamzer—a bastard; the word may be used jokingly or in earnest, depending upon the context.

maskil—literally, in Hebrew, "intelligent," "knowing"; in the nineteenth century, a follower of the *haskole* (which see); *maskilim* is the plural form.

matse—(plural, "matses") the unleavened bread eaten during the Passover holiday (sometimes spelled "matzo").

megile—literally, a scroll; applied more specifically to the five short books of the Bible: Song of Songs, Ruth, Lamentations, Ecclesiastes, and Esther. (Sometimes spelled *megillah.)*

melamed—a teacher of young children in religious school; *melamdim* is the plural form.

mentsh—this word involves a whole philosophy of life. The meaning of mentsh is a human being in the moral and ethical sense; not merely a person, but a person with worth and dignity, one who can be respected. *Mentshn* is the plural form.

mezuze—a piece of parchment containing twenty-two lines from Deuteronomy. It is rolled up in a wooden, metal, or glass cylinder and attached to the doorpost of Jewish homes. It is kissed upon entering and leaving the house. (Sometimes spelled *mezuzah.*)

milkhiks—Jewish religious dietary laws distinguish between two chief types of food: *milkheks* (dairy) and *fleyshiks* (meat) which may not be eaten together.

mitsve—an act performed as prescribed by Jewish religion or law or in the interest of fellow Jews; hence, a good deed.

moyel—circumciser

pan—the Polish and Ukrainian equivalent of "mister"; also "sir," "gentleman," "lord," "master."

pilpul—subtle argumentation, hair splitting; casuistry.

pood—a Russian weight, equivalent to thirty-six pounds.

purim—the Feast of Lots. This joyful holiday symbolizes the victory of the Jews over their persecutors. It celebrates the events described in the Bible's "Book of Esther."

rashi—Rabbi Solomon, the son of Isaac, one of the foremost commentators on the Bible; lived in Troyes, France (1040-1105). (Acronym for *Ra*bbi *Sh*loyme ben *I*tskhok.)

rebe—here used as a term synonymous with *melamed.* Also the title used for a *khasidic* rabbi.

rebitsin—literally, the rabbi's wife; often sarcastically applied to a woman who gives herself airs.

reb—the Yiddish equivalent of "mister."

rosh khoydesh—literally, the first day of the month. The first day of each month is a festive occasion in the Jewish religion. Special prayers are said, particularly in benediction of the new moon.

sambatyen—according to a Jewish legend, the ten lost tribes of Israel live in a distant land, at the end of the world, behind the high Dark Mountains and the River Sambatyen. This river rages and roars, spewing huge boulders which make it impossible to cross except on the Sabbath, when it rests—but when a pious Jew is not permitted to walk the distance to cross it. According to other legends, the inhabitants of that distant land are called the "Little Red Jews."

sandek—the godfather of a boy; the *sandek* holds the baby boy on his knee for circumcision.

seyder—the home service and meal on several nights during the week of Passover.

shabes—literally, the Sabbath. The festivity of the Jewish Sabbath on which, for one day, the man of the house is king and his wife is queen, is quite different from the spirit of somberness which is sometimes associated with the Christian Sabbath.

shames—the attendant in a synagogue.

shevues—the Feast of Weeks, or Pentecost (sometimes spelled "shavuoth").

shlimazl—an unlucky person whose life is a series of misfortunes; the word often has an amusing connotation.

shmalts—chicken fat which has been rendered until liquefied.

sholem aleykhem—a traditional Jewish greeting, meaning, "peace be with you," but through repeated usage simply signifying "Hello." Also, the nom-de-plume of Sholem Rabinovitsh.

shoyfer—a ram's horn which is blown in the synagogue on *Yinkiper*, the Day of Atonement, and *Rosh-Hashone*, the first day of the new year (sometimes spelled *shofar*).

shtibl—a *khasidic* house of prayer.

shul—a synagogue.

sidre—the portion of the Pentateuch (*khumesh*) which is read at the services on *shabes*.

simkhes-toyre—the festival of the rejoicing of the receiving of the *toyre*.

tales—a prayer shawl.

talmud-toyre—traditionally, a tuition-free elementary school maintained by the community for the poorest children.

tamuz—the fourth month of the Jewish calendar. It corresponds to June-July. (Sometimes spelled *tammuz*.)

tfiln—phylacteries. The *tfiln* consist of two leather boxes containing passages from the Pentateuch. One box is worn on the head and the other is strapped to the left arm, while the appropriate prayers are recited.

tishe bov—a fast day which occurs on the ninth day of the month of *Ov* (sometimes spelled *Ab*), a day on which both the first and the second Temples were destroyed. (Sometimes spelled *Tisha b'Ab*.)

tkhine—a prayerbook of supplication for women containing lachrymose comments on various aspects of daily life.

toyre— (*torah*) in rabbinic literature *toyre* is used in a variety of senses, all based on the general understanding of *toyre* as the guidance and teaching imparted to Israel by Divine Revelation. In its narrow, literal sense, *toyre* designates the Pentateuch, as distinct from the other two main sections of the Bible — the Prophets and Hagiographa — but in a wider sense, is also applied to Scripture as a whole, including the Oral law, and finally to religious learning in general.

treyf—unkosher, unfit for eating according to Jewish dietary laws.

tsadik—literally, a righteous man. In *khasidic* and kabalistic lore, the *tsadik* plays an important role. The legends state that in each generation there are thirty-six *tsadikim* whose identity is secret and who are outwardly simple people—but the world rests on their righteousness. They are often endowed with magical powers. (Sometimes spelled *tzaddik*.)

tsitses—fringes appended to each of the four corners of a garment. Since modern dress rarely includes four-cornered garments, a special one, or *talis katan,* "small *talis*" (so-called to differentiate it from the large *talis* worn at prayer), is worn during the day by observant male Jews (including children) beneath their outer clothing in order to fulfill the biblical precept "and they shall put upon the fringe of the corner a thread of blue."

yeshiva—an institution of higher Talmudic learning.

yakhnehoz—this odd nickname of Alter's is composed of the first letters of several words: *ya,* for wine; *k,* for kidesh; *ne,* for candle; *ha,* for *havdole,* which is a *shabes* benediction; and, *z* for time. These are an indication of the wares he handled, namely goods serving the religious needs of the people and yielding but little income. There is a saying: "He sells *yakhnehoz,*" meaning useless, profitless items.

yinkiper—the Day of Atonement (often spelled *yom kippur*).

yortsayt—anniversary of death.

zeyde—grandfather.

כתבים
מוטל סופר ספרים

אױסגעהאקטע בילדער
פֿאָרד אײנם פֿון דאָם אנדערע

דאָס ערשטע בוך
פֿישקע דער קרומער.